Racing & Football Outlook

JUMPS RACING GUIDE 2018-19

**Interviews • Statistics • Results
Previews • Training centre reports**

Raceform

Contributors: Richard Birch, James Burn, David Carr, Tom Collins, Jack Haynes, Dylan Hill, Bruce Jackson, Tony Jakobson, Andrew King, Justin O'Hanlon, James Stevens, Mark Storey, Nick Watts

Designed and edited by Nick Watts and Dylan Hill

Published in 2018 by Raceform Ltd
27 Kingfisher Court, Hambridge Road, Newbury RG14 5SJ

Copyright © Raceform Ltd 2018

All rights reserved. No part of this publication may be reproduced, stored in a retrieval system, or transmitted in any form or by any means, electronic, mechanical, photocopying, recording, or otherwise, without prior written permission of the publishers.

A catalogue record for this book is available from the British Library.

ISBN 978-1910497821

Printed by CPI Group (UK) Ltd, Croydon, CR0 4YY

RACING & FOOTBALL OUTLOOK
Est. 1909

Contents

Introduction		4
Profiles for punters	Tom George	6
	Tom Lacey	13

2018-19 Preview

Nick Watts' 30 horses to follow	20
Ante-post	28
Jerry M	42
Downsman	46
Hastings	50
Borderer	54
Southerner	58
John Bull	61
Aborigine	65
Hunter chasers	68
Tom Collins	70
Richard Birch	73
Time Test	76

2017-18 Review

Big-Race Review	79
Novice Review	103

Statistics, Races and Racecourses

Comprehensive stats for top ten trainers	119
Jockey & trainer standings	140
Fixtures	145
Big-race dates	155
Big-race trends	156
Track facts for all Britain's Flat courses	176
Record and standard times	220

Final furlong

Picture quiz	232
Betting guide & Rule 4 deductions	236
Horse index	238

2018-19 RFO Jumps Racing Guide

RACING & FOOTBALL OUTLOOK
Est. 1909

Editor's introduction

IT seems a long time ago now and it would be forgiveable to think the memory is playing tricks after the long, dry summer we had, but rewind the clock seven months and we were looking at heavy ground at Cheltenham.

The best-laid plans and all that. Trainers and punters had probably spent months looking for good-ground horses and even a week before the meeting there were plenty of people saying conditions must turn soon, but it didn't happen.

It didn't happen in time for Aintree either and it left us having kittens here at Outlook Towers. Sitting on a great position with 50-1 ante-post vouchers about Tiger Roll – we hope plenty of you took our advice in last year's jumps guide – we were counting the money as he cantered around Aintree and soared over the National fences until the soft ground saw his legs turn to jelly as the petrol gauge hit empty at the Elbow. Given normal spring ground, he'd surely have hacked up.

Nonetheless, to our relief, Tiger Roll held on by the slimmest of margins and, despite the conditions, Cheltenham will be remembered for plenty of good things still getting the job done as well.

Buveur D'Air found it tough but battled home in front, Footpad showed his class in spectacular fashion, while Samcro and Laurina were magnificent in a couple of the novice hurdles.

Now the task is to work out who those good things will be 12 months on and you couldn't be in better hands to steer you through the winter.

Our ante-post previews have not only produced 50-1 Tiger Roll in recent times but also the 2017 Champion Chase winner Special Tiara at 25-1. Don't miss this year's advice, which covers the King George and the National as well as the four big championship races from Cheltenham.

One man hoping to make a splash at that level is Tom George, who has a leading Champion Hurdle hope in Summerville Boy after the horse ended George's 16-year wait for another festival winner by landing the Supreme. George features in our stable tours along with Tom Lacey, who enjoyed a breakthrough campaign last term and continues to deliver stunning profits for his followers.

Our regional reporters have also been speaking to all the trainers in their area to bring you all the latest news on fresh arrivals and horses to follow from the rest of the leading names in the training ranks.

As well as all that, Nick Watts has picked out his 30 horses to follow from either side of the Irish Sea, while we have the views of RFO regulars Richard Birch and Tom Collins, a comprehensive guide to last season's big races by Dylan Hill and a rundown of the leading speed figures from last season.

Then there are reams of statistics that should help your punting, including figures for last season's top ten trainers broken down by month, jockey, race type and course plus lists of the leading trainers and jockeys for every course in Britain.

We have every angle covered to make it a profitable season, although to keep up to date make sure you also buy your copy of the RFO every Tuesday.

TIGER ROLL (right): put us through the wringer but got the job done at 50-1

Profiles for punters
Tom George

TOM GEORGE: all smiles at Cheltenham after Summerville Boy's win

Profile by James Stevens

IT took 16 years for Tom George to finally return to the Cheltenham Festival winners' enclosure, but you'd get good odds about him enduring such a wait this time as he suddenly overlooks one of the most powerful yards in Britain.

Supreme Novices' Hurdle winner Summerville Boy is the star of the show, his tough victory over Kalashnikov confirming him as a top-class hurdler and a contender for this season's Champion Hurdle.

Then, just a day later, Black Op found only the incredible Samcro too good in the Ballymore Novices' Hurdle before going one better at Grade 1 level at Aintree.

George is certainly better placed to build on Cheltenham Festival success at the very highest level than he was when Galileo broke through for him by winning the Royal & SunAlliance Hurdle in 2002, although that was a hugely important victory in establishing the trainer as one of the most innovative trainers in the game.

Keen to explore new bloodstock options to provide value for his owners, George had found Galileo among 17 horses he bought from Poland, among whom were 14 individual winners. After that he was also one of the first trainers to really take advantage of opportunities in France, most notably with the hugely popular Nacarat.

Galileo's win came nine years after George had taken out his licence at Down Farm, the family farm where he had always known he wanted to become a trainer, leaving to take up roles with the likes of Francois Doumen and Martin Pipe before he came back to start on his own.

The first half-century of winners came two seasons later in 2003-04 and George was then hugely consistent for many years before taking a big step forward in the last two seasons, his peak tally of 71 coming in 2016-17 before last season's big-race successes.

There's a feeling that George has battled hard and done things the hard way, which is matched by the way he views his horses.

"All our horses have worked their way up to being good," he says. "We don't have horses who just come here as champions. It's a testament to all the people that work here."

As an example, George cites last year's King George runner-up Double Shuffle and stable stalwart God's Own, who has been at the yard for six seasons and has competed honourably at the top level for much of that, winning three Grade 1 races and achieving his best Champion Chase placing of third last season in his third attempt at the race.

"Just look at God's Own, who is still competing at the very highest level at ten," says his proud trainer. "These horses have started with humble beginnings and just kept improving which is always great to see.

"Double Shuffle is a great success story. He did nothing in his first three runs but we've managed to make him a top-class chaser. Everyone treats each horse like a good one and they've got the chance to prove how good they are."

While George mentions humble beginnings, his consistent success has been rewarded by more spending power courtesy of the likes of the Brookhouse family and Paul and Clare Rooney.

"A lot of the owners like to have their own jockeys now," he says, "which I haven't got a problem with, so we've built up a very good pool of riders here. Adrian

GALILEO: a breakthrough winner for Tom George in the 2002 'Ballymore'

Heskin, Noel Fehily and Paddy Brennan will ride for us, Johnny Burke is here quite a few times as is Ciaran Gethings. My son Noel will also continue riding for us – he's still got a very useful 7lb claim so we'll hope to take advantage of that."

Even more important than the riding talent is the equine talent at George's disposal and, on that front, it's no wonder he's hugely optimistic about the season ahead.

George says: "Last season was great – it's brilliant to get winners at the big festivals – and we're excited about this year. We've started well already but we're just getting everything ready for November time and we've got everything sorted.

"I think we're probably down a few horses this year than last year, but we're coming into this year with some of the best horses in the country. We aren't an enormous yard but we've certainly got some top horses. I'm happy with the team and looking forward to getting going."

The horses

Activial 8yo gelding
Lord Du Sud – Kissmirial

He's been at quite a few different yards and was a very good hurdler for Harry Fry a few seasons ago. He's new to us and I hope we can find his best form again. He's had his problems, but he's settled in really well here, which is good to see – I think he's enjoying the place.

Air Navigator 7yo gelding
Yeats – Lox Lane

He's a huge horse who's always been built for chasing. We had to send him over hurdles last season to give him that experience, but we knew they wouldn't suit him and they just seemed to get in the way. He'd had some really good bumper form before that – he won twice and was second in a Listed race at Cheltenham – and he'll come into his own this season over fences. We've been schooling him over fences for a while and he seems to jump them very well.

Black Op 7yo gelding
Sandmason – Afar Story

He's an exciting horse. He did brilliantly over hurdles considering he's so enormous and hurdles just got in the way for him. He put up a great performance in the Ballymore at Cheltenham, where he was the only one who gave Samcro something to think about. He needs a truly run race and he had to take up the running pretty early when he then went to Aintree, so to win anyway proves he's tough and pretty smart. He's set to go novice chasing and he's looked good when we've schooled him – he's very rangy. He'll start off over 2m4f but he'll get further. We have quite a few options for him and can go any way we want.

Boyhood 7yo gelding
Oscar – Glen Dubh

He won a couple of times last season, but he was stopped early as he had a bit of a splint problem after Cheltenham on New

BLACK OP: in front a long way from home at Aintree but still got the job done

DOUBLE SHUFFLE: far from straightforward but very smart on his day

Year's Day. He still appears pretty well handicapped, but I'm not sure how long we'll keep him over hurdles before he goes chasing. He's a young horse who is heading in the right direction.

Casa Tall 4yo gelding
No Risk At All – Gribouille Parcs

I really like this horse. He came here from France in the middle of last season after winning twice, but he found the Fred Winter a baptism of fire and then Perth possibly came a bit too soon after Cheltenham and he was caught on the run-in when fourth. He's only four but he's a great jumper of fences and I think he'll go novice chasing. He gets all the allowances and I think he'll do very well.

Clondaw Castle 6yo gelding
Oscar – Lohort Castle

He won a couple of novice hurdles last season and we wanted to run him at Cheltenham, but in his prep run he had to run on very heavy ground and then he got splints which finished his season early. He was always going to be a chaser and should come into his own over fences. I think he'll improve a lot this year and might even make it up to Graded level.

Double Shuffle 8yo gelding
Milan – Fiddlers Bar

He's not straightforward and it's hard to get him spot on every time, but we had

GOD'S OWN (centre): beating Vautour and Simonsig at Punchestown in 2016

him in unbelievable form for the King George at Kempton last season and it was a great run to finish second to Might Bite. He struggles on very soft ground and that was the best ground he got last year – it was too soft for him at Aintree and the same happened at Sandown. I'm sure there's another really big day for him as he's still improving physically, he's stronger than last year and he's bred to improve with age. I'd have thought the the Charlie Hall would be a good starting point as a flat track is what he wants.

Espoir De Teillee 6yo gelding
Martaline – Belle De Lyphard

Roger Brookhouse has sent this horse to us after he won a bumper and a maiden hurdle for Neil Mulholland. He showed a lot of promise in that hurdles win, doing it really convincingly, and hasn't run since. It's great to have him here and I think he'll be one to watch.

Fanfan Du Seuil 3yo gelding
Racinger – Nina Du Seuil

He's a very nice horse who has come here from France. He won his juvenile hurdle over there and has done nothing wrong. He's a big, rangy horse and will jump a fence one day for sure.

God's Own 10yo gelding
Oscar – Dantes Term

He's been an incredible horse for us and is still going strong. He had a great season last term considering everything went against him as he never had his ground at all. To finish third in the Champion Chase on unsuitable ground at the age of ten is pretty amazing and he's a great warrior. He hasn't won in a while, but he's full of enthusiasm and I think he's looking better than he's ever done. He'll have a similar campaign again and I think he'll start off in the Haldon Gold Cup at Exeter.

Rocklander 9yo gelding
Oscar – Rua Lass

He had a good year last season, winning a couple of novice chases and running a great race in the novice handicap at the Cheltenham Festival. There should be plenty more improvement to come from him this season and he should feature in those big 2m4f handicap chases at Cheltenham. He's a second-season chaser and rated 145, which is just about right for those type of races.

Seddon 5yo gelding
Stowaway – Andreas Benefit

He's an exciting prospect. He won his bumper up at Musselburgh very well and his finishing position in the Champion Bumper probably doesn't do him justice as I thought it was a great run. He got lots of daylight and was far too keen, but he was still running well before flattening out. It could have been a different result if he'd settled. He's a fast horse and he'll be running in 2m novice hurdles. He's a great jumper and should do very well.

Singlefarmpayment 8yo gelding
Milan – Crevamoy

He loves it at Cheltenham and has gone down by the smallest of margins a couple of times there, firstly at the Cheltenham Festival in 2017 and then at the April meeting last season. That last run was the end of a lot of hard work as he took a really heavy fall in the Ladbrokes Trophy when he was running a big race and he never really got over it. We put a lot of effort into

SINGLEFARMPAYMENT: in his element at Cheltenham and will be back in March

SUMMERVILLE BOY: could he spark more wild celebrations by winning the Champion Hurdle?

saying one day at Cheltenham that none of those who finished in front of him would beat him in a truly run race. He finally got one in the Supreme and did amazingly to win after a bad mistake two out – I remember thinking he'd do well to finish in the first four after that. He's done really well over the summer and came back about five kilos heavier. He's strengthened up physically and matured phenomenally. He'll jump fences eventually, but he's so quick we don't need to go down that route yet and the initial plan is to stay over hurdles. He's a very sharp horse and he'll spot something before everything else in the race. The Fighting Fifth would be our first major target but he'll probably have a run before that.

The Big Bite 5yo gelding
Scorpion – Thanks Noel

He's an exciting novice hurdler. He's been very backward, but he won a couple of bumpers spread across two season and was mid-division in the Champion Bumper. His owners have been very patient with him and I hope they'll be rewarded with a good season as he's strengthened up really well.

The Worlds End 7yo gelding
Stowaway – Bright Sprite

He was a Grade 1 winner as a novice hurdler but last season just proved a nightmare for him. He never got his ground, not even once - he's okay on good to soft but he was always coming in on soft or heavy ground and, with a horse like him, there are only so many races you can go to. Considering the situation he was in, I thought he had a good season as he wasn't beaten too far in the Stayers' Hurdle and kept on improving throughout the year. We were always up against it and I'm sure things will be easier this time around as we'll have far more options now he's going novice chasing. We started schooling him at the back of last season and he'll do well.

schooling him and finally got him right and it very nearly paid off. I'm sure he can keep that up now. We'll keep going back to Cheltenham and it would be great to win at the festival with him.

Summerville Boy 6yo gelding
Sandmason – Suny House

He was beaten a few times early last season as it took a long time to get him to switch off, but I remember Noel [Fehily]

Profiles for punters
Tom Lacey

TOM LACEY: going from strength to strength and well worth another visit

Profile by Dylan Hill

IT'S not often one of these stable tours works out quite as well as the one we did with Tom Lacey last season, so please forgive us for going back to the same fantastic source of profits.

When we spoke to Lacey 12 months ago, he had just had by far his best ever season, sending out 21 winners at a profit of £87.32 to £1 level stakes.

Since then he has taken another giant leap forward. The last campaign saw him increase that winning tally to 39 winners and anyone following the yard as we advised would have again found themselves massively better off – to the tune of £79.80 to the same £1 level stakes.

Those bare statistics are impressive enough, but the story behind Lacey's campaign makes it even more remarkable as he lost a major owner in the autumn and several of his more established performers with them.

"You never know what's around the corner," reflects Lacey, 48, who trains in a 206-acre establishment in the Herefordshire countryside that he bought four years ago as a derelict fruit farm and built up himself. "I was never too worried because I still knew we had a good team with lots of youngsters coming through, but it was an incredible season. Everything just clicked."

WINNING TEAM: *gracing the winner's enclosure at Aintree*

The fact it was done with so many horses means there may well be more to come. Of 20 individual winners last season, the winningmost age group was those who are now five-year-olds, with nine of them doing the business. Three winners – one of whom, Thistle Do Nicely, has since joined Jamie Snowden – were a year younger and another five are now six-year-olds, also young enough to continue to progress.

However, the trainer also has the ability to improve older horses. The nine-year-old Alberto's Dream had failed to win in nearly two years for Tom Symonds and was switched to Lacey's yard with a mark of 80, but he won four in a row this year and is now rated 115.

Similarly, Jester Jet – rated 98 when joining from Tony Carroll in 2017 – went on to become part of a stunning breakthrough for Lacey at the Grand National meeting in April when she won the 2m4f handicap hurdle on the second day, followed 24 hours later by Thomas Patrick winning on the big day itself. Lacey also had Kateson and Meep Meep finishing second and fourth in the two Grade 2 bumpers at Aintree.

Having those proven class acts in the ranks means Lacey is now on a much surer footing than 12 months ago and, inevitably, the exposure brought about by such success has led to greater interest.

"We've got more horses this season," Lacey confirms, "but I'm keen to put a cap at 50. I have no ambitions to have 100 horses or anything like that – I want to be able to do a thorough job with each horse. It's more about improving the quality."

That quality now has Lacey talking of Gold Cups, Grand Nationals and various Cheltenham Festival races for his horses, although you can be sure his horses will be running in those sort of races only if their progress between now and then has merited it.

"The big stage itself doesn't reel me in," he admits. "I'm more than happy ducking and diving, but of course owners have ambitions for their horses and you see where they end up. But you can't run them in big races if they're not good enough – you ruin horses that way."

Should Lacey's horses see him reluctantly end up on the big stage, it would be somewhat in keeping with the way he set out as a trainer.

Having fallen into racing at the age of 16 when his headmaster suggested he take a job at a local yard, Lacey rose to become head lad for Brian Meehan but admits he had no ambitions to become a trainer. Instead he had found a niche in the buying, selling and pre-training of horses until circumstances again took over.

"It got to the point where I stopped being able to sell them for what I thought they were worth," he says. "I had to start running them myself just so they'd proved themselves outside the point-to-point arena."

It's certainly proved an extremely smart decision and, whether by accident or design, it's clear that Lacey is a trainer going places – and one punters should be keeping firmly on their side.

2018-19 RFO Jumps Racing Guide

The horses

Alberto's Dream 9yo gelding
Fantastic Spain – Molly's Folly

His owners switched him to our yard at the start of the year as he'd been struggling a bit, but he was down on a good mark and we managed to win four times with him. I think the handicapper might just have caught up with him now, but he might be able to win once or twice.

Coningsby 5yo gelding
Midnight Legend – Motcombe

I think he's been really harshly treated by the handicapper. He was second twice over hurdles last season, but a mark of 128 is unbelievable for what he's achieved. He's going to have to improve this season, although in fairness he's done well over the summer. He'll be going novice chasing.

Dorking Boy 4yo gelding
Schiaparelli – Megasue

He won on his bumper debut at Market Rasen in April and we ran him in the Grade 1 at Punchestown after that as there were no nice bumpers left in Britain and his owners love to have runners there. He finished eighth and I thought he ran very well for a long way – he definitely wasn't disgraced as it was probably the hottest bumper of the season. He's schooled nicely over hurdles and we'll start him off over 2m and see where we end up.

Dorking Cock 4yo gelding
Winged Love – Kiss Jolie

He's a nice horse with plenty of ability and was fourth in the big sales bumper at Newbury on his only run last season. He'll be going novice hurdling this season and

TORNADO FLYER (centre): winning what Tom Lacey feels was the hottest bumper of the season at Punchestown, with Lacey's Dorking Boy in eighth

will still be learning the ropes, but I'm sure he'll be able to win.

Equus Amadeus 5yo gelding
Beat Hollow – Charade

He was very promising last season and was placed in a couple of good novice hurdles in the spring, including at Sandown on the last day of the season. However, we started him over fences at Southwell in September and he was very disappointing. He'd been very free in the past and we've done a lot of work teaching him to settle, but Aidan [Coleman] got him dropped out in rear that day and I don't think he ever switched on. We'll stick to fences and I'm sure he'll prove a lot better than that.

Flashing Glance 5yo gelding
Passing Glance – Don And Gerry

He had an issue that caused him to miss a lot of last season, but he came back in the spring and did really well to win at Ludlow. We started him chasing this summer and I was very pleased with his run at Southwell in August when third behind All Set To Go. We then stepped him up in trip at Worcester and he pulled too hard. I'm looking forward to being able to run him through the winter this time, although he wouldn't want the ground too soft – I think good to soft would be ideal.

Jester Jet 8yo mare
Overbury – Hendre Hotshot

She's done nothing but improve since she came here last year and won at Aintree's Grand National meeting before coming a close second at Haydock in May. She's schooled nicely over fences and I'd like to think there's more to come from her this season. She'll be ready to make her chasing debut at the end of October, probably at Worcester, and hopefully we'll be looking at Listed mares' chases.

JESTER JET: a terrific winner at Aintree and could progress again over fences

POLYDORA (left): hard to catch right but won twice over hurdles last season

Kateson 5yo gelding
Black Sam Bellamy – Silver Kate

He was solid all last season and was unlucky not to win more than one bumper. He finished second three times after that win at Chepstow, including in the Grade 2 bumper at Aintree behind Portrush Ted. He's schooled over hurdles and will probably step up in trip as the season goes on. His owners have mentioned the Albert Bartlett but he's got a bit of strengthening up to do first. I think he's really come into his own next season.

Kimberlite Candy 6yo gelding
Flemensfirth – Mandys Native

He was inconsistent last season, but he won well at Chepstow on his last run and that was the first time he'd jumped his fences with any enthusiasm and confidence. He'd been so backward earlier in the season and his hurdles form hadn't actually worked out, but I'm really looking forward to him now as he's had a good summer and really strengthened up. He'll be one for staying handicap chases.

Meep Meep 5yo mare
Flemensfirth – Charming Leader

She won a bumper on her debut at Chepstow in March and I was delighted with her run when fourth at Aintree after that. She'll be running in mares' novice hurdles this season and there's a good programme for her. The mares' novice at the Cheltenham Festival would be a possibility, but she wants plenty of juice in the ground.

Polydora 6yo gelding
Milan – Mandysway

He won a couple of times over hurdles and should be a good prospect for fences this season as he's summered nicely and schooled well. He's a hard horse to catch

THOMAS PATRICK: could be a real flag-bearer for Tom Lacey in top races

right, though, as he's highly sensitive to pollen and dust, so we can't make any big plans for him.

Sebastapol 4yo gelding
Fame And Glory – Knockcroghery

He looks like a really good horse and the dream would be the Supreme Novices' Hurdle at Cheltenham. He won his only bumper at Ayr in April and he'll have no problem jumping hurdles as he won a point-to-point. He has plenty of speed and I see no point in stepping him up beyond the minimum trip. He's very exciting.

Sir Egbert 5yo gelding
Kayf Tara – Little Miss Flora

He progressed throughout last season, winning on his final run at Taunton, and he's done really well again physically over the summer. He'll be going chasing and even though he went up 6lb after Taunton I still think he's nicely handicapped. I'd love to find a novice handicap for him, but there aren't enough of them if you can pass a message on to the BHA!

Thomas Patrick 6yo gelding
Winged Love – Huncheon Siss

He'd been retrained as a riding horse when we got him and he was a complete dope, which is why we had to start him over hurdles last season to sharpen him up mentally. He was always going to be a chaser, though, and he really flourished once we got him over fences towards the end of last season. He won on his chasing debut at Chepstow in February and we thought it was worth throwing him straight into the Devon National, but Richard [Johnson] didn't think he enjoyed the hustle and bustle and he also got a bad overreach. We switched to front-running after that and he won twice more, including back in really top company at Aintree. He's got the Ladbrokes Trophy as an option for the first half of the season and if we go down that route I'd probably give him a run over hurdles first to protect his mark of 148. However, he'll also have entries in the Grand Sefton and the Becher Chase because I've got the Grand National in the back of my mind for him, while we'll also put him in the Gold Cup. All his form last year was on soft ground, but he's a year stronger and he's learned to race now so I'd like to think he'd cope with quicker ground.

Triopas 6yo gelding
Stowaway – Aine Dubh

He was really progressive last winter, winning four times in November and December, and will be novice chasing this season. He actually finished a good third on his chasing debut at Wincanton in January, but we decided there was no point risking his novice status after that so he went back over hurdles and we waited until May before running him over fences again when it was one race too many and he was pulled up. He could do with running in some small-field novice chases to boost his confidence.

Vado Forte 5yo gelding
Walk In The Park – Gloire

He was a big improver last season. He found things tough at first as he'd come back from a bumper at Kempton with a stress fracture and needed some time off. He can also be very keen, but once he started to learn he won three of his last four races, including the Sussex Champion Hurdle at Plumpton. I'd like to send him over fences, but he'll be sticking to hurdles as his owners are keen to go down that route and there are a lot of big handicaps for him. I think he'll be just right for the Greatwood at Cheltenham in November if they get soft ground as they'll go a hell of a gallop in that race.

VADO FORTE: has won three of his last four and will go for big 2m handicaps

2018-19 RFO Jumps Racing Guide

Nick Watts' 30 horses to follow

ACEY MILAN 4 b g
Milan – Strong Wishes (Strong Gale)
21114-

Acey Milan was a very good bumper horse last season, winning two Listed events at Cheltenham and Newbury. Although he couldn't convert favouritism in the Champion Bumper, he didn't fare badly in fourth and it doesn't diminish his hurdling prospects for this season one iota. He should do well in novice hurdles and, as he handles deep ground, he will be effective through the winter. He will probably be best over 2m4f or further in time.

Anthony Honeyball, Dorset

ANOTHER STOWAWAY 6 b g
Stowaway – Another Pet (Un Desperado)
U222P-2

Another Stowaway didn't manage to win last season, but he put in several good efforts, notably when running the smart On The Blind Side to three-quarters of a length at Aintree early in the campaign. He wasn't as good thereafter, but he did get a taste of fences in May at Kempton when an encouraging second behind Amour De Nuit and that bodes well for his novice chase campaign this season. He's unlikely to go to the top but is capable of winning good races from 2m4f-3m.

Tom George, Slad

BELLSHILL 8 b g
King's Theatre – Fairy Native (Be My Native)
151-

Has Bellshill finally come of age? Last season he won the Bobbyjo Chase and the Punchestown Gold Cup and in between he ran a remarkable race in the Irish National, leading his rivals a merry dance right up until the final fence. He travelled like a class horse in that race, backed it up at Punchestown and now the platform is there for him to go for all the top staying events, including the Gold Cup. Although a four-time Grade 1 winner, he's never done it at Cheltenham – yet. He goes on any ground and is a sound jumper.

Willie Mullins, Closutton

CLAN DES OBEAUX 6 b g
Kapgarde – Nausicaa Des Obeaux (April Night)
2123-

Clan Des Obeaux seems to have been around forever but is still tender in terms of years. Paul Nicholls has rightly minded him thus far, but he has still achieved plenty, winning a graduation chase easily at Haydock before finishing a good second in the Caspian Caviar at Cheltenham. On his final start he dipped his toe in Grade 1 waters and wasn't disgraced in being beaten just over ten lengths by Might Bite. That experience won't be lost on him, but a handicap off a mark of 157 could still be an option for him before resuming in Grade 1s.

Paul Nicholls, Ditcheat

COMMANDER OF FLEET 4 b g
Fame And Glory – Coonagh Cross (Saddlers' Hall)
11-

A son of the ill-fated Fame And Glory, Commander Of Fleet burst on to the scene in stunning fashion at Punchestown in April, running away with a bumper to win by eight and a half lengths. He had previously won his only point start for Pat Doyle before transferring to Gordon Elliott and he looks a smart prospect for staying novice hurdles this term. Were he to go the right way, then an Albert Bartlett bid could be on the cards next March. Both of his wins have come on yielding to soft ground, but there's no reason why he wouldn't be effective on good.

Gordon Elliott, Co Meath

DANNY KIRWAN 5 b g
Scorpion – Sainte Baronne (Saint Des Saints)
110-

Danny Kirwan won his sole Irish point last October and was quickly whisked off to Ditcheat to pursue his career. Things started well with a win at Kempton in February and his trainer was most effusive in his praise for him. Missing Cheltenham was a wise move and, although he couldn't justify favouritism in the Grade 2 bumper at Aintree's Grand National meeting, that shouldn't be held against him as he is still essentially a work in progress. With a bit more time and experience under his belt, he could be an exciting hurdling prospect – and one for the spring festivals.

Paul Nicholls, Ditcheat

DAPHNE DU CLOS 5 b m
Spanish Moon – Katarina Du Clos (Panoramic)
121/-

Daphne Du Clos missed all of last season and hasn't been seen since February 2017. However, if Nicky Henderson can get her back to her best, she will be very exciting, as her bumper performances indicate. On her British debut she was just touched off by the smart Cap Du Soleil and then at Newbury a couple of months later she saw off Western Ryder, now rated 145, with contemptuous ease. That is quite some time ago now, but there is no trainer better at bringing a horse back from an absence and there is a lovely mares' programme for her to follow now hurdling.

Nicky Henderson, Lambourn

DEBECE 7 b g
Kayf Tara – Dalamine (Sillery)
4-F

Debece was put in last season as a novice chaser to follow, but unfortunately injury saw him miss most of the campaign and he only returned at Aintree's Grand National meeting where he ran in a competitive 3m hurdle. He ran a cracker as well, finishing fourth behind Mr Big Shot having jumped the last upsides. His next outing at Haydock in May saw him take a crashing fall, which is hardly ideal, but if he can be kept low-key over fences early on and get his confidence up he is still a smart long-term prospect for staying chases.

Tim Vaughan, Glamorgan

DIDTHEYLEAVEUOUTTO 5 ch g
Presenting – Pretty Puttens (Snurge)
110-

It is a long time since the days of Straw Bear, but Nick Gifford has got another very smart horse on his hands here. Didtheyleaveuoutto won his first two starts easily, first at Lingfield and then in a Listed event at Ascot before Christmas. He was high up in the betting for Cheltenham after that and was a big fancy for the bumper there until rain turned the going soft and scuppered his chances. He still ran well, travelling strongly before weakening on the going and ending up tenth. On good ground, he could go to the very top over hurdles this season.

Nick Gifford, Findon

FOOTPAD 6 b g
Creachadoir – Willamina (Sadler's Wells)
11111-

Footpad may not be the most original choice as a horse to follow for the season, but he simply has to go in as he is a joy to watch and can win wherever his trainer decides to send him this season. That could easily be over the minimum trip – Mullins has never won a Queen Mother Champion Chase and, as the Arkle winner, he would deserve to have a crack. However, he will undoubtedly stay much further, so the Ryanair could be a realistic option for him as well. Perhaps three miles could even be on the cards? Wherever he goes, he is one just to watch and admire.

Willie Mullins, Closutton

GILGAMBOA 10 b g
Westerner – Hi Native (Be My Native)
52111-

A Grade 1-winning novice chaser in his youth, Gilgamboa was an exciting addition to the hunter chase ranks last season, winning three times in succession. On the latter occasion he got the better of a great tussle with the smart Burning Ambition, who subsequently went off favourite for the Foxhunter at Cheltenham. He didn't qualify for the festival last season, but he will do so next year and, although he will be 11 by then, he does bring plenty of class to what might be quite a modest division. Expect him to prosper.

Enda Bolger, Co Limerick

GREAT FIELD 7 b g
Great Pretender – Eaton Lass (Definite Article)
1-

Let's hope Great Field has an uninterrupted campaign this time around. He had anything but last season, managing to hit the track only once, and it's a testament to his class that it was a winning performance as he beat the smart Doctor Phoenix in a Grade 2 at Naas. With nothing much to challenge Altior in the 2m division at this moment in time should Footpad go up in trip, could Great Field be the one to challenge in the Champion Chase? Having been unbeaten in his last five races, including a Grade 1, he might well be.

Willie Mullins, Closutton

KALASHNIKOV 5 br g
Kalanisi – Fairy Lane (Old Vic)
11212-

Kalashnikov was a star for his young trainer last season and big things can be expected of him as he now embarks on a chasing career. He was awesome in the Betfair Hurdle at Newbury in February and looked for all the world like he was going to follow up in the Supreme at Cheltenham only to be cruelly run down by Summerville Boy up the hill. There was no disgrace in that, however, and he was merely confirming himself as a high-class hurdler. There could be more to come over fences and he looks an Arkle candidate.

Amy Murphy, Newmarket

KILBRICKEN STORM 7 b g
Oscar – Kilbricken Leader (Supreme Leader)
1311313-

A very consistent staying novice hurdler last season, Kilbricken Storm also has class as a win in the Albert Bartlett in March proves. On his final outing of the campaign he was beaten only half a length into third behind Next Destination and Delta Work and he looks a natural RSA Chase candidate – or one for the four-miler even. He will be going over fences this season and stamina looks his chief asset, so maybe an extreme trip will see him at his best. A similar type in essence to Colin Tizzard's Gold Cup winner Native River.

Colin Tizzard, Dorset

KING'S ODYSSEY 9 b g
King's Theatre – Ma Furie (Balleroy)
3333-

At first glance King's Odyssey may appear a strange one to put in, but there was evidence last season that he was getting to grips with tough handicaps at long last and a handicap mark of 139 still makes him interesting for the Caspian Caviar Gold Cup – or any 2m4f event when the mud is flying. Last season he finished third on every start with the pick of his efforts probably coming in the Plate at the Cheltenham Festival behind The Storyteller. It's easy to predict his campaign and hopefully he can turn places into wins.

Evan Williams, Glamorgan

KING'S SOCKS 6 b g
King's Best – Alexandrina (Monsun)
35P-

King's Socks has been a bit of a talking horse in his career and didn't come up to scratch last season, so he has a few questions to answer. That said, he ran with a lot of promise in the Plate at Cheltenham for one so inexperienced, finishing fifth of 22 behind The Storyteller. Go back to his French form and he was second behind Footpad in a Grade 1 hurdle – and that was only in 2016. So, as a young horse and with the benefit of last season's experience to draw upon, it's fair to expect better now and a handicap mark of 139 is sure to help.

David Pipe, Wellington

MEEP MEEP 5 ch m
Flemensfirth – Charming Leader (Supreme Leader)
14-

With the vastly improved programme for mares now, it's worth putting a few in this list and Tom Lacey's five-year-old Meep Meep looks like she could be a good one. She won easily on her debut at Chepstow and was then pitched into Grade 2 company at Aintree, where she ran with great credit to come fourth behind Getaway Katie Mai. She really hit the line hard that day and wasn't beaten far, so you can expect a longer trip to suit her when she goes hurdling. She is definitely up to running in Graded hurdles.

Tom Lacey, Ledbury

MENGLI KHAN 5 b g
Lope De Vega – Danielli (Danehill)
111O233-

Mengli Khan reportedly goes chasing this season and he could be one of Ireland's top novice chase prospects. Aside from when running out at Leopardstown in December, he was very consistent last term, winning a Grade 1 in the Royal Bond at Fairyhouse and coming third in the Supreme and at Punchestown. He is unlikely to be quite good enough for a Champion Hurdle bid, so it does make sense for him to go over the larger obstacles, and on good ground it would be easy to see him go right to the very top.

Gordon Elliott, Co Meath

MISSED APPROACH 8 b g
Golan – Polly's Dream (Beau Sher)
P6321P-

Missed Approach is not always the most consistent but is a very effective stayer at his best, as he showed when repelling some very well-supported Irish horses in the Kim Muir at Cheltenham last March. He was unable to replicate that in the bet365 Gold Cup, but it could pay to ignore that as he did have a tough race at the festival. He will be the perfect age for a Grand National bid next season and he's already proved his staying abilities when a good second at Musselburgh in February over a trip of 4m1f. A good stayer when he gets in a rhythm, he could be ideal for Aintree.

Warren Greatrex, Lambourn

ON THE BLIND SIDE 6 b g
Stowaway – Such A Set Up (Supreme Leader)
1116-

On The Blind Side started off last season in great style, winning his first three races and looking every inch a Cheltenham Festival contender. He had to miss that, however, and didn't reappear until Aintree on Grand National day. He was sent off favourite – and a short one at that (11-8) – but he couldn't get the job done and eventually came home sixth behind Black op. That was a tough race to come back in and it doesn't alter the fact that he will be a great chase prospect for this season over 2m4f. He has already won a point-to-point and the JLT could be his race.

Nicky Henderson, Lambourn

ON TOUR 10 b g
Croco Rouge – Galant Tour (Riberetto)
1U9F62-6-

On Tour is getting on in years maybe, but he is lightly raced and goes well at Aintree, where he has form figures of 212. His best effort came on Grand National day last season when beating all bar Thomas Patrick under a fine waiting ride by Adam Wedge. The pair of them were unlucky earlier in the season at Newbury, where they unseated in a handicap won by Gold Present when going very nicely indeed. If his mark of 140 drops slightly then he will be back in business and he could easily pop up somewhere at a nice price.

Evan Williams, Glamorgan

PENHILL 7 b g
Mount Nelson – Serrenia (High Chaparral)
12-

We don't see Penhill very often and that is unlikely to change this season either. He's not the easiest to keep sound, but Willie Mullins is used to that – he dealt with Quevega for many years – and there's no need to run him too often when he goes so well fresh. The Stayers' Hurdle was very much run to suit him last season as there was no pace on up front and a whole host of horses had a chance going to the last, but he had the flat speed to get past them and that is a huge weapon. Although he couldn't follow up at Punchestown, he wasn't at his peak that day.

Willie Mullins, Closutton

POINT OF PRINCIPLE 5 b g
Rip Van Winkle – L'Ancresse (Darshaan)
242175-

Point Of Principle is a very well-bred five-year-old whose dam, L'Ancresse, almost won at the Breeders' Cup in her career. He got off to a slow start last season but got off the mark over hurdles at the fourth attempt, nosing out the useful Dame De Compagnie, before finishing a good seventh behind Santini in a Grade 1 at Aintree. Although below-par at Chepstow on his final start of the campaign, he could well have been over the top by then. A mark of 135 gives him scope if he stays hurdling, but chasing could be the way forward. Either way, he is interesting.

Tim Vaughan, Glamorgan

RELEGATE 5 b f
Flemensfirth – Last Of The Bunch (Silver Patriarch)
1117-

Although she disappointed on her final start of the campaign at Punchestown, Relegate had already enjoyed a great season and it doesn't diminish her prospects this time around. She sprang a surprise at the Cheltenham Festival in the hands of Katie Walsh, winning the Champion Bumper by a neck from stablemate Carefully Selected having been a long way behind at one stage. She now goes hurdling and should stay further than two miles. It is easy to see her returning to Prestbury Park in March with a big chance again.

Willie Mullins, Closutton

SANTINI 6 b g
Milan – Tinagoodnight (Sleeping Car)
1131-

What a lovely chasing prospect – Santini should be at the forefront of everyone's mind for the RSA Chase in March no matter which way they go with Samcro. He won three of his four hurdle races last season and the only time he was beaten it came in a gruelling Albert Bartlett, in which he was still a very encouraging third. It shows he is made of stern stuff to come back from that and still land a Grade 1 at Aintree. A big horse whose future is definitely over fences, he will be hard to beat wherever he goes during the season.

Nicky Henderson, Lambourn

TESTIFY 7 b g
Witness Box – Tanya Thyne (Good Thyne)
1110P--

One of the most enjoyable aspects of last season was the re-emergence of Donald McCain and he has a perfect candidate for handicap chases in the north in Testify. He won his first three starts over fences last season, culminating in a Grade 2 win at Haydock, and although below-par after that at both the major spring festivals that shouldn't detract from what he does in the early part of this season. Put simply, give him Haydock, give him soft or heavy ground and he will do the business, probably more than once.

Donald McCain, Cholmondeley

THE BIG BITE 5 b g
Scorpion – Thanks Noel (Tel Quel)
1/10-

The Big Bite is a very lightly raced type who won a bumper for Tom Lacey in March 2017 before transferring to Tom George. On his first start for George he won a bumper at Huntingdon on Boxing Day under Ciaran Gethings and was then sent for an ambitious tilt at the Champion Bumper at Cheltenham which didn't come to fruition, although he was hardly disgraced in finishing 11th of 23 behind Relegate. He will go hurdling this season and will do well over a trip according to his breeding – he is closely related to RSA Chase winner Cooldine.

Tom George, Slad

TIME TO MOVE ON 5 ch g
Flemensfirth – Kapricia Speed (Vertical Speed)
11-

Although he won't come into his own until he goes over fences in a year or two, there should be plenty of fun to be had with Time To Move On. This unbeaten bumper horse won two from two last season, both at Exeter, and on both occasions he put distance between himself and his rivals – always the sign of a good horse. Connections were keen on a crack at the spring festivals after his second win in February and it didn't happen for him, but he should be back this season and will do well hurdling over a longer trip.

Fergal O'Brien, Naunton

WE HAVE A DREAM 4 b g
Martaline – Sweet Dance (Kingsalsa)
4411111-

Nicky Henderson has the dual Champion Hurdle winner in his yard in Buveur D'Air, but it would be no surprise to see this one challenging him at Cheltenham next March. Yes, it isn't easy for juvenile hurdlers to make the step up, but he did everything right last season, winning in gritty fashion at Musselburgh on sticky ground and then putting in a much more fluent performance when easily scoring at Aintree in a Grade 1 on his final start of the campaign. He deserves to have a crack at the highest level before being sent chasing.

Nicky Henderson, Lambourn

YANWORTH 8 ch g
Norse Dancer – Yota (Galetto)
1F216-

Yanworth isn't everyone's cup of tea, but it's hard to argue about a horse who has won 12 of his 19 starts including two Grade 1s. It was understandable that his trainer decided to have a crack at an open-looking Stayers' Hurdle with him, but this season he ought to return to fences off what could be a very lenient chase mark of 148. That is 13lb lower than his hurdles mark and one he can exploit – either in something like the BetVictor Gold Cup or even the Ladbrokes Trophy if his stamina holds out for that longer trip.

Alan King, Barbury Castle

Top ten horses

Acey Milan	Mengli Khan
Bellshill	Missed Approach
Didtheyleaveuoutto	On Tour
Great Field	We Have A Dream
Meep Meep	Yanworth

RACING & FOOTBALL OUTLOOK

2018-19 RFO Jumps Racing Guide

Ante-post preview
Dylan Hill & Nick Watts

King George

LOOK down the ante-post list for the King George at this time of year and it tends to read like a who's who of the very best chasers in Britain and Ireland, which could fool you into thinking the race will be far more competitive than actually proves to be the case.

In fact, of the eight horses who are currently no bigger than 16-1 with any firm, I'd be amazed if more than two or three of them actually turn up at Kempton on Boxing Day.

This race surely won't be on **Altior**'s agenda. It would take a setback for stablemate Might Bite for connections to even consider it and even then I doubt they would perform such a u-turn considering they have been saying for some time that he will stick to the minimum trip.

Another crack two-miler, **Footpad**, is more likely to step up in trip, but I doubt it will happen this quickly or indeed this season at all. He'll probably run over 2m4f at some point, perhaps even in the Ryanair, but this comes early enough in the cam-

King George
Kempton, December 26

	Bet365	Betfair	Betfred	Coral	Hills	Lads	P Power	Skybet
Might Bite	2	9-4	5-2	5-2	5-2	5-2	9-4	2
Waiting Patiently	6	7	6	5	7	5	6	6
Douvan	10	11	10	12	-	12	10	12
Native River	8	12	-	10	4	10	12	10
Altior	10	16	12	-	10	-	16	14
Footpad	10	16	10	10	-	10	16	12
Road To Respect	12	16	16	-	-	-	16	14
Presenting Percy	14	16	8	-	8	-	16	14
Politologue	16	16	-	16	-	16	20	16
Sizing John	14	20	20	14	-	12	16	20
Terrefort	20	25	25	16	-	20	16	25
Bristol De Mai	25	16	25	20	-	25	16	25
Top Notch	14	25	16	20	-	20	20	20
Thistlecrack	16	20	25	25	-	25	20	25

each-way 1/4 odds, 1-2-3
Others on application, prices correct at time of going to press

NATIVE RIVER: unlikely to confirm Gold Cup form on a sharper track

paign for second-season chasers anyway.

Then there are several Irish chasers in the field, yet this has become a rare port of call for Irish-trained horses and I'd expect the likes of **Road To Respect** and **Presenting Percy** to stay at home. The same goes for other potential raiders at bigger prices like **Balko Des Flos**, **Monalee**, **Bellshill** and **Disko**.

Douvan is more likely to make the trip. Willie Mullins and Rich Ricci brought over Champagne Fever and Vautour, both of whom finished second, so perhaps they feel like they have unfinished business in this race.

However, I couldn't back Douvan even if his participation was more or less guaranteed. He showed a lot of his old sparkle in the Champion Chase, but he had raced so freely that he probably wouldn't have lasted home. Any more of that and he'll have no chance of getting this extra mile.

His next run at Punchestown was pretty disappointing. Un De Sceaux hadn't won a top-class 2m chase in the spring for several years, always looking like he needed a longer trip or softer ground, yet he looked like an absolute superstar that day. I think it perhaps said more about the opposition and, while Min had an excuse – he was having his third quick run after Cheltenham and Aintree – Douvan should surely have done better.

The other reason to expect the competition to thin out is that, while even more connections have been mentioning a crack at the King George this year than usual, that is because there is now a £1 million bonus for any horse winning this race in between the Betfair Chase and the Gold Cup.

Of course, only one horse can still be in the running for the triple crown after Haydock, though, and I find it hard to believe **Native River**, for example, would be running here if he's been beaten in the first leg of the treble.

Kempton simply won't suit the Gold Cup hero. Cheltenham, especially on soft ground, brought his stamina into play and that can also be an asset in the King George, in which the horses tend to get racing from a long way out, but he doesn't have enough speed to make all the running around this much sharper track.

MIGHT BITE, on the other hand, looks tailormade for this course and distance and all this preamble has been a way of justifying lumping on last year's winner at 5-2. Yes, it's a short price, but I'd be surprised if he doesn't go off significantly shorter on the day and I expect him to win.

MIGHT BITE: looked an improved and more mature horse at Aintree

Might Bite would have won all three runs at Kempton had he not fallen at the last when miles clear in the Kauto Star Novices' Chase in 2016 and he put that ghost to bed when winning last year. He wasn't very impressive that day, but at least he got the job done and it's worth bearing in mind it was basically his first run outside novice company, with his prep run having come in a four-runner intermediate chase at Sandown.

The nine-year-old has definitely improved since then, just getting outstayed in the Gold Cup – stop the race at this 3m trip and he looked every inch the winner – and then slamming Bristol De Mai at Aintree. Both times he also looked a much more mature horse than the one who so nearly threw away victory in the RSA two seasons ago.

On that form I'd expect him to win the Betfair Chase on anything other than bottomless ground and, if conditions are that desperate at Haydock, I'd trust Nicky Henderson to do the sensible thing and take him out rather than risk losing him for Kempton. Coming here via a win in that race or a quieter preparation, he could well go off odds-on or close to it in this race.

The main danger at Haydock will be **Bristol De Mai**, who has a stunning record at that track. He can also do it elsewhere, with his Charlie Hall win last season having worked out well, and he was plagued by physical issues after following up in the Betfair so is perhaps best forgiven his poor subsequent efforts.

If he comes back to form for Nigel Twiston-Davies, he could also be the best outsider for the King George at 25-1 as he has won well on right-handed tracks before, notably in the Grade 1 Scilly Isles Novices' Chase.

Also in the field at Haydock could be **Sizing John** and **Politologue** if connections follow through on their words this autumn, but I can't see either making an impact and that would then knock them out of the King George running.

Politologue surely wouldn't want such an extreme test of stamina – it's not that long ago he was seen as a weak finisher over shorter – and Sizing John has an awful lot to prove after injury, as does **Thistlecrack**.

As a younger horse with far fewer miles in his legs, I'd be more confident of **Waiting Patiently** coming back to his best and this race has been earmarked for him.

However, I have concerns about his stamina as he was apparently legless after the line in the Ascot Chase when the way he travelled was what caught the eye. Even if he gets home, just beating a 12-year-old Cue Card doesn't entitle him to be beating Might Bite. [DH]

Champion Hurdle

HAVING expected to see the reigning champion **Buveur D'Air** win easily in last season's Champion Hurdle, it was a bit of a disappointment to see him only scrape home from Melon.

He was 4-6 in what didn't look a great field, but he came very close to getting chinned and anyone thinking they have a horse for this season's renewal wouldn't have seen too much to fear in that display.

It could be that a light campaign, in which soft races were hand-picked for him, didn't give him sufficient preparation for a festival race.

Nicky Henderson pondered that possibility several times during the season, but he has no-one to blame but himself, sending him for a non-event at Sandown in February instead of taking him to Ireland for a proper, competitive work-out on the same day.

There's no doubt the Champion Hurdle will be on the cards for Buveur D'Air again and he will bid to emulate See You Then, who completed a hat-trick in the race for Henderson in 1987.

However, prices of around 3-1 don't really appeal at this stage as there are bound to be contenders emerging as we go through the season.

As is often the case at Cheltenham, the main danger may lurk from within.

WE HAVE A DREAM is a horse I liked a lot last season and, although he missed Cheltenham, a record of five wins from five races including two Grade 1 races at Chepstow and Aintree makes for impressive reading.

The only time he looked less than impressive was on tacky ground at Musselburgh in February but he still managed to beat the ill-fated Act Of Valour by four and a half lengths, while his Aintree performance after that was a joy to behold.

The problem, as it is for all juveniles going out into the big, wide world, is how will he cope against the big boys? You only have to look back to last season to see how much Defi Du Seuil struggled after looking amazing during his Triumph Hurdle-winning campaign.

However, We Have A Dream could be different as he's a sound jumper who travels very smoothly in his races. He also loves good ground.

Champion Hurdle

Cheltenham, March 12

	Bet365	Betfair	Betfred	Coral	Hills	Lads	P Power	Skybet
Buveur D'Air	3	10-3	3	3	7-2	3	3	5-2
Samcro	4	7-2	4	3	4	3	10-3	4
Melon	6	8	6	8	5	8	8	6
Summerville Boy	14	12	12	10	12	12	12	14
Laurina	12	14	12	12	14	12	14	12
Min	14	-	12	16	14	16	-	16
We Have A Dream	16	20	16	20	20	16	20	16
Global Citizen	33	33	-	25	33	25	33	33
Mick Jazz	33	33	-	33	25	33	33	25
If The Cap Fits	25	33	-	33	33	33	33	33
Saldier	33	33	-	33	33	25	33	33
Mengli Khan	33	33	-	25	33	25	33	40
Getabird	33	20	-	20	33	20	25	40
Farclas	33	20	25	20	33	20	20	40

each-way 1/4 odds, 1-2-3
Others on application, prices correct at time of going to press

If Henderson can bring him along slowly, then he could be ready for a Champion Hurdle crack by next March and the 33-1 with Betfair holds some appeal.

The other one to consider at this stage is last season's Supreme winner **Summerville Boy**, who stays over hurdles according to Tom George.

He looked to have his limitations when beaten into third by Western Ryder at Cheltenham in December, but he came back to win the Grade 1 Tolworth Hurdle at Sandown the following month before his Cheltenham win, which was impressive considering his jumping was sloppy at times.

He lost about three lengths at the second-last and was untidy at the final flight as well. Normally that would signal the end of a horse's challenge, but it seemed to galvanise him and he reeled in Kalashnikov to win by a neck.

Summerville Boy would have won comfortably without the errors and if he can brush up his jumping then he has to be a big player.

It's great that George was quick to map out Summerville Boy's campaign, which wasn't the case with **Samcro**. The Ballymore winner has quotes from all the leading firms for this race but there must be a good chance he will go chasing.

That's also a possibility for another useful novice in **If The Cap Fits** as well as last year's runner-up **Melon**, who would be very beatable even at his best.

There is always the potential for a horse to go chasing, not really enjoy it and then come back to hurdles and thrive, as Buveur D'Air did in 2017.

If there is such a candidate, I'd be most interested in **Mengli Khan**, who was only a couple of lengths off Summerville Boy at Cheltenham.

That was a good effort from a horse who is pumping in some consistent performances now, but he looks a decent type for the Racing Post Arkle so it may all be academic. Even a top price of 40-1 isn't enough to put him up now.

There's not much else that appeals. It's hard to know where **Laurina** will end up and the likelihood is that she will remain in mares' company, while **Mick Jazz** has won plenty of prize-money but it would be a poor Champion Hurdle that he wins. [NW]

MENGLI KHAN (centre): still has potential at this level but will start over fences

GREAT FIELD: let's hope he stays fit as alternatives to Altior are hard to find

Champion Chase

IF **Altior** goes for this race again then it is mighty hard to come up with a convincing angle as to who can beat him.

In this space 12 months ago I put **Min** up as a plausible alternative to the favourite and turning into Cheltenham's home straight he had a chance.

Not for long though. Altior, who hadn't been going particularly well, was manoeuvred off the rail and put the race to bed in a matter of strides, which was a brilliant effort on ground he hated. He took all Min had to throw at him and he threw it back – and more.

If the pair ever met again there's no reason why Min would ever come out on top.

The same owner also has **Douvan** in the mix and he was running well in the Champion Chase when crashing out four from home.

However, there is no telling where he would have finished and his subsequent effort at Punchestown has to go down as disappointing as he was beaten comfortably by stablemate Un De Sceaux.

It's possible he just isn't quite as good as he was. Bear in mind he was a French-bred who came to hand early – his first festival win came aged five – and he's had a few injuries to contend with.

He's had two stabs at this race already and it would be a surprise if he could make it third time lucky.

Footpad would have a greater chance of dethroning Altior for Willie Mullins, but all the noises emanating from the camp suggest he might be going up in trip this season.

Let's not forget this is a horse who was placed over hurdles in a 3m Grade 1 event at Punchestown, so he does stay a good deal further, and Mullins might try to turn him into a Gold Cup horse – and if not that then the Ryanair at least.

Mullins does have another potential contender in his midst, however, with **GREAT**

FIELD lurking at 25-1 with Paddy Power.

He's evidently not the easiest to keep sound as he managed just one race last season, but it was still a winning one as he gave Doctor Phoenix 4lb and a beating, making all as he usually does.

Doctor Phoenix is no slouch and would have given Un De Sceaux a race at Fairyhouse subsequent to this had he not fallen two out when challenging, so there was merit in his display.

That was his fifth win in succession and he might be the type of horse who can trouble Altior as he sets off fast and gets faster – while his jumping, which has been a touch suspect in the past, appears to have got better.

A rating of 164 still gives him 11lb to find with Altior and that's not going to be easy to find, but of those currently quoted he has more chance than most.

Sceau Royal, **Diego Du Charmil**, **Petit Mouchoir** and **San Benedeto** make little appeal and such is the hold Altior has on this division that we could be looking at a very small field for this race come March.

That could be a plus for Great Field, however, as it could allow him to get an uncontested lead. He has to be the each-way pick at the prices. [NW]

ALTIOR: will be hard to dethrone in the Champion Chase

Champion Chase
Cheltenham, March 13

	Bet365	Betfair	Betfred	Coral	Hills	Lads	P Power	Skybet
Altior	6-4	13-8	**7-4**	5-4	**7-4**	11-8	6-4	5-4
Footpad	4	**9-2**	4	4	4	4	4	4
Douvan	12	**14**	10	10	10	10	**14**	12
Un De Sceaux	12	-	-	-	14	-	-	-
Min	12	20	12	12	10	10	**25**	16
Great Field	16	20	-	**25**	20	20	**25**	16
Fox Norton	-	**25**	-	-	-	-	**25**	-
Sceau Royal	25	-	-	-	-	-	-	25
Diego Du Charmil	-	-	-	-	33	-	-	25
Petit Mouchoir	**33**	**33**	20	20	**33**	25	**33**	**33**
Politologue	14	25	25	20	14	16	**50**	25
Saint Calvados	33	40	-	25	25	25	**50**	40
Special Tiara	40	40	33	33	50	33	**50**	50
Brain Power	50	40	33	33	33	33	**66**	40

each-way 1/4 odds, 1-2-3
Others on application, prices correct at time of going to press

Stayers' Hurdle

THERE have been many multiple Stayers' Hurdle winners over the years and **PENHILL** could be another one.

The lightly raced seven-year-old doesn't stand a great deal of racing, but he has compiled a great record for Willie Mullins with seven wins from 11 outings since going hurdling.

Those wins include an Albert Bartlett triumph and this race last season on his return to the track after a long layoff.

It's true that he was soundly beaten by stablemate Faugheen subsequent to that in a Grade 1 at Punchestown, but he seems the type of horse who finds it difficult to back up so not too much should be read into the defeat.

Bearing in mind his fragility, it seems unlikely that he will go chasing but many of the horses in this market may do – making his price quite an attractive one.

Faugheen has been talked about as having a belated chasing campaign, while **Identity Thief**, **Next Destination** and **Bacardys** all have that option.

Sam Spinner and **Supasundae** will stay hurdling and, while Sam Spinner

PENHILL (left): gets the better of Supasundae at Cheltenham in March

may have done better last year if setting a stronger tempo, Supasundae would again be feared more, especially if conditions are quicker.

He is a very versatile horse who can cope with varying trips and is another who loves Cheltenham as well.

Stayers' Hurdle

Cheltenham, March 14

	Bet365	Betfair	Betfred	Coral	Hills	Lads	P Power	Skybet
Faugheen	5	5	**6**	5	5	9-2	9-2	5
Penhill	6	6	6	**7**	**7**	**7**	6	**7**
Supasundae	10	10	10	**12**	**12**	10	**12**	**12**
Apple's Jade	8	**14**	-	12	**14**	12	**14**	12
Next Destination	12	16	10	10	16	10	**20**	16
Call Me Lord	14	-	-	10	14	12	**20**	16
Identity Thief	14	**20**	**20**	16	16	**20**	16	16
Bacardys	16	14	20	**25**	16	**25**	16	16
Wholestone	16	**25**	-	**25**	20	**25**	20	**25**
Sam Spinner	20	16	**33**	20	**33**	16	20	25
Delta Work	**33**	-	-	-	16	-	-	20
Pallasator	-	-	-	33	33	33	-	**33**
Kilbricken Storm	16	-	16	**40**	20	**40**	-	20
Apple's Shakira	**40**	-	-	33	33	25	-	33

each-way 1/4 odds, 1-2-3
Others on application, prices correct at time of going to press

PALLASATOR: a reformed character who took well to hurdles last season

Although Penhill got the better of the argument last season, Supasundae wouldn't have been suited by the rain that fell prior to the race and that may have blunted his speed a touch.

However, it's worth bearing in mind that Penhill is no slouch either having won plenty of 1m4f handicaps on the Flat in his days with Luca Cumani.

Apple's Jade could conceivably be a player in this if only connections would point her at it.

She beat Supasundae in a 3m Grade 1 at Leopardstown's Christmas meeting, but rather inexplicably she then reverted to mares' company – probably expecting easier pickings – and came unstuck at Cheltenham and Punchestown, losing out on both occasions to Benie Des Dieux.

At Cheltenham, in particular, she looked short of pace, making all at quite a modest gallop and never able to repel them when things got desperate up the run-in.

She was beaten only a length and a half at the line and if Jack Kennedy had his time again he would have gone a much stronger clip.

Either way, she did battle on to the line and whichever way you spin it she simply needs further.

If she gets that opportunity this season she will be a player, but it's anyone's guess whether connections will do as they should have done last season. Gigginstown's racing manager Eddie O'Leary even mentioned using the Irish Champion Hurdle over 2m as a Cheltenham prep this year, which is baffling.

Her trainer, Gordon Elliott, also has **PALLASATOR** in his yard and he is the most interesting of those at big prices.

A Doncaster Cup winner on the Flat, he has taken surprisingly well to hurdles, so much so that he won a Grade 2 at Fairyhouse in April, staying on well after a mistake at the last to see off Jetz.

Since then he's been to Ascot and won the Queen Alexandra easily and, while he was below par after that, it could be that extreme trips bring out the best in him now and dropping back was a shock to the system.

Pallasator will be ten next year, but he has never been over-raced and if there is one championship race at Cheltenham where age isn't necessarily a barrier it is this one.

A few bookmakers have got him in their lists at 33-1 and he most certainly has the class to figure in something like this if his head can be kept right.

The omens are good on that front at the moment and Elliott should be congratulated on taming this sometimes out-of-control horse, who may just have more to give yet. [NW]

Gold Cup

SHOULD we be taking a chance on a horse whose festival form figures read 003?

Not in most cases, but I'll make an exception for **BELLSHILL**, whose previous efforts at Cheltenham in March are easy enough to explain away.

In 2015 he was tenth of 23 in the Champion Bumper, which wasn't a disgrace in a race that often comes too soon for some horses, and the following year he ran in the wrong race behind Altior in the Supreme. For a thorough stayer, it was no surprise he couldn't keep up.

His third run at the meeting in 2017 was much better as he finished third in the RSA Chase behind Might Bite. Yes, he was beaten a comfortable ten lengths, but it was only his fourth start over fences and he came into the race after a tired fall at Leopardstown a month earlier – not the ideal prep for a festival.

In the circumstances it was a good run and since then he's just got better and better.

Last season he opened up with an easy win in the Bobbyjo Chase and then ran a remarkable race in the Irish National under 11st 5lb, giving weight away all round.

He looked in a different league for most of the race, jumping well, travelling superbly and looking as though he had all his rivals cooked approaching the last only to spook at something, climb over the fence, interfere with several others and drop to fifth – but still beaten only a length!

BELLSHILL: now has the maturity to deal with the challenge of Cheltenham

ANIBALE FLY: did well to finish third in the Gold Cup coming off a terrible fall

Impressively, he then backed up that effort with a Grade 1 win at Punchestown – the fourth of his career, beating Djakadam and Road To Respect a shade cosily.

He's now up to a mark of 168 and should be treated as a legitimate Gold Cup contender, potentially taking in a race such as the King George or Leopardstown Christmas Chase along the way.

A top price of 25-1 with Betfair is more than reasonable for a horse who proved in the RSA that he doesn't necessarily hate Cheltenham.

The market is in fact led by the previous two winners of the RSA Chase in **Presenting Percy** and **Might Bite**, followed closely by reigning champion **Native River**.

Out of the three, I would expect Might Bite to make the most impact again as it was only unusually soft ground on Gold Cup day that stopped him in his tracks after the last following a tremendous tussle with Native River. Given the likelihood of better ground next year, I'd expect him to prove himself the better horse.

He went to Aintree after that and put up an imperious display and looks reliable enough that it's hard to believe pundits were once describing him as irresolute and a bit of a fruitcake!

Might Bite will be ten next year so it may well be the last chance for him if he is to win the Gold Cup – not many do it at 11. He won't be far away.

Presenting Percy was hugely impressive in the RSA Chase last season and, if he makes it to the Gold Cup, he will be bidding for a third straight win at the festival. He jumps well, he stays very well and he loves Cheltenham, so it is all there for him.

There's not much to quibble about with his chance save for his price – he is joint favourite already yet things will be tougher for him this season after beating the likes of Monalee and Elegant Escape in the RSA. Still, it's hard not to see him being a major player when March arrives.

Willie Mullins, trainer of Bellshill, also has **Footpad** high up in the betting but I would surprised if he was immediately hiked up to staying trips.

There's no doubt he stays further than two miles, but so do most Champion Chase winners and the Ryanair must be a more likely destination.

One at a bigger price who could place again is **ANIBALE FLY**, who is a big price for a horse who was third last season.

That was a highly commendable run given he had taken an absolutely crashing fall on his previous outing in the Irish Gold Cup.

He got to within eight and a half lengths of Native River and Might Bite at the line and, while he never threatened to beat those two, he had some good horses behind him.

He must be brave as he ran in the Grand National to round off his campaign, finishing fourth after being given quite a strange ride by Barry Geraghty, who kept him wide throughout, giving away ground.

As an eight-year-old, he will be in his prime during this campaign. [NW]

PRESENTING PERCY: a big player

Cheltenham Gold Cup

Cheltenham, March 15

	Bet365	Betfair	Betfred	Coral	Hills	Lads	P Power	Skybet
Presenting Percy	6	6	6	6	6	6	6	6
Might Bite	5	13-2	5	5	5	5	5	5
Native River	6	13-2	8	7	7	7	7	5
Footpad	12	16	-	10	16	12	16	16
Sizing John	14	20	14	16	14	16	16	12
Bellshill	16	16	25	20	14	20	20	20
Douvan	20	25	-	20	-	16	25	25
Shattered Love	25	25	-	25	25	20	25	25
Terrefort	25	33	33	25	25	25	25	33
Monalee	33	25	20	33	20	25	20	33
Thistlecrack	20	-	-	25	25	33	-	20
Al Boum Photo	33	-	-	33	25	33	-	33
Balko Des Flos	40	25	20	20	25	20	25	25
Anibale Fly	40	25	-	40	25	33	33	25

each-way 1/4 odds, 1-2-3
Others on application, prices correct at time of going to press

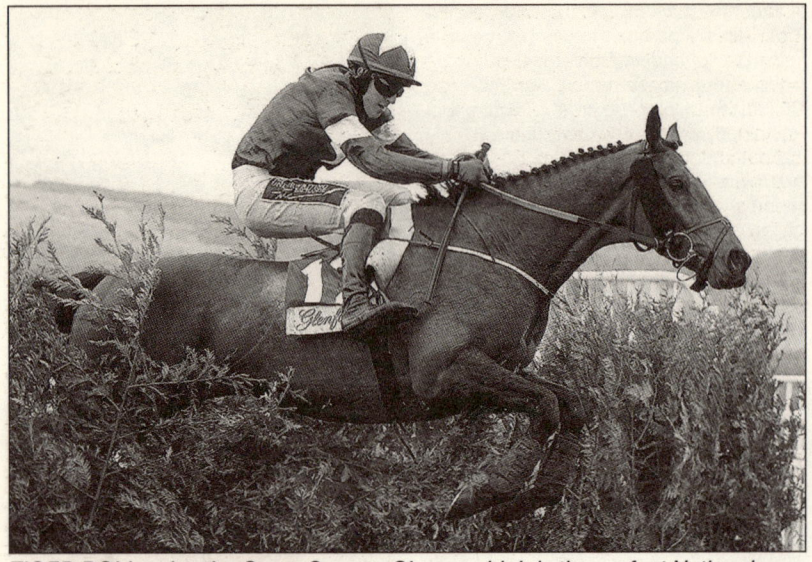

TIGER ROLL: wins the Cross Country Chase, which is the perfect National prep

Grand National

TIGER ROLL'S win in this race last year turned out to be much closer than looked likely all the way up the straight and it's precisely because of the dramatic nature of the finish that he is worth backing to follow up this season and become the first back-to-back winner of the great race since Red Rum in 1974.

The reason for that long wait is that past winners – indeed, any horse who has run well in the great race – tend to get hammered by the handicapper 12 months on.

However, in winning by just a nose, Tiger Roll ensured the assessor couldn't go too far overboard, certainly not to the extent that might have been the case had he sluiced up by ten lengths.

Make no mistake, that's the sort of margin for which Gordon Elliott's eight-year-old was value in April. It was only the fact his stamina began to ebb away that allowed Pleasant Company to reel him in, but on good ground there's no question he would see out the race better. And, if it comes up testing again, his jockey knows the need to hang on to him for a fraction longer this time.

Tiger Roll is already favourite, but you can still get 20-1 and bookmakers could have been forgiven for pricing him up a good deal shorter than that. He's the sort of horse who would be likely to go off in single figures on the day.

The mission for Elliott is to get him there in one piece, but Tiger Roll has proved himself to be a remarkably sound and durable type down the years. After all, it's now four and a half years since he won the Triumph Hurdle and he's barely missed a beat since.

Victories in the National Hunt Chase and the Cross Country Chase at the Cheltenham Festival have also followed since and a warm-up in the latter race will surely be on the agenda for him again, which is perfect as that has proved the ideal prep run in recent times, with Silver Birch winning this race after his Cheltenham second and Cause Of Causes finishing second at

Aintree when attempting the same double Tiger Roll pulled off.

You're not getting much more generous odds about several horses behind Tiger Roll in the betting yet none of them have anything like the same credentials.

Another former winner, **One For Arthur**, has plenty to prove this season after 18 months on the sidelines; **Bellshill** will be giving away lumps of weight if this season goes as well as expected; **Pleasant Company** has surely missed his chance; **Step Back** has been hammered by the handicapper for his bet365 Gold Cup win; and **General Principle** will never get as lucky again as he did in winning the Irish National.

Ballyoptic would have been more interesting in different hands. When it comes to getting a horse well handicapped, Nigel Twiston-Davies rather blotted his copybook last season when **Blaklion** soared up the handicap rather than keep his powder dry until the weights came out. It made no difference in the end as he departed early, but I suspect there will be better-handicapped horses than Ballyoptic and Blaklion.

For a second interest, I'll instead go with Willie Mullins' National Hunt Chase hero **RATHVINDEN**, a strong stayer with a touch of class who just might serve up another Mullins-Elliott thriller. [DH]

Betting advice

King George
Might Bite 2pts 5-2
(generally available)

Champion Hurdle
We Have A Dream 1pt 20-1
(generally available)

Champion Chase
Great Field 1pt 25-1
(Coral, Paddy Power)

Stayers' Hurdle
Penhill 1pt 7-1
(generally available)

Pallasator 1pt 33-1
(generally available)

Gold Cup
Bellshill 1pt 25-1
(Betfred)

Anibale Fly 1pt 40-1
(Bet365, Coral)

Grand National
Tiger Roll 1pt 20-1
(generally available)

Rathvinden 0.5pt 40-1
(Betfair, Paddy Power)

Grand National
Aintree, April 6

	Bet365	Betfair	Betfred	Coral	Hills	Lads	P Power	Skybet
Tiger Roll	**20**	**20**	**20**	16	**20**	16	**20**	16
Bellshill	20	**25**	20	**25**	**25**	**25**	**25**	20
Pleasant Company	**25**	**25**	**25**	20	**25**	20	**25**	**25**
One For Arthur	25	25	25	25	**33**	25	25	25
General Principle	25	25	25	25	25	25	**33**	**33**
Step Back	**33**	**33**	**33**	**33**	25	**33**	**33**	20
Ballyoptic	**33**	**33**	**33**	**33**	**33**	**33**	**33**	25
Anibale Fly	**40**	25	25	33	33	33	25	33
Mall Dini	33	33	33	33	33	**40**	33	33
Blaklion	**40**	33	33	33	33	33	33	33
Rathvinden	33	**40**	33	33	33	33	**40**	33
Ms Parfois	25	**40**	25	33	33	**40**	-	33

each-way 1/4 odds, 1-2-3
Others on application, prices correct at time of going to press

UN DE SCEAUX: a remarkable campaigner who keeps coming back for more

Ireland
by Jerry M

THE 2017-18 jumps season saw the domination of *WILLIE MULLINS* and *GORDON ELLIOTT* reach unprecedented levels, but it also gave us a battle for the trainer's championship that will live long in the memory.

It was perhaps the training equivalent of some of the battles for jockeys' championships which enthralled racing fans and broader sports fans in the past, such as Cauthen v Eddery in 1987 or Dunwoody v Maguire in 1993-94.

The endgame of a battle which had tipped both ways during the season was the backdrop to a Punchestown Festival that could hardly have been more dramatic and at which reigning champion Mullins achieved feats that would have stretched credulity had Sam Goldwyn or David O Selznick dreamed them up.

As the week began, Elliott's lead over Mullins stood at €521,413, but by close of business on Saturday Mullins had outscored him over the week by a startling €1.3 million and had the championship retained with a day to spare.

Mullins earned more prize-money over

those five days than some high-profile trainers had earned over the entire season. Anybody who had questions in the back of their mind about whether the title was still important to Mullins certainly got their answer.

Some familiar old faces are likely to be stalwarts once more for the Closutton trainer, although Djakadam sadly won't be among them having been retired this summer after an injury.

Un De Sceaux is back, though, and proved as good as ever last season, with his defeat in the Ryanair Chase at Cheltenham the only blot on his copybook. His defeat of Douvan at Punchestown was stunning and he will be aimed at all of the good chases at around 2m4f.

The return of **Douvan** was terrific to see even despite his Punchestown defeat. The manner in which he was travelling in the Champion Chase before his fall gave signs that the real Douvan was back and the upcoming campaign for him is eagerly awaited.

We shouldn't forget former Champion Hurdle winner **Faugheen**, whose victory in the Champion Stayers' Hurdle at Punchestown could see him reinvented over the coming campaign.

In company with Cheltenham winner **Penhill**, that would leave Mullins with a very strong hand among the staying hurdlers.

For the champion trainer, though, no horse will set the heart racing more than **Footpad**. It was not just that he was the best 2m novice chaser last season by some margin in an unbeaten campaign, it was the manner in which he did it with numerous displays of strong galloping and brilliant jumping.

How he will be campaigned is a bit of an unknown, with his trainer hinting at the end of last season that he might well step up in trip this year. A clash between him and Altior over 2m is an exhilarating prospect, but so would a potential clash with Might Bite at Kempton over Christmas.

At Gold Cup level, if Footpad is otherwise campaigned, principal hopes may lie with Punchestown Gold Cup winner **Bellshill**, although **Total Recall** was far from out of the reckoning in the Gold Cup when he fell and could be a real dark horse in that division this season.

Champion Hurdle runner-up **Melon** would appear to be the stable's principal hope in that division and doesn't have to improve very much to win one if nothing better than last year's field turns up.

However, unbeaten mare **Laurina** is very much in the 'could be anything' category and, if Mullins decides not to go the mares' route with her – he already has **Benie Des Dieux** as a possible for those big races – she could well throw several spanners in the works against the best two-milers.

Among the younger recruits, **Getabird** could well be an exciting recruit to novice chasing and if fences can help him settle he could be a potential star.

Next Destination, whose only defeat came at the hands of Samcro at Cheltenham, is very likely to be among the leading staying novice chasers.

As for Elliott, his meteoric rise is mostly due to him now being the principal trainer for Gigginstown House Stud, who have spent all summer considering what to do with probably the most exciting horse in training in **Samcro**.

His season ended in the damp squib of his unexpected fall in the Champion Hurdle at Punchestown, the race which was likely to tell us whether he would go chasing or have a crack at the Champion Hurdle this year.

It should really be a no-brainer as the Champion Hurdle, if not there for the taking, looks extremely winnable and there is plenty of time to go chasing. No decision in the early part of the season is awaited with more anticipation, but whatever path he does take he remains an extremely exciting prospect.

What Elliott actually achieved last season has to be measured against the fact that last season he lost top-class novice hurdle prospect Fayonagh to fatal injury and the same fate befell Triumph Hurdle runner-up Mega Fortune and exciting novice hurdler Lucky Pass, all before the month of October was out. All of those could have made a big difference in the

CHAMPAGNE CLASSIC: back from injury and a useful novice chase prospect

prize-money battle in Grade 1 races.

As it turns out, the season's successes were founded largely on a numbers game, helping Elliott to farm a lot of the valuable Grade A handicaps, and outside Samcro the depth of challenge he will have at the top level is a little bit more difficult to identify.

If that horse goes chasing, Champion Hurdle third **Mick Jazz** is probably Elliott's main contender in that division, although Triumph Hurdle winner **Farclas** could well fit into that mould. One of them could well pick up a Grade 1 somewhere down the line.

The form of **Apple's Jade** tailed off a bit in the spring with underwhelming performances at Cheltenham and Punchestown, but she clearly is one of the top staying hurdlers on her day.

Elliott's hopes of having a Grade 1 chaser have been hit by the fact the injury Death Duty suffered at Leopardstown over Christmas will see him miss the season, but JLT winner **Shattered Love** could go down the Gold Cup route.

There's betters news on the injury front with the 2017 Martin Pipe Hurdle winner **Champagne Classic** returning from a season off. He will head some useful prospects for staying novice chases, joined by Punchestown winner **Dortmund Park** and the highly promising **Cracking Smart**.

Elliott's link with Gigginstown always gives him plenty of depth in that staying division, with **Tiger Roll** having proved the point when he stepped up to win the Grand National last term. He will have Aintree on his agenda, as could Irish National winner **General Principle** and perhaps even the returning **Don Poli**.

JOSEPH O'BRIEN's first full season as a trainer was a huge success, ending with 67 winners and a pair of Grade 1 successes at the Dublin Racing Festival in February with novice hurdler **Tower Bridge** and surprise Irish Gold Cup winner **Edwulf** ridden by Derek O'Connor, a horse who had come parlously close to death at Cheltenham the previous March.

Those two horses will both pay their way this season, the former as a staying novice chase prospect most probably.

There are a lot of promising horses with potential yet to be tapped, such as **Alighted** and **Triplicate**, who could have lucrative seasons.

HENRY DE BROMHEAD looks likely to continue the steady increase in quality horses he has enjoyed over the past number of years.

Principal among this year's hopes in the chase division is going to be **Monalee** and where he fits in is likely to become clear in the early part of the season. His second in the RSA Chase at Cheltenham didn't disguise the suspicion that his stamina might just be stretched over 3m, so he might have to come down to shorter trips.

In that event, the stable could have an incredibly strong hand in a Ryanair Chase which will already include last year's impressive winner **Balko Des Flos**.

Identity Thief reinvented himself last spring, winning the Grade 1 staying hurdle at Aintree. Although disappointing at Punchestown, he is a horse of terrific potential.

For *JESSICA HARRINGTON*, her biggest disappointment of last season was having to rub 2017 Gold Cup winner **Sizing John** off for the season after his poor display at Leopardstown last Christmas. He's back, though, and will take his place at the competitive top table of staying chasers.

Harrington has a quandary with **Supasundae**, who won the Irish Champion Hurdle at Leopardstown and effectively picked up the pieces in the Punchestown Champion Hurdle after the falls of Samcro and Melon. In between, his second to Penhill in the Stayers' Hurdle at Cheltenham showed that his stamina does tend to run out over 3m. Training him as a Champion Hurdle horse would add yet another potentially interesting layer to that division.

NOEL MEADE enjoyed a good season and his standard-bearer for the upcoming campaign is likely to be Gold Cup fourth **Road To Respect**, for whom good ground at Cheltenham would have aided his task significantly.

The other stable star is **Disko**, who wasn't seen out after November as a slow-recovering stress fracture to his back frustratingly kept him on the sidelines. He still retains great potential.

One of the leading candidates for Gold Cup honours is going to be **Presenting Percy** for the small Athenry stable of *PAT KELLY*.

Despite having only a handful of horses in his care, Kelly has plotted Cheltenham success in each of the last three years and with this horse in the last two. His performance in winning last season's RSA Chase was that of a future Gold Cup winner.

Invincible Irish
Bellshill
Getabird
Supasundae

IDENTITY THIEF: has reinvented himself as a staying hurdler

Berkshire by Downsman

NICKY HENDERSON has been training for 40 years, but rarely – if ever – in that period can he have boasted such a strong team.

Champion trainer for a fifth time last term, Henderson is long odds-on for another crown and that is no surprise given the depth of talent at Seven Barrows.

Altior is perhaps top of the tree having won the Supreme, Arkle and Champion Chase at the last three Cheltenham Festivals.

His campaign is likely to begin in the Tingle Creek at Sandown in December, with the Clarence House and Game Spirit also options en route to Cheltenham and another Champion Chase bid.

Connections may mull stepping up in trip, but that seems unlikely to come in the King George VI Chase so Aintree's Melling Chase in the spring could be the best spot to test the son of High Chaparral's stamina.

The reason Henderson won't be tempted to step up Altior all the way to three miles is that he has King George winner and Gold Cup runner-up **Might Bite** in the staying chase division and he will Boxing Day at Kempton ringed in red on his calendar.

Before then, Haydock's Betfair Chase, which offers the winner a £1 million bonus if they go on to add the King George and the Gold Cup, is firmly in the equation.

The nine-year-old will be ten come Cheltenham and has stats to overcome on that score, but, unlike most double-digit performers, he has few miles on the clock for a staying chaser.

Ultra-impressive when last seen in the Bowl at Aintree, he behaved impeccably last term and should again take high rank.

Dual Champion Hurdle winner **Buveur**

SCEAU ROYAL: likely to start off in the Shloer Chase at Cheltenham

D'Air completes Henderson's 'big three'.

A third hurdling title, which would equal the mighty Istabraq, is on his agenda, which also includes Newcastle's Fighting Fifth and the Christmas Hurdle at Kempton.

Right behind that terrific trio are **Terrefort**, who could take in the Ladbrokes Trophy, **Gold Present**, who has a major handicap chase on decent ground in him, and **Brain Power**, a horse Henderson is not giving up on after a full summer MOT.

Brave Eagle is also one to follow and could even develop into a Scottish Grand National horse, while **We Have A Dream** – a Grade 1-winning juvenile last season – will be treated as a Champion Hurdle horse until he shows connections otherwise.

Stablemate **Call Me Lord** could emerge as a dark horse for staying hurdles and **Chef Des Obeaux**, **Claimantakinforgan**, **Lough Doug Spirit**, **Mr Whipped**, **On The Blind Side** and **Santini** are novice chasers to note. Do not be surprised if the last-named is talked of as a Gold Cup contender in 12 months.

As for some less heralded names, the handsome **Mister Fisher** could be a force for novice hurdles, as could **Downtown Getaway**, a strong and robust gelding who has done nicely since the spring. **Birchdale**, an impressive point winner, is also expected to flourish.

ALAN KING endured a relatively quiet campaign last season, largely because of the wettest winter he has known, but his Barbury Castle base boasts a typically powerful team for the forthcoming months.

Sceau Royal, who won the Grade 1 Henry VIII Novices' Chase but missed the spring festivals, is back in good form and is likely to start in the Shloer Chase at Cheltenham in November, which will determine whether he is a Champion Chase player.

Mia's Storm was another novice chaser who looked promising last year and is fresh and well after a couple of falls. She could start over hurdles before going chasing again, but good ground is essential.

King says we will "most definitely" see more from **Redicean**, who won his first three over hurdles before flopping in the Triumph, and his star juvenile hurdler from the previous campaign, **Master Blueyes**, is back from injury. The pair give the yard depth in the 2m hurdling division to replace the injured Elgin.

King reckons he has a good bunch of novice chasers, with **Talkischeap**, who is thought better on a sounder surface, among them, while the trainer, notoriously strong in the juvenile department, recommends **Giving Glances** as one for that sphere.

Missed Approach was a second Cheltenham Festival scorer for WARREN GREATREX, who will aim the Kim Muir winner at the Grand National with the Becher a possible starting point.

The Aintree showpiece is also the plan for the consistent **Theatre Territory**, perhaps inevitably given she is owned by the Waley-Cohens.

La Bague Au Roi should shine in mares' novice chases, while soft-ground novice chases over staying trips should suit **Lovenormoney** who is thought capable of improvement when sent over fences.

Keeper Hill's kissing spine issues have been operated on and he could have unfinished business as he has a "lot of ability" according to his trainer, while **Western Ryder** will remain over hurdles with the Greatwood perhaps his first target. Highly regarded, he could be better than he showed last term.

Emitom, who has enjoyed a good off-season, is also adored by Greatrex, who is amazed **Begbie** has not won a bumper. They are likely types for novice hurdling.

Grand National-winning trainer OLIVER SHERWOOD had to overcome a difficult winter when his string were not right, but he ended things well and has had his best ever summer.

Euxton Lane is among the Lambourn stalwart's leading lights and he goes chasing after a fine novice hurdle campaign, which ended with him being rated 1lb higher than his former stablemate and connections' late Aintree hero Many Clouds. He is one to keep on your side.

Jurby will also go over fences in the

HITHERJACQUES LADY (in front): will be going chasing this season

famous Trevor Hemmings silks. A likeable type, he has had some schooling sessions with jumping expert Yogi Breisner and is a proper galloper.

The Organist will be aimed at the Pertemps Final as 3m on goodish ground is her bag, although going back over fences has not been ruled out.

That is most definitely the plan for **Hitherjacques Lady**, a "super jumper" who thrives in testing conditions.

Another capable mare is **Got Away**, who was running a big race at Punchestown when coming down. Only five, she has also had a stint with Breisner and "could be anything".

Captain Peacock should continue to be effective on decent ground, while **Papagana** is a well-regarded Ffos Las winner thought above average.

The exciting **Sevarano** and **Shaughnessy** are two bumper horses to look out for over hurdles, as is **Manning Estate**, who has thrived over the summer, while **Southern Sam** is a promising signing from the point-to-point sphere.

JAMIE SNOWDEN enjoyed his best ever season and is determined to build on that and find a top-level horse.

The progressive **Hogan's Height** is one who could step up for Snowden. He is being targeted at the Ladbrokes Trophy, although he could start in a novice hurdle or Carlisle's intermediate chase in early November.

Double Treasure's future is also set to be back over fences, but Snowden will see how high he can fly in novice hurdles first and Chepstow's Persian War is inked in for him. **Carntop** is also regarded as a useful prospect for that division.

Snowden has high hopes for **Dans Le Vent**, saying: "He's on workable mark and has a good handicap in him, so he could start in Chepstow's Silver Trophy."

Scorpion Sid is probably the yard's brightest hope going over fences, but **Naranja** and **Kalahari Queen** are mares to note for novice chasing while **Monbeg Theatre** and **Three Ways** are also expected to pay their way.

Of the youngsters, smart bumper horse **Thebannerkingrebel** could shine over hurdles after a summer breathing operation, while **Kiltealy Briggs** – second in an Irish point in the spring and from the family of Grand National hero Ballabriggs – is the first horse Snowden will train for Max McNeill.

Alrightjack is another baby to note as

48

he is an unraced Norse Dancer three-year-old out of Best Mate's half-sister Katmai.

Like Snowden, *HARRY WHITTINGTON* is another trainer on the up and he enters the 2018-19 campaign with the best team of horses he has ever had.

Leading them is Grade 2 winner **Saint Calvados**, who is earmarked for the Haldon Gold Cup before a possible clash with Altior in the Tingle Creek. He shone on flat tracks last season, but Whittington is convinced this imposing five-year-old can handle undulating venues as well.

Bigmartre was also a decent novice chaser and connections are thinking back from the Grand Annual, while the Topham is another long-term goal.

The Dubai Way, a three-time winner over hurdles, is arguably the leading hope going over fences this time around as he is "built for chasing".

Sussex National winner **Vinnie Lewis**, another to have done well for a summer break, could exploit his status as a novice hurdler, although long-distance slogs over fences also suit him.

The greatest staying handicap chase of all is the dream for **Emerging Force**, who returns after a minor tendon injury, but before any Grand National bid he could go down the Pertemps route, which is also the plan for the promising **Court Liability**.

Simply The Betts – the "trainer's favourite" – could provide some fun off 130 in good 2m handicap hurdles, while Whittington is convinced we haven't seen the best of **Charlemar**, who goes chasing.

Anemoi – a half-brother to Prix de Diane heroine Laurens – is regarded as an exciting type for hurdles, while **Genius** and **Rouge Vif** are once-raced bumper winners to remember.

MARK BRADSTOCK has won the Hennessy, the bet365 Gold Cup and the Cheltenham Gold Cup and now has the Grand National in his sights with **Step Back**.

He has had a very good summer and connections reckon they have a much better handle on his muscle enzyme problems. He could start in the Becher.

Research in the US has led the team to a view **Coneygree** will be better going right-handed, so Down Royal's Champion Chase and the Sodexo Gold Cup at Ascot are starting options for the 2015 Gold Cup hero if he stays sound.

Jaisalmer, who suffers with ulcers, might be hard to catch in small-field novice chases when on song.

CHARLIE MANN has raided the German market with success in the past and is hoping **Capone**, a son of Nathaniel, will prove another shrewd purchase.

The trainer has plenty of time for former pointer **Ivilnoble**, while **Pickamix** will be worth a second look in staying chases on a sound surface and **Like The Sound** is another to keep an eye on.

Zen Master's schooling over fences has been good and **The Lincoln Lawyer** is one for juvenile hurdles.

NEIL KING is hoping to build on a fruitful summer haul and is relying on the popular **Lil Rockerfeller** to fly the flag for him.

The smart hurdler, who bolted up on the Flat at Glorious Goodwood, could be even better over fences judged on his exciting schooling.

Grand National fifth **Milansbar** will have that race and other staying chases on deep ground on his schedule.

That pair rescued a season that was disappointing for King, who says **Canyon City** was among those wrong all last year but should be a well-handicapped horse now and is in great order.

The Boss's Dream is another said to be better than his mark, while King also thinks plenty of **Nearly Perfect** and feels **Mercers Court** will win again soon.

Silents Steps has some useful form and should be easy to place as a novice over hurdles and fences.

Farne, a big, scopey type, is another mare to follow and might be a black-type performer, while Flat recruit **Cubswin** could thrive when switched over hurdles.

Best of Berkshire
Euxton Lane
Missed Approach
Naranja

KILBRICKEN STORM (left): *a good staying hurdler who will go chasing now*

The West by Hastings

ALL roads will be leading to Cheltenham for **Native River** next March when *COLIN TIZZARD*'s eight-year-old will be attempting to lift the coveted Gold Cup once again.

But first there is the little matter of the £1 million bonus temptingly put up for any horse that can land chasing's 'triple crown' – the Betfair Chase at Haydock in November, the King George at Kempton and the Gold Cup.

Native River's sporting owners, Brocade Racing, must think they have a chance of bagging the big-money bonus if their pride and joy can land the first leg at Haydock, although going right-handed around Sunbury's twisting and turning chase course on Boxing Day might be stretching it.

At last season's festival the Tizzard star simply galloped and jumped his rivals into submission in chasing's Blue Riband before passing the post with more than four lengths to spare over Might Bite – and there did not seem to be any fluke about the result on the day.

Confidence is high at Venn Farm Stables that there is more to come from the horse as he returned from his elongated summer break looking stronger than ever and the obvious first stop of the campaign is Haydock, but it would be no great surprise if he gave Kempton the swerve at Christmas if beaten there.

Whatever route is chosen by connections this side of the new year, it seems a sure bet that Native River will warm up for his second tilt at Gold Cup glory in the Betfair Denman Chase at Newbury in February as it perfectly paved the way last season.

If Tizzard has a young chasing star waiting in the wings it might well be **Kilbricken Storm**, who sprang a 33-1 surprise in the Grade 1 Albert Bartlett Novices' Hurdle at Cheltenham and then went down only narrowly when third in a similar event at Punchestown.

Given that he is already seven years old and won an Irish point before joining current connections, he should be ready to take to fences quickly and he has the make and shape to go right to the top of the novice chasing tree.

Anyone looking for a darker horse among the Tizzard team could do worse than **White Moon**, who, as his name suggests, is a striking grey individual.

He started off well last term by winning with ease at Wincanton and Exeter but then blew out at Sandown and was not seen again in public.

He had shown enough in his two successes in Britain to suggest he could prove a cut above average when switched to chasing, especially when conditions ride soft or heavy.

Despite missing out on the trainers' championship again, *PAUL NICHOLLS* still had plenty to smile about as he bagged 127 domestic winners and over £2.5 million in prize-money last term.

Politologue proved his stable star as he was successful on four occasions in Grade 1 and Grade 2 company.

He signed off with victory in the Melling Chase at Aintree over 2m4f, which had Nicholls and the horse's owner, John Hales, thinking in terms of another step up in trip to three miles for the Betfair Chase so Haydock is likely to be his first port of call this season.

There have to be doubts about a horse who travels so well in his races getting the longer trip in my opinion, though, and it will be no surprise if connections settle on aiming him at all the top 2m4f races in the aftermath.

Of the younger horses at Ditcheat, one name on many lips at the yard over the summer was **Danny Kirwan**.

He simply hosed up on his British debut in a bumper at Kempton but then flopped on very deep ground in Grade 2 company at Aintree in April.

The former winning Irish pointer has come back from his summer holiday looking a much stronger individual than in the spring and it will be a huge shock if he does not make his mark in the top novice hurdles and end up at the major festivals next year.

Trevelyn's Corn cost £400,000 at the Cheltenham sales last December after winning his only point in Ireland, so plenty will be expected of him when the core season gets underway this autumn.

He is a chaser for the future, but before that one of the staying novice hurdles at Cheltenham next March is likely to be on his radar.

As usual Nicholls has an array of

DANNY KIRWAN: looks a lot stronger

potential stars and improvers in the novice chasing division, none more so than **Master Tommytucker**, who won twice at Exeter over hurdles at the end of last term and surprised even his trainer.

Getting carried away with a couple of victories in ordinary company can be the quickest way to the poor house, but he would not have won any prizes for looks on either occasion and has definitely filled out and seems much stronger now. He could be anything when switched to fences.

Great things were expected over fences from **Movewiththetimes** last season, but he proved something of a damp squib in his four attempts over fences which is something of a surprise.

He had finished a close second behind Ballyandy in the ultra-competitive Betfair Hurdle at Newbury on his final start over hurdles and if the Nicholls team can get him back to something along those lines he is surely a nicely handicapped horse over fences.

One or more of the better 2m4f handicap chases should be within his compass.

Both *DAVID PIPE* and *PHILIP HOBBS* saw their fortunes dip last term, but there is every reason to believe that the pair will leave those disappointments well behind in the mists of time and they should be followed this autumn and winter as some of their inmates are bound to be well handicapped as a result.

Pipe has never tried to hide the high regard in which he holds **King's Socks**, but the road with the six-year-old has been a rather bumpy one to say the least.

However a wind operation over the summer might well prove the key that unlocks the door to a successful season this time around.

Given that the Pipe name is inextricably linked with the race now known as the BetVictor Gold Cup – David's legendary father won the prize many times and his son took the spoils with Great Endeavour a few years back – at Cheltenham in November, it would not be a shock if King's Socks became the latest on the Pond House roll of honour.

MOVEWITHTETIMES: looks handicapped to win a big race this season

DEFI DU SEUIL (left): could easily bounce back over hurdles or fences

The mares' programme over hurdles and fences has been significantly boosted in recent years and Pipe has a potential top contender in the division in **Queens Cave**.

She ran out a comfortable winner of a Uttoxeter bumper on her debut and then was only just touched off in a Listed event at Sandown. She could be anything over hurdles.

Hobbs also found himself in the relative doldrums for much of last season with just 63 winners on the board and the master of Sandhill Stables will be relying on a number of young-bloods to get the yard's name back in the ascendancy.

However, one name many may recall is that of **Defi Du Seuil**, who went through the 2016-17 season unbeaten, culminating in victory in Cheltenham's JCB Triumph Hurdle and another Grade 1 hurdle at Aintree, but managed only two uninspiring starts last term.

He is still held in some regard at the yard and there is more than a chance he could get back in the winning groove over the autumn and winter, with connections having the options of remaining over hurdles or switching to fences.

HARRY FRY is always a trainer to keep on your side as he runs his horses only in races in which they have a proper chance and **Bullionaire**, who only made it to the racecourse once last term, is a name to follow.

He landed a bumper with considerable ease at Newbury last year and was beaten only a couple of lengths when next seen at Ascot in December despite running with the choke out.

As long as his tendency to be too keen can be ironed out, he could run up a little sequence over hurdles.

Western wonders
Bullionaire
Danny Kirwan
Kilbricken Storm

The North by Borderer

NORTHERN jumping fortunes are unquestionably on the up – whatever the once-a-year racegoers at Cheltenham may think.

Festival success at Prestbury Park in March remains elusive for the moment but there were a string of big Saturday winners to celebrate and three Grade 1 victories showed that it's perfectly possible to find a top-class jumper north of the Trent.

The best hurdler in the area was **Sam Spinner**. Indeed, he was arguably the best stayer trained anywhere in Britain, bolting up in a handicap at Haydock on Betfair Chase day and then making serene progress into top company with a cosy victory in the Long Walk Hurdle at Ascot.

His form dipped in the spring, but he is reported to be stronger than ever this autumn, encouraging the hope that he'll hold his form longer through the season. He is set to kick off in the West Yorkshire Hurdle at Wetherby, with the Stayers' Hurdle at Cheltenham the long-term aim.

However, should he come up slightly shy of the top stayers this time around, the obvious alternative is to go chasing – he'd be just about the best hurdler to be sent over fences anywhere in 2018-19.

Sam Spinner is one of only a handful of jumpers trained by *JEDD O'KEEFFE*, a Russian language graduate with a largely Flat string in Middleham, whereas *NICKY*

SAM SPINNER: form tailed off a bit last season but he should still be a force

RICHARDS has a stable full of them at the Cumbrian yard from which his family have been raiding all parts for more than half a century.

It was a vintage season for the Greystoke team, whose British prize-money tally was the highest for a decade – and that was without counting the haul of euros earned by **Simply Ned** on his trips to Ireland.

The crack chaser is usually there or thereabouts in the top 2m events at Leopardstown and he got rewarded for his consistency when awarded the Grade 1 Paddy's Rewards Club Chase in the stewards' room last December.

Expect more of the same from him this season as well as stablemate **Guitar Pete**, a smart 2m4f chaser who landed the Caspian Caviar Gold Cup in December and will have more top handicaps on his agenda.

Baywing, runaway winner of the Towton Novices' Chase on bottomless ground at Wetherby in 2017, is in his element when the mud is flying and underlined the point with a gutsy victory in the Eider Chase on heavy going at Newcastle last spring. He's an obvious candidate for the Welsh Grand National, not to mention the Grand National itself if we have a wet spring.

Duke Of Navan, who won the valuable 2m chase at Doncaster on Sky Bet Chase day, also has more good prizes in him.

Richards has a strong team of novice chasers, notably **On A Promise**, **Uncle Alastair** and the exciting **Chapel Stile**, who won his last three hurdle races in gritty fashion and could be one for the National Hunt Chase which his half-brother Rathvinden took last March.

There was nothing gritty about the north's third Grade 1 victory of the season. Rather, **Waiting Patiently** simply oozed class, making a horse as good as Cue Card look one-paced as he eased to the front full of running in the Ascot Chase last February.

It was impossible to know how much he had in reserve as he passed the post a comfortable winner and we were none the wiser by the end of the season as a slight setback forced him on to the sidelines.

Yet there's no doubt that the seven-year-old, who is unbeaten in six races over fences, is genuinely top-class and the word from Malton trainer *RUTH JEFFERSON* is that he could be back as early as November.

Though he's run his best races at 2m4f and on a soft surface, neither his trip nor his ground requirements are set in stone and the bookmakers who rate him Might Bite's main danger in the King George VI Chase at Kempton may not be far wide of the mark.

There are also a couple of high-class chasers across Malton in *BRIAN ELLISON*'s yard, including another possible King George candidate in **Definitly Red**.

He's certainly better than a laboured sixth behind Native River in the Cheltenham Gold Cup might suggest – he was never travelling with any fluency and it could be that some tough races were catching up with him.

If he's freshened up by a summer break and comes back to the form he showed when winning Grade 2 events there and at Aintree previously, he'll be a danger to all but the very best over staying trips.

Stablemate **Forest Bihan** is a two-miler to watch if he can recapture earlier efforts. Beating Simply Ned a length and three-quarters when they took each other at levels at Kelso was an outstanding effort and there was nothing wrong with his fourth place under top-weight at Doncaster in January.

Across Yorkshire, high up on the hills overlooking Bingley, *SUE SMITH* topped the 40-winner mark for the 13th time in 16 seasons.

The ultra-consistent stayer **Vintage Clouds** made the frame in the Welsh and Scottish Grand Nationals last season and the National itself is likely to be the aim this term.

Stablemate **I Just Know** was the yard's runner in the world's most famous chase last April and, though he got no further than the first Becher's, he has time on his side as he's only eight. He'd shown he was potentially smart in the way he bolted up in the North Yorkshire Grand National at Catterick previously.

CLOUDY DREAM (left): high-class chaser has been moved to Donald McCain

Sky Bet Chase winner **Wakanda** and Eider Chase fourth **Hainan** are others to look out for from a yard whose horses come into their own over fences and over longer distances.

That augurs exceptionally well for **Midnight Shadow**, Smith's big, raw five-year-old who beat seasoned campaigners to land the Scottish Champion Hurdle over just 2m at Ayr in April.

There won't be many horses in Britain who go chasing with better prospects than him.

One of the north's most dependable sources of winners is back firing on all cylinders in Cheshire as *DONALD McCAIN* returned to the top ten in the trainers' table and came within two of reaching a century for the first season since 2013-14.

The 2018-19 campaign promises to be just as successful, if not more so, particularly with Brian Hughes formally signed to the yard.

Second-season chaser **Testify** looks just the sort to land a decent soft-ground handicap in the winter.

Cracking novice chase prospects **Uppertown Prince** and **Dear Sire**, who's already won over fences, ought to pay their way, while progressive 2m hurdler **William Of Orange** could still have more improvement in him.

Lastbutnotleast is better than she showed on her last two runs and remains one to be interested in for mares' races, while promising novice hurdler **Fin And Game** is a decent prospect for handicaps and the juveniles **Breakfast** and **Ormesher** are already up and running with power to add.

As well as the usual influx of young Irish point-to-pointers, McCain's 2017-18 team is also boosted by the arrival of high-class chaser **Cloudy Dream** and useful novice **Mount Mews**, who have been given a change of scenery and sent to Bankhouse Stables by Trevor Hemmings.

ROSE DOBBIN had much her best season in ten years as a trainer with 25 winners in 2017-18 and she promises to do at least as well in the new campaign, if not better.

Smart novice hurdler **Coole Hall**, who wasn't himself on his final appearance last term, is just the sort to make a mark now he's being sent over fences, while Bigirononhiship has been given plenty of time to recover from bruised bones and ought to be really competitive in staying handicap chases.

A number of promising young horses have also joined South Hazelrigg Farm, but the name to look out for in the second half of the season is the highly promising **Jonniesofa**. He injured his suspensory ligament again but is worth waiting for.

Even more anticipation surrounds the expected return of *LUCINDA RUSSELL*'s **One For Arthur**, who won the Grand National in 2017 and was favourite to win it again 12 months only to miss the whole season due to injury.

The early word on his condition is good, with a November comeback planned and then one more run before another crack at the National.

He's an unexposed chaser who was firmly on the up when last we saw him and should still have plenty more to offer.

But this is no one-horse stable. Russell actually increased her total of winners in One For Arthur's absence last term and she has plenty of others to look forward to this season.

Smart novice **Big River** is due out in early November and could have the Scottish Grand National as a long-term target.

Forest Des Aigles is another progressive handicapper to look out for over fences, while three-time hurdle winner **Grand Morning** is a fine prospect for long-distance novice chases.

Nor is Russell the only Scottish trainer with reason to look forward to 2018-19.

Seeyouatmidnight did make it to last year's National and ran so well for such a long way that *SANDY THOMSON* will retain hope of finding winning opportunities for his talented but fragile flag-bearer.

Bedrock's third in Grade 1 novice company at Aintree and fourth in the Galway Hurdle suggests he can land something decent for *IAIN JARDINE*, while unbeaten bumper horse **I'm To Blame** could go places for *KEITH DALGLEISH*.

Angels of the north
Testify
One For Arthur
Sam Spinner

SEEYOUATMIDNIGHT: on the gallops at Sandy Thomson's yard

Midlands
by John Bull

DAN SKELTON has cemented his position among the leading jumps trainers in Britain, enjoying by far his best season with 156 winners last term, and more of the same can be expected after another fast start.

Skelton has enjoyed a fruitful summer and attention now turns to his winter stars, with **Roksana** among his leading lights.

The six-year-old produced a career-best when second to Santini in the Grade 1 Doom Bar Sefton Novices' Hurdle at Aintree on her final start of last season and is set to return to action in the late autumn.

The yard enjoyed Cheltenham Festival success with Mohaayed in the Randox Health County Hurdle last season and he is open to further improvement, with a step up to Graded company among options for the talented son of Intikhab.

An interesting recruit for the Skelton team is **Alnadam**, who was bought for £130,000 at the Goffs UK Spring sale in May.

The son of Poliglote was an impressive eight-length winner on his sole point-to-point start at Dromahane in May and could prove a real star.

OLLY MURPHY has an ever-expanding team and is set for his best season yet with several smart types.

Brewin'Upastorm defeated subsequent Grade 2 Aintree scorer Portrush Ted by nine lengths at Hereford in January before finishing fourth in a hot Listed bumper at Newbury the following month.

Murphy told John Bull: "He's summered really well. We'll start him off in a 2m maiden hurdle in the autumn over two miles and look to step him up in trip as the season goes on.

ROKSANA (right): one of Dan Skelton's top prospects for the season

ROBIN ROE (left): an interesting recruit to the Olly Murphy yard

"His bumper form looks strong, he's done well for a break and I'm really looking forward to seeing him back on the track."

One new recruit for Murphy is the talented **Robin Roe**, who has been off the track since falling in the Challow Novices' Hurdle in December 2016 when trained by Skelton. He will start off over hurdles before going novice chasing.

A novice hurdle campaign is in the offing for **Sangha River**.

Murphy said: "Sangha River will start off in a maiden hurdle in the late autumn but he doesn't want the ground too soft and is more of a horse for the spring. He's got a big engine and his work at home is second to none."

Hunters Call landed the Grade 3 Racing Welfare Handicap Hurdle at Ascot on his yard debut in December but missed the remainder of the season following a setback.

A repeat bid at Ascot is among options, with Murphy feeling the eight-year-old remains fairly treated.

Murphy commented: "The plan is to go straight for the Greatwood if I can get him ready in time, but if not we'll go straight back to Ascot for the race he won last year. I still think he's well handicapped and believe there will be another nice race in him this season."

Calipso Collonges won four of his five starts since joining Murphy last season and is set to go chasing.

Murphy said: "He's come up through the ranks and life will be a little tougher for him this season, but he always looked a chaser in the making so that's the route we'll go with him. He'll start off in a beginners' chase and will give his connections plenty of fun again this season. He stays very well."

Murphy also nominated a couple of younger horses to follow for the campaign among a team of more than 30 novice hurdlers set to be unleashed by the Warwickshire trainer.

He said: "**Garrettstown** won a bumper in really nice fashion at Chepstow last season and he could be a smart 2m4f novice hurdler, while **Thomas Darby** won a similar contest at Huntingdon and the form has worked out very well."

Popular veteran **Gas Line Boy** will once again have his followers for *IAN WILLIAMS* following a fine campaign in the 2017-18 season.

The 12-year-old landed the Grand

FAGAN: now with Alex Hales and bound for hunter chases in the spring

Sefton at Aintree and ran fine races when third in the veterans' handicap chase series final at Sandown and seventh in the Grand National.

Seven De Baune was an impressive bumper winner at Uttoxeter in May and is a potential star of the future, while **Michael's Mount**, a progressive five-year-old who landed two novice hurdles last season, and **Secret Legacy**, fairly treated off a mark of 122, are others definitely worth following.

A novice chaser worthy of note from the Alvechurch yard is **King Of Realms**.

The talented six-year-old boasts a progressive profile, finishing second behind two nice types before winning easily at Doncaster in the winter, and remains a horse of considerable potential despite a below-par final effort in handicap hurdle company at Cheltenham in April.

The Foxhunter at the Cheltenham Festival is the aim for *ALEX HALES*'s new recruit **Fagan**.

Second in the Albert Bartlett in 2016, Fagan was last seen pulling up when favourite in the Scottish National in April and joined Hales for £26,000 the following month.

The talented grey will be ridden by amateur jockey Ben Brackenbury, as will another recruit **Smooth Stepper**, who could contest the Becher Chase in December and Kim Muir in March.

Hales said: "We're very lucky to have them. Fagan is a lovely horse, has some top form and should be ideal for the leading hunter chases in the spring.

"Smooth Stepper is a real old-fashioned type and a great jumper. The Becher Chase could be a starting point for him – he'd relish the test over the National fences."

Hopes are high for **Huntsman Son**, who finished fourth in the Imperial Cup last season and is set to embark on a novice chase campaign for owner Bill Booth with a race at Uttoxeter earmarked as a possible starting point in October.

Hales said: "He's a really nice horse and

had a fantastic campaign last year. He's built for chasing, has plenty of toe and should excel over fences with the stamina for three miles."

The Close Brothers Novices' Handicap Chase could be a target for him at the Cheltenham Festival in March, while the Pertemps Final is a potential aim for the progressive **Florrie Knox**.

Duel At Dawn, a well-built son of Presenting, boasts some strong form from last season, including when a five-length second to Ms Parfois in a Listed novice chase at Warwick, and could be one for big staying handicaps in the spring.

Hereford maiden hurdle winner **Royal Sunday** and juvenile hurdling recruit **For Pleasure** are also worth following from the Edgcote yard.

ALASTAIR RALPH is another trainer on the up, the former assistant to Henry Daly boasting a 24 per cent strike-rate last season with an impressive 14 winners from 59 runners.

A mark of 124 could seriously underestimate **Billingsley**, the apple of the trainer's eye, who won two heavy-ground novice hurdles at Chepstow last year and is very much open to improvement with a lightly raced and unexposed profile.

Daario Naharis could prove a shrewd purchase for owner Bill Hawkins with the £20,000 Goffs buy finishing a close third behind the aforementioned Thomas Darby at Huntingdon in May.

Another horse for the notebook is **Redemption Song** from KEVIN FROST's yard near Market Drayton.

The imposing daughter of Mastercraftsman had wind surgery in March and returned with a promising third over hurdles at Worcester in August.

She is set for a chasing campaign and will be seen to best effect over three miles.

Midlands magic
Fagan
Roksana
Thomas Darby

DUEL AT DAWN (right): could have a big staying handicap in him

The South by Southerner

RETIREMENT for stable star Sire De Grugy and the aching loss of the breathtaking Ar Mad in a fall at Sandown's final meeting would be a bodyblow to many a stable.

However, the loss of his two Grade 1 performers is not stopping *GARY MOORE* looking for more success at the top table with not only the rising young stars but also an ex-Willie Mullins hurdler.

Step forward **Diakali**, who joined Moore at his Lower Beeding estate at the start of the year, his owner Nick Peacock having had horses with him for some time.

Diakali initially ran ingloriously in the Aintree Hurdle and bet365 Hurdle at Sandown, but two runs in June changed everything.

The nine-year-old pulverised novice chase fields under typical front-running rides from Richard Johnson and has Moore planning top targets this winter.

Punters will point to odds on 1-2 and 8-13 suggesting Diakali just won some weak summer jumping heats as he should, but it would be foolish to underestimate a horse who four years ago came within a head and a nose of winning the Grade 1 Aintree Hurdle for Mullins against no less than The New One and Rock On Ruby, while a year earlier he had won a Grade 1 at Auteuil.

Moore plans to run him under a double penalty after his summer break, probably at the Showcase meeting at Cheltenham on October 27.

"He has ambitious targets," said Moore. "He's rated 156 and yes, he's not getting any younger, but I could see him running in the Arkle next March – he has bags of speed."

Sussex Ranger, who dropped away two out in the Triumph Hurdle last season, is out to prove that run was all wrong, which his trainer believes was the case. He'll run in four-year-old hurdles before the turn of the year, while the Gerry Feilden at Newbury is also on his radar.

Benatar, third in the JLT at Cheltenham after winning the Grade 2 Noel Chase at Ascot last season, is being aimed at the BetVictor Gold Cup, for which he might warm up in a graduation chase. Moore could step him up in trip if he settles better into his races this season.

Another Cheltenham Festival runner, **Traffic Fluide**, who went on to win the Grade 2 Silver Trophy there in April, has even bigger targets as a horse who thrives in the spring.

The Randox Health Grand National is the ultimate target this season, but the eight-year-old has to qualify for the Aintree showpiece with a placing in a race over 3m, which Moore hopes to achieve in October before a winter break when the ground turns soft.

The message is not to give up on **Casse Tete**, who could make no impression in some top handicap chases including the Ultima Handicap at Cheltenham. Equally Moore is not expecting fireworks in his early races as the six-year-old needs racing to sharpen up, but he still has Cheltenham aspirations again for him.

Eragon De Chanay, seventh in the Fred Winter, is another to keep on your side with Moore expecting improvement from a step up in trip and when racing right-handed.

Moore has done well with his buys out of France and is hoping the trend continues with three to note.

Episode is a strong filly who was placed in a provincial bumper and has jumped well in schooling; **Tazka** is a nice three-year-old who also placed in a bumper; and **Editeur Du Gite**, winner of a Compiegne bumper, gets a good word as a big

2018-19 RFO Jumps Racing Guide

BENATAR (right): being aimed at the BetVictor Gold Cup at Cheltenham

horse who will be at home on galloping tracks.

Another youngster Moore points out is **Twenty Twenty**, a juvenile hurdler who is a half-brother to Supasundae.

CHRIS GORDON had a season to remember last year, although had some of his 40 seconds won he probably wouldn't remember the campaign!

Unfortunately this year's hopes have been torn apart by his star hurdler Remiluc, runner-up in the County Hurdle, being out for the season with a leg injury.

Gordon still has hopes of **Highway One O One** stepping up to the plate in novice chases after providing another of the stable's big-race seconds when beaten by Ballymoy in the novice championship final at Sandown in April.

The six-year-old son of Stowaway, who is certainly built to impress over fences and had pointing form before joining Gordon from John Costello in Ireland, made a winning start over fences in September.

Talking of the legendary Costello, Gordon has another from that source who is showing promise for bumpers in **It's Only Money**.

With Gordon using bumpers to bring along his young horses rather than rev them up for success, there were a couple of promising sorts from that field last season who are ready to go novice hurdling.

They are **Baddesley Knight**, who still won his Plumpton bumper, and **Commanche Red**, who ran in the Grade 2 bumper at Aintree after a fluent Kempton win. Forget his Aintree showing as heavy rain turned conditions against him there and he remains one to follow. Both are chasers further down the line.

EMMA LAVELLE has moved further west from Andover to Philip Makin's old yard in Ogbourne Maizey, but she remains one of Southerner's best contacts and her young novice chasers, most of whom are stayers in the making, are exciting the team.

Enniscoffey Oscar, who won the Grade 2 River Don Novices' Hurdle last season, is expected to start at 2m4f and come

DIDTHEYLEAVEUOUTTO: exciting season ahead in novice hurdles

into his own over 3m. He needs top of the ground.

Gunfleet is another marked down as a 3m novice chaser for the season after the six-year-old won two hurdle races to finish last term.

Flemcara, who has kept on improving, is another staying chaser in the making and for the midwinter as he likes nothing better than deep ground, while **De Rasher Counter**, who is versatile with all ground coming alike and should prove best over 2m4f, is also going chasing.

Junction Fourteen, who took a horrible fall at Fontwell which shook his confidence, is on his way back and wants decent ground, with Aintree's Grand Sefton a possibility.

Buster Thomas, a half-brother to the retired stable stalwart Shotgun Paddy, could be well handicapped for 2m4f chases on decent ground after Lavelle realised the seven-year-old did not want soft ground or longer trips. He is a really good jumper.

Another familiar name to follow is **Full Irish**, who has had a wind operation and has shown his best form fresh with cut in the ground and going left-handed.

Look out for two of the stable's bumper horses as **Boomerang**, who won a decent summer bumper at Newton Abbot, is a good jumper and doesn't need the quick ground, and **Dissavril**, impressive in her bumper at Market Rasen before nothing went right at Aintree, is reported to have done well over the break and loves her jumping despite not being overly big.

NICK GIFFORD has his Champion Bumper tenth **Didtheyleaveuoutto** back from owner JP McManus after his summer holiday at Martinstown with an exciting season ahead of the five-year-old, who won his Ascot and Lingfield bumpers in style.

The Findon trainer also has potential Grand National contender **Glen Rocco** back after missing a season.

Southern stars
Diakali
Benatar
Didtheyleaveuoutto

2018-19 RFO Jumps Racing Guide

Newmarket by Aborigine

LUCY WADHAM believes that her progressive six-year-old mare **Banjo Girl** could use a Listed race at Bangor in November as a springboard to greater things this season.

Wadham has held this daughter of Presenting in high esteem from an early stage and she justified that faith by winning three of her seven starts last season.

A win at Southwell in November preceded wins at Fakenham and Fontwell before she was again to the fore in Listed company when third to Dame De Compagnie at Cheltenham, leading approaching the last before fading on the climb to the finish.

The racecourse vet reported afterwards that she had suffered from heat stress as a result of the high temperatures, so her run can definitely be upgraded.

Wadham gave her a well-deserved break during the summer and is very pleased with the way Banjo Girl has done during her holiday.

The plan is to find a small race somewhere before the mare goes for black type at Bangor.

Wadham has always had a way with mares and also holds out high hopes for **Shantung**.

This five-year-old daughter of Shantou has been plying her trade in bumpers and caught the eye when third to Morningreferendum at Warwick in February.

Her campaign will start off in bumpers before she turns her attention to hurdles. She looks a very exciting prospect.

Potters Legend is another powerful string to Wadham's jumping bow.

Though he took some time to get his head in front last season, he ran some cracking races. He was looking all over the winner when falling at the last at Fakenham and then revealed his true potential by winning a competitive staying chase final at Haydock in great style, coasting clear of Horatio Hornblower.

Even though he has taken a hike in the

POTTERS LEGEND: a rise in the weights won't stop him from winning again

weights, this fine individual has a lot more mileage left in him.

Sticking to the chasers, Wadham has been nursing her high-class stayer **Le Reve** back to fitness after injury sidelined him last season.

Wadham told Aborigine: "He's run with credit in the Grand National but his target this year will be the veterans' final at Sandown in January as he loves the course."

Wadham also expects **Shanroe Santos** to pay his way.

Although the nine year-old won only once last year, hacking up at Carlisle in heavy ground, he also inished a good second to Vinnie Lewis in Plumpton's Sussex National.

Wadham said: "There's a decent handicap chase to be won with him, but the trouble is that he tends to make the odd mistake even though jumping well most of the time."

AMY MURPHY is a rising star in Newmarket and **Kalashnikov** quickly put her into the jumping limelight last season.

This good-looking individual soon made his mark, winning his first three races under rules and going on to add the Betfair Hurdle at Newbury, in which he was most impressive in beating Bleu Et Rouge by four and a half lengths.

However, he met his nemesis in Summerville Boy, who had beaten him in the Tolworth and just did so again in the Supreme Novices' Hurdle at Cheltenham.

MERCIAN PRINCE: reduced mark

It looked like Kalashnikov had stolen the race that day when Jack Quinlan took him to the front three out, but Summerville Boy fought back after the last to score.

Murphy tells me Kalashnikov has done wonderfully well over the summer and the plan is to send him novice chasing, although no specific target has yet been chosen.

Murphy also holds out high hopes for her 25-1 Cheltenham winner **Hawthorn Cottage**.

The five-year-old mare stepped up appreciably on previous form when making virtually all the running to beat Definitelyanoscar by half a length in a bumper at the course in April and will go novice hurdling.

Murphy could have a rewarding time with **Mercian Prince**.

Twice a winner over fences at Kempton and Wetherby, he was slightly out of his depth at the Cheltenham Festival and then up at Ayr. Back in more modest company, he should have little difficulty in using his reduced handicap mark to good effect.

RICHARD SPENCER has won at Royal Ascot and Glorious Goodwood in his fledgling career and has the Cheltenham Festival on his mind once again for his stalwart performer **Sir Jack Yeats**, although it could be in a different race.

Last season the seven-year-old paid his way with hunter chase wins at Market Rasen and Kelso in February, which earned him a tilt at the Foxhunter at Cheltenham. He ran well to finish 12th to Pacha Du Polder and was then seventh to Balnaslow in the Aintree version, jumping with his usual fluency until he ran out of steam after a busy couple of months.

Spencer is pleased with the way he has come through the summer and said: "He may continue in hunter chases, but I feel that he has the ability to make his mark on the cross-country circuit and we could go down that route in time."

JAMES EUSTACE always keeps a few potential jumps winners on the move from his Park Lodge Stables.

The five-year-old Irish-bred gelding **Debacle** was never going to achieve much on the Flat, but he can pay his way over hurdles this season and, from looking at him, chasing ought to be his forte in time.

Given plenty of time to come to hand, he had just two runs last year and will come on for his first run this season at Stratford in a hot contest for a novice hurdle. That qualified him for handicaps and his shrewd trainer will place him to good advantage.

Closest Friend caught the eye when putting in his best effort to date when second to Grow Nasa Grow at Market Rasen. Eustace feels a chase win should soon come his way.

Stablemate **Macksville** has been knocking on the door over hurdles and is worth following, while unraced Lawman gelding **See The City** has plenty of potential.

Hot off the Heath
Banjo Girl
Debacle
Hawthorn Cottage

TONY JAKOBSON

BRILLIANT ALL-WEATHER ADVICE FOR THE WINTER

There will be good jumps angles too so you really will be getting the best of all worlds to keep your punting in top shape!

0906 911 0232

BT UK calls cost £1 per minute. ROI call 1560 719760 (Eircom calls €1.25/min). Calls from mobiles and other networks will vary. To subscribe to Tony's daily tips, text RFOJAKO to UK: 84080 / ROI: 57856 (£1.50 / €2 per text plus standard network rate).

Hunter chasers by Nick Watts

THE amazing **Pacha Du Polder** could have been going to the Cheltenham Festival next year on a four-timer if things had worked out slightly differently.

He has won the last two renewals of the Foxhunter and it might have been three if Victoria Pendleton had just a little more race-riding experience going into 2016. On that occasion the pair finished fifth, beaten less than three lengths, and while Pendleton emerges with huge credit a more experienced pilot probably would have won.

Pacha Du Polder will be a 12-year-old next year, but that doesn't rule him out of things.

However, his trainer Paul Nicholls has another interesting candidate for hunter chases this season in **Silsol**.

He is a 153-rated hurdler who took the scalp of Native River in a Grade 2 at Wetherby in 2016. Not quite so good over fences, he still managed to come fifth in the Welsh National last season and fourth in the Midlands National.

A strong stayer, he will find things easier in this sphere and could easily be heading to Cheltenham with a couple of wins next to his name already.

Alex Hales also has an interesting newcomer to these ranks in **Fagan**.

It's a slight concern that he has left the Gordon Elliott yard – presumably if he was still thought capable of good things he wouldn't have – but, that said, a switch to a smaller yard can help certain horses and there is no doubt his past form is good.

Second in the 2016 Albert Bartlett to Unowhatimeanharry, he managed to finish second to the useful Ballyandy and Black Corton last season before being sent off favourite for the Scottish National only to disappoint and pull up.

SILSOL: a very smart hurdler and not far off that level over fences

BURNING AMBITION: only eighth at Cheltenham but can do better now

He cost Hales £26,000 this spring and, as an eight-year-old – and a lightly raced one at that – he should still have some good years ahead of him in theory at least.

If Silsol and Fagan do make it to the big spring festivals, they are likely to have to deal with **Gilgamboa**, something they wouldn't have had to do last season.

He wasn't eligible for Cheltenham, but this former Grade 1-winning chaser still made quite a splash in this division, winning three Irish hunter chases in a row.

An easy defeat of Foxrock at Thurles in January was impressive, as was his win at Punchestown the following month, although that was much harder fought.

The young pretender Burning Ambition looked as though he was coming to win that race but, galvanised after jumping the last by the now-retired Nina Carberry, Gilgamboa fought back strongly and was well on top at the line.

That was it for him and he wasn't seen thereafter, but he is the one they all have to aim at this season as no hunter will have the class that he possesses.

Although he didn't place at Cheltenham, **Burning Ambition** is still very much one to keep on your side.

Pierce Power's seven-year-old looked as though he didn't stay the trip in the Foxhunter, finishing a respectable eighth of 24.

However, he also lacked experience going into the race and, with another year on his back, he may be a different proposition this time.

Before then he had been impressive, especially when one of the easiest winners you will have seen all season when taking Limerick's hunter chase at their Christmas meeting.

It's interesting he was entered in Aintree's Foxhunter's after Cheltenham (even though he ended up not going) as that is a race that might suit him perfectly. It is run over a much shorter trip than its Cheltenham counterpart and Burning Ambition does travel particularly well.

His jumping at Cheltenham in the face of a big field was also secure, so he could have the perfect attributes for success at Liverpool, particularly if connections can again call upon the services of Jamie Codd – one of the best amateur riders in the game and the man who rode him into eighth at the festival.

Tipping Point with Tom Collins

Six horses who will pay their way this season

THE Flat season is coming to an end and it's almost time for tweed, soft ground and stamina-sapping, thrilling contests to engulf us for the next six to seven months.

People will often say that they can't wait for Christmas or ask what you are doing for Christmas this year, but the first thing that springs to my mind when the festive December holiday is mentioned is Boxing Day and the abundance of equine brilliance that graces our television screens while we tuck into leftovers from the day before. Sad, I know.

However, the season starts well before then and powerhouses Nicky Henderson, Paul Nicholls, Willie Mullins, Gordon Elliott and the like will already hope they have racked up a vast amount of winners leading into the new year.

Indeed, it will be interesting to see whether Henderson can fend off Nicholls for a third season in a row to become champion trainer once more – or whether the up-and-coming Dan Skelton, who built up a huge advantage over the summer, can cause a relative upset.

Though there's even less chance of an upset in Ireland, the trainers' battle is no less intriguing given the battle between Mullins and Elliott last term. The pair will dominate again and there looks to be very little between them in terms of strength.

The ever-consistent Richard Johnson bids to add another jockey's title to his name in Britain since the retirement of the legendary Sir Anthony McCoy.

Ruby Walsh, Davy Russell and perhaps Rachael Blackmore look set to tussle for the Irish version. What a brilliant result it would be to see Blackmore come out on top. That would be the story of the season, without question.

On the horse front, the Racing Post's horse tracker will start to become active again – there isn't anything better than to see a good thing declared for the next day via email – and the likes of Altior, Buveur D'Air, Samcro and Might Bite are sure to get the pulse racing at the best festivals.

Away from the absolute superstars, here are six others who look worth following across the course of the season.

Al Boum Photo 6yo gelding
1F2F1O- (Willie Mullins)

Al Boum Photo improved beyond recognition last season, with the pinnacle coming in the Grade 1 Ryanair Gold Cup when he beat the JLT Novices' Chase winner Shattered Love by a length.

He was unlucky to record just that sole success in a Grade 1 last year as he was only narrowly denied in the Flogas Novice Chase in February, fell heavily two out in the RSA at Cheltenham and incredibly ran out at the final fence at Punchestown.

Paul Townend had given him a cracking ride that day and he looked for all the world like scoring for the first time over 3m or further, but a moment of madness led to his rider veering dramatically off course and costing him the race.

It won't take him long to win over that kind of trip this year and he's one to follow en route to the Cheltenham Festival.

Dostal Phil 5yo gelding
4- (Philip Hobbs)

Dostal Phil is a completely unexposed gelding who won his only start in France as a three-year-old when beating a 123-rated performer cosily before joining Philip Hobbs with a big reputation.

The son of Coastal Path has clearly had his problems for new connections as he made the track just once last year when finishing fourth in a decent novice hurdle at Bangor in October.

He was sent off the 4-5 favourite that day but never really travelled or jumped with much fluency. In the circumstances he did quite well to finish relatively close to the leaders and all three who finished in front of him have won since.

He looks a hurdler to follow this season with another summer under his belt.

Fleminport 5yo gelding
37114- (Jonjo O'Neill)

Fleminport may need another season as he's sure to be a cracking chaser, but he looked an improving sort last season and seems to be pretty ground versatile.

He denied useful sorts Tossapenny and Clash Of D Titans in maiden and novice hurdles earlier this year before being sent off favourite for a Uttoxeter handicap hurdle won by Clyne. The fact he was so short in the market suggests how much ability he might have and the winner is obviously no slouch.

Once Jonjo O'Neill sends him over fences, I'll be following him closely.

AL BOUM PHOTO: one to watch over staying trips this season

MEEP MEEP: finished fourth in this bumper won by Getaway Katie Mai

Lust For Glory 5yo mare
13-1 (Nicky Henderson)

This five-year-old mare could be something special.

Winner of a Lisronagh point-to-point in Ireland under Jamie Codd last October, Lust For Glory was sold to Nicky Henderson for £240,000 a month later and ran encouragingly on both starts for her new connections.

Well backed for an Ascot bumper, she looked extremely athletic in the preliminaries but blew her chance by pulling too hard early on. She travelled really well, mind you, but just couldn't live with the first two in the final furlong.

Unsurprisingly she made amends when making her racecourse reappearance at Ludlow in May, showing a really nice turn of foot to burst clear. She could be the real deal.

Meep Meep 5yo mare
14- (Tom Lacey)

Meep Meep made the track for the first time in March when well supported for a Chepstow bumper and duly obliged with a strong, staying performance.

Tom Lacey's attractive mare was sent straight to Aintree on the back of that performance for the Grade 2 mares' bumper at the Grand National meeting and showed clear improvement and a copious amount of talent when plugging on to take fourth behind the impressive Getaway Katie Mai.

Subsequently unsold at the horses in training sale, Meep Meep remains with Lacey and is one to follow this year, especialyl if stepped up to staying trips.

Seddon 5yo gelding
10- (Tom George)

Tom George clearly ranks Seddon highly and he didn't look far wrong when he hacked up on debut at Musselburgh by five lengths last February.

A top bumper was immediately given as the next target by the trainer, so it was no surprise to see him run at the Cheltenham Festival on his second and final start of the campaign.

He finished 12th that day under Adrian Heskin, but he travelled really smoothly throughout and coming round the home bend you could have been mistaken for thinking he was going to go close.

In the end he flattened out and just didn't have the speed to live with the protagonists, but he'll be seen to good effect this season over longer trips.

2018-19 RFO Jumps Racing Guide

RACING & FOOTBALL OUTLOOK
Est. 1909

Richard Birch
Read Birchy every week in the RFO

Keep Baywing on your radar for staying chases

REGULAR readers of my weekly Get It Ready! column will not be surprised to see **Baywing** among my list of ten horses to follow for the 2018-19 jumps season.

The Nicky Richards-trained stayer has proved a punting colossus for me over the last few seasons and remains unexposed in marathon chases.

Remember how easily he won the Eider Chase at Newcastle last February? Always travelling strongly and jumping with slick precision, he showed a remarkable turn of foot at the end of a 4m endurance test to slam West Of The Edge by four lengths.

He won that race with plenty in hand and looks a natural for the Welsh Grand National, which is always run in the deep-ground conditions which Baywing needs.

And if the ground came up soft at Aintree I honestly believe he has the class to make a serious impact in the Grand National itself. After all, how many horses can you think of who storm up the hill and show acceleration after the final fence in an Eider, which traditionally sees a slow-motion finish?

Broken Quest, who showed rapid improvement during the spring to win three consecutive handicap hurdles at Huntingdon, Kempton and Sandown, didn't look the same horse afterwards in heavy Ayr and Wincanton defeats.

I have a hunch his hard race at Sandown left a mark and he will be all the better for a good summer break.

Only six, he has the size and scope to make up into a decent handicapper over fences this campaign and seems sure to be suited by a step up to 3m.

The Nick Williams-trained **Dentley De Mee** caught my eye on several occasions last term, particularly when a seven-length runner-up to Sam's Gunner in the valuable EBF Final at Sandown in the spring.

He travelled through that race like the best horse at the weights and maybe his rider Chester Williams committed him for home too soon.

Dentley De Mee will start the season on a mark of 128 and there is abundant potential for him to be rated considerably higher in 12 months.

Glittering Love is an intriguing horse for handicap chases this season.

Owned by Paul and Clare Rooney, the six-year-old cut little ice in novice hurdles prior to embarking on a stint in point-to-points for Nicky Richards's daughter Joey.

He duly won four of his five starts between the flags and can resume his career

73

off a mark of just 92, which gives Richards plenty of options with him.

Glittering Love could stay over hurdles and rack up a sequence prior to switching to chasing or go straight over the bigger obstacles off his basement rating. Whichever way Richards points him, I expect him to win a stack of handicaps over the course of the season.

Leith Hill Legasi, a one-paced staying chaser who loves the mud, drew a blank last year and, as a result, starts the season on a very attractive mark of 77.

Charlie Longsdon's mare, given a wind operation last spring, jumps beautifully and is as game as they game, albeit slow. She shouldn't be difficult to place off her mark and I expect her to win two or three.

Nigel Twiston-Davies enjoyed a memorable 2017-18, highlighted by the success of Bristol De Mai.

Stablemate **Natter Jack Croak** is nowhere near that class, but the six-year-old son of Gold Well was a massive eye-catcher on his first start for the stable since switching from the Rebecca Curtis yard.

He shaped really nicely in fourth place behind First Assignment at Huntingdon in January, travelling like a well-handicapped horse for much of the journey.

Natter Jack Croak missed eight months after that and may just have needed his first run back at Perth at the end of September, but he was able to run off just 111 that day and it will be a major disappointment if he isn't rated 125 or higher by April.

BAYWING: could be good enough to win a Grand National on soft ground

YANMARE (right): remember him for December's marathon chase at Exeter

On A Promise proved a big money-spinner last term with three wins from four starts, his sole defeat in handicap hurdles coming behind a well-treated Pop Rockstar at Wetherby in December.

Although he stays particularly well, On A Promise is blessed with a wonderful cruising speed and I expect him to make further improvement when sent over fences.

The six-year-old grey can start in limited handicaps off 120 and it will be no surprise if he works his way quickly up the staying ladder. He is a very exciting prospect for such races in the north.

Evan Williams places his horses particularly well and **Virginia Chick** proved the latest showcase of his talents when landing four of his last five starts in 2017-18.

Still lightly raced and open to more improvement, the six-year-old will find things tougher off 123, but he possesses all the qualities required to take a further big step forward and is well worth following.

So, too, is the Venetia Williams-trained **Yalltari**, who should develop into a lovely staying chaser this term.

A grand stamp of a horse with plenty of physical scope, the son of Kayf Tara goes into the new season unbeaten in handicap hurdles, his victories coming in the mud at Hereford, Exeter and Uttoxeter.

He gives the impression there will be significant improvement when switched to fences and he has every chance of staying 3m. A most exciting prospect.

Yanmare wasn't as prolific last season as he had been the previous year, but that wasn't entirely unexpected as he had moved up the handicap.

He still has potential in marathon chases, though, and while even a major handicap like the Eider couldn't be ruled out at this stage the race which looks tailormade for him once again is the 3m6f handicap chase run on the first Friday in December at Exeter.

Jamie Bargary produced one of the rides of the season to get Yanmare home in that contest last year and it will be a surprise if Twiston-Davies hasn't got his eye firmly focused on a repeat. A mark of 106 looks eminently workable.

Time Test

Gold Cup the race of the year on the eye and the clock

THE Cheltenham Gold Cup won by **Native River** was an epic for the eye and on the clock.

In torching a field of high-class staying chasers with a powerful front-running performance hallmarked by economic jumping, Native River earned a Time Test mark of 92 in what was comfortably the best race of the season.

Only **Might Bite** could live with him and his mark of 87, also a career-best, would have been good enough to have comfortably landed the previous year's Gold Cup.

Native River is still only eight and, after a light campaign of two races last season, he appears well placed for a crack at the triple crown of the Betfair Chase, the King George and the Gold Cup.

Henderson has similar aspirations with Might Bite, who is a year older than his Cheltenham conqueror but came to chasing a season later, and if both stay fit their rivalry has the potential to define the jumps season, with shades of Denman and Kauto Star about it given their contrasting styles.

Both have been similarly pegged in the Gold Cup market alongside **Presenting Percy**, who has yet to record an eyecatching Time Test figure over fences with his victory in the RSA Chase earning just 26.

Some substance to his championship claims comes from the fact he excelled when given an extreme test over hurdles, with his mark of 71 when winning the Pertemps Final in 2017 the highest by a staying hurdler that season, although ready preference would have to be for the established performers at this stage.

Just as likely to shake things up is **Balko Des Flos**, who achieved a Time Test mark of 81 in upsetting **Un De Sceaux** (80) in the Ryanair Chase.

A second in the Grade 1 Christmas Chase at Leopardstown last Christmas pointed to his potential over further and the Galway Plate winner could easily develop into a serious Gold Cup contender.

The Hennessy Gold Cup was rebranded the Ladbrokes Trophy last season, but its enduring quality was underlined by the fact it produced a figure of 83 from runner-up **Whisper**, who was denied on the line when trying to give loads of weight to winner **Total Recall**. That was the fourth best on the clock all season in a race won by Native River two years ago, with only the first three from the Gold Cup ahead of him.

Politologue does not seem to like Cheltenham but does well elsewhere and the career-best mark of 79 he posted in winning Aintree's Melling Chase suggests last year's Tingle Creek winner could have potential over longer trips, a hope shared by trainer Paul Nicholls, who has the Betfair Chase in mind.

Turning to the 2m division, it is strange to think a horse that has won his last 14 starts might be a little vulnerable but that is how it feels about Champion Chase winner **Altior**, who is unbeaten for the last four years and has never lost over hurdles or fences.

After an injury-interrupted season, he did not look especially comfortable at times in the season's premier 2m chase, at one point looking like getting beaten before ultimately surging away powerfully.

That may just be his style of racing these days, but a Time Test figure of 77 is lower than he notched in the previous campaign and any regression could be ruthlessly exploited by Racing Post Arkle winner **Footpad**.

Like the brilliant Altior, Footpad is unbeaten over fences and his 14-length defeat of Brain Power at Cheltenham earned him a mark of 83, the best by any 2m chaser last season. The six-year-old has a silken way of jumping and time on his side.

While a golden season might await over fences, it is hard to be so enthusiastic about the hurdlers.

The best hurdling number on the clock last season belonged to the admirable veteran **The New One** (75) for his win in the Welsh Champion Hurdle, which says plenty about the lack of competitiveness at the top end.

When **Buveur D'Air** quit novice chasing two years ago, it opened the path to two Champion Hurdle wins, the first delivering a Time Test mark of 85. But he needed to hit just 70 to strike again last March and the pool of high-class rivals capable of thwarting the hat-trick looks small.

In such a barren division, it looks a wise move to keep Supreme Novices' Hurdle winner **Summerville Boy** (67) to hurdles as he doesn't have much to find on that evidence, although the suspicion is that Buveur D'Air remains capable of reaching greater heights.

FOOTPAD: Arkle win was better than anything Altior has ever achieved

Strictly on the ratings, the biggest threat to the champion promises to come from **Supasundae** if he drops back in trip at Cheltenham.

Runner-up to **Penhill** in a slowly run Stayers' Hurdle in March, the Irish Champion Hurdle winner notched the best Time Test rating of his career (72) when beating **Wicklow Brave** (68) in the Punchestown Champion Hurdle over this trip.

That race would have been a lot more revealing had **Melon** and **Samcro** not fallen three out. Melon had matched Buveur D'Air's mark of 70 when beaten a neck in the Champion Hurdle, but Ballymore Novices' Hurdle winner Samcro is yet to record anything significant on the clock.

Having beaten Penhill over 3m at Punchestown, **Faugheen** is being remodelled as a staying hurdler and may even prove the answer in a weak-looking division, although that victory came in another slowly run race and his best Time Test rating of last season – 64 earned in landing the Morgiana – was a long way below his peak of 77 from four seasons ago.

Top chasers of 2017-18

	Horse	Speed rating	Distance in furlongs	Going	Track	Date achieved
1	**Native River**	92	26	SFT	Cheltenham	Mar 16
2	Might Bite	87	26	SFT	Cheltenham	Mar 16
3	Anibale Fly	83	26	SFT	Cheltenham	Mar 16
3	Footpad	83	16	HY	Cheltenham	Mar 13
3	Whisper	83	26	GS	Newbury	Dec 2
6	Waiting Patiently	82	21	SFT	Ascot	Feb 17
7	Balko Des Flos	81	21	SFT	Cheltenham	Mar 15
8	Un De Sceaux	80	16	YS	Punchestown	Apr 24
9	Cue Card	79	21	SFT	Ascot	Feb 17
9	Politologue	79	20	SFT	Aintree	Apr 13
9	Road To Respect	79	26	SFT	Cheltenham	Mar 16

Top hurdlers of 2017-18

	Horse	Speed rating	Distance in furlongs	Going	Track	Date achieved
1	**The New One**	75	16	SFT	Ffos Las	Oct 21
2	Supasundae	72	16	SFT	Punchestown	Apr 27
3	Buveur D'Air	70	16	HY	Cheltenham	Mar 13
3	Melon	66	16	HY	Cheltenham	Mar 13
5	Wicklow Brave	68	16	SFT	Punchestown	Apr 27
5	William Henry	68	21	SFT	Kempton	Jan 13
7	Beer Goggles	67	24	SFT	Aintree	Nov 11
7	Bleu Et Rouge	67	16	SFT	Newbury	Feb 10
7	Kalashnikov	67	16	SFT	Newbury	Feb 10
7	Summerville Boy	67	16	HY	Cheltenham	Mar 13

2018-19 RFO Jumps Racing Guide

RACING & FOOTBALL OUTLOOK

Est. 1909

Big-race review by Dylan Hill

1 bet365 Charlie Hall Chase (Grade 2) (3m45y)
Wetherby November 4 (Soft)
1 **Bristol De Mai** 6-11-6 Daryl Jacob
2 **Blaklion** 8-11-0 Gavin Sheehan
3 **Definitly Red** 8-11-4 Danny Cook
6/1, 5/1, 8/1. ½l, 23l. 8 ran. 6m 28.20s (Nigel Twiston-Davies).

The strongest evidence that Betfair Chase winner **Bristol De Mai** can be a top-class chaser away from Haydock as he won with more authority than the narrow winning margin given he was always travelling far more strongly than main rival **Blaklion** and found plenty having idled and been joined at the last. Blaklion was receiving 6lb and confirmed he was a much-improved horse when running away with the Becher Chase next time, while subsequent dual Grade 2 winner **Definitly Red** was well beaten in third. **Cue Card** fell when upsides Bristol De Mai five out.

2 JNwine.com Champion Chase (Grade 1) (3m)
Down Royal (IRE) November 4 (Soft)
1 **Outlander** 9-11-10 Jack Kennedy
2 **Road To Respect** 6-11-10 Sean Flanagan
3 **Zabana** 8-11-10 Davy Russell
16/1, 7/2, 25/1. ½l, 14l. 8 ran. 6m 16.10s (Gordon Elliott).

Outlander had lost his way after winning the Lexus in 2016, but treatment for a back problem brought him back to his best and he again proved himself a high-class chaser with a gutsy win over **Road To Respect**. The pair had a tremendous duel from two out, but Outlander was just too strong for his younger rival, who would improve again on better ground when winning at Leopardstown over Christmas. He was 14l clear of **Zabana** and **Alpha Des Obeaux**, with **Sub Lieutenant**, **More Of That** and **Our Duke** further back.

3 BetVictor Gold Cup (Handicap Chase) (Grade 3) (2m4f78y)
Cheltenham November 18 (Soft)
1 **Splash Of Ginge** 9-10-6 Tom Bellamy
2 **Starchitect** 6-11-2 Tom Scudamore
3 **Le Prezien** 6-11-8 Barry Geraghty
25/1, 10/1, 6/1. nk, 2½l. 17 ran. 5m 24.50s (Nigel Twiston-Davies).

A surprise winner but a strong field behind, with two progressive second-season chasers filling the places and the last two winners of the Cheltenham Festival novice handicap, **Ballyalton** and **Tully East**, also to the fore. Ultimately, though, it proved the handicapper had taken too much of a chance with **Splash Of Ginge**, who was let loose off 134 having once won a Grade 3 course-and-distance handicap off 145 and would go close at the Cheltenham Festival off 137. The unfortunate **Starchitect**, denied another big prize when fatally breaking down in the Caspian Caviar Gold Cup, was particularly unlucky after mistakes at the last two fences, finishing second ahead of subsequent Grand Annual winner **Le Prezien** with Ballyalton, **Romain De Senam** and Tully East next. **Guitar Pete** was always in rear after being badly hampered at the first.

4 Unibet Morgiana Hurdle (Grade 1) (2m40y)
Punchestown (IRE) November 19 (Soft To Heavy)

79

1 **Faugheen** 9-11-10 Paul Townend
2 **Jezki** 9-11-10 Mark Walsh
3 **Swamp Fox** 5-11-10 David Mullins
4/11F, 6/1, 20/1. 16l, 37l. 4 ran. 4m 0.00s (W P Mullins).

A winning return for **Faugheen** after more than 18 months off the track, but the lack of serious opposition probably led connections to run him over the wrong trip for much of the campaign as he couldn't win again until stepped up to 3m at Punchestown. The 2015 Champion Hurdle winner made all the running and wasn't hard pushed to beat fellow veteran **Jezki**, with young gun **Campeador** well beaten when falling at the last.

5 Betfair Chase (Grade 1) (registered as the Lancashire Chase) (3m1f125y)
Haydock November 25 (Heavy)
1 **Bristol De Mai** 6-11-7 Daryl Jacob
2 **Cue Card** 11-11-7 Harry Cobden
3 **Outlander** 9-11-7 Jack Kennedy
11/10F, 2/1, 5/1. 57l, 9l. 6 ran. 7m 1.00s (Nigel Twiston-Davies).

A demolition job from **Bristol De Mai**, the type rarely seen in a Grade 1, although the performance might not have been quite as extraordinary as it seemed at the time. Bristol De Mai revelled in the heavy ground and kept up a relentless gallop that proved far too much for his rivals from a long way out, although the fact the winner couldn't strike again all season suggests that was as much due to their own failures to cope with conditions as his brilliance. **Cue Card** was among those to come up short in a distant second, although he still plugged on bravely ahead of **Outlander** and **Tea For Two**.

6 Christy 1965 Chase (Grade 2) (2m5f8y)
Ascot November 25 (Good To Soft)
1 **Top Notch** 6-11-4 Nico de Boinville
2 **Double Shuffle** 7-11-1 Jonathan Burke
3 **Frodon** 5-11-5 Sean Bowen
5/2J, 12/1, 8/1. 8l, 2¼l. 9 ran. 5m 15.60s (Nicky Henderson).

The best of three Grade 2 victories for **Top Notch** over the season and good enough to suggest he could still be a force at the top level as he put a high-class field to the sword. Always prominent, Top Notch took over in front after the third-last and soon stormed clear of **Double Shuffle**, who franked the form with his King George second. **Frodon** was third ahead of **Flying Angel**, with that quartet clear of **Smad Place** and **Josses Hill**, who enjoyed making the running in a far less competitive field when second to Top Notch in the Peterborough Chase next time.

7 Coral Hurdle (registered as the Ascot Hurdle) (Grade 2) (2m3f58y)
Ascot November 25 (Good To Soft)
1 **Lil Rockerfeller** 6-11-0 Trevor Whelan
2 **L'Ami Serge** 7-11-6 Nico de Boinville
3 **Wakea** 6-11-4 Mr J C Barry
9/4, 7/2, 50/1. 1½l, hd. 5 ran. 4m 41.20s (Neil King).

Second in the 2017 Stayers' Hurdle, **Lil Rockerfeller** couldn't get close to that level last season and even this victory owed plenty to the 6lb he received from **L'Ami Serge**, although whether that rival would have gone past him even with less weight is open to question. Lil Rockerfeller at least showed his battling qualities to come out on top, with L'Ami Serge finding little on the run-in and only just holding the rallying **Wakea** for second. **Defi Du Seuil** was a massive disappointment in fourth.

8 Ladbrokes Long Distance Hurdle (Grade 2) (3m52y)
Newbury December 1 (Soft)
1 **Beer Goggles** 6-11-0 Richard Johnson
2 **Unowhatimeanharry** 9-11-6 B Geraghty
3 **Taquin Du Seuil** 10-11-0 Aidan Coleman
40/1, 7/4, 33/1. 2¼l, 3¾l. 6 ran. 6m 2.90s (Richard Woollacott).

A poignant win in retrospect for the late Richard Woollacott, whose star stayer **Beer Goggles** pulled off a major upset, taking advantage of a declining force in **Unowhatimeanharry** and some other below-par rivals. Beer Goggles made all the running and Unowhatimeanharry could never haul him back, hindered by a 6lb penalty. **Thistlecrack**, returning from a long absence, was badly in need of the run in fifth, though he still finished ahead of the disappointing **Wholestone**.

9 Ladbrokes Trophy (Handicap Chase) (Grade 3) (3m1f214y)
Newbury December 2 (Good To Soft)
1 **Total Recall** 8-10-8 Paul Townend
2 **Whisper** 9-11-8 Davy Russell
3 **Regal Encore** 9-10-11 Richie McLernon
9/2F, 8/1, 66/1. nk, 9l. 20 ran. 6m 29.60s (W P Mullins).

An agonising finish saw **Whisper** overhauled in the final strides by handicap blot **Total Recall** when on the brink of one of the great weight-carrying victories of recent times. Improving rapidly having just won the Munster National on his first run for Willie Mullins, Total Recall was thrown in given he was good enough to prove competitive in the Gold Cup and stayed on strongly from the last to get up close home. Conceding 14lb to such a good horse proved too much for Whisper, whose performance suggested he could also be very much a Gold Cup horse, though he may have missed his chance after missing the second half of the season through injury. The pair pulled 9l clear of **Regal Encore**, a big handicap winner at Ascot later in the season, and the rest were well strung out, including Kim Muir winner **Missed Approach** in sixth and other good subsequent winners **Potters Legend**, **Bigbadjohn** and **Vyta Du Roc**. **American** struggled to cope with the big field and was pulled up.

10 Unibet Fighting Fifth Hurdle (Grade 1) (2m98y)
Newcastle December 2 (Soft)
1 **Buveur D'Air** 6-11-7   Barry Geraghty
2 **Irving** 9-11-7   Sean Bowen
3 **Flying Tiger** 4-11-7   Tom Scudamore
1/6F, 9/2, 9/1. 3½l, 1l. 5 ran. 4m 10.10s (Nicky Henderson).

A ridiculously straightforward win for **Buveur D'Air** that was more about the total lack of opposition than his own brilliance. Only one rival was rated within two stone of the Champion Hurdle winner and that was **Irving**, so past his best that he would be retired after only one more run, though he at least ran on into second past **Flying Tiger**.

11 Bar One Racing Hatton's Grace Hurdle (Grade 1) (2m4f)
Fairyhouse (IRE) December 3 (Soft)
1 **Apple's Jade** 5-11-3   Jack Kennedy
2 **Nichols Canyon** 7-11-10   Paul Townend
3 **Supasundae** 7-11-10   Robbie Power
EvensF, 2/1, 14/1. 9l, 1¾l. 7 ran. 5m 7.20s (Gordon Elliott).

A stunning performance from **Apple's Jade**, who repeated her 2016 victory but looked a much better mare than 12 months earlier. Seemingly benefiting from a recent prep run – five of her six defeats, including both below-par efforts in the spring, have come after at least 45 days off, whereas her average time

TOP NOTCH: hugely impressive when winning at Ascot last November

SIZING JOHN: possibly flattered by his Punchestown win with rivals out of sorts

between wins during a season is 23 days – Apple's Jade made all the running and drew clear of **Nichols Canyon**, who had won first time out in all three previous seasons over hurdles, and dual subsequent Grade 1 winner **Supasundae**. **Cilaos Emery** and **Mick Jazz** travelled well but didn't seem to get home, with **Augusta Kate** tailed off behind.

12 Betfair Tingle Creek Chase (Grade 1) (1m7f119y)
Sandown December 9 (Good To Soft)
1 **Politologue** 6-11-7   Harry Cobden
2 **Fox Norton** 7-11-7   Robbie Power
3 **Ar Mad** 7-11-7   Joshua Moore
7/2, 8/13F, 8/1. ½l, 5l. 6 ran. 3m 54.30s
(Paul Nicholls).

A thrilling win for **Politologue** and one for which he probably didn't get the credit he deserved until backing it up with a second Grade 1 success at Aintree. Politologue improved massively to dominate the first half of the season over 2m in Altior's absence, splitting wins in the Haldon Gold Cup and Desert Orchid Chase with this battling victory as he jumped well and held off **Fox Norton** having taken over in front two out. Though seemingly even better over further, Fox Norton had thrived over this trip in the spring before adding a second successive Shloer Chase and he ran another fine race in second, pulling 5l clear of **Ar Mad** and **Charbel**.

13 John Durkan Memorial Punchestown Chase (Grade 1) (2m4f40y)
Punchestown (IRE) December 10 (Heavy)
1 **Sizing John** 7-11-10   Robbie Power
2 **Djakadam** 8-11-10   Paul Townend
3 **Sub Lieutenant** 8-11-10 Davy Russell
2/1, 5/4F, 7/1. 7l, 2¾l. 6 ran. 5m 34.30s
(Mrs John Harrington).

One more magic moment for triple Gold Cup hero **Sizing John** before his season fell apart, although even this performance may not have been as special as it appeared at the time with **Djakadam** and **Sub Lieutenant** out of sorts for much of the season. Still, Djakadam was at least a dual winner of the race and a Punchestown specialist, as he would underline when second again in the Gold Cup in April, yet Sizing John was much too good for him, hitting the front three out and comfortably easing clear. **A Toi Phil** was fourth, while **Shaneshill** was found to be coughing after he was pulled up.

14 Caspian Caviar Gold Cup (Handicap Chase) (Grade 3) (2m4f166y)
Cheltenham December 16 (Soft)
1 **Guitar Pete** 7-10-2 Ryan Day
2 **Clan Des Obeaux** 5-11-12 Harry Cobden
3 **King's Odyssey** 8-10-11 Adam Wedge
9/1, 3/1F, 9/1. 2¾l, 5l. 10 ran. 5m 16.90s (Nicky Richards).

A desperately sad race as **Starchitect** fatally broke down in the straight when all set to improve on his BetVictor Gold Cup second, handing a somewhat hollow victory to **Guitar Pete**. Running in a weaker race and jumping much better than he had that day, Starchitect was all set to win easily when he went wrong before the second-last. Guitar Pete was left in fourth at the time but picked up well to run down **Clan Des Obeaux**, who had got behind early before making ground and looked in need of further. **King's Odyssey** was next ahead of **Ballyalton**, who didn't seem to run to his BetVictor form with **Romain De Senam** much closer in fifth, while **Le Prezien** stumbled badly three out to lose his chance.

15 Unibet International Hurdle (Grade 2) (2m179y)
Cheltenham December 16 (Soft)
1 **My Tent Or Yours** 10-11-0 B Geraghty
2 **The New One** 9-11-6 S Twiston-Davies
3 **Melon** 5-11-6 David Mullins
5/1, 5/2, 7/4F. 1¼l, 1l. 7 ran. 4m 7.90s (Nicky Henderson).

A last and long-overdue success for **My Tent Or Yours**, who had been second in three Champion Hurdles since his previous win over jumps in 2013 when beating **The New One** in the Christmas Hurdle and amazingly saw off the same rival here. My Tent Or Yours made the most of the 6lb he received from The New One, who came out best at the weights and again showed he was still a force over this trip in testing conditions when confirming this form with fourth-placed **Ch'Tibello** to win his fourth successive Haydock Champion Hurdle Trial. At the other end of the scale, **Melon** was still very much a work in progress in third on only his fifth run over hurdles, while **Old Guard** was fifth ahead of **John Constable**, those six covered by just 4¼l.

16 JLT Reve De Sivola Long Walk Hurdle (Grade 1) (3m97y)
Ascot December 23 (Good To Soft)
1 **Sam Spinner** 5-11-7 Joe Colliver
2 **L'Ami Serge** 7-11-7 Daryl Jacob
3 **Unowhatimeanharry** 9-11-7 B Geraghty

MY TENT OR YOURS: a last and long-overdue success

9/2, 5/1, 6/4F. 2¾l, 8l. 8 ran. 6m 2.90s (Jedd O'Keeffe).

The weakness of the British staying hurdlers was shown at Cheltenham and Aintree, but **Sam Spinner** suggested he was perhaps the best of them with this victory despite his spring disappointments. Unlike at Cheltenham, Sam Spinner made this a proper test and was able to show his true capability, showing the class and courage to pick up again in the straight just as the race looked to have been set up for **L'Ami Serge** to pick off his rivals from the rear, as he did when winning the Aintree Hurdle. The pair pulled 8l clear of **Unowhatimeanharry** and **The Worlds End**, who had more favourable conditions than at any other stage in the season but still came up well short. **Thomas Campbell**, a dual handicap winner at Cheltenham earlier in the season, had his limitations exposed in fifth ahead of the disappointing **Lil Rockerfeller**.

17 32Red King George VI Chase (Grade 1) (3m)
Kempton December 26 (Soft)
1 **Might Bite** 8-11-10 Nico de Boinville
2 **Double Shuffle** 7-11-10 A P Heskin
3 **Tea For Two** 8-11-10 Lizzie Kelly
6/4F, 50/1, 20/1. 1l, 2l. 8 ran. 6m 6.60s
(Nicky Henderson).

Might Bite made a successful first step into open company but didn't make the impression many had anticipated as he struggled to win a race that seemed to fall apart behind him. Might Bite wouldn't see out the Gold Cup trip as strongly as Native River on soft ground and was perhaps also affected by the conditions here as he failed to pick up as well as he may have done on a quicker surface, though he still travelled strongly and was always well on top. **Double Shuffle** produced a career-best effort over a course and distance he relishes to take second ahead of **Tea For Two**, but the other big players were all well below their best. The 2016 winner **Thistlecrack**, later found to have suffered a stress fracture, was a one-paced fourth on his first run over fences for nearly a year, **Whisper** was a distant fifth, **Bristol De Mai** needed treatment for stomach ulcers after his bitterly disappointing sixth and **Fox Norton** was pulled up having looked a non-stayer.

18 Unibet Christmas Hurdle (Grade 1) (2m)
Kempton December 26 (Soft)
1 **Buveur D'Air** 6-11-7 Barry Geraghty
2 **The New One** 9-11-7 Sam Twiston-Davies
3 **Mohaayed** 5-11-7 Harry Skelton
2/11F, 5/1, 20/1. 2¼l, 3¾l. 4 ran. 3m 57.50s
(Nicky Henderson).

The New One at least ensured **Buveur D'Air** would face one serious rival before Cheltenham, but the Champion Hurdle winner was still just 2-11 to prevail and justified those odds comfortably. Though better over further, The New One set only a moderate gallop before aiming to catch out Buveur D'Air with a sudden injection of speed turning for home,

YOUNG GUNS: Road To Respect (right) and Balko Des Flos come to the fore

but the favourite closed him down smartly between the last two before cruising clear. The proximity of **Mohaayed** and **Chesterfield** in such a slowly run race was clearly tough for the handicapper to assess and they showed they hadn't been as flattered as appeared to be the case when going on to finish first and fourth in the County.

19 Paddy's Rewards Club Chase (Grade 1) (2m1f)
Leopardstown (IRE) December 27 (Yielding)
2 **Min** 6-11-12 Paul Townend
1 **Simply Ned** 10-11-12 Mark Walsh
3 **Ordinary World** 7-11-12 Davy Russell
2/7F, 16/1, 12/1. ½l, 15l. 6 ran. 4m 9.90s (Nicky Richards).

A Grade 1 success for **Simply Ned** that owed everything to his connections' willingness to have a go as he was one of very few to take on **Min** and was rewarded by a strangely below-par display from the 2-7 favourite that opened the door to a surprise. The third highest-rated horse in the line-up despite his mark of just 151, Simply Ned was rightly awarded the race in the stewards' room having been carved up on the run-in as Min struggled to hold him at bay, though Min's 12-length success over Simply Ned back at the course in a Grade 2 in February was a fairer reflection of their relative ability.

20 Leopardstown Christmas Chase (Grade 1) (3m)
Leopardstown (IRE) December 28 (Yielding)
1 **Road To Respect** 6-11-10 Sean Flanagan
2 **Balko Des Flos** 6-11-10 Denis O'Regan
3 **Outlander** 9-11-10 Rachael Blackmore
8/1, 66/1, 16/1. 1¼l, 2¼l. 12 ran. 6m 8.40s (Noel Meade).

This race gained more headlines for its flops, with **Sizing John**, **Yorkhill** and **Djakadam** all well below their best, but that shouldn't mask the fact it was probably the strongest staying chase form in Ireland over the winter – certainly until Bellshill's Punchestown win in April – with two progressive young horses in **Road To Respect** and **Balko Des Flos** fighting out the finish. As both relished quicker ground than they faced at other times of the season, Road To Respect overcame a tendency to jump left as he mastered the front-running Balko Des Flos, a big improver on only his second run over 3m. **Outlander**, who sandwiched this effort with his Grade 1 win at Down Royal and Irish Gold Cup second, was a rock-solid yardstick in third, with that trio upwards of 5½l clear of **Minella Rocco**, **Valseur Lido** and **Alpha Des Obeaux**. Sizing John trailed home in seventh and was found to be clinically abnormal post-race, though he still finished ahead of Yorkhill, who began his desperately disappointing season. Djakadam and **Edwulf** were both pulled up.

21 Squared Financial Christmas Hurdle (Grade 1) (3m)
Leopardstown (IRE) December 28 (Soft)
1 **Apple's Jade** 5-11-3 Davy Russell
2 **Supasundae** 7-11-10 Robbie Power
3 **Bapaume** 4-11-5 Noel Fehily
4/6F, 7/1, 20/1. ½l, 4¾l. 6 ran. 6m 18.80s (Gordon Elliott).

A race overshadowed by the sad death of **Nichols Canyon**, who fell at the fifth, and what followed was fairly underwhelming anyway, with **Apple's Jade** less impressive stepping up in trip than she had been in the Hatton's Grace and understandably not doing enough to sway connections from their intended Cheltenham target of the Mares' Hurdle. Ridden much less positively, having set only a modest early gallop and then taken a lead off **Supasundae**, she struggled to master that rival in the straight and, while the runner-up franked the form when second again in the Stayers' Hurdle at Cheltenham, he still didn't convince he sees out a strongly run race at the trip and probably proved best all the way back at 2m. **Bapaume**, who struggled all season before finally getting back on track in France in the summer, wasn't beaten far in third ahead of **Augusta Kate** and **Jezki**.

22 Ryanair Hurdle (Grade 1) (2m)
Leopardstown (IRE) December 29 (Soft)
1 **Mick Jazz** 6-11-10 Davy Russell
2 **Cilaos Emery** 5-11-10 David Mullins
3 **Campeador** 5-11-10 Barry Geraghty
14/1, 6/1, 12/1. 1¾l, 21l. 5 ran. 4m 4.90s (Gordon Elliott).

One of the most notorious races of the season, with 2-11 favourite **Faugheen** running so badly that many felt he had been doped, though he may not have been able to cope with **Mick Jazz** anyway in light of the underrated winner's subsequent Champion Hurdle third. **Cilaos Emery** was left to make the running and also benefited from a shorter trip than when catching the eye in the Hatton's Grace, but Mick Jazz was always cruising and proved too classy. The pair were well clear of **Campeador**.

23 Coral Welsh Grand National (Handicap Chase) (Grade 3) (3m5f110y)
Chepstow January 6 (Heavy)
1 **Raz De Maree** 13-10-10   James Bowen
2 **Alfie Spinner** 13-10-2   Richard Patrick
3 **Final Nudge** 9-11-6   Aidan Coleman
16/1, 33/1, 12/1. 6l, 9l. 20 ran. 8m 12.10s
(Gavin Cromwell).

This was even more of a test of stamina than usual in desperate conditions and only the older legs proved up to the challenge, with **Raz De Maree** seeing off fellow 13-year-old **Alfie Spinner**. Just 1lb higher than when second to Native River 12 months earlier, Raz De Maree stayed on by far the strongest in the straight having briefly been outpaced, heading Alfie Spinner two out and pulling clear. **Final Nudge** was just the best of the youngsters, edging out **Vintage Clouds** and **Silsol** in a tight battle for third.

THE DUTCHMAN: wins what looked a strong Peter Marsh Chase

24 Peter Marsh Chase (Limited Handicap) (Grade 2) (3m1f125y)
Haydock January 20 (Heavy)
1 **The Dutchman** 8-10-6   Harry Cobden
2 **Captain Redbeard** 9-10-10 Sam Coltherd
3 **Hainan** 7-10-11   Danny Cook
13/2, 12/1, 6/1. 13l, ¾l. 13 ran. 7m 22.50s
(Colin Tizzard).

A stunning performance from **The Dutchman**, who proved well ahead of his mark as he saw off a trio of in-form rivals with a resolute display of jumping and galloping from the front. Few courses need as much stamina as Haydock on heavy ground and just five horses managed to finish, but the three behind him were all course winners in similar conditions over the season, with **Captain Redbeard** and **Hainan** filling the places ahead of **Yala Enki**, who was the only horse to cope with a gruelling surface in the Grand National Trial next time.

25 Royal Salute Whisky Clarence House Chase (Grade 1) (2m167y)
Ascot January 20 (Soft)
1 **Un De Sceaux** 10-11-7   Paul Townend
2 **Speredek** 7-11-7   Sean Bowen
3 **Kylemore Lough** 9-11-7   Noel Fehily
4/9F, 16/1, 8/1. 7l, 14l. 5 ran. 4m 26.40s
(W P Mullins).

A third successive Clarence House for **Un De Sceaux**, who was much too good for a field lacking the best 2m talent. The novice **Brain Power** was his most serious rival according to the market despite having already looked short of the best in his own division and he took a crashing fall two out when looking likely to finish second. Un De Sceaux was already in charge by that point having just headed long-time leader **Speredek**, who finished a clear second after **Kylemore Lough** was hampered by Brain Power's fall.

26 BetBright Trial Cotswold Chase (Grade 2) (3m1f56y)
Cheltenham January 27 (Heavy)
1 **Definitly Red** 9-11-6   Danny Cook
2 **American** 8-11-2   Noel Fehily
3 **Bristol De Mai** 7-11-6   Daryl Jacob
7/1, 9/2, 7/4F. 8l, 2¼l. 8 ran. 6m 54.00s
(Brian Ellison).

Definitly Red had already won a Grade 2 when beating a dodgy stayer in Cloudy Dream at Aintree, but this was a much deeper race and he did really well to defy a 6lb penalty. Definitly Red was always prominent and was ridden clear between the last two fences, proving too strong for the highly regarded

AGRAPART: not his first big win at Cheltenham but struggles to back it up

American, who was much better back in a smaller field. **Bristol De Mai**, unable to dominate and not jumping as fluently as usual, was well below his best in third and subsequently had a wind operation, but **The Last Samuri**, getting 6lb from the winner and having proved he handles these conditions when second in the Becher, was a close fourth to give more depth to the form. **Tea For Two** was pulled up.

27 galliardhomes.com Cleeve Hurdle (Grade 2) (2m7f213y)
Cheltenham January 27 (Heavy)
1 **Agrapart** 7-11-6   Lizzie Kelly
2 **Wholestone** 7-11-6   Daryl Jacob
3 **Colin's Sister** 7-10-13   Paddy Brennan
9/1, 9/2, 10/1. 3l, 8l. 9 ran. 6m 25.60s
(Nick Williams).

A decent renewal with placed horses **Wholestone** and **Colin's Sister** going on to finish third and fourth in an admittedly modest Stayers' Hurdle, though it might not be wise to read too much into **Agrapart**'s victory. Heavy ground brought his bottomless stamina to the fore and he duly managed a second Grade 2 win at Cheltenham in testing conditions following the 2017 Relkeel Hurdle, but he was then a beaten favourite in the Rendlesham in both seasons, this time at 4-7 behind Donna's Diamond. Wholestone, who had beaten Agrapart in the latest edition of the Relkeel, again travelled like the better horse but was just outstayed, still pulling 8l clear of Colin's Sister, while **The Worlds End** was another who travelled well but finished tamely.

28 BHP Insurance Irish Champion Hurdle (Grade 1) (2m)
Leopardstown (IRE) February 3 (Soft)
1 **Supasundae** 8-11-10   Robbie Power
2 **Faugheen** 10-11-10   Paul Townend
3 **Mick Jazz** 7-11-10   Davy Russell
8/1, 9/10F, 8/1. 2¼l, 4¾l. 8 ran. 4m 0.90s
(Mrs John Harrington).

A result that only began to make sense after Punchestown as **Supasundae**, using the race as a prep run for the Stayers' Hurdle, managed to beat several Champion Hurdle hopes despite the much shorter trip. Supasundae, always close to the front-running **Faugheen**, proved too strong from the final flight and it would transpire that connections had probably got his trip wrong given he won

WAITING PATIENTLY: favoured by sitting off a strong pace as he beat Cue Card

a second 2m Grade 1 in April. That said, this probably didn't take a great deal of winning, with Faugheen looking short of speed and benefiting from the step up to 3m at Punchestown while **Mick Jazz** failed to run to form and **Melon** resented a first-time hood. **Jezki** split the last-named pair in fourth, while **Identity Thief** needed his first run of the season in sixth ahead of the struggling five-year-olds **Defi Du Seuil** and **Bapaume**.

29 Unibet Irish Gold Cup (Grade 1) (3m)
Leopardstown (IRE) February 4 (Soft)
1 **Edwulf** 9-11-10 Mr Derek O'Connor
2 **Outlander** 10-11-10 Jack Kennedy
3 **Djakadam** 9-11-10 Mr P W Mullins
33/1, 6/1, 13/2. nk, 10l. 10 ran. 6m 24.90s
(Joseph Patrick O'Brien).

A heartwarming win for **Edwulf**, who had nearly died at the 2017 Cheltenham Festival and remarkably bounced back from being pulled up on his only start since then. Soft ground was the key to Edwulf's victory, his stamina coming to the fore as testing conditions strung out the field and helped him to run down **Outlander** from the final fence. **Killultagh Vic**, another horse with an amazing story in only his third chase and first for more than two years, may well have won but for falling at the last, but his lack of experience was exposed in stronger races to confirm this as ordinary form for the grade. **Anibale Fly** was also potentially unlucky, falling two out when close enough given how well he stayed on in the Gold Cup, while **Djakadam** was left an underwhelming third ahead of **Our Duke**, **Valseur Lido** and **Alpha Des Obeaux**, with **Minello Rocco** well beaten when also coming down at the last.

30 Betfair Hurdle (Handicap) (Grade 3) (2m69y)
Newbury February 10 (Soft)
1 **Kalashnikov** 5-11-5 Jack Quinlan
2 **Bleu Et Rouge** 7-11-10 Barry Geraghty
3 **Spiritofthegames** 6-11-0 Bridget Andrews
8/1C, 10/1, 20/1. 4½l, 8l. 24 ran. 4m 8.90s
(Amy Murphy).

Kalashnikov boasted some of the strongest

2m novice hurdle form all season, finishing second to Summerville Boy in the Tolworth and the Supreme, and a mark of 141 clearly underestimated him as he blew away his rivals in devastating fashion. The rest were well strung out in testing conditions and the fact that two of the first five, **Spiritofthegames** and **Remiluc**, were to the fore in the County Hurdle suggests those in prominent positions ran better than suggested by the lengths they were beaten, with **Bleu Et Rouge** running a particularly fine race in second under top weight given he was the only horse to finish within 12l of the winner.

31 Betfair Denman Chase (Grade 2) (2m7f86y)
Newbury February 10 (Soft)
1 **Native River** 8-11-6   Richard Johnson
2 **Cloudy Dream** 8-11-3   Brian Hughes
3 **Saphir Du Rheu** 9-11-0 S Twiston-Davies
8/11F, 11/4, 100/30. 12l, 24l. 3 ran. 6m 11.70s
(Colin Tizzard).

A much later start to the campaign for **Native River**, who had already won the Hennessy and the Welsh National when taking this race in 2017, but he was quickly back up to speed in repeating that success. Always jumping well in front, Native River made all the running and needed only hands-and-heels riding to come clear of **Cloudy Dream**, who travelled strongly but was comprehensively outstayed.

32 Betfair Exchange Chase (Grade 2) (registered as the Game Spirit Chase) (2m92y)
Newbury February 10 (Soft)
1 **Altior** 8-11-6   Nico de Boinville
2 **Politologue** 7-11-6   Sam Twiston-Davies
3 **Valdez** 11-11-0   Wayne Hutchinson
1/3F, 5/2, 25/1. 4l, 13l. 3 ran. 4m 19.60s
(Nicky Henderson).

Altior was potentially vulnerable on his return from a long layoff, his return having been delayed by a wind operation, but instead he gave a stunning reminder of his brilliance by toying with a top-class rival in **Politologue**. Paul Nicholls had warned that Politologue would also come on for the run after a mid-season break, but even so the way Altior travelled all over him before cantering clear on the run-in confirmed he was in a different league.

33 Betfair Ascot Chase (Grade 1) (2m5f8y)
Ascot February 17 (Soft)
1 **Waiting Patiently** 7-11-7   Brian Hughes
2 **Cue Card** 12-11-7   Paddy Brennan
3 **Frodon** 6-11-7   Bryony Frost
2/1F, 9/1, 9/1. 2¾l, 15l. 7 ran. 5m 25.90s
(Ruth Jefferson).

One of the races of the season as **Cue Card** served it up to a top young talent in **Waiting Patiently** and went down fighting in memorable fashion. Having produced arguably his best performance of the last two seasons when easily winning the race in 2017, Cue Card again proved ideally suited by the conditions, but this time he found one just too good in Waiting Patiently, who was perhaps favoured by being held up off a searching gallop. The pair pulled 15l clear of **Frodon** and the below-par **Top Notch**, while the early pace proved too much for **Speredek**, who was pulled up.

34 Betway Kingwell Hurdle (Grade 2) (1m7f65y)
Wincanton February 17 (Soft)
1 **Elgin** 6-11-6   Wayne Hutchinson
2 **Ch'Tibello** 7-11-2   Harry Skelton
3 **Call Me Lord** 5-11-2   Aidan Coleman
5/1, 6/4F, 13/8. 2½l, 2l. 6 ran. 3m 55.70s
(Alan King).

Elgin had been sharply progressive in top 2m handicaps earlier in the season, most notably when winning the Greatwood, and this put him right near the top of a 2m hurdling division rather short of talent in Britain beyond Buveur D'Air only for a summer injury to rule him out of the coming season. Elgin comfortably gave 4lb to rock-solid yardstick **Ch'Tibello**, with the form tying in closely with The New One's performances against that horse. **Call Me Lord** also franked the form when second in the Imperial Cup next time before winning at this level on the final day of the season.

35 Ultima Handicap Chase (Grade 3) (3m1f)
Cheltenham March 13 (Heavy)
1 **Coo Star Sivola** 6-10-10   Lizzie Kelly
2 **Shantou Flyer** 8-11-6   James Bowen
3 **Vintage Clouds** 8-10-12   Danny Cook
5/1F, 14/1, 7/1. nk, 6l. 18 ran. 6m 47.50s
(Nick Williams).

Third time lucky for **Coo Star Sivola**, who had been placed at the Cheltenham Festival in the previous two years but took this easier opportunity in an ordinary renewal. Seemingly an improved horse since stepping up to 3m, Coo Star Sivola was always going well and looked value for more than the narrow margin as he idled on the run-in having looked set to win easily when taking command between the last two, though he still has plenty to prove at a higher level having been pulled up in a Grade 1 at Aintree next time. **Shantou Flyer** had been held all season off similar marks but ran his usual solid race in second, as did **Vintage Clouds**, while it was remarkable that **Beware The Bear** was beaten just 9l in fourth having been well behind for much of the contest, running on past many tired horses.

36 Unibet Champion Hurdle Challenge Trophy (Grade 1) (2m87y)
Cheltenham March 13 (Heavy)
1 **Buveur D'Air** 7-11-10   Barry Geraghty
2 **Melon** 6-11-10   Paul Townend
3 **Mick Jazz** 7-11-10   Davy Russell
4/6F, 7/1, 25/1. nk, 3l. 11 ran. 4m 5.00s (Nicky Henderson).

A second successive Champion Hurdle for **Buveur D'Air**, who had been dominating a desperately weak division since reverting to hurdles in early 2017 but was pushed far harder than at any point in that time by the much-improved **Melon**. Buveur D'Air was probably better than the bare form, though, as he was the only horse ridden close to a strong early pace able to survive up front and pulled out extra on the run-in after Melon, settling better off the solid gallop, had come through to head him at the last. **Mick Jazz** ran a fine race in third and was 9l clear of **Identity Thief**, who stayed on from the rear to point to his step up in trip at Aintree, with **Elgin** the next best of the British runners in fifth. **Faugheen** dropped out tamely to finish sixth ahead of **Wicklow Brave** and **Ch'Tibello**, who was found to be sore after the race. **Yorkhill** was pulled up.

37 OLBG Mares' Hurdle (Grade 1) (registered as the David Nicholson Mares' Hurdle) (2m3f200y)
Cheltenham March 13 (Heavy)
1 **Benie Des Dieux** 7-11-5   R Walsh
2 **Midnight Tour** 8-11-5   Davy Russell
3 **Apple's Jade** 6-11-5   Jack Kennedy

BENIE DES DIEUX (far side): benefited from stamina coming to the fore

9/2, 33/1, 1/2F. ½l, 1l. 9 ran. 5m 10.10s
(W P Mullins).

A below-par performance from red-hot favourite **Apple's Jade** opened the door to her rivals and **Benie Des Dieux**, reverting to hurdles after three chase wins to pull off a Cheltenham and Punchestown double, took full advantage despite finding the distance of both races probably short of her best. With heavy ground bringing stamina to the fore, Benie Des Dieux needed almost every yard to run down the surprise package **Midnight Tour**, who had quickened past the sluggish Apple's Jade. **La Bague Au Roi** wouldn't have been far away but for blundering at the last, fading into seventh.

38 Coral Cup (Handicap Hurdle) (Grade 3) (2m5f26y)
Cheltenham March 14 (Soft)
1 **Bleu Berry** 7-11-2 Mark Walsh
2 **Topofthegame** 6-11-9 S Twiston-Davies
3 **Barra** 7-10-10 Jack Kennedy
20/1, 9/1, 16/1. nk, 1¼l. 26 ran. 5m 20.80s
(W P Mullins).

Top winter handicap form was well represented, with big-race winners **Topofthegame** and **William Henry** second and fourth, but neither could defy a rise against the unexposed **Bleu Berry**. Unplaced on his only run since a promising novice campaign, Bleu Berry stormed home to pip Topofthegame and **Barra**, improving for stepping up in trip in a race in which stamina came to the fore. William Henry was sent off joint-favourite, still looking fairly treated with his Lanzarote win working out, including by fourth-placed Topofthegame's victory in a Grade 3 handicap at Sandown, but that latter win had come over further and William Henry didn't see this out as well as the first three.

39 Betway Queen Mother Champion Chase (Grade 1) (1m7f199y)
Cheltenham March 14 (Soft)
1 **Altior** 8-11-10 Nico de Boinville
2 **Min** 7-11-10 Paul Townend
3 **God's Own** 10-11-10 Paddy Brennan
EvensF, 5/2, 40/1. 7l, 11l. 9 ran. 4m 7.60s
(Nicky Henderson).

Having waited all season for a clash between **Altior** and **Douvan**, there was more frustration for racing fans when Douvan fell four out, although the way Altior powered up the hill to a third successive Cheltenham Festival victory suggests he would have been very hard to stop anyway. Douvan was going well in front at the time of his departure whereas Altior

BLEU BERRY: Coral Cup hero

wasn't always travelling smoothly, especially coming down the hill to the third-last, but it had been a similar story when he won the Arkle in 2017 and once again he devoured the uphill finish to draw clear of **Min**, who ran a terrific race in second. Min pulled 11l clear of **God's Own**, who had finished much closer than that to the winner in his two previous attempts at the race. **Politologue**, not for the first time, seemed to under-perform at Cheltenham in fourth, while **Special Tiara** was pulled up and **Charbel** fell at the sixth.

40 Pertemps Network Final (Handicap Hurdle) (Grade 3) (2m7f213y)
Cheltenham March 15 (Soft)
1 **Delta Work** 5-10-10 Davy Russell
2 **Glenloe** 7-10-8 Barry Geraghty
3 **Connetable** 6-10-7 Harry Cobden
6/1, 9/2F, 33/1. nse, 2¾l. 23 ran. 6m 9.50s
(Gordon Elliott).

A thrilling race won by an exciting young stayer in **Delta Work**, who edged out plunge horse **Glenloe** and proved a match for the best novices around at Punchestown. Both of the first two had plenty go wrong, with Delta Work struggling to get a clear run and Glenloe blundering at the last when in front, but they still quickened clear of **Connetable** and **Taj Badalandabad** as they locked horns up the run-in, with that pair the only horses to finish within 8l of them. **Who Dares Wins**, a close third in a 2m4f handicap at Aintree next time, and **A Great View**, successful at Punchestown after blundering away his chance two out here, were next and both gave this form significant boosts.

41 Ryanair Chase (Grade 1) (registered as the Festival Trophy) (2m4f166y)
Cheltenham March 15 (Soft)
1 **Balko Des Flos** 7-11-10   Davy Russell
2 **Un De Sceaux** 10-11-10   Paul Townend
3 **Cloudy Dream** 8-11-10   Brian Hughes
8/1, 8/11F, 10/1. 4½l, 8l. 6 ran. 5m 23.60s (Henry De Bromhead).

An impressive win for **Balko Des Flos**, though it came in a strange race in which he had been a massive drifter with conditions believed to have gone against him – which seemed to be the case on similar ground at Aintree. Balko Des Flos probably benefited from those behind him running well below their best, which was certainly true of **Cue Card**, who hadn't recovered from his Ascot exertions and was pulled up in what would prove to be his final race, while a combination of the trip and testing ground seemed to take away **Un De Sceaux**'s spark, not helped by a couple of notable jumping errors. **Cloudy Dream** had lost his way after a couple of hard slogs over 3m, with **Frodon** another who went on to struggle in the spring, while fourth-placed **Sub Lieutenant** was the only other runner in a disappointing field.

42 Sun Bets Stayers' Hurdle (Grade 1) (2m7f213y)
Cheltenham March 15 (Soft)
1 **Penhill** 7-11-10   Paul Townend
2 **Supasundae** 8-11-10   Robbie Power
3 **Wholestone** 7-11-10   Aidan Coleman
12/1, 6/1, 14/1. 2l, 3l. 15 ran. 6m 20.40s (W P Mullins).

A modest renewal but a brilliant winner in **Penhill**, who won with remarkable authority given most of the field still held every chance between the last two – and did so despite not having run all season after a setback in the summer. A lack of early pace benefited the speed horses and Penhill was by far the quickest as he stormed through from last to first to win going away from **Supasundae**, a dual Grade 1 winner at 2m by the end of the season who also had the race run to suit but had nothing like the speed of the winner. Bizarrely, the moderate gallop was most disadvantageous for the front-running **Sam Spinner**, whose jockey got the fractions all wrong, leaving him a sitting duck in the straight as he finished fifth behind **Wholestone** and **Colin's Sister**, while **Yanworth** was sixth ahead of **The Worlds End** and **L'Ami Serge**, who was particularly unsuited by the gallop. **Bacardys** was disputing fifth and staying on when falling at the last and those nine were much better than the rest as there was a 6l gap back to **Augusta Kate**, with the 2017 second and third, **Lil Rockerfeller** and **Unowhatimeanharry**, and the non-staying **The New One** behind.

43 Brown Advisory & Merriebelle Stable Plate (Handicap Chase) (Grade 3) (2m4f166y)
Cheltenham March 15 (Soft)
1 **The Storyteller** 7-11-4   Davy Russell
2 **Splash Of Ginge** 10-10-5   Jamie Bargary
3 **King's Odyssey** 9-10-10   Adam Wedge
5/1F, 25/1, 14/1. 1¾l, 5l. 22 ran. 5m 28.20s (Gordon Elliott).

A very similar race to the major course handicaps over similar trips earlier in the season, with BetVictor Gold Cup winner **Splash Of Ginge** going desperately close and the consistent **King's Odyssey** and **Ballyalton** not far behind, but **The Storyteller** was just too good for them. Hugely flattered by his subsequent Grade 1 win at Punchestown but still well handicapped off 147, The Storyteller was always going well and produced a well-timed challenge to run down the front-running Splash Of Ginge in the final 100 yards. The handicapper had eased King's Odyssey (1lb) and Ballyalton (5lb) since the Caspian Caviar Gold Cup yet both could only fill the same positions ahead of **King's Socks**, who travelled well before seemingly failing to stay, and **Guitar Pete**, who lost his chance with a bad mistake four out. That sextet were 9l clear of the rest.

44 Randox Health County Handicap Hurdle (Grade 3) (2m179y)
Cheltenham March 16 (Soft)
1 **Mohaayed** 6-10-8   Bridget Andrews
2 **Remiluc** 9-10-11   Harry Reed
3 **Whiskey Sour** 5-10-13   David Mullins
33/1, 50/1, 7/1. 2¾l, ¾l. 24 ran. 4m 18.00s (Dan Skelton).

A most unusual renewal with only one five-year-old – normally the dominant age group – in the first 12 and two massive outsiders

THUMBS UP: Bridget Andrews and Mohaayed after winning the County Hurdle

finishing first and second, but it still looked a good race with the handicapper having failed to latch on to the improving **Mohaayed**. Left unchanged after his third to Buveur D'Air in the Christmas Hurdle, Mohaayed showed that was far too lenient by staying on too strongly for **Remiluc**, a course-and-distance winner in January, and **Whiskey Sour**, who had both led in the straight. **Chesterfield**, dropped 4lb for running in the same Kempton race as Mohaayed to a mark 3lb lower than when winning the 2017 Scottish Champion Hurdle, franked the form when going close in that race again, while **Lagostovegas** and **Spiritofthegames** dead-heated for fifth with a 7l gap back the rest.

45 Timico Cheltenham Gold Cup (Grade 1) (3m2f70y)
Cheltenham March 16 (Soft)
1 **Native River** 8-11-10 Richard Johnson
2 **Might Bite** 9-11-10 Nico de Boinville
3 **Anibale Fly** 8-11-10 Barry Geraghty
5/1, 4/1F, 33/1. 4½l, 4l. 15 ran. 7m 2.60s (Colin Tizzard).

An epic duel between **Native River** and **Might Bite**, who were in the first two positions throughout with Native River's staying power proving too much for the stronger-travelling runner-up. Native River benefited from a much quieter season than when third in 2017 and duly proved himself a much better horse than had looked the case 12 months earlier as he jumped superbly in front and maintained a searching gallop that saw just four horses finish within 38l. Softer ground also played a big part with Native River clearly the stronger stayer, though Might Bite still ran a mighty race in second as he loomed alongside Native River between the last two before struggling home from the final fence.

No other horse was remotely able to land a blow, though **Anibale Fly** stayed on strongly to get to within 4l in third. It was 4l back to **Road To Respect**, another horse unsuited by the conditions but still a fine fourth ahead of **Djakadam**, who took a step back in the right direction in fifth and was 18l clear of **Definitly Red**, **Tea For Two** and **Edwulf** with **American** last of the nine finishers. **Total Recall** was still in contention when falling three out, but **Killultagh Vic**'s jumping had long been found out by then and he was pulled up along with **Outlander**.

46 Johnny Henderson Grand Annual Challenge Cup Handicap Chase (Grade 3) (2m62y)
Cheltenham March 16 (Soft)
1 **Le Prezien** 7-11-8   Barry Geraghty
2 **Gino Trail** 11-11-10   Jamie Moore
3 **Top Gamble** 10-11-7   Davy Russell
15/2, 25/1, 8/1. 4½l. nk. 22 ran. 4m 21.80s (Paul Nicholls).

Outpaced in this race on good ground 12 months earlier, subsequent BetVictor Gold Cup third **Le Prezien** found the combination of softer ground and a return to 2m ideal. Le Prezien still had plenty to do turning for home, but he stormed up the hill to see off veterans **Gino Trail** and **Top Gamble**. The best-handicapped horse in the race was probably **Theinval**, who found conditions against him in fourth but would finally win a big handicap at Ayr, while there was a 6l gap back to the rest.

47 BoyleSports Irish Grand National (Handicap Chase) (Grade A) (3m5f)
Fairyhouse (IRE) April 2 (Heavy)
1 **General Principle** 9-10-0   J J Slevin
2 **Isleofhopendreams** 11-10-1   D Mullins
3 **Forever Gold** 11-9-5   Adam Short
20/1, 16/1, 20/1. hd. ½l. 30 ran. 9m 2.20s (Gordon Elliott).

A remarkably fortunate win for **General Principle**, who might well have been only fifth but for **Bellshill** jinking at the last yet ended up getting the best of a blanket finish. Bellshill, running a mighty race off a mark of 158 to point to his Grade 1 breakthrough at Punchestown, made much of the running and was still narrowly in front when he swerved to his left, taking out **Arkwright** and **Folsom Blue**, with **Isleofhopeanddreams** inheriting the lead only to stop in front and allow General Principle to get up on the line. Folsom Blue was desperately unlucky given he was brought almost to a standstill yet still managed to summon another effort and was beaten just 1¾l, being placed ahead of Bellshill in the stewards' room.

48 Betway Bowl Chase (Grade 1) (3m210y)
Aintree April 12 (Good To Soft)
1 **Might Bite** 9-11-7   Nico de Boinville
2 **Bristol De Mai** 7-11-7   Daryl Jacob
3 **Clan Des Obeaux** 6-11-7   Harry Cobden
4/5F, 5/1, 8/1. 7l. 3¼l. 8 ran. 6m 38.20s (Nicky Henderson).

An emphatic win from **Might Bite**, who gained compensation for his Gold Cup defeat with another tremendous performance. Might Bite jumped better than the front-running **Bristol De Mai**, producing an exhibition round, and comfortably took his main rival's

POLITOLOGUE: managed his second Grade 1 win in the Melling Chase

THRILLER: five horses strung across the track at the line in the Irish National

measure as he eased clear from the second-last. Bristol De Mai put a couple of tame efforts behind him without quite matching his early-season efforts, finishing second ahead of a pair of eyecatchers in **Clan Des Obeaux**, who travelled notably well but was reported to have blown up two out after a long layoff, and **Sizing Codelco**, who made several mistakes yet was beaten little more than 13l. **Sub Lieutenant** produced a much better effort in fifth, but **Tea For Two** was a big letdown and **Definitly Red** unseated his rider early on.

49 Betway Aintree Hurdle (Grade 1) (2m4f)
Aintree April 12 (Soft)
1 **L'Ami Serge** 8-11-7 Daryl Jacob
2 **Supasundae** 8-11-7 Robbie Power
3 **Clyne** 8-11-7 Adam Wedge
5/1, 11/10F, 25/1. 3l, 3¾l. 9 ran. 5m 5.20s (Nicky Henderson).

A desperately weak renewal with a late setback to Buveur D'Air robbing the race of any Champion Hurdle representation and **L'Ami Serge** took full advantage. L'Ami Serge was suited by a breakneck gallop, allowing him to pick off tiring rivals without getting drawn into a battle after he had travelled with typical panache. **Supasundae** was second ahead of **Clyne**, who was perhaps flattered by his rider chasing down tearaway leader **Diakali** much earlier than the others, while **My Tent Or Yours** failed to stay the trip in testing conditions and **The New One** was pulled up.

50 JLT Melling Chase (Grade 1) (2m3f200y)
Aintree April 13 (Soft)
1 **Politologue** 7-11-7 Sam Twiston-Davies
2 **Min** 7-11-7 Paul Townend
3 **Sizing Granite** 10-11-7 Robbie Power
11/1, 11/10F, 20/1. nk, 20l. 6 ran. 5m 18.50s (Paul Nicholls).

A second Grade 1 win of the season for **Politologue**, who bounced back to form to confirm the giant strides he had made earlier in the campaign. A weak finisher over this trip as a novice to prompt his drop to 2m, Politologue also proved he was now a much stronger horse by outstaying **Min**, who may have just paid the price for racing more keenly early on but still fought hard and was a long way clear of the rest. Despite winning on soft ground at Cheltenham, **Balko Des Flos** was kept wide in search of a better surface and those tactics perhaps caught up with him as he folded tamely in the straight, losing third to the staying-on **Sizing Granite**, while **Cloudy Dream** was tailed off and **Le Prezien** pulled up.

51 Randox Health Grand National (Handicap Chase (Grade 3) (4m2f74y)
Aintree April 14 (Heavy)
1 **Tiger Roll** 8-10-13 Davy Russell
2 **Pleasant Company** 10-10-11 D Mullins
3 **Bless The Wings** 13-10-6 Jack Kennedy
10/1, 25/1, 40/1. hd, 11l. 38 ran. 9m 40.10s (Gordon Elliott).

95

JOE FARRELL: Scottish National hero on the beach with trainer Rebecca Curtis

A stunning finish saw **Tiger Roll** just hold off **Pleasant Company**, who would have been well clear just a few yards after the line as the winner fell in a hole in testing conditions having quickened into what seemed a decisive lead at the Elbow. Conditions therefore masked the superiority of Tiger Roll, who travelled with real class throughout and may well be able to make his mark at the top level on this evidence, especially with Gold Cup third **Anibale Fly** adding some class to the form in fourth behind the evergreen veteran **Bless The Wings**. The leading quartet were 21l clear of **Milansbar**, with other big gaps back to the likes of **Gas Line Boy** and **Vieux Lion Rouge**, who had both finished higher in 2017, as well as Welsh National winner **Raz De Maree**. **Childrens List** travelled notably well before running out of stamina, as did **Seeyouatmidnight** to a lesser extent, while **Baie Des Iles** was still in contention when badly hampered eight fences from home. **Blaklion** was brought down at the first, while **Total Recall** was pulled up after jumping poorly and **The Last Samuri** was badly on edge before the race for the second year in a row and also pulled up.

52 Ryanair Stayers' Hurdle (registered as the Liverpool Hurdle) (Grade 1) (3m149y)
Aintree April 14 (Soft)
1 **Identity Thief** 8-11-7　　Sean Flanagan
2 **Wholestone** 7-11-7　　Daryl Jacob
3 **Sam Spinner** 6-11-7　　Joe Colliver
14/1, 7/2, 6/5F. 5l, 10l. 10 ran. 6m 20.70s (Henry De Bromhead).

An unusual renewal in which the winner didn't emerge from the Stayers' Hurdle at Cheltenham, underlining the weakness of that race, with Champion Hurdle fourth **Identity Thief** instead stepping up from 2m to win comfortably. Identity Thief travelled remarkably well and, having cruised to the front between the last two, he found plenty under pressure to beat the dogged **Wholestone**, with **Sam Spinner** well below his best in third after some very slow jumps. It was another 8l back to **The Worlds End**, who threatened briefly before fading, while **Old Guard** was tailed off in last and **Lil Rockerfeller** was pulled up.

53 Coral Scottish Grand National (Handicap Chase) (Grade 3) (3m7f176y)
Ayr April 21 (Good)
1 **Joe Farrell** 9-10-6 Adam Wedge
2 **Ballyoptic** 8-11-6 Tom Bellamy
3 **Vintage Clouds** 8-10-12 Danny Cook
33/1, 9/1, 12/1. nse, 4l. 29 ran. 8m 0.50s (Rebecca Curtis).

A thrilling race fought out between a couple of well-handicapped novices in **Joe Farrell** and **Ballyoptic**. Joe Farrell was still at the right end of the handicap despite going up 11lb for winning his previous outing at Newbury and he made light of a massive step up in grade, racing prominently and just holding off the late thrust of Ballyoptic, who was conceding 14lb to the winner but found more for the step up in trip to mark himself out as a real staying talent on a flat track. **Vintage Clouds** was a fine third, perhaps even improving on a better surface, with the first three pulling 7l clear of **Doing Fine** and dual winner **Vicente**, both of whom had conditions to suit but couldn't take advantage. **Beware The Bear** and the favourite **Fagan** were among those pulled up.

54 QTS Scottish Champion Hurdle (Limited Handicap) (Grade 2) (2m)
Ayr April 21 (Good)
1 **Midnight Shadow** 5-10-4 Danny Cook
2 **Claimantakinforgan** 6-11-3 N de Boinville
3 **Chesterfield** 8-10-6 Daniel Sansom
25/1, 11/2F, 6/1. 1¼l, ½l. 16 ran. 3m 41.50s (Sue Smith).

A fiercely competitive handicap dominated by a couple of novices, with **Claimantakinforgan** much the better of them at the weights but just unable to concede 13lb to **Midnight Shadow**. Claimantakinforgan improved for the switch to quicker ground after finishing fifth in the Supreme but could never quite get to the more prominently ridden Midnight Shadow, who had himself shown fair form at Grade 1 level. **Chesterfield**, 1lb lower than when winning the race in 2017, was a close third ahead of **Charli Parcs** and **Brelade**, two former Grade 1 performers who had also slipped down the weights.

55 BoyleSports Champion Chase (Grade 1) (2m)
Punchestown (IRE) April 24 (Yielding To Soft)
1 **Un De Sceaux** 10-11-12 Mr P W Mullins
2 **Douvan** 8-11-12 Paul Townend
3 **A Toi Phil** 8-11-12 Jack Kennedy
9/2, 4/5F, 33/1. 3¾l, 7l. 9 ran. 4m 16.00s (W P Mullins).

Un De Sceaux hadn't won over 2m in the spring since 2015, but softer ground than had ever been the case in that time helped him to set the record straight, albeit in a race that took less winning than appeared likely beforehand with **Douvan** and **Min** in opposition. Un De Sceaux also benefited from a wonderfully positive ride, making the running at a strong pace and jumping superbly as his pursuers struggled to bridge the gap. Douvan got closest, but his jumping lacked any fluency under pressure and Min was well below his best having run so well at Cheltenham and Aintree, finishing only fourth behind **A Toi Phil**.

56 Coral Punchestown Gold Cup (Grade 1) (3m120y)
Punchestown (IRE) April 25 (Yielding)
1 **Bellshill** 8-11-10 David Mullins
2 **Djakadam** 9-11-10 Mr P W Mullins
3 **Road To Respect** 7-11-10 Sean Flanagan
4/1, 5/1, 7/2F. ¾l, 8l. 12 ran. 6m 43.00s (W P Mullins).

Bellshill confirmed his arrival as a genuine Grade 1 chaser as he confirmed the promise of his Irish National run to win with more in hand than the margin suggested. Always going well, Bellshill was ridden clear at the last and just seemed to idle as **Djakadam**, back to form to finish second in this race for the fourth successive year, closed him down. The pair pulled 8l clear of **Road To Respect**, who seemed to run a bit flat, and the well-backed **Sub Lieutenant**, confirming his return to form after Aintree. **Killultagh Vic** was next ahead of **Sizing Granite**, who would certainly have been placed but for a bad mistake two out, with that sextet clear of **Edwulf** and **Outlander**. **Total Recall** was pulled up.

57 Ladbrokes Champion Stayers' Hurdle (Grade 1) (3m)
Punchestown (IRE) April 26 (Yielding To Soft)
1 **Faugheen** 10-11-10 David Mullins
2 **Penhill** 7-11-10 Paul Townend
3 **Shaneshill** 9-11-10 Danny Mullins
11/2, 2/1F, 33/1. 13l, 4¾l. 12 ran. 6m 4.10s (W P Mullins).

A remarkable renaissance from **Faugheen**, who produced a performance up there with his best as the step up to 3m apparently made all the difference. Faugheen made all the running at a good enough gallop that just three of the 12-strong field came home within 30l of him, yet he still finished strongly to pull clear of **Penhill**, who was going well when looming up two out but didn't get home as well. Faugheen had been gifted a healthy lead at the start, but he had greatly extended that advantage by the line and those who raced closest to him, **Bacardys** and **La Bague Au Roi**, paid the price as they fell away on the final circuit, with **Shaneshill** staying on into third ahead of **Identity Thief**, **Bapaume** and **Diamond Cauchois**. **Yorkhill** was never a factor yet kept on well enough into eighth ahead of **Bleu Et Rouge**.

58 Betdaq 2% Commission Punchestown Champion Hurdle (Grade 1) (2m)
Punchestown (IRE) April 27 (Soft)
1 **Supasundae** 8-11-12 Robbie Power
2 **Wicklow Brave** 9-11-12 Mr P W Mullins
3 **Bleu Berry** 7-11-12 Mark Walsh
7/1, 12/1, 40/1. 3¼l, 19l. 7 ran. 4m 0.90s
(Mrs John Harrington).

An eagerly awaited clash between Champion Hurdle runner-up **Melon** and superstar novice **Samcro** failed to materialise as, amazingly, both fell independently at the same hurdle three out, helping **Supasundae** to a second Grade 1 win of the year. Back down in trip after Cheltenham and Aintree, Supasundae looked good from that point, reeling in **Wicklow Brave**, who had made all to win the race in 2017, although he came up short in better races in the grade and the suspicion remains that he will to continue to do so. Coral Cup winner **Bleu Berry** was hampered by the fallers three out and left with no chance.

59 bet365 Gold Cup (Handicap Chase) (Grade 3) (3m4f166y)
Sandown April 28 (Good To Soft)
1 **Step Back** 8-10-0 Jamie Moore
2 **Rock The Kasbah** 8-11-0 R Johnson
3 **Present Man** 8-10-9 Bryony Frost
7/1, 12/1, 25/1. 13l, 14l. 20 ran. 7m 32.90s
(Mark Bradstock).

A demolition job from the novice **Step Back**, who romped home on only his fourth run over fences. Step Back pressed on early having led from the fifth and very few were able to live with him from there, with **Rock The Kasbah** his only serious rival for much of the final circuit before he drew clear from the

STEP BACK: had rivals strewn all over Esher with this demolition job

second-last. Rock The Kasbah still finished a clear second ahead of **Present Man**, who was also prominently ridden, with **Relentless Dreamer** the best of those coming through from the rear in fourth ahead of **Carole's Destrier**. **Blaklion** was never jumping well and was pulled up.

60 bet365 Celebration Chase (Grade 1) (1m7f119y)
Sandown April 28 (Good To Soft)
1 **Altior** 8-11-7 Nico de Boinville
2 **San Benedeto** 7-11-7 Sam Twiston-Davies
3 **God's Own** 10-11-7 Paddy Brennan
2/11F, 33/1, 11/1. 3¼l, 3¾l. 6 ran. 3m 56.90s
(Nicky Henderson).

Not a vintage performance from **Altior**, but yet again he was never stronger than at the finish as he stormed clear of **San Benedeto**. Altior, after quickening into the lead three out, had taken time to shake off San Benedeto until the run-in, but the runner-up probably took more beating than looked likely beforehand given the quality of those he had behind him as **God's Own** was third with further gaps back to **Special Tiara** and Grade 1 novice winner **Diego Du Charmil**.

61 bet365 Select Hurdle (Grade 2) (2m5f110y)
Sandown April 28 (Good To Soft)
1 **Call Me Lord** 5-11-0 Nico de Boinville
2 **Lil Rockerfeller** 7-11-6 Wayne Hutchinson
3 **Wholestone** 7-11-6 Daryl Jacob
6/4J, 8/1, 6/4J. 16l, 6l. 6 ran. 5m 30.50s
(Nicky Henderson).

This race seemed to fall apart slightly with form horse **Wholestone** failing to recover from his exertions at Cheltenham and Aintree, but it was still a fine performance from **Call Me Lord**. Relishing the step up to 2m5½f, Call Me Lord did plenty wrong, racing keenly early and blundering at the last, but in between he had travelled strongly and put the race to bed in hugely impressive fashion. **Old Guard** was another rival to run below his best in fourth, though even his best form – he had beaten 16l runner-up **Lil Rockerfeller** far more narrowly in the National Spirit Hurdle at Fontwell – suggests he had no chance with the winner.

62 Irish Stallion Farms EBF Annie Power Mares' Champion Hurdle (Grade 1) (2m4f)
Punchestown (IRE) April 28 (Yielding To Soft)
1 **Benie Des Dieux** 7-11-7 Paul Townend
2 **Augusta Kate** 7-11-7 David Mullins

CALL ME LORD: pulled hard but that didn't stop him

3 **Apple's Jade** 6-11-7 Jack Kennedy
3/1, 16/1, 5/6F. 3l, 2½l. 8 ran. 4m 54.70s
(W P Mullins).

A Grade 1 double for **Benie Des Dieux**, who was more impressive than at Cheltenham as she travelled more strongly before being ridden clear from the last, albeit in a race in which her only serious rival, **Apple's Jade**, was again nowhere near her best in third. Apple's Jade was the only other true Grade 1 mare in the field, with **Augusta Kate**, who ran on into second, well beaten in four races at this level since her soft Grade 1 win in 2017 at the expense of **Let's Dance**, whose fourth place here took her record in the highest grade to 0-7.

Big-race index

All horses placed or commented on in our big-race review section, with race numbers

A Great View	40, 55
A Toi Phil	13
Agrapart	27
Alfie Spinner	23
Alpha Des Obeaux	2, 20, 29
Altior	32, 39, 60
American	9, 26, 45
Anibale Fly	29, 45, 51
Apple's Jade	11, 21, 37, 62
Ar Mad	12
Arkwright	47
Augusta Kate	11, 21, 42, 62
Bacardys	42, 57
Baie Des Iles	51
Balko Des Flos	20, 41, 50
Ballyalton	3, 14, 43
Ballyoptic	53
Bapaume	21, 28, 57
Barra	38
Beer Goggles	8
Bellshill	47, 56
Benie Des Dieux	37, 62
Beware The Bear	35, 53
Bigbadjohn	9
Blaklion	1, 51, 59
Bless The Wings	51
Bleu Berry	38, 58
Bleu Et Rouge	30, 57
Brain Power	25
Brelade	54
Bristol De Mai	1, 5, 17, 26, 48
Buveur D'Air	10, 18, 36
Call Me Lord	34, 61
Campeador	4, 22
Captain Redbeard	24
Carole's Destrier	59
Ch'Tibello	15, 34, 36
Charbel	12
Charli Parcs	54
Chesterfield	18, 44, 54
Childrens List	51
Cilaos Emery	11, 22
Claimantakinforgan	54
Clan Des Obeaux	14, 48
Cloudy Dream	31, 41, 50
Clyne	49
Colin's Sister	27, 42
Connetable	40
Coo Star Sivola	35
Cue Card	1, 5, 33, 41
Defi Du Seuil	7, 28
Definitly Red	1, 26, 45, 48
Delta Work	40
Diakali	49
Diamond Cauchois	57
Diego Du Charmil	60
Djakadam	13, 20, 29, 45, 56
Doing Fine	53
Double Shuffle	6, 17
Douvan	39, 55
Edwulf	20, 29, 45, 56
Elgin	34, 36
Fagan	53
Faugheen	4, 22, 28, 36, 57
Final Nudge	23
Flying Angel	6
Flying Tiger	10
Folsom Blue	47
Forever Gold	47
Fox Norton	12, 17
Frodon	6, 33, 41
Gas Line Boy	51
General Principle	47
Gino Trail	46
Glenloe	40
God's Own	39, 60
Guitar Pete	3, 14, 43
Hainan	24
Identity Thief	28, 36, 52, 57
Irving	10
Isleofhopendreams	47
Jezki	4, 21, 28
Joe Farrell	53
John Constable	15
Josses Hill	6
Kalashnikov	30
Killultagh Vic	29, 45, 56
King's Odyssey	14, 43
King's Socks	43
Kylemore Lough	25
L'Ami Serge	7, 16, 42, 49
La Bague Au Roi	37, 57
Lagostovegas	44
Le Prezien	3, 14, 46, 50
Let's Dance	62
Lil Rockerfeller	7, 16, 42, 52, 61
Melon	15, 28, 36, 58
Mick Jazz	11, 22, 28, 36
Midnight Shadow	54
Midnight Tour	37
Might Bite	17, 45, 48
Milansbar	51

Min.	19, 39, 50, 55
Minella Rocco	20, 29
Missed Approach	9
Mohaayed	18, 44
More Of That	2
My Tent Or Yours	15, 49
Native River	31, 45
Nichols Canyon	11, 21
Old Guard	15, 52, 61
Ordinary World	19
Our Duke	2, 29
Outlander	2, 5, 20, 29, 45, 56
Penhill	42, 57
Pleasant Company	51
Politologue	12, 32, 39, 50
Potters Legend	9
Present Man	59
Raz De Maree	23, 51
Regal Encore	9
Relentless Dreamer	59
Remiluc	30, 44
Road To Respect	2, 20, 45, 56
Rock The Kasbah	59
Romain De Senam	3, 14
Sam Spinner	16, 42, 52
Samcro	58
San Benedeto	60
Saphir Du Rheu	31
Seeyouatmidnight	51
Shaneshill	13, 57
Shantou Flyer3	5
Silsol	23
Simply Ned	19
Sizing Codelco	48
Sizing Granite	50, 56
Sizing John	13, 20
Smad Place	6
Special Tiara	39, 60
Speredek	25, 33
Spiritofthegames	30, 44
Splash Of Ginge	3, 43
Starchitect	3, 14
Step Back	59
Sub Lieutenant	2, 13, 41, 48, 56
Supasundae	11, 21, 28, 42, 49, 58
Swamp Fox	4
Taj Badalandabad	40
Taquin Du Seuil	8
Tea For Two	5, 17, 26, 45, 48
The Dutchman	24
The Last Samuri	26, 51
The New One	15, 18, 42, 49
The Storyteller	43
The Worlds End	16, 27, 42, 52
Theinval	46
Thistlecrack	8, 17
Thomas Campbell	16

FAUGHEEN: had an eventful season

Tiger Roll	51
Top Gamble	46
Top Notch	6, 33
Topofthegame	38
Total Recall	9, 45, 51, 56
Tully East	3
Un De Sceaux	25, 41, 55
Unowhatimeanharry	8, 16, 42
Valdez	32
Valseur Lido	20, 29
Vicente	53
Vieux Lion Rouge	51
Vintage Clouds	23, 35, 53
Vyta Du Roc	9
Waiting Patiently	33
Wakea	7
Whiskey Sour	44
Whisper	9, 17
Who Dares Wins	40
Wholestone	8, 27, 42, 52, 61
Wicklow Brave	36, 58
William Henry	38
Yala Enki	24
Yanworth	42
Yorkhill	20, 36, 57
Zabana	2

Novice review by Dylan Hill

1 **Ballymore Novices' Hurdle (Grade 2) (registered as the Hyde Novices' Hurdle) (Grade 2) (2m5f26y)**
Cheltenham November 17 (Good To Soft)
1 **On The Blind Side** 5-11-0 N de Boinville
2 **Momella** 5-10-7 Harry Skelton
3 **Poetic Rhythm** 6-11-5 Paddy Brennan
9/2, 7/1, 9/2. 2½l, nse. 6 ran. 5m 13.50s
(Nicky Henderson).

A really strong Grade 2 won by a high-class horse in **On The Blind Side**, who was probably the leading British novice in the first half of the season before unfortunately seeing his spring campaign ruined by a setback. On The Blind Side was outpaced at the top of the hill, but he got into overdrive and picked off **Momella** and **Poetic Rhythm** on the run-in before adding a second Grade 2 under a penalty at Sandown. The placed horses also did plenty for the form, with Momella third in a Grade 1 at Aintree and Poetic Rhythm winning an admittedly weak Challow Hurdle. **Vision Des Flos** was a disappointing fourth and would need a wind operation to show his improvement in the spring.

2 **JCB Triumph Trial Juvenile Hurdle (registered as the Prestbury Juvenile Hurdle) (Grade 2) (2m87y)**
Cheltenham November 18 (Soft)
1 **Apple's Shakira** 3-10-5 Barry Geraghty
2 **Gumball** 3-10-12 Richard Johnson
3 **Eragon De Chanay** 3-10-12 Josh Moore
EvensF, 5/4, 28/1. 17l, 5l. 6 ran. 4m 9.10s
(Nicky Henderson).

A stunning British debut from **Apple's Shakira** and the best of her three Cheltenham victories that saw her head back there for the Triumph Hurdle a warm favourite as she thrashed subsequent Grade 1 runner-up **Gumball**. That said, Gumball showed all his best form on flat tracks and was pulled up on his only other run at Cheltenham in the Triumph Hurdle, so Apple's Shakira still has plenty to prove in terms of her quality after her disappointing spring.

3 **Ladbrokes Novices' Chase (registered as the Berkshire Novices' Chase) (Grade 2) (2m3f187y)**
Newbury December 1 (Good To Soft)
1 **Willoughby Court** 6-11-1 N de Boinville
2 **Yanworth** 7-11-1 Barry Geraghty
3 **Adrien Du Pont** 5-11-1 Harry Cobden
15/8, 5/6F, 11/2. 3l, 3½l. 5 ran. 4m 57.90s
(Ben Pauling).

Willoughby Court's reputation took a knock when only third behind Yanworth in the Dipper at Cheltenham next time out on what would prove his final run of the season, but heavy ground was probably his undoing that day and he looked like much the more accomplished of the pair over fences in this clash. Having won what is now the Ballymore at Cheltenham in 2017, Willoughby Court jumped well and hit the front around halfway before proving much too strong for **Yanworth**, who wasn't as fluent and won what proved a much weaker Grade 2 in the Dipper before reverting to hurdles.

4 **randoxhealth.com Henry VIII Novices' Chase (Grade 1) (1m7f119y)**
Sandown December 9 (Good To Soft)
1 **Sceau Royal** 5-11-2 Daryl Jacob
2 **North Hill Harvey** 6-11-2 Harry Skelton
3 **Finian's Oscar** 5-11-2 Robbie Power
11/1, 11/2, 13/8F. 11l, 50l. 5 ran. 3m 53.50s
(Alan King).

WILLOUGHBY COURT: looked a really accomplished chaser at Newbury

A terrific performance from **Sceau Royal**, who was much too good for a high-class field of novices and may well have pushed Footpad closer than any other novice on this evidence but for injury. Sceau Royal travelled remarkably well and quickened clear in superb fashion up the hill having already been in command when subsequent Arkle runner-up **Brain Power** fell at the last. **North Hill Harvey** had just beaten Sceau Royal when receiving 5lb at Cheltenham in October but found the winner had improved past him, finishing second as **Capitaine** also came down when held at the second-last. **Finian's Oscar** didn't jump well enough as he finished a distant third and needed much further.

5 32Red Kauto Star Novices' Chase (Grade 1) (3m)
Kempton December 26 (Soft)
1 **Black Corton** 6-11-7 Bryony Frost
2 **Elegant Escape** 5-11-7 Tom O'Brien
3 **West Approach** 7-11-7 Tom Scudamore
4/1, 11/2, 11/1. 1½l, 21l. 7 ran. 6m 9.40s
(Paul Nicholls).

Black Corton finished behind **Elegant Escape** in all three of their other meetings over the season but got his head in front when it mattered most, with a Grade 1 victory on the line. The sharper track was probably the key to Black Corton's victory as he made much of the running and was always holding the more stamina-laden Elegant Escape, who proved one-paced in the straight. However, the pair would both have surely finished behind the ill-fated **Fountains Windfall** had that one not fallen four out, while favourite **Mia's Storm** also came down although she was already struggling on unfavourably soft ground. In the end **West Approach** plugged on for a distant third, with **Ballyoptic** another let down by his jumping in fourth.

6 Betfred Challow Novices' Hurdle (Grade 1) (2m4f118y)
Newbury December 30 (Heavy)
1 **Poetic Rhythm** 6-11-7 Paddy Brennan
2 **Mulcahys Hill** 5-11-7 A P Heskin
3 **Kilbricken Storm** 6-11-7 Harry Cobden
15/8F, 16/1, 11/4. shd, 23l. 6 ran. 5m 24.30s
(Fergal O'Brien).

A desperately weak Grade 1 in which **Poetic**

103

CLASSY CLASH: subsequent Grade 1 winners Black Op (left) and Santini

Rhythm probably wasn't required to step up on the form of his Cheltenham third behind On The Blind Side. With that one a notable absentee and subsequent Albert Bartlett winner **Kilbricken Storm** running stones below his best with his trainer Colin Tizzard's horses out of form, Poetic Rhythm faced just one serious rival in **Mulcahys Hill**, who led for most of the way and may well have won but for a mistake at the last.

7 Coral Future Champions Finale Juvenile Hurdle (Grade 1) (2m11y)
Chepstow January 6 (Heavy)
1 **We Have A Dream** 4-11-0 Daryl Jacob
2 **Sussex Ranger** 4-11-0 Jamie Moore
3 **Mercenaire** 4-11-0 Lizzie Kelly
8/11F, 3/1, 10/1. 1½l, 11l. 5 ran. 4m 6.70s
(Nicky Henderson).

Only five runners but they included the horse who would prove to be the best British juvenile of the season, **We Have A Dream**, who ran out a ready winner. Having made all in his first two races, We Have A Dream was ridden with far more restraint this time and just nudged into the lead at the last, winning with a bit in hand, although **Sussex Ranger** ran a fine race to keep him honest in second and pulled 21l clear of the rest.

8 32Red Tolworth Novices' Hurdle (Grade 1) (1m7f216y)
Sandown January 6 (Heavy)
1 **Summerville Boy** 6-11-7 Noel Fehily
2 **Kalashnikov** 5-11-7 Jack Quinlan
3 **Mont Des Avaloirs** 5-11-7 Sean Bowen
8/1, 2/1, 4/1. 4l, 9l. 5 ran. 4m 3.50s
(Tom George).

One of the most informative Tolworths of recent times with the first two filling the same places in the Supreme, though the key point about the improvement made by **Summerville Boy** was missed by most at the time with excuses instead made for runner-up **Kalashnikov**. Summerville Boy had been beaten on all three runs over hurdles, but he made a huge step forward when showing too much staying power for Kalashnikov, who showed he handled these conditions better than many felt with his efforts later in the season.

Mont Des Avaloirs was a good third, but **Western Ryder** was disappointing behind.

9 Lawlor's Of Naas Novice Hurdle (Grade 1) (2m4f)
Naas (IRE) January 7 (Soft To Heavy)
1 **Next Destination** 6-11-10   Paul Townend
2 **Cracking Smart** 6-11-10   Davy Russell
3 **Duc Des Genievres** 5-11-7   David Mullins
8/15F, 9/2, 25/1. 1l, 3l. 8 ran. 5m 10.10s
(W P Mullins)

A really strong Grade 1 won in gritty style by **Next Destination** even though he would prove better again over further. Next Destination was made to work much harder by **Cracking Smart** than when first and second again in a Grade 2 at Navan before Christmas on heavy ground and would show he really needed a softer surface over this trip at Cheltenham, but he was still good enough to put the race to bed before closed down by a strong-staying and potentially high-class runner-up close home. **Duc Des Genievres** was third ahead of **Jetz**, who franked the form when beaten just a head by Tower Bridge in another Grade 1 at Leopardstown next time, and the first four were 13l clear of the rest, including **Blow By Blow**, who won his next two including the Martin Pipe Hurdle at Cheltenham.

10 Ballymore Classic Novices' Hurdle (Grade 2) (2m4f56y)
Cheltenham January 27 (Heavy)
1 **Santini** 6-11-5   Jeremiah McGrath
2 **Black Op** 7-11-5   Tom Scudamore
3 **Aye Aye Charlie** 6-11-5   Paddy Brennan
4/1, 8/1, 16/1. ¾l, 29l. 9 ran. 5m 23.10s
(Nicky Henderson).

A good clash between two subsequent Grade 1 winners and the extra stamina of **Santini**, who was always set to be stepped up in trip in the spring, proved decisive on heavy ground. Santini steadily wore down **Black Op** on the run-in and won with a bit in hand, although he may not have got there had Black Op not made a mistake at the last. The pair pulled 29l clear of **Aye Aye Charlie**, with **Mulcahys Hill** a disappointing fourth.

11 Betfred TV Scilly Isles Novices' Chase (Grade 1) (2m4f10y)
Sandown February 3 (Soft)
1 **Terrefort** 5-11-1   Daryl Jacob
2 **Cyrname** 6-11-4   Sean Bowen
3 **No Comment** 7-11-4   Tom O'Brien
15/8F, 9/4, 8/1. nk, 30l. 5 ran. 5m 16.90s
(Nicky Henderson).

A disappointing turnout for a Grade 1, but **Terrefort** and **Cyrname** at least served up a terrific finish as they proved vastly superior to the opposition. Terrefort was ultimately just too strong and would prove himself a top-class novice at Cheltenham and Aintree, but he was pushed all the way by Cyrname, who was much better suited by this right-handed track than Aintree in the Manifesto having gained his three wins last season at Kempton and Huntingdon going the same way. **No Comment** ran a hugely promising chasing debut and was a lot closer until stumbling two out, but **Kalondra** and **West Approach** were very disappointing.

12 Frank Ward Solicitors Arkle Novice Chase (Grade 1) (2m1f)
Leopardstown (IRE) February 3 (Soft)
1 **Footpad** 6-11-10   Paul Townend
2 **Petit Mouchoir** 7-11-10   Davy Russell
3 **Any Second Now** 6-11-10   Mark Walsh
4/9F, 3/1, 8/1. 5l, 19l. 5 ran. 4m 13.90s
(W P Mullins).

Footpad had finished behind **Petit Mouchoir** every time they met over hurdles, but this first clash over fences showed that chasing had been the making of him as he ran out a clearcut winner. Impressive in a course-and-distance Grade 1 over Christmas, Footpad faced a tougher opponent but rose to the task, massively extending his superiority over **Any Second Now** from that race as he made all the running and eased to victory. Petit Mouchoir had the excuse of a setback since his chase debut but actually produced probably his best performance of the season in finishing a clear second.

13 Deloitte Novice Hurdle (Grade 1) (2m)
Leopardstown (IRE) February 4 (Soft)
1 **Samcro** 6-11-10   Jack Kennedy
2 **Duc Des Genievres** 5-11-9   Noel Fehily
3 **Paloma Blue** 6-11-10   Davy Russell
4/6F, 9/1, 16/1. 5½l, 3¾l. 11 ran. 4m 8.70s
(Gordon Elliott).

Samcro, aimed at the Ballymore all season, showed he also had the speed for 2m with a remarkably comfortable win in a race that had plenty of depth. Samcro wasn't remotely stretched to beat the likes of **Paloma Blue** and **Debuchet** further than they were beaten in the Supreme, with **Duc Des Genievres** getting closest to him in second. **Sharjah**, who had been all set to win a course-and-distance Grade 1 over Christmas when falling at the last, was well below his best in seventh, but **Real Steel**, left in front that day when also falling, and **Whiskey Sour**, who had gone on to pick up the pieces, were also well beaten here, suggesting he would have struggled to get close to Samcro anyway.

14 Flogas Novice Chase (Grade 1) (2m5f)
Leopardstown (IRE) February 4 (Soft)
1 **Monalee** 7-11-10 Noel Fehily
2 **Al Boum Photo** 6-11-10 David Mullins
3 **Invitation Only** 7-11-10 Paul Townend
11/4J, 9/1, 7/2. ¾l, hd. 11 ran. 5m 34.80s (Henry De Bromhead).

A fiercely competitive race featuring two subsequent Cheltenham Festival winners and two further Grade 1 winners, all of whom were beaten by **Monalee**. Doing particularly well to win over a trip short of his best, Monalee made all the running and outstayed **Invitation Only**, with **Al Boum Photo** finishing strongly to split the pair. **Dounikos** ran a huge race to finish just ¾l back in fourth and three more horses finished within 8l, with **Snow Falcon** in fifth ahead of **Tombstone** and **The Storyteller**. **Rathvinden** would also have been involved but for unseating his rider two out, but **Sutton Place** was pulled up.

15 Betway Kingmaker Novices' Chase (Grade 2) (2m54y)
Warwick February 10 (Soft)
1 **Saint Calvados** 5-10-12 Aidan Coleman
2 **Diego Du Charmil** 6-11-0 Bryony Frost
3 **North Hill Harvey** 7-11-5 Harry Skelton
4/9F, 11/1, 11/4. 22l, 17l. 4 ran. 4m 6.90s (Harry Whittington).

Saint Calvados blotted his copybook in the Arkle, but the form of this performance was franked later in the season and suggests he could yet prove a superstar. An easy winner of novice handicaps on his first two runs over fences, Saint Calvados proved equally dominant taking on better novices and made all the running in devastating fashion, jumping superbly. **North Hill Harvey** was disappointing in third, but it's perhaps understandable that he couldn't cope given subsequent Grade 1

CHEF DES OBEAUX (right): a much better horse than he showed in the spring

winner **Diego Du Charmil** was also left toiling.

16 Albert Bartlett Novices' Hurdle (registered as the Prestige Novices' Hurdle) (Grade 2) (2m6f177y)
Haydock February 17 (Heavy)
1 **Chef Des Obeaux** 6-11-0 Noel Fehily
2 **Uppertown Prince** 6-11-0 Will Kennedy
3 **Golan Fortune** 6-11-0 Jamie Moore
13/8F, 12/1, 7/2. 15l, 1¼l. 8 ran. 6m 0.30s
(Nicky Henderson).

A competitive race won in stunning fashion by **Chef Des Obeaux**, who proved himself a much better horse than he would subsequently show at Cheltenham and Aintree. Always handy as several rivals were outpaced, Chef Des Obeaux powered clear from the third-last to beat **Uppertown Prince**, who got closer to Santini in the Grade 1 Sefton at Aintree. **Golan Fortune** brought strong handicap form to the table but was only third ahead of **Just Your Type**, an impressive winner next time, while **Shannon Bridge**, a short-head second to Enniscoffey Oscar in another Grade 2 at Doncaster, was already struggling when a mistake three out ended his challenge.

17 Betdaq #ChangingForTheBettor Adonis Juvenile Hurdle (Grade 2) (2m)
Kempton February 24 (Good)
1 **Redicean** 4-11-1 Wayne Hutchinson
2 **Malaya** 4-10-10 Sam Twiston-Davies
3 **Beau Gosse** 4-11-3 Daryl Jacob
10/11F, 4/1, 4/1. 7l, 10l. 7 ran. 3m 49.50s
(Alan King).

This wasn't particularly competitive, but **Redicean** still faced a useful rival in **Malaya** and beat her with remarkable ease to justify his lofty place in the Triumph Hurdle market. Below his best on soft ground that day, Redicean was ideally suited by good ground and a sharp track here as he deployed a stunning turn of foot that saw him burst clear of Malaya, who franked the form by winning a strong juvenile handicap at Ascot next time.

18 Sky Bet Dovecote Novices' Hurdle (Grade 2) (2m)
Kempton February 24 (Good)
1 **Global Citizen** 6-11-2 Daryl Jacob
2 **Scarlet Dragon** 5-11-2 W Hutchinson
3 **Michael's Mount** 5-11-2 Tom O'Brien
5/1, 13/2, 7/1. 9l, 3¾l. 10 ran. 3m 47.10s
(Ben Pauling).

A runaway win from the impressive **Global Citizen** but one that may just have flattered him bearing in mind subsequent events at Aintree. Soon in front, Global Citizen was clear turning for home and stormed home ahead of **Scarlet Dragon**, who ran on from the rear on a promising hurdling debut, but both were then disappointing at the Grand National meeting, where third-placed **Michael's Mount** was also a well-beaten favourite in a handicap. **Mont Des Avaloirs** was a below-par fourth on much quicker ground than in the Tolworth.

19 Sky Bet Supreme Novices' Hurdle (Grade 1) (2m87y)
Cheltenham March 13 (Heavy)
1 **Summerville Boy** 6-11-7 Noel Fehily
2 **Kalashnikov** 5-11-7 Jack Quinlan
3 **Mengli Khan** 5-11-7 Jack Kennedy
9/1, 5/1, 14/1. nk, 1¾l. 18 ran. 4m 5.00s
(Tom George).

This looked a poor renewal beforehand, with the total of four last-time-out winners the lowest this century even though there was a big field of 20 runners, but **Summerville Boy** was much the best of them despite the narrow margin. Summerville Boy looked to have lost all chance with a blunder two out and then lost his momentum again with a mistake at the last, but he still produced a storming run up the hill to get past **Kalashnikov**, who lacked the gears to put the race to bed when sent for home after the second-last. Royal Bond winner **Mengli Khan** was best of the Irish in third ahead of **Paloma Blue**, while **Claimantakinforgan**, an improver on better ground at Ayr, was fifth ahead of **Western Ryder** and **Lostintranslation**, all three staying on well from the rear with Western Ryder most unlucky after being hampered when making progress two out. **Sharjah** and **Debuchet** were next, while **Getabird** raced too keenly and faded tamely. **Slate House** was held in seventh when falling at the last.

20 Racing Post Arkle Novices' Chase (Grade 1) (1m7f199y)
Cheltenham March 13 (Heavy)
1 **Footpad** 6-11-4 R Walsh
2 **Brain Power** 7-11-4 Nico de Boinville
3 **Petit Mouchoir** 7-11-4 Davy Russell
5/6F, 14/1, 4/1. 14l, ¾l. 5 ran. 4m 2.40s
(W P Mullins).

An outstanding performance from **Footpad**, with the only disappointment being that he wasn't remotely tested because of the way the race was run. There was a pitifully small field, with several connections understandably scared off by Footpad, and while the opposition still looked strong – five of the previous 15 renewals hadn't contained a single hurdler rated as highly as Footpad, **Brain Power** and **Petit Mouchoir** over timber and **Saint Calvados** had also looked a star – two of those rivals compromised their own chances by tearing off in front at a suicidal gallop, with Petit Mouchoir doing well to finish within 15l in the circumstances in third and Saint Calvados 38l further back in fourth. Footpad, given a terrific ride as Ruby Walsh dispensed with his usual front-running tactics to sit a distant third for much of the race, proved his versatility as he eased through and stormed up the hill. Brain Power staggered home in comparison despite also being held up, but he still did enough to pick up the pieces in second.

21 National Hunt Challenge Cup (Amateur Riders' Novices' Chase) (Grade 2) (3m7f170y)
Cheltenham March 13 (Soft)
1 **Rathvinden** 10-11-6   Mr P W Mullins
2 **Ms Parfois** 7-10-13   Mr William Biddick
3 **Sizing Tennessee** 10-11-6   Mr B O'Neill
9/2, 11/2, 8/1. ½l, 21l. 16 ran. 8m 50.30s (W P Mullins).

This was a serious test of stamina in testing conditions so a huge credit to **Rathvinden** and **Ms Parfois** for providing a stirring duel at the end of it, with Rathvinden just proving strongest in the final 50 yards. Rathvinden came up short over shorter trips but showed that stamina is his strong suit as he wore down the gallant Ms Parfois, who franked the form with a fine run at Aintree. The pair pulled 21l clear of **Sizing Tennessee**, who was still in front between the last two before fading on the run-in, and **Impulsive Star**. **Pylonthepressure** and **No Comment** were the only others to finish and both caught the eye despite being beaten a long way, with Pylonthepressure doing well to stay in contention for so long after jumping violently right-handed and No Comment travelling strongly before failing to stay.

22 Close Brothers Novices' Handicap Chase (Listed) (2m4f78y)
Cheltenham March 13 (Soft)
1 **Mister Whitaker** 6-11-2   Brian Hughes
2 **Rather Be** 7-11-8   Jeremiah McGrath
3 **Rocklander** 9-11-7   A P Heskin
13/2, 12/1, 25/1. hd, 3¼l. 19 ran. 5m 29.00s (Mick Channon).

This race had been raised to a 0-145 handicap and therefore attracted far more Graded performers than usual at the top of the handicap, but more progressive types still came to the fore with **Mister Whitaker**, up 19lb for two wins and a second in three previous handicaps, defying his latest 8lb rise. Mister Whitaker didn't have a clear run two out and lost ground, but he produced a strong finish to edge past **Rather Be** with **Rocklander** a gallant third, that trio pulling 8l clear of **Barney Dwan**, who travelled well but couldn't pick up on the ground, and **Ibis Du Rheu**. The best of those to have earned their marks in Graded company – Rocklander and Ibis Du Rheu had failed to complete in single runs at that level – was the favourite **Any Second Now** back in eighth, with Grade 2 winner **Testify** last of the 11 finishers and **De Plotting Shed** another notable disappointment when pulled up.

23 Ballymore Novices' Hurdle (Grade 1) (2m5f26y)
Cheltenham March 14 (Soft)
1 **Samcro** 6-11-7   Jack Kennedy
2 **Black Op** 7-11-7   Noel Fehily
3 **Next Destination** 6-11-7   R Walsh
8/11F, 8/1, 4/1. 2¾l, 5l. 14 ran. 5m 18.20s (Gordon Elliott).

A consummate performance from the brilliant **Samcro**, who was an easy winner of what looks set to prove a strong renewal with two subsequent Grade 1 winners in the places. Samcro was always travelling strongly and carried himself to the front between the last two when still on the bridle, staying on well to beat **Black Op**, who couldn't cope with the winner's speed after the second-last but rallied strongly. It was 5l back to **Next Destination**, who looked badly in need of further as he stormed up the hill having been outpaced, pipping **Scarpeta** for third with **Duc Des Genievres** and **Vision Des Flos**, who travelled well and led two out but failed to get home, also finishing within 10l. That sextet pulled 14l clear of **Aye Aye Charlie**.

24 RSA Insurance Novices' Chase (Grade 1) (3m80y)
Cheltenham March 14 (Soft)
1 **Presenting Percy** 7-11-4   Davy Russell
2 **Monalee** 7-11-4   Noel Fehily
3 **Elegant Escape** 6-11-4   Harry Cobden
5/2F, 100/30, 9/1. 7l, 7l. 10 ran. 6m 32.40s (Patrick G Kelly).

A stunning performance from **Presenting Percy**, who was much too good for the Flogas one-two **Monalee** and **Al Boum Photo** to follow up his victory in the 2017 Pertemps Final. Held up in rear, Presenting Percy jumped well throughout and smoothly drew clear of

SAMCRO: easily shook off two subsequent Grade 1 winners

Monalee, with Al Boum Photo staying on in third when he fell at the last. While made to look ordinary, that pair were still set to frank the form before the carnage at Punchestown the following month and proved themselves much better than the British novices behind them. **Black Corton** was slightly let down by his jumping on this tougher test and couldn't confirm Kempton form with **Elegant Escape**, who just edged out **Ballyoptic** in third – that rival seemingly less effective on a more undulating track than when second in the Scottish National – with Black Corton close behind. There were only five finishers, with **Dounikos** pulled up.

25 Boodles Fred Winter Juvenile Handicap Hurdle (Grade 3) (2m87y)
Cheltenham March 14 (Soft)
1 **Veneer Of Charm** 4-11-0 Jack Kennedy
2 **Style De Garde** 4-11-8 Nico de Boinville
3 **Nube Negra** 4-11-6 Harry Skelton
33/1, 12/1, 15/2F. 3l, 1l. 22 ran. 4m 10.70s
(Gordon Elliott).

This was dominated by three horses who did plenty wrong, hinting at the potential for more to come, but the bare form was nothing special and the fact that all three were well beaten subsequently suggests they were perhaps lucky to get away with it in a poor renewal. **Veneer Of Charm** was still very green as he took command but straightened up in time to see off **Style De Garde**, who raced keenly, and **Nube Negra**, who didn't get home having travelled best. However, **Padleyourcanoe**, seemingly exposed having earned his mark in three runs in open handicaps, was beaten less than 7l in fourth at 33-1 to point to the shortcomings in the form, with several less battle-hardened types disappointing and an incident at the third, when **Lisp** fell and badly hampered **Mitchouka** and **Oxford Blu**, taking out three fancied runners.

26 Weatherbys Champion Bumper (Grade 1) (2m87y)
Cheltenham March 14 (Soft)
1 **Relegate** 5-10-12 Ms K Walsh
2 **Carefully Selected** 6-11-5 Danny Mullins
3 **Tornado Flyer** 5-11-5 Paul Townend
25/1, 6/1, 14/1. nk, 3¼l. 23 ran. 4m 4.30s
(W P Mullins).

A stunning win from the mare **Relegate**, who stormed from last to first to pip **Carefully**

Selected having struggled to go the pace for the first mile until her stamina kicked in. Any other outcome would have been most unjust as Carefully Selected had been gifted a big lead during a botched start, allowing his rider to wait in front before kicking clear off the home turn, and he would prove unable to confirm his superiority over the third and fifth, **Tornado Flyer** and **Blackbow**, as that trio filled the first three places at Punchestown, with quicker ground perhaps proving Relegate's undoing that day. **Acey Milan** ran a cracker to finish among that group in fourth, the only British runner in the first seven, while **Mercy Mercy Me** was the only runner to go on to Aintree after finishing eighth and disappointed there behind Portrush Ted.

27 JLT Novices' Chase (Grade 1) (2m3f198y)
Cheltenham March 15 (Soft)
1 **Shattered Love** 7-10-11   Jack Kennedy
2 **Terrefort** 5-11-3   Daryl Jacob
3 **Benatar** 6-11-4   Jamie Moore
4/1, 3/1F, 10/1. 7l, 5l. 9 ran. 5m 11.80s (Gordon Elliott).

A really strong renewal with **Shattered Love** much too good for a pair of subsequent Aintree Grade 1 winners. Shattered Love had won a 3m Grade 1 winner at Leopardstown over Christmas – albeit when helped by the fall of main rival Monalee – and her proven stamina came in handy in the conditions, but runner-up **Terrefort** also won over further at Aintree and it was much more than staying power behind the underrated mare's triumph as she travelled all over her rivals and drew clear from the second-last. **Benatar** did remarkably well to finish third having pulled hard in the early stages, showing the improvement he had made since a narrow verdict over **Finian's Oscar** in a Grade 2 at Ascot earlier in the season with that rival only fifth on this occasion, **Kemboy**, who went on to win a novice handicap at Punchestown,

SHATTERED LOVE: less heralded than stablemate Samcro but she also had a pair of Grade 1 winners behind her when hacking up in the JLT

splitting them in fourth. It was another 6l back to **West Approach**, while **Bigmartre**, who would win a desperately weak Grade 2 at Ayr the following month but had his limitations exposed in this stronger company, was seventh ahead of **Modus**. **Invitation Only** was still going well when a bad blunder four out caused him to be pulled up, though he was beaten by Shattered Love anyway in the Ryanair Gold Cup even as the mare struggled to maintain her form in the spring.

28 Trull House Stud Mares' Novices' Hurdle (Grade 2) (2m179y)
Cheltenham March 15 (Soft)
1 **Laurina** 5-11-7 　　　　　　Paul Townend
2 **Cap Soleil** 5-11-7 　　　　Paddy Brennan
3 **Champayne Lady** 6-11-2 Denis O'Regan
4/7F, 10/1, 80/1. 18l, shd. 14 ran. 4m 15.40s
(W P Mullins).

An astonishingly straightforward victory for **Laurina**, who demolished her rivals without coming off the bridle with even a terrible mistake at the last doing nothing to stop her. The quality of the opposition was certainly questionable, especially with **Maria's Benefit** – the best rival Laurina faced in this race or a subsequent Grade 1 win at Fairyhouse – going off far too fast in front and running herself into the ground, but Laurina looked all quality as she sauntered into the lead between the last two and moved clear effortlessly. With Maria's Benefit legless up the hill, **Cap Soleil** and **Champayne Lady** came from well off the pace to battle for second.

29 JCB Triumph Hurdle (Grade 1) (2m179y)
Cheltenham March 16 (Soft)
1 **Farclas** 4-11-0 　　　　　　　Jack Kennedy
2 **Mr Adjudicator** 4-11-0 　　　 Paul Townend
3 **Sayo** 4-11-0 　　　　　　　　Danny Mullins
9/1, 8/1, 33/1. 1¾l, 3½l. 9 ran. 4m 17.00s
(Gordon Elliott).

Beaten by **Mr Adjudicator** in a Grade 1 at Leopardstown that developed into a sprint on his previous start, **Farclas** reversed those placings in a more strongly run race as the Irish form held sway. Staying on powerfully in what proved a stiff test of stamina, Farclas had to be switched a couple of times in the straight but came through to lead at the last and pulled clear of Mr Adjudicator in the final 50 yards, while **Sayo** ran a mighty race on only his second run over hurdles in third to complete a clean sweep of the places for Irish-trained runners. That said, it's questionable just what that trio had left to beat with **Apple's Shakira** disappointing in fourth, **Redicean** finding conditions against him in sixth and We Have A Dream out injured to leave a meagre field of just nine. **Saldier**, another running for only the second time over hurdles, would improve massively for the experience after coming home a distant fifth, while **Sussex Ranger** and **Gumball** were both disappointing. **Stormy Ireland** paid the price for setting a strong pace and was set for fifth when she fell at the last.

30 Albert Bartlett Novices' Hurdle (Grade 1) (2m7f213y)
Cheltenham March 16 (Soft)
1 **Kilbricken Storm** 7-11-5 　Harry Cobden
2 **Ok Corral** 8-11-5 　　　　　Barry Geraghty
3 **Santini** 6-11-5 　　　　　　Nico de Boinville
33/1, 16/1, 11/4F. 3l, 1½l. 20 ran. 6m 13.60s
(Colin Tizzard).

A surprise result as **Kilbricken Storm** made full use of his proven stamina, helped by the riders of his nearest rivals perhaps being guilty of injudicious tactics, although another fine run at Punchestown next time would confirm he had been badly underrated because of a poor run in the Challow Hurdle when his trainer's horses were wrong. The winner of a truly run course-and-distance Grade 2 in December, albeit in what amounted to a match against a subsequently disappointing rival in Count Meribel, Kilbricken Storm was ridden far closer to the pace than **Ok Corral** and **Santini** and never looked like relinquishing the decisive lead he inherited when the front-running **Fabulous Saga** fell away. Ok Corral finished best and may even have got up but for a mistake at the last, while Santini kept on well in third ahead of **Ballyward**, **Tower Bridge** and **Robin Waters** with Fabulous Saga also holding on well enough to finish within 12l in seventh. It was 14l back to subsequent Punchestown winner **Dortmund Park**, with **Poetic Rhythm** and **Real Steel** also among the also-rans, while **Mulcahys Hill** and **Chef Des Obeaux** were pulled up.

31 Ryanair Gold Cup (Novice Chase) (Grade 1) (2m4f)
Fairyhouse (IRE) April 1 (Soft To Heavy)
1 **Al Boum Photo** 6-11-10 　David Mullins
2 **Shattered Love** 7-11-3 　　Jack Kennedy
3 **Invitation Only** 7-11-10 　Paul Townend
11/2, 13/8F, 5/1. 1l, 7l. 9 ran. 5m 35.90s
(W P Mullins).

A competitive field despite all the nine runners remarkably being prepared by just two trainers and **Al Boum Photo** bounced back from his RSA fall to see off **Shattered Love**. There was little between the pair, but a slow jump by Shattered Love at the last just as she looked to have taken control of the race handed the initiative to Al Boum Photo and he stayed on strongly to win. **Invitation Only** didn't jump well enough, notably at the second-last, and weakened from that point to finish third, with another 8l back to **Up For Review**. **The Storyteller** was below his best in fifth, with **Tombstone** next.

32 Rathbarry & Glenview Studs Novice Hurdle (Grade 2) (2m)
Fairyhouse (IRE) April 2 (Heavy)
1 **Getabird** 6-11-10   Paul Townend
2 **Draconien** 5-11-4   Noel Fehily
3 **Hardline** 6-11-10   Davy Russell
EvensF, 16/1, 6/1. 12l, 1¾l. 9 ran. 4m 38.10s (W P Mullins).

Getabird finished the season with a rather patchy profile, not coming close in three runs at Grade 1 level, but this was the second of two Grade 2 wins and put him up there with the season's best novices. Too good for Mengli Khan at Punchestown in January, Getabird made all the running here and stormed clear from the second-last, thumping **Draconien**, who franked the form by winning at Punchestown next time when Getabird was struck into. **Hardline** was third ahead of **Sharjah**, with that quartet 13l clear of the rest.

33 Big Buck's Celebration Manifesto Novices' Chase (Grade 1) (2m3f200y)
Aintree April 12 (Good To Soft)
1 **Finian's Oscar** 6-11-4   Robbie Power
2 **Rene's Girl** 8-10-11   Harry Skelton
3 **Calino D'Airy** 6-11-4   Sean Flanagan
5/2, 8/1, 33/1. 2l, 3¼l. 6 ran. 5m 16.00s (Colin Tizzard).

Without any of the four who finished in front of him in the JLT to worry about and helped by the early fall of **Brain Power**, **Finian's Oscar** made the most of a golden opportunity without convincing at all with his jumping. Finian's Oscar was last of the five still standing on the home turn after several mistakes, but none of those ahead of him had the ability to put the race to bed and he stayed on powerfully to lead on the run-in. **Rene's Girl**, who had won two Listed mares' chases, was second ahead of **Calino D'Airy**, while **Cyrname** hung right throughout and faded into a disappointing fourth ahead of **Modus**.

34 Doom Bar Anniversary 4-Y-O Juvenile Hurdle (Grade 1) (2m209y)
Aintree April 12 (Good To Soft)
1 **We Have A Dream** 4-11-0   Daryl Jacob
2 **Gumball** 4-11-0   Richard Johnson

GETABIRD: patchy profile but not far off the best novice hurdlers on his day

3 **Apple's Shakira** 4-10-7   Barry Geraghty
2/1, 20/1, 13/8F. 7l, 10l. 10 ran. 4m 15.80s
(Nicky Henderson).

Having missed Cheltenham through injury, **We Have A Dream** comprehensively proved himself the best of the British juveniles and won well enough to suggest he could have been a major player against the Irish. Always prominent, We Have A Dream took over in front four out and drew clear from the second-last, leaving his rivals toiling and putting far more distance into **Apple's Shakira** than Farclas had in the Triumph. **Gumball** finished a good second, slightly holding down the form after a couple of poor efforts, although he benefited from the return to a flat track and slightly better ground. Apple's Shakira was tried in a hood after racing keenly at Cheltenham but did no better in third ahead of **Cristal Icon** and **Nube Negra**, with a 14l gap back to the rest including **Beau Gosse**, **Malaya** and **Padleyourowncanoe**.

35 Betway Top Novices' Hurdle (Grade 1) (2m103y)
Aintree April 13 (Soft)
1 **Lalor** 6-11-4   Richard Johnson
2 **Vision Des Flos** 5-11-4   Robbie Power
3 **Bedrock** 5-11-4   Ross Chapman
14/1, 11/4, 33/1. 2½l, ¾l. 13 ran. 4m 15.80s
(Kayley Woollacott).

Disappointing since winning the Grade 2 bumper at Aintree 12 months earlier, **Lalor** finally built on that promise on his second run after a wind operation as he won what would prove a much stronger Grade 1 than it looked at the time, travelling strongly in front and drawing clear of **Bedrock** from the last. Only the disappointing **Slate House** came here from the Supreme, but there was still strong Cheltenham form represented by the Ballymore sixth **Vision Des Flos**, who had looked sure to improve for the drop to 2m that day and showed that was the case at Aintree and Punchestown, staying on strongly here to get up for second ahead of the tiring Bedrock. The first three pulled 9l clear of **Mind's Eye** and **Coolanly**, while **Midnight Shadow** franked the form by winning the Scottish Champion Hurdle, albeit off a low mark, after finishing seventh. **Global Citizen** was sent off a warm favourite, but he was only sixth with Dovecote runner-up **Scarlet Dragon** ninth.

36 Betway Mildmay Novices' Chase (Grade 1) (3m210y)
Aintree April 13 (Soft)
1 **Terrefort** 5-11-4   Daryl Jacob

LALOR: finally built on bumper promise

2 **Ms Parfois** 7-10-11   Noel Fehily
3 **Elegant Escape** 6-11-4   Harry Cobden
3/1F, 9/2, 4/1. 3¾l, 9l. 9 ran. 6m 49.90s
(Nicky Henderson).

A really strong race dominated by Cheltenham runners-up **Terrefort** and **Ms Parfois**, with the speedier Terrefort able to last home over this longer trip in hugely impressive fashion as he mastered the runner-up between the last two and powered clear. Ms Parfois had been beaten by **Black Corton** in the Reynoldstown but had suggested that was a below-par effort when going close at Cheltenham and confirmed herself a much better mare than that with a fine effort in second, although Black Corton was well below his best in fourth as he finished 18l behind old rival **Elegant Escape**. **Captain Chaos** ran much better than the bare form, fading into fifth having set a strong gallop that found

CARNAGE: Paul Townend begins to steer Al Boum Photo around the last

out several talented horses, with **Coo Star Sivola**, **Testify** and **Snow Falcon** (broke a blood vessel) pulled up.

37 Doom Bar Sefton Novices' Hurdle (Grade 1) (3m149y)
Aintree April 13 (Soft)
1 **Santini** 6-11-4   Nico de Boinville
2 **Roksana** 6-10-11   Harry Skelton
3 **Tower Bridge** 5-11-4   J J Slevin
6/4F, 9/1, 8/1. 1½l, 6l. 13 ran. 6m 40.80s (Nicky Henderson).

Redemption for **Santini**, who had probably run better than the bare form when a beaten favourite in the Albert Bartlett and made amends by grinding out victory. Ridden much more prominently than at Cheltenham, Santini led three out and held off **Roksana**, who had won the EBF Mares' Final at Newbury and proved herself a high-class staying mare in second. **Tower Bridge**, 3¼l behind Santini at Cheltenham, was a 7½l third this time, not helped by a mistake three out, although Albert Bartlett runner-up **Ok Corral** failed to back up that form by managing only fifth behind **Uppertown Prince**. **Count Meribel** and **Chef Des Obeaux** were pulled up.

38 Betway Mersey Novices' Hurdle (Grade 1) (2m4f)
Aintree April 14 (Soft)
1 **Black Op** 7-11-4   Noel Fehily
2 **Lostintranslation** 6-11-4   Robbie Power
3 **Momella** 6-10-11   Harry Skelton
3/1, 12/1, 10/1. ½l, 3l. 12 ran. 5m 4.70s (Tom George).

A gutsy win from Ballymore runner-up **Black Op**, who probably wasn't at his best but fought hard to beat **Lostintranslation**. Trainer Tom George's first winner since Cheltenham, Black Op struggled to make his superiority tell as he made a couple of mistakes in the straight, but he forged clear in the final 100 yards and was well on top at the line. Lostintranslation improved for the step up in trip after his Supreme seventh and was a good second ahead of **Momella** and **Aye Aye Charlie**, who got significantly closer to Black Op than he had in the Ballymore to emphasise Black Op's sub-par effort. **Western Ryder** failed to stay in fifth ahead of **On The Blind Side**, who had beaten Momella at Cheltenham to show just how much he ran below his best after a long layoff.

39 Doom Bar Maghull Novices' Chase (Grade 1) (1m7f176y)
Aintree April 14 (Soft)
1 **Diego Du Charmil** 6-11-4   Harry Cobden
2 **Petit Mouchoir** 7-11-4   Davy Russell
3 **Shantou Rock** 6-11-4   Harry Skelton
5/1, 4/5F, 13/2. 2½l, 6l. 6 ran. 4m 2.20s (Paul Nicholls).

With little depth to the race, this boiled down to a virtual match between **Diego Du Charmil** and **Petit Mouchoir**, who was let down by his headstrong tendencies for the second time in a row when turned over at odds-on. Petit Mouchoir got extremely lit up and even demolished a rail before the start, and that may well have contributed to his disappointing effort as he was left behind by Diego Du Charmil, who posted a career-best effort over fences after an autumn setback had set back his earlier progress even allowing for doubts over just how much he achieved. **Shantou Rock** was third ahead of **Lady Buttons**.

40 Herald Champion Novice Hurdle (Grade 1) (2m100y)

Punchestown (IRE) April 24 (Yielding To Soft)
1 **Draconien** 5-11-12 Noel Fehily
2 **Vision Des Flos** 5-11-12 Robbie Power
3 **Mengli Khan** 5-11-12 Jack Kennedy
25/1, 11/1, 11/2. 2¼l, 7l. 10 ran. 4m 3.70s
(W P Mullins).

A big upset as **Draconien**, put in his place by **Getabird** at Fairyhouse and the Willie Mullins fourth string according to the betting, swooped late for a comfortable victory. With Getabird down the field having been struck into, Draconien benefited from being produced late off a strong gallop and took advantage of what became a fairly soft opening at the top level as he ran down **Vision Des Flos** and **Mengli Khan**, whose bad mistake at the last cost him a shot at second. **Whiskey Sour** looked in need of further as he ran on for a never-nearer fourth, with **Sharjah** and **Hardline** among those behind. **Paloma Blue** weakened quickly after a mistake two out and was found to have pulled a shoe.

41 Growise Champion Novice Chase (Grade 1) (3m120y)

Punchestown (IRE) April 24 (Yielding To Soft)
1 **The Storyteller** 7-11-10 Davy Russell
2 **Monbeg Notorious** 7-11-10 D O'Regan
3 **Jury Duty** 7-11-10 Mark Walsh
16/1, 33/1, 16/1. 6l, 1¼l. 11 ran. 6m 42.00s
(Gordon Elliott).

One of the most incredible races of the season as Paul Townend, mistakenly thinking the final fence had to be bypassed, hooked **Al Boum Photo** around the obstacle when in front and took out his nearest pursuer **Finian's Oscar**, handing a hollow victory to The Storyteller. Even before then there had been drama at the second-last when **Monalee**, who looked likely to confirm previous form with Al Boum Photo and **Invitation Only**, fell and badly hampered Invitation Only, who unseated his rider. Finian's Oscar was keeping on well when forced out, looking much improved with the slightly slower tempo at 3m helping his jumping on what would sadly prove to be his final run, while **The Storyteller** also ran a fine race on his first run over 3m even if a lucky winner. It was 6l back to **Monbeg Notorious** and **Jury Duty**, while **Rathvinden** was outpaced but stayed on well into fourth ahead of the below-par **Shattered Love**.

42 Irish Daily Mirror Novice Hurdle (Grade 1) (3m)

Punchestown (IRE) April 25 (Yielding)
1 **Next Destination** 6-11-10 Paul Townend
2 **Delta Work** 5-11-9 Davy Russell
3 **Kilbricken Storm** 7-11-10 Harry Cobden
5/4F, 7/1, 5/1. nk, nk. 11 ran. 6m 16.00s
(W P Mullins).

A terrific three-way battle with **Next Destination**, relishing the step up to this trip for the first time, just beating a pair of Cheltenham Festival winners in **Delta Work** and **Kilbricken Storm**. Still seemingly caught out when the tempo increased, Next Destination had to be driven to challenge turning for home but galloped on strongly and held off the Pertemps Final winner Delta Work, who showed he belonged at this level with a terrific run in second. Kilbricken Storm proved there was no fluke about his Cheltenham success with a game third, pulling 20l clear of the Albert Bartlett fourth **Ballyward**, with a third Cheltenham Festival winner, **Blow By Blow**, among those further back.

43 Ryanair Novice Chase (Grade 1) (2m)

Punchestown (IRE) April 26 (Yielding To Soft)
1 **Footpad** 6-11-10 Daryl Jacob
2 **Optimus Prime** 6-11-10 Noel Fehily
3 **Asthuria** 7-11-3 David Mullins
2/5F, 25/1, 20/1. 12l, 5l. 6 ran. 4m 14.20s
(W P Mullins).

Another stunning performance from **Footpad**, who reverted to his usual front-running tactics and broke the hearts of his opponents with a relentless display of galloping and jumping. Faultless in front, Footpad burned off his market rivals **Petit Mouchoir** and **Castlegrace Paddy**, the former admittedly perhaps finding this third quick run too much after Cheltenham and Aintree, with **Optimus Prime** and **Asthuria** staying on from behind and perhaps flattered to finish so close.

DORTMUND PARK: made the most of yet more drama at Punchestown

44 Profile Systems Champion Novice Hurdle (Grade 1) (2m4f)
Punchestown (IRE) April 27 (Soft)
1 **Dortmund Park** 5-11-10 Jack Kennedy
2 **Whiskey Sour** 5-11-10 David Mullins
3 **Burrows Saint** 5-11-10 Robbie Power
16/1, 11/2, 33/1. 10l, 2l. 9 ran. 5m 9.80s (Gordon Elliott).

This race fell apart at the second-last when **Debuchet** fell and hampered **Scarpeta** and **Getabird** to such an extent that both had to be pulled up immediately, helping **Dortmund Park** to make his breakthrough at the top level after twice coming up short previously. With three leading contenders wiped out, including arguably the two form horses in Scarpeta and Getabird, the incident clearly made things a great deal easier for Dortmund Park, but it was still a good effort to beat the rest so easily as he followed an emerging pattern of horses improving on their second runs after wind surgery. **Whiskey Sour** saw out the longer trip well, even doing his best work late as he ran on into a clear second from **Burrows Saint** and **Real Steel**, but **Pallasator** and **Duc Des Genievres** were both disappointing.

45 AES Champion Four-Year-Old Hurdle (Grade 1) (2m)
Punchestown (IRE) April 28 (Yielding To Soft)
1 **Saldier** 4-11-0 Robbie Power
2 **Mr Adjudicator** 4-11-0 Paul Townend
3 **Saglawy** 4-11-0 Rachael Blackmore
10/1, 100/30, 8/1. 3l, 3½l. 7 ran. 3m 57.10s (W P Mullins).

The first two from the Triumph locked horns again but, even with **Farclas** below his best, **Mr Adjudicator** still couldn't take advantage as **Saldier** improved past him. Fifth at Cheltenham on just his second run over hurdles, Saldier had since finished third at Fairyhouse but reversed all that form when taking a massive step forward, travelling well to lead at the last and running on strongly. Mr Adjudicator had to switch to make his challenge but probably wouldn't have won anyway, finishing second ahead of Fairyhouse winner **Saglawy** and **Msassa** as Willie Mullins trained the first four even though his shortest-priced runner, **Stormy Ireland**, was a big disappointment, unseating her rider at the last having faded out of contention. Farclas was only fifth, with **Mitchouka** well beaten behind.

Novice index

All horses placed or commented on in our novice review section, with race numbers

Acey Milan	26
Adrien Du Pont	3
Al Boum Photo	14, 24, 31, 41
Any Second Now	12, 22
Apple's Shakira	2, 29, 34
Asthuria	43
Aye Aye Charlie	10, 23, 38
Ballyoptic	5, 24
Ballyward	30, 42
Barney Dwan	22
Beau Gosse	17, 34
Bedrock	35
Benatar	27
Bigmartre	27
Black Corton	5, 24, 36
Black Op	10, 23, 38
Blackbow	26
Blow By Blow	9, 42
Brain Power	4, 20, 33
Burrows Saint	44
Calino D'Airy	33
Cap Soleil	28
Capitaine	4
Captain Chaos	36
Carefully Selected	26
Castlegrace Paddy	43
Champayne Lady	28
Chef Des Obeaux	16, 30, 37
Claimantakinforgan	19
Coo Star Sivola	36
Coolanly	35
Count Meribel	37
Cracking Smart	9
Cristal Icon	34
Cyrname	11, 33
De Plotting Shed	22
Debuchet	13, 19, 44
Delta Work	42
Diego Du Charmil	15, 39
Dortmund Park	30, 44
Dounikos	14, 24
Draconien	32, 40
Duc Des Genievres	9, 13, 23, 44
Elegant Escape	5, 24, 36
Eragon De Chanay	2
Fabulous Saga	30
Farclas	29, 45
Finian's Oscar	4, 27, 33, 41
Footpad	12, 20, 43
Fountains Windfall	5
Getabird	19, 32, 40, 44
Global Citizen	18, 35
Golan Fortune	16
Gumball	2, 29, 34
Hardline	32, 40
Ibis Du Rheu	22
Impulsive Star	21
Invitation Only	14, 27, 31, 41
Jetz	9
Jury Duty	41
Just Your Type	16
Kalashnikov	8, 19
Kalondra	11
Kemboy	27
Kilbricken Storm	6, 30, 42
Lady Buttons	39
Lalor	35
Laurina	28
Lisp	25
Lostintranslation	19, 38
Malaya	17, 34
Maria's Benefit	28
Mengli Khan	19, 40
Mercenaire	7
Mercy Mercy Me	26
Mia's Storm	5
Michael's Mount	18
Midnight Shadow	35
Mind's Eye	35
Mister Whitaker	22
Mitchouka	25, 45
Modus	27, 33
Momella	1, 38
Monalee	14, 24, 41
Monbeg Notorious	41
Mont Des Avaloirs	8, 18
Mr Adjudicator	29, 45
Ms Parfois	21, 36
Msassa	45
Mulcahys Hill	6, 10, 30
Next Destination	9, 23, 42
No Comment	11, 21
North Hill Harvey	4, 15
Nube Negra	25, 34
Ok Corral	30, 37
On The Blind Side	1, 38
Optimus Prime	43
Oxford Blu	25
Padleyourowncanoe	25, 34
Pallasator	44
Paloma Blue	13, 19, 40
Petit Mouchoir	12, 20, 39, 43

VISION DES FLOS: produced a string of high-class efforts in the spring

Poetic Rhythm	1, 6, 30
Presenting Percy	24
Pylonthepressure	21
Rather Be	22
Rathvinden	14, 21, 41
Real Steel	13, 30, 44
Redicean	17, 29
Relegate	26
Rene's Girl	33
Robin Waters	30
Rocklander	22
Roksana	37
Saglawy	45
Saint Calvados	15, 20
Saldier	29, 45
Samcro	13, 23
Santini	10, 30, 37
Sayo	29
Scarlet Dragon	18, 35
Scarpeta	23, 44
Sceau Royal	4
Shannon Bridge	16
Shantou Rock	39
Sharjah	13, 19, 32, 40
Shattered Love	27, 31, 41
Sizing Tennessee	21
Slate House	19, 35
Snow Falcon	14, 36
Stormy Ireland	29, 45
Style De Garde	25
Summerville Boy	8, 19
Sussex Ranger	7, 29
Sutton Place	14
Terrefort	11, 27, 36
Testify	22, 36
The Storyteller	14, 31, 41
Tombstone	14, 31
Tornado Flyer	26
Tower Bridge	30, 37
Up For Review	31
Uppertown Prince	16, 37
Veneer Of Charm	25
Vision Des Flos	1, 23, 35, 40
We Have A Dream	7, 34
West Approach	5, 11, 27
Western Ryder	8, 19, 38
Whiskey Sour	13, 40, 44
Willoughby Court	3
Yanworth	3

Trainer Statistics

2018-19 RFO Jumps Racing Guide

By race type

	Hurdles W	R	%	£1 stake	Chases W	R	%	£1 stake
Handicap	39	287	14	-74.22	27	147	18	-23.02
Novice	44	179	25	-44.97	32	93	34	+41.71
Maiden	12	60	20	-13.26	0	0	-	+0.00

By jockey

	Hurdles W	R	%	£1 stake	Chases W	R	%	£1 stake	Bumpers W	R	%	£1 stake
Harry Skelton	78	358	22	-80.04	45	162	28	+31.70	5	31	16	-12.39
Bridget Andrews	15	120	13	-31.11	2	24	8	-11.50	1	7	14	+1.00
Noel Fehily	0	3	-	-3.00	3	3	100	+2.45	0	0	-	+0.00
David England	1	13	8	-11.00	1	4	25	+1.00	0	0	-	+0.00
Fergus Gregory	1	3	33	+2.50	0	0	-	+0.00	0	0	-	+0.00
Mr L Williams	0	1	-	-1.00	1	1	100	+1.88	0	1	-	-1.00
Henry Brooke	0	3	-	-3.00	1	3	33	+1.33	0	0	-	+0.00
Mr S Davies-T	1	7	14	-5.17	0	2	-	-2.00	0	2	-	-2.00
Ian Popham	1	16	6	+5.00	0	6	-	-6.00	0	0	-	+0.00
Daryl Jacob	0	1	-	-1.00	0	0	-	+0.00	0	0	-	+0.00

By month

	Hurdles W	R	%	£1 stake	Chases W	R	%	£1 stake	Bumpers W	R	%	£1 stake
May 2017	19	56	34	-11.04	5	16	31	-2.50	1	2	50	+2.00
June	5	29	17	-16.20	3	9	33	-0.67	0	3	-	-3.00
July	10	30	33	+5.82	4	13	31	+0.43	0	0	-	+0.00
August	8	24	33	-3.56	6	13	46	+12.56	0	0	-	+0.00
September	4	36	11	-5.55	3	14	21	-0.75	1	3	33	-1.39
October	7	57	12	-36.17	7	30	23	+25.96	0	6	-	-6.00
November	12	65	18	-4.51	8	26	31	-3.70	1	5	20	+2.00
December	11	62	18	-24.42	6	16	38	+9.27	0	3	-	-3.00
January 2018	7	48	15	-12.37	2	17	12	-12.78	0	3	-	-3.00
February	7	49	14	-14.06	4	19	21	-2.47	1	5	20	+3.00
March	4	50	8	-2.75	2	16	13	-3.50	1	3	33	-1.50
April	3	39	8	-23.00	3	21	14	-8.00	1	8	13	-3.50

By horse

	Wins-Runs	%	£1 level stakes	Win prize	Total prize
Rene's Girl	3-7	43	+22.00	£64,982.25	£91,320.85
Mohaayed	2-5	40	+30.03	£61,823.50	£78,359.50
Cobra De Mai	5-10	50	+12.83	£35,128.11	£58,410.36
North Hill Harvey	2-5	40	+1.83	£35,572.50	£51,872.50
Roksana	3-5	60	+8.41	£29,278.00	£51,054.68
Momella	3-5	60	+7.75	£30,314.30	£47,366.81
Value At Risk	2-6	33	+6.00	£34,105.40	£45,029.40
Oldgrangewood	1-5	20	+2.00	£31,280.00	£44,590.00
Optimus Prime	3-5	60	+0.45	£24,987.33	£39,488.73
Shantou Rock	1-5	20	-0.50	£7,279.50	£37,372.66
Spiritofthegames	1-5	20	-1.75	£7,596.00	£36,302.50
Ch'Tibello	0-5	-	-5.00	£0.00	£35,939.30
Ashoka	2-9	22	+9.00	£29,015.60	£33,181.22

Dan Skelton

All runners

	Wins-Runs	%	Win prize	Total prize	£1 level stakes
Hurdle	97-545	18	£546,075.13	£958,485.37	-147.82
Chase	53-210	25	£505,680.98	£756,654.24	+13.85
Bumper	6-41	15	£13,775.76	£21,650.34	-14.38
TOTAL	156-796	20	£1,065,531.87	£1,736,789.95	-148.35

By course - last four seasons

	Hurdles W	R	%	£1 stake	Chases W	R	%	£1 stake	Bumpers W	R	%	£1 stake
Aintree	6	45	13	-27.58	2	24	8	-16.25	0	4	-	-4.00
Ascot	0	26	-	-26.00	2	17	12	+1.00	0	3	-	-3.00
Ayr	6	26	23	-2.76	3	16	19	-3.00	1	2	50	+1.75
Bangor-On-Dee	12	45	27	-5.90	8	19	42	+15.43	1	7	14	-2.67
Carlisle	2	5	40	-2.38	0	2	-	-2.00	0	2	-	-2.00
Cartmel	0	7	-	-7.00	1	3	33	-0.13	0	0	-	+0.00
Catterick	5	17	29	-7.77	2	10	20	+0.25	1	1	100	+0.91
Cheltenham	11	98	11	-12.63	3	37	8	-20.17	0	5	-	-5.00
Chepstow	6	34	18	-2.50	0	14	-	-14.00	2	12	17	+4.00
Doncaster	4	46	9	-34.54	2	14	14	-9.00	0	5	-	-5.00
Exeter	3	15	20	-10.53	1	4	25	-2.43	0	0	-	+0.00
Fakenham	9	38	24	-6.09	6	21	29	-5.33	1	2	50	+5.00
Ffos Las	2	19	11	-9.50	1	6	17	-0.50	0	3	-	-3.00
Fontwell	6	39	15	-17.52	9	21	43	+7.99	1	11	9	-3.00
Haydock	6	50	12	-16.00	1	16	6	-13.13	0	0	-	+0.00
Hereford	2	12	17	-5.60	2	7	29	+2.38	0	1	-	-1.00
Hexham	2	5	40	-0.14	1	2	50	-0.50	0	0	-	+0.00
Huntingdon	10	68	15	-26.85	6	29	21	-1.25	2	17	12	-7.90
Kelso	0	3	-	-3.00	1	2	50	+3.00	0	0	-	+0.00
Kempton	7	75	9	-48.03	2	28	7	-23.43	0	9	-	-9.00
Leicester	2	12	17	-4.25	3	14	21	+3.10	0	0	-	+0.00
Lingfield	3	11	27	+2.50	2	3	67	+9.50	0	0	-	+0.00
Lingfield (A.W)	0	0	-	+0.00	0	0	-	+0.00	0	1	-	-1.00
Ludlow	18	70	26	-6.14	2	16	13	-6.75	1	13	8	-1.00
Market Rasen	28	89	31	+30.06	11	40	28	-4.17	1	11	9	-6.67
Musselburgh	1	7	14	-4.63	0	2	-	-2.00	0	0	-	+0.00
Newbury	5	44	11	-15.13	3	12	25	+6.50	0	1	-	-1.00
Newcastle	1	7	14	-4.63	1	5	20	-3.71	1	1	100	+0.80
Newton Abbot	4	34	12	-21.65	3	20	15	-10.15	0	0	-	+0.00
Perth	1	2	50	+5.50	0	2	-	-2.00	0	0	-	+0.00
Plumpton	6	26	23	-10.56	1	7	14	-5.27	0	0	-	+0.00
Sandown	0	29	-	-29.00	1	9	11	-4.00	0	2	-	-2.00
Sedgefield	12	36	33	-6.85	4	14	29	+7.24	0	4	-	-4.00
Southwell	14	75	19	-26.53	6	25	24	-6.76	0	16	-	-16.00
Southwell (A.W)	0	0	-	+0.00	0	0	-	+0.00	1	1	100	+0.50
Stratford	12	71	17	-23.24	5	31	16	-11.50	2	7	29	+4.00
Taunton	8	48	17	-25.15	0	4	-	-4.00	2	4	50	+4.00
Towcester	5	21	24	-8.17	2	7	29	-3.97	1	5	20	-1.00
Uttoxeter	15	62	24	+3.99	8	33	24	-11.51	1	10	10	-6.00
Warwick	14	87	16	-39.21	10	34	29	+2.28	5	19	26	+3.25
Wetherby	15	46	33	+0.73	10	26	38	+9.64	3	8	38	+1.04
Wincanton	6	25	24	+1.75	2	9	22	+0.00	0	2	-	-2.00
Worcester	12	71	17	-29.82	9	39	23	+9.60	2	12	17	-8.01

By race type

	Hurdles W	R	%	£1 stake	Chases W	R	%	£1 stake
Handicap	19	146	13	-42.04	11	76	14	-28.05
Novice	44	130	34	-2.88	12	55	22	-26.04
Maiden	18	35	51	+21.74	0	0	-	+0.00

By jockey

	Hurdles W	R	%	£1 stake	Chases W	R	%	£1 stake	Bumpers W	R	%	£1 stake
Nico de Boinville	40	125	32	+4.46	15	67	22	-18.36	5	25	20	-6.64
Daryl Jacob	9	22	41	+2.06	7	18	39	-1.31	0	0	-	+0.00
Jeremiah McGrath	7	48	15	-17.09	7	27	26	-9.50	0	10	-	-10.00
Barry Geraghty	12	25	48	-1.78	0	0	-	+0.00	0	1	-	-1.00
James Bowen	10	35	29	+16.50	0	0	-	+0.00	0	2	-	-2.00
Ned Curtis	3	22	14	-5.64	1	2	50	-0.27	4	10	40	+0.75
Noel Fehily	6	16	38	+2.44	0	1	-	-1.00	0	0	-	+0.00
Mr Hugo Hunt	3	6	50	+2.13	0	1	-	-1.00	0	1	-	-1.00
Alan Doyle	0	4	-	-4.00	0	0	-	+0.00	2	3	67	+1.58
David Bass	2	6	33	+0.07	0	0	-	+0.00	0	1	-	-1.00

By month

	Hurdles W	R	%	£1 stake	Chases W	R	%	£1 stake	Bumpers W	R	%	£1 stake
May 2017	4	16	25	-3.49	3	13	23	+0.00	2	5	40	+1.50
June	5	9	56	+1.15	3	7	43	-1.17	3	5	60	+3.60
July	3	7	43	-0.13	0	5	-	-5.00	0	1	-	-1.00
August	1	2	50	+2.33	1	3	33	+2.50	0	0	-	+0.00
September	1	3	33	-1.09	0	0	-	+0.00	0	0	-	+0.00
October	3	17	18	-7.75	0	5	-	-5.00	0	3	-	-3.00
November	13	47	28	-4.16	7	27	26	-13.53	2	7	29	-3.17
December	19	51	37	+21.08	7	27	26	+2.05	0	4	-	-4.00
January 2018	14	38	37	+11.70	4	13	31	-4.31	2	8	25	+0.00
February	10	44	23	-17.15	3	8	38	-2.51	0	8	-	-8.00
March	8	43	19	-22.90	3	16	19	-7.60	2	7	29	+0.25
April	12	50	24	+2.93	5	17	29	-4.22	1	8	13	-6.39

By horse

	Wins-Runs	%	£1 level stakes	Win prize	Total prize
Buveur D'Air	4-4	100	+1.08	£413,705.62	£413,705.62
Might Bite	3-4	75	+1.74	£251,967.24	£390,739.75
Altior	3-3	100	+1.52	£331,730.40	£331,730.40
L'Ami Serge	1-5	20	+1.00	£140,525.00	£191,825.00
We Have A Dream	5-5	100	+4.56	£129,652.82	£129,652.82
Terrefort	3-4	75	+5.38	£95,456.80	£127,511.80
Top Notch	3-5	60	+1.74	£99,809.90	£112,364.90
Santini	3-4	75	+8.00	£80,946.32	£95,526.14
My Tent Or Yours	1-2	50	+4.00	£74,035.00	£87,410.00
Gold Present	2-4	50	+13.00	£81,974.00	£81,974.00
Whisper	1-3	33	-1.33	£12,512.00	£71,967.00
Call Me Lord	2-5	40	+1.00	£46,962.50	£71,753.30
Apple's Shakira	3-5	60	-0.76	£47,821.00	£65,044.61

2018-19 RFO Jumps Racing Guide

Nicky Henderson

All runners

	Wins-Runs	%	Win prize	Total prize	£1 level stakes
Hurdle	93-327	28	£1,495,146.15	£1,877,735.33	-17.50
Chase	36-141	26	£1,089,522.73	£1,559,155.37	-38.79
Bumper	12-56	21	£27,690.44	£40,713.59	-20.20
TOTAL	141-524	27	£2,612,359.32	£3,477,604.29	-76.49

By course - last four seasons

	Hurdles				Chases				Bumpers			
	W	R	%	£1 stake	W	R	%	£1 stake	W	R	%	£1 stake
Aintree	16	69	23	+19.69	7	36	19	-3.09	2	11	18	+6.00
Ascot	16	85	19	-25.16	8	35	23	-2.20	2	13	15	-3.09
Ayr	1	20	5	-18.09	2	14	14	-6.00	2	3	67	+2.23
Bangor-On-Dee	3	20	15	-15.42	1	5	20	-3.56	1	7	14	-5.00
Carlisle	1	1	100	+0.91	0	0	-	+0.00	0	0	-	+0.00
Catterick	0	2	-	-2.00	2	3	67	+1.73	0	0	-	+0.00
Cheltenham	26	198	13	-63.48	9	92	10	-58.25	1	12	8	-5.00
Chepstow	5	20	25	-1.44	1	5	20	+2.00	0	2	-	-2.00
Doncaster	17	44	39	+8.55	8	21	38	+0.62	0	7	-	-7.00
Exeter	4	13	31	-4.21	1	6	17	+5.00	0	5	-	-5.00
Fakenham	6	20	30	-6.79	2	6	33	-3.31	4	5	80	+3.15
Ffos Las	8	18	44	-3.39	0	4	-	-4.00	2	5	40	+0.50
Fontwell	4	20	20	-5.14	1	7	14	-5.09	1	8	13	-6.20
Haydock	5	26	19	-8.97	2	7	29	-1.09	1	2	50	+1.75
Hereford	3	4	75	+3.13	0	1	-	-1.00	0	0	-	+0.00
Hexham	1	3	33	-1.17	1	1	100	+0.20	0	0	-	+0.00
Huntingdon	16	49	33	-0.10	8	15	53	+1.54	2	18	11	-14.44
Kelso	1	1	100	+0.36	1	1	100	+2.25	1	3	33	+3.50
Kempton	28	117	24	-17.85	16	55	29	-6.84	6	24	25	-2.43
Kempton (A.W)	0	0	-	+0.00	0	0	-	+0.00	1	4	25	+1.00
Leicester	1	7	14	-5.20	1	8	13	-6.86	0	0	-	+0.00
Lingfield	3	5	60	-0.65	1	1	100	+0.40	0	0	-	+0.00
Lingfield (A.W)	0	0	-	+0.00	0	0	-	+0.00	2	8	25	-2.00
Ludlow	15	48	31	-1.56	2	13	15	-4.63	7	19	37	-0.72
Market Rasen	12	34	35	-3.41	3	10	30	+5.10	5	11	45	+8.13
Musselburgh	7	18	39	-2.96	0	2	-	-2.00	0	1	-	-1.00
Newbury	26	96	27	-6.21	4	39	10	-25.37	4	23	17	-5.63
Newcastle	2	3	67	+0.08	1	1	100	+2.75	0	0	-	+0.00
Newton Abbot	5	14	36	+4.20	1	4	25	-2.09	1	2	50	+0.25
Perth	0	6	-	-6.00	0	4	-	-4.00	0	1	-	-1.00
Plumpton	3	12	25	+0.33	3	5	60	-0.42	0	3	-	-3.00
Sandown	27	88	31	+22.73	10	37	27	-7.76	1	3	33	+0.00
Southwell	5	24	21	-10.15	0	5	-	-5.00	8	14	57	+8.13
Stratford	2	22	9	-17.10	3	10	30	+1.07	0	7	-	-7.00
Taunton	9	26	35	+5.74	1	3	33	-1.56	1	3	33	-1.00
Towcester	8	16	50	+6.29	1	4	25	-2.27	2	10	20	-4.60
Uttoxeter	13	37	35	-5.17	4	18	22	-7.46	2	7	29	-1.22
Warwick	8	27	30	+1.45	3	6	50	-0.83	2	17	12	-11.09
Wetherby	1	6	17	-4.56	1	5	20	-3.83	1	2	50	+1.75
Wincanton	2	12	17	+6.00	2	5	40	-0.38	0	3	-	-3.00
Worcester	14	39	36	+5.28	3	11	27	-3.21	5	18	28	+5.33

By race type

	Hurdles				Chases			
	W	R	%	£1 stake	W	R	%	£1 stake
Handicap	10	103	10	-50.52	26	157	17	-33.42
Novice	28	95	29	-11.08	39	120	33	-22.54
Maiden	3	24	13	-18.84	0	0	-	+0.00

By jockey

	Hurdles				Chases				Bumpers			
	W	R	%	£1 stake	W	R	%	£1 stake	W	R	%	£1 stake
S Twiston-Davies	14	91	15	-39.11	30	104	29	-14.43	3	20	15	-12.71
Bryony Frost	11	38	29	+4.45	15	46	33	+14.02	0	4	-	-4.00
Harry Cobden	11	58	19	-31.61	12	67	18	-23.31	1	8	13	-4.75
Sean Bowen	3	14	21	-6.13	5	22	23	-11.67	0	3	-	-3.00
Mr L Williams	3	9	33	-2.03	3	11	27	-5.67	0	0	-	+0.00
Mr David Maxwell	0	0	-	+0.00	4	9	44	+1.68	0	0	-	+0.00
Nick Scholfield	1	2	50	+0.10	2	5	40	+0.75	0	0	-	+0.00
Barry Geraghty	0	2	-	-2.00	3	16	19	-4.75	0	0	-	+0.00
Alexander Thorne	1	5	20	+1.00	0	1	-	-1.00	1	1	100	+10.00
Miss H Tucker	0	0	-	+0.00	1	2	50	+24.00	0	0	-	+0.00

By month

	Hurdles				Chases				Bumpers			
	W	R	%	£1 stake	W	R	%	£1 stake	W	R	%	£1 stake
May 2017	1	11	9	-9.56	9	19	47	+0.11	0	0	-	+0.00
June	3	5	60	+9.00	4	12	33	-0.70	0	0	-	+0.00
July	0	2	-	-2.00	5	10	50	+8.32	0	0	-	+0.00
August	0	0	-	+0.00	3	9	33	-5.19	0	0	-	+0.00
September	1	3	33	-1.43	1	2	50	-0.60	0	1	-	-1.00
October	6	33	18	-17.41	13	34	38	+9.63	2	5	40	-0.33
November	5	39	13	-26.79	11	46	24	-10.95	1	5	20	-1.75
December	7	37	19	-15.47	6	46	13	-24.97	0	4	-	-4.00
January 2018	1	10	10	-8.17	2	18	11	-8.59	0	1	-	-1.00
February	6	36	17	-3.92	12	34	35	-2.70	1	5	20	-2.38
March	5	21	24	-2.26	4	28	14	+13.57	1	9	11	+2.00
April	10	41	24	-10.81	7	42	17	-5.50	0	6	-	-6.00

By horse

	Wins-Runs	%	£1 level stakes	Win prize	Total prize
Politologue	4-6	67	+15.53	£316,857.70	£349,934.70
Black Corton	8-12	67	+11.58	£128,505.59	£149,216.53
Old Guard	3-9	33	+1.25	£88,717.40	£109,891.61
Frodon	1-8	13	-0.50	£42,712.50	£107,516.26
Le Prezien	1-5	20	+3.50	£62,645.00	£89,005.00
Clan Des Obeaux	1-4	25	+0.00	£32,490.00	£81,972.71
Topofthegame	1-4	25	+2.50	£56,270.00	£80,038.50
Diego Du Charmil	2-6	33	+1.40	£63,251.24	£76,706.89
Cyrname	3-7	43	+0.02	£49,512.28	£70,957.78
San Benedeto	0-6	-	-6.00	£0.00	£66,727.50
Alcala	5-8	63	+12.65	£62,774.00	£65,767.27
Braqueur D'Or	3-12	25	-1.13	£24,064.24	£62,984.37
Present Man	2-5	40	+5.57	£38,068.80	£54,954.20

Paul Nicholls

All runners

	Wins-Runs	%	Win prize	Total prize	£1 level stakes
Hurdle	45-238	19	£396,301.88	£647,569.17	-88.81
Chase	77-300	26	£1,191,045.93	£1,830,933.27	-27.57
Bumper	5-36	14	£24,760.64	£34,521.15	-14.46
TOTAL	127-574	22	£1,612,108.45	£2,513,023.59	-130.84

By course - last four seasons

	Hurdles W	R	%	£1 stake	Chases W	R	%	£1 stake	Bumpers W	R	%	£1 stake
Aintree	4	42	10	-11.75	9	77	12	-28.88	1	8	13	-5.00
Ascot	8	53	15	-9.88	16	70	23	-2.11	1	6	17	-3.25
Ayr	3	15	20	-2.88	4	23	17	+11.75	1	2	50	+4.00
Bangor-On-Dee	1	3	33	-0.75	4	10	40	+3.47	0	0	-	+0.00
Carlisle	1	1	100	+2.50	4	6	67	+3.85	0	0	-	+0.00
Cartmel	0	0	-	+0.00	0	3	-	-3.00	0	0	-	+0.00
Catterick	0	2	-	-2.00	1	2	50	+0.50	0	1	-	-1.00
Cheltenham	13	129	10	-7.47	17	162	10	+31.23	3	5	60	+5.50
Chepstow	14	60	23	-8.35	7	44	16	-13.42	3	10	30	-2.83
Doncaster	6	24	25	-5.54	7	31	23	-2.83	1	1	100	+0.67
Exeter	23	68	34	-1.91	12	41	29	-12.71	1	6	17	+0.00
Fakenham	2	6	33	-0.13	2	10	20	-3.00	0	0	-	+0.00
Ffos Las	1	5	20	+4.00	1	3	33	-1.43	0	2	-	-2.00
Fontwell	8	30	27	-5.54	21	38	55	+17.69	0	2	-	-2.00
Haydock	4	34	12	-17.84	9	21	43	+7.60	0	2	-	-2.00
Hereford	1	5	20	-3.33	0	4	-	-4.00	0	0	-	+0.00
Hexham	0	0	-	+0.00	2	2	100	+2.40	0	0	-	+0.00
Huntingdon	1	6	17	-3.13	4	11	36	+8.38	1	1	100	+4.50
Kelso	2	4	50	+2.13	5	14	36	-3.66	0	0	-	+0.00
Kempton	12	68	18	-11.54	19	75	25	-4.42	1	7	14	-4.38
Kempton (A.W)	0	0	-	+0.00	0	0	-	+0.00	1	6	17	+5.00
Leicester	1	2	50	+0.88	3	6	50	-0.80	0	0	-	+0.00
Ludlow	2	13	15	-9.04	4	19	21	-6.16	1	3	33	-0.38
Market Rasen	2	8	25	-5.17	4	17	24	+5.91	0	1	-	-1.00
Musselburgh	4	16	25	+2.27	6	10	60	+4.45	0	0	-	+0.00
Newbury	6	54	11	-20.00	12	74	16	-3.25	0	3	-	-3.00
Newcastle	3	5	60	+6.88	0	2	-	-2.00	0	0	-	+0.00
Newton Abbot	18	55	33	-8.64	23	66	35	-16.96	1	4	25	-1.25
Perth	1	2	50	-0.64	3	7	43	+3.30	0	0	-	+0.00
Plumpton	3	13	23	-2.17	3	6	50	+2.13	0	0	-	+0.00
Sandown	7	60	12	-15.59	13	97	13	-21.83	0	3	-	-3.00
Sedgefield	0	1	-	-1.00	1	1	100	+0.18	0	0	-	+0.00
Southwell	2	3	67	+2.30	1	2	50	+0.00	0	0	-	+0.00
Stratford	5	13	38	-2.30	2	14	14	-9.57	1	1	100	+4.00
Taunton	33	104	32	-2.20	10	40	25	-9.06	3	12	25	-2.75
Uttoxeter	0	1	-	-1.00	0	13	-	-13.00	0	0	-	+0.00
Warwick	3	18	17	-9.63	8	22	36	+2.09	1	4	25	-0.25
Wetherby	3	5	60	+7.16	1	7	14	-5.09	0	0	-	+0.00
Wincanton	49	126	39	+5.23	21	71	30	-7.29	6	24	25	+0.69
Worcester	5	19	26	-1.75	7	22	32	-3.99	0	0	-	+0.00

By race type

	Hurdles				Chases			
	W	R	%	£1 stake	W	R	%	£1 stake
Handicap	32	220	15	+4.25	31	146	21	+21.25
Novice	19	93	20	-19.80	13	47	28	+5.16
Maiden	3	29	10	-15.47	0	0	-	+0.00

By jockey

	Hurdles				Chases				Bumpers			
	W	R	%	£1 stake	W	R	%	£1 stake	W	R	%	£1 stake
Will Kennedy	25	161	16	+3.48	18	100	18	+3.53	1	11	9	-8.13
Brian Hughes	9	41	22	-3.32	12	44	27	+5.75	3	8	38	-1.13
Lorcan Murtagh	10	64	16	-7.38	1	10	10	-1.00	2	9	22	+4.00
Miss A McCain	7	21	33	+6.88	0	0	-	+0.00	0	1	-	-1.00
A P Heskin	1	3	33	-1.67	3	5	60	+3.25	0	0	-	+0.00
Mr D O'Connor	0	0	-	+0.00	1	2	50	+7.00	0	0	-	+0.00
Wayne Hutchinson	0	1	-	-1.00	1	2	50	+0.50	0	0	-	+0.00
Aaron McGlinchey	1	4	25	+2.00	0	0	-	+0.00	0	0	-	+0.00
Harry Stock	0	3	-	-3.00	0	0	-	+0.00	1	1	100	+1.20
Mr Theo Gillard	1	17	6	+0.00	0	1	-	-1.00	0	0	-	+0.00

By month

	Hurdles				Chases				Bumpers			
	W	R	%	£1 stake	W	R	%	£1 stake	W	R	%	£1 stake
May 2017	2	27	7	-21.18	4	19	21	-7.38	1	2	50	+0.88
June	0	16	-	-16.00	1	10	10	-7.50	0	1	-	-1.00
July	3	15	20	-4.51	2	8	25	+14.00	1	3	33	+6.00
August	10	20	50	+45.64	2	7	29	+7.50	1	2	50	+2.00
September	4	13	31	+6.75	1	7	14	-3.00	0	0	-	+0.00
October	3	35	9	-13.00	2	12	17	+7.00	0	2	-	-2.00
November	5	39	13	+14.50	4	13	31	+13.00	0	6	-	-6.00
December	10	39	26	+14.33	8	25	32	+7.75	0	4	-	-4.00
January 2018	7	39	18	-7.25	8	22	36	+4.03	1	2	50	+0.20
February	2	26	8	-12.50	2	12	17	-0.13	0	0	-	+0.00
March	6	33	18	-6.81	2	17	12	-5.25	3	9	33	-2.13
April	2	32	6	-23.00	0	16	-	-16.00	0	5	-	-5.00

By horse

	Wins-Runs	%	£1 level stakes	Win prize	Total prize
Dear Sire	5-13	38	+13.50	£51,723.80	£67,147.74
William Of Orange	2-8	25	+7.50	£37,448.00	£41,451.20
Testify	3-5	60	+3.78	£34,166.00	£34,166.00
Tawseef	3-7	43	+17.00	£27,336.40	£33,547.15
The Clock Leary	3-8	38	+4.00	£21,754.40	£27,014.15
Derintoher Yank	2-13	15	+2.00	£11,046.60	£26,036.75
What Happens Now	4-11	36	+3.28	£17,508.00	£25,559.41
Chti Balko	1-7	14	-3.25	£8,122.50	£23,539.00
Same Circus	2-7	29	+4.38	£17,659.50	£23,507.40
Ubaltique	2-8	25	+0.50	£19,494.00	£22,692.18
Henry's Joy	1-6	17	-0.50	£18,768.00	£21,482.54
Uppertown Prince	2-5	40	+11.11	£7,509.48	£20,496.30
Lofgren	2-9	22	-3.75	£9,708.30	£18,469.82

Donald McCain

All runners

	Wins-Runs	%	Win prize	Total prize	£1 level stakes
Hurdle	54-334	16	£305,349.45	£464,665.29	-23.02
Chase	36-168	21	£227,088.91	£336,204.42	+14.03
Bumper	7-36	19	£21,455.70	£33,956.84	-11.06
TOTAL	97-538	18	£553,894.06	£834,826.55	-20.04

By course - last four seasons

	Hurdles W	R	%	£1 stake	Chases W	R	%	£1 stake	Bumpers W	R	%	£1 stake
Aintree	2	49	4	-42.67	1	36	3	-26.00	0	6	-	-6.00
Ascot	0	1	-	-1.00	0	1	-	-1.00	0	0	-	+0.00
Ayr	7	33	21	-9.57	6	30	20	-6.68	1	8	13	-3.50
Bangor-On-Dee	36	158	23	+63.84	12	65	18	-16.92	2	25	8	-17.50
Carlisle	16	106	15	-4.13	8	48	17	-6.45	2	11	18	-6.55
Cartmel	16	61	26	+15.48	3	36	8	-26.00	0	0	-	+0.00
Catterick	17	90	19	-17.39	6	36	17	+4.38	1	9	11	-4.50
Cheltenham	0	8	-	-8.00	1	17	6	-8.00	0	1	-	-1.00
Chepstow	1	8	13	-3.00	0	5	-	-5.00	0	1	-	-1.00
Doncaster	3	35	9	-17.00	1	18	6	-6.00	0	2	-	-2.00
Exeter	0	3	-	-3.00	0	3	-	-3.00	0	0	-	+0.00
Fakenham	1	7	14	-1.50	1	5	20	-2.50	0	0	-	+0.00
Ffos Las	0	0	-	+0.00	0	0	-	+0.00	0	1	-	-1.00
Fontwell	1	2	50	+0.38	1	4	25	+1.50	0	0	-	+0.00
Haydock	6	45	13	-19.00	8	22	36	+17.03	0	3	-	-3.00
Hereford	0	5	-	-5.00	0	3	-	-3.00	0	1	-	-1.00
Hexham	10	64	16	-35.96	0	12	-	-12.00	0	7	-	-7.00
Huntingdon	2	18	11	-5.50	0	4	-	-4.00	0	1	-	-1.00
Kelso	11	76	14	-24.25	9	38	24	+1.71	1	5	20	-2.80
Kempton	0	2	-	-2.00	0	5	-	-5.00	0	0	-	+0.00
Leicester	1	8	13	-1.50	2	9	22	-1.50	0	0	-	+0.00
Ludlow	0	38	-	-38.00	1	15	7	-5.00	0	4	-	-4.00
Market Rasen	2	42	5	+0.25	2	28	7	-9.00	0	5	-	-5.00
Musselburgh	12	68	18	+3.80	6	35	17	-6.25	2	4	50	+4.00
Newbury	0	8	-	-8.00	0	3	-	-3.00	0	0	-	+0.00
Newcastle	4	35	11	-10.58	2	17	12	-10.13	0	7	-	-7.00
Newcastle (A.W)	0	0	-	+0.00	0	0	-	+0.00	0	3	-	-3.00
Newton Abbot	0	5	-	-5.00	0	2	-	-2.00	0	0	-	+0.00
Perth	10	51	20	-11.07	7	26	27	+20.00	2	6	33	+0.38
Plumpton	0	1	-	-1.00	0	1	-	-1.00	0	0	-	+0.00
Sandown	0	5	-	-5.00	0	7	-	-7.00	0	0	-	+0.00
Sedgefield	32	163	20	-5.84	10	58	17	-11.63	2	14	14	-4.50
Southwell	0	16	-	-16.00	1	10	10	-6.50	0	0	-	+0.00
Southwell (A.W)	0	0	-	+0.00	0	0	-	+0.00	3	5	60	+1.87
Stratford	4	24	17	+4.38	2	14	14	-1.13	1	3	33	+6.00
Taunton	0	3	-	-3.00	0	1	-	-1.00	0	0	-	+0.00
Towcester	1	15	7	-6.00	0	6	-	-6.00	0	0	-	+0.00
Uttoxeter	6	66	9	-14.50	1	27	4	-23.75	0	10	-	-10.00
Warwick	0	10	-	-10.00	1	10	10	-6.00	0	0	-	+0.00
Wetherby	5	52	10	-25.50	2	21	10	-3.50	0	5	-	-5.00
Wincanton	0	0	-	+0.00	1	1	100	+3.50	0	0	-	+0.00
Worcester	5	52	10	-19.80	6	27	22	+17.73	0	6	-	-6.00

By race type

	Hurdles W	R	%	£1 stake	Chases W	R	%	£1 stake
Handicap	13	105	12	-16.88	33	215	15	-10.63
Novice	14	70	20	-22.42	9	53	17	-21.39
Maiden	2	28	7	-24.14	0	0	-	+0.00

By jockey

	Hurdles W	R	%	£1 stake	Chases W	R	%	£1 stake	Bumpers W	R	%	£1 stake
S Twiston-Davies	5	69	7	-42.25	17	81	21	-5.13	4	19	21	-1.40
Jamie Bargary	5	56	9	-14.50	10	78	13	-12.63	1	14	7	-5.00
Daryl Jacob	9	23	39	+7.83	4	17	24	+5.98	0	2	-	-2.00
Mr Zac Baker	2	10	20	+2.00	5	22	23	+5.63	0	0	-	+0.00
Tom Bellamy	3	7	43	+2.24	2	22	9	+7.50	0	1	-	-1.00
Mark Grant	3	12	25	-1.13	0	5	-	-5.00	0	3	-	-3.00
Tom Humphries	3	18	17	-6.38	0	4	-	-4.00	0	6	-	-6.00
Jack Savage	0	5	-	-5.00	0	0	-	+0.00	2	5	40	+0.50
Jonathan Burke	0	0	-	+0.00	0	0	-	+0.00	1	1	100	+2.50
Gavin Sheehan	0	0	-	+0.00	1	3	33	-0.25	0	0	-	+0.00

By month

	Hurdles W	R	%	£1 stake	Chases W	R	%	£1 stake	Bumpers W	R	%	£1 stake
May 2017	1	12	8	-3.00	2	12	17	-3.25	0	3	-	-3.00
June	0	7	-	-7.00	1	5	20	+1.00	0	2	-	-2.00
July	0	9	-	-9.00	2	6	33	-0.63	0	0	-	+0.00
August	0	1	-	-1.00	1	3	33	-0.25	0	0	-	+0.00
September	1	8	13	-6.60	5	8	63	+14.87	0	1	-	-1.00
October	5	27	19	-9.68	4	31	13	-5.75	1	5	20	-1.50
November	6	29	21	-9.13	8	37	22	+15.23	2	8	25	+8.00
December	3	25	12	-10.63	5	39	13	-7.50	1	9	11	-6.00
January 2018	3	24	13	-11.75	2	31	6	-16.50	2	7	29	-2.40
February	4	22	18	-0.14	4	21	19	+13.00	0	8	-	-8.00
March	2	21	10	+2.38	1	25	4	-21.00	3	5	60	+6.50
April	6	30	20	-5.15	4	31	13	-14.13	0	8	-	-8.00

By horse

	Wins-Runs	%	£1 level stakes	Win prize	Total prize
Bristol De Mai	2-5	40	+4.10	£170,290.00	£224,211.71
Wholestone	1-8	13	-4.75	£28,475.00	£133,546.57
The New One	2-7	29	-2.00	£70,968.90	£129,723.90
Blaklion	1-5	20	-2.25	£81,442.91	£127,567.57
Splash Of Ginge	1-6	17	+20.00	£91,120.00	£116,092.75
Ballyoptic	2-7	29	-0.75	£34,490.21	£100,170.57
Ballymoy	3-5	60	+6.24	£70,087.48	£70,316.44
Mr Antolini	2-4	50	+24.00	£48,640.10	£62,616.10
Cogry	1-7	14	+0.50	£31,280.00	£51,003.50
Ballyhill	1-8	13	+2.00	£42,712.50	£47,126.40
Arthur's Gift	3-9	33	+2.63	£33,907.00	£41,822.35
Crievehill	2-8	25	+0.50	£22,078.80	£41,121.41
Calett Mad	4-7	57	+4.33	£38,312.50	£40,795.90

Nigel Twiston-Davies

All runners

	Wins-Runs	%	Win prize	Total prize	£1 level stakes
Hurdle	31-215	14	£387,946.24	£639,952.51	-70.68
Chase	39-249	16	£790,270.07	£1,217,242.51	-24.91
Bumper	9-56	16	£20,914.70	£34,389.63	-17.40
TOTAL	79-520	15	£1,199,131.01	£1,891,584.65	-112.99

By course - last four seasons

	Hurdles W	R	%	£1 stake	Chases W	R	%	£1 stake	Bumpers W	R	%	£1 stake
Aintree	3	34	9	-16.00	5	46	11	-16.25	0	4	-	-4.00
Ascot	1	19	5	-14.50	0	13	-	-13.00	0	2	-	-2.00
Ayr	0	2	-	-2.00	0	15	-	-15.00	0	1	-	-1.00
Bangor-On-Dee	3	21	14	-11.67	5	21	24	-3.19	2	10	20	-3.50
Carlisle	2	3	67	+3.38	0	5	-	-5.00	0	0	-	+0.00
Cartmel	0	6	-	-6.00	1	4	25	-1.25	0	0	-	+0.00
Catterick	0	1	-	-1.00	0	0	-	+0.00	0	0	-	+0.00
Cheltenham	11	84	13	-38.23	11	118	9	-24.17	2	10	20	+5.00
Chepstow	7	34	21	+1.46	6	37	16	+8.33	3	12	25	+3.60
Doncaster	1	21	5	-15.00	2	18	11	+0.75	0	4	-	-4.00
Exeter	1	17	6	-8.00	2	17	12	-8.25	1	2	50	+0.50
Fakenham	0	4	-	-4.00	2	10	20	+0.88	0	1	-	-1.00
Ffos Las	18	77	23	+4.35	9	41	22	+0.74	3	15	20	+1.75
Fontwell	0	2	-	-2.00	0	1	-	-1.00	0	1	-	-1.00
Haydock	10	37	27	+5.74	7	46	15	-9.32	0	2	-	-2.00
Hereford	1	9	11	-4.00	3	9	33	+1.25	0	6	-	-6.00
Hexham	0	0	-	+0.00	0	1	-	-1.00	0	0	-	+0.00
Huntingdon	3	36	8	-24.17	2	20	10	-13.20	0	8	-	-8.00
Kelso	1	3	33	-1.17	2	5	40	+3.25	0	0	-	+0.00
Kempton	4	23	17	-12.14	7	32	22	+1.25	0	4	-	-4.00
Leicester	5	22	23	+5.13	9	32	28	+23.33	0	0	-	+0.00
Lingfield	5	15	33	+6.08	3	11	27	+19.50	0	0	-	+0.00
Ludlow	6	59	10	-43.92	5	44	11	-24.54	0	5	-	-5.00
Market Rasen	6	22	27	+9.06	2	9	22	+4.75	0	3	-	-3.00
Musselburgh	1	1	100	+5.00	0	1	-	-1.00	0	0	-	+0.00
Newbury	5	27	19	+10.03	1	38	3	-31.00	1	10	10	-7.63
Newcastle	0	4	-	-4.00	1	9	11	-5.25	0	0	-	+0.00
Newton Abbot	4	15	27	-0.18	4	16	25	+2.75	0	3	-	-3.00
Perth	8	41	20	-13.93	6	28	21	-6.41	2	6	33	+10.00
Plumpton	0	7	-	-7.00	1	1	100	+5.50	0	1	-	-1.00
Sandown	6	26	23	+53.25	4	29	14	-4.59	0	0	-	+0.00
Sedgefield	1	1	100	+1.20	0	2	-	-2.00	0	0	-	+0.00
Southwell	4	28	14	-10.00	3	12	25	+7.00	0	7	-	-7.00
Stratford	8	37	22	+5.63	2	26	8	-21.00	0	4	-	-4.00
Taunton	2	18	11	-2.50	3	12	25	+4.50	0	1	-	-1.00
Towcester	2	25	8	-16.00	2	15	13	+2.38	1	10	10	-3.00
Uttoxeter	11	68	16	-21.18	11	55	20	+5.32	1	13	8	-10.90
Warwick	3	56	5	-41.52	10	52	19	-6.52	2	22	9	-12.00
Wetherby	4	20	20	-7.05	4	19	21	-1.50	1	1	100	+0.50
Wincanton	1	13	8	-6.50	2	13	15	+4.00	0	3	-	-3.00
Worcester	7	50	14	-14.88	5	23	22	+1.00	3	10	30	+10.91

By race type

	Hurdles				Chases			
	W	R	%	£1 stake	W	R	%	£1 stake
Handicap	13	116	11	-42.63	25	189	13	-57.70
Novice	21	106	20	-1.90	11	75	15	-23.88
Maiden	6	21	29	+0.82	0	0	-	+0.00

By jockey

	Hurdles				Chases				Bumpers			
	W	R	%	£1 stake	W	R	%	£1 stake	W	R	%	£1 stake
Harry Cobden	20	94	21	+29.86	20	93	22	+14.80	0	14	-	-14.00
Robbie Power	6	25	24	-4.18	4	32	13	-20.50	0	0	-	+0.00
Tom Scudamore	7	34	21	-6.89	3	25	12	-11.00	0	4	-	-4.00
Paddy Brennan	2	7	29	+0.00	2	21	10	-7.25	0	2	-	-2.00
B J Cooper	0	12	-	-12.00	4	24	17	-15.96	0	3	-	-3.00
Richard Johnson	0	0	-	+0.00	2	8	25	-0.27	1	2	50	+0.25
Mitchell Bastyan	2	9	22	-1.75	1	4	25	-1.38	0	1	-	-1.00
James Bowen	1	11	9	-7.75	0	1	-	-1.00	1	1	100	+3.00
Tom O'Brien	1	19	5	-13.00	1	18	6	-16.33	0	3	-	-3.00
Danny Cook	0	0	-	+0.00	0	1	-	-1.00	0	0	-	+0.00

By month

	Hurdles				Chases				Bumpers			
	W	R	%	£1 stake	W	R	%	£1 stake	W	R	%	£1 stake
May 2017	1	2	50	+1.00	1	3	33	-0.25	0	1	-	-1.00
June	1	2	50	-0.39	0	3	-	-3.00	0	0	-	+0.00
July	0	2	-	-2.00	1	6	17	+7.00	0	0	-	+0.00
August	0	0	-	+0.00	0	5	-	-5.00	0	0	-	+0.00
September	0	3	-	-3.00	0	3	-	-3.00	0	0	-	+0.00
October	8	35	23	-4.31	4	38	11	-28.92	1	6	17	-3.75
November	8	41	20	-5.05	6	46	13	-28.17	0	2	-	-2.00
December	6	37	16	-7.00	5	33	15	-15.13	0	3	-	-3.00
January 2018	1	21	5	-18.13	3	25	12	-11.75	0	4	-	-4.00
February	7	29	24	+1.68	7	24	29	+10.82	1	9	11	-5.00
March	6	31	19	+25.48	5	36	14	-10.50	0	4	-	-4.00
April	1	34	3	-30.00	5	34	15	-1.00	0	7	-	-7.00

By horse

	Wins-Runs	%	£1 level stakes	Win prize	Total prize
Native River	2-2	100	+5.73	£398,296.92	£398,296.92
Kilbricken Storm	3-5	60	+36.00	£101,183.07	£106,142.67
Finian's Oscar	3-7	43	-0.26	£87,741.50	£105,926.00
Ultragold	1-6	17	+9.00	£78,582.00	£94,720.50
Elegant Escape	2-7	29	+0.67	£35,560.00	£88,487.84
Cue Card	0-4	-	-4.00	£0.00	£75,389.00
Fox Norton	1-3	33	-1.20	£42,712.50	£75,169.50
The Dutchman	1-5	20	+2.50	£42,913.50	£64,538.70
Tempestatefloresco	4-7	57	+11.81	£57,657.90	£59,565.90
Sizing Tennessee	1-8	13	-5.00	£17,372.50	£44,853.02
Vision Des Flos	1-6	17	-3.13	£14,237.50	£43,782.50
West Approach	2-7	29	-1.38	£25,122.20	£39,694.95
Silverhow	2-7	29	+1.13	£31,391.00	£39,017.63

2018-19 RFO Jumps Racing Guide

Colin Tizzard

All runners

	Wins-Runs	%	Win prize	Total prize	£1 level stakes
Hurdle	39-237	16	£306,451.73	£498,258.04	-41.71
Chase	37-256	14	£958,570.02	£1,464,626.38	-88.89
Bumper	2-36	6	£3,963.78	£9,514.18	-29.75
TOTAL	78-529	15	£1,268,985.53	£1,972,398.60	-160.35

By course - last four seasons

	Hurdles W	R	%	£1 stake	Chases W	R	%	£1 stake	Bumpers W	R	%	£1 stake
Aintree	4	16	25	+32.29	8	31	26	+69.20	0	0	-	+0.00
Ascot	3	18	17	-1.67	3	35	9	-21.06	0	5	-	-5.00
Ayr	0	2	-	-2.00	0	8	-	-8.00	0	0	-	+0.00
Bangor-On-Dee	0	4	-	-4.00	0	5	-	-5.00	0	2	-	-2.00
Carlisle	0	1	-	-1.00	1	6	17	-1.00	0	0	-	+0.00
Cheltenham	7	58	12	+4.55	12	117	10	-44.27	0	6	-	-6.00
Chepstow	6	60	10	-17.75	8	67	12	-31.25	0	19	-	-19.00
Doncaster	0	0	-	+0.00	0	1	-	-1.00	0	0	-	+0.00
Exeter	11	70	16	-22.94	12	61	20	-15.92	0	8	-	-8.00
Fakenham	0	2	-	-2.00	1	4	25	-0.75	0	0	-	+0.00
Ffos Las	0	0	-	+0.00	1	3	33	-0.25	0	2	-	-2.00
Fontwell	9	46	20	-8.51	10	40	25	-1.92	1	10	10	-6.00
Haydock	0	5	-	-5.00	4	17	24	+0.46	0	0	-	+0.00
Hereford	1	12	8	-8.25	0	4	-	-4.00	0	2	-	-2.00
Huntingdon	1	1	100	+1.88	2	4	50	+7.25	0	2	-	-2.00
Kelso	0	0	-	+0.00	0	1	-	-1.00	0	0	-	+0.00
Kempton	5	27	19	+9.25	6	36	17	+22.85	0	4	-	-4.00
Leicester	0	0	-	+0.00	0	3	-	-3.00	0	0	-	+0.00
Lingfield	1	3	33	+0.75	2	8	25	-1.50	0	0	-	+0.00
Ludlow	4	12	33	-1.99	0	13	-	-13.00	0	1	-	-1.00
Market Rasen	0	3	-	-3.00	0	2	-	-2.00	0	0	-	+0.00
Newbury	3	24	13	-8.25	10	36	28	+13.20	1	7	14	-3.00
Newcastle	2	3	67	+15.00	1	3	33	+10.00	0	0	-	+0.00
Newton Abbot	5	44	11	-23.88	4	35	11	-1.88	1	4	25	-1.00
Plumpton	6	36	17	-11.63	5	22	23	-5.29	0	3	-	-3.00
Sandown	2	19	11	-13.15	1	35	3	-29.50	0	0	-	+0.00
Southwell	1	1	100	+3.00	0	3	-	-3.00	0	1	-	-1.00
Stratford	1	4	25	+5.00	0	4	-	-4.00	0	0	-	+0.00
Taunton	11	61	18	-3.85	5	37	14	+2.00	0	5	-	-5.00
Towcester	0	1	-	-1.00	0	0	-	+0.00	0	2	-	-2.00
Uttoxeter	2	5	40	+17.00	1	12	8	+1.00	0	0	-	+0.00
Warwick	2	19	11	-9.00	1	16	6	-12.00	0	4	-	-4.00
Wetherby	2	3	67	+8.73	2	12	17	+0.25	0	0	-	+0.00
Wincanton	13	102	13	-45.85	17	76	22	+22.58	0	29	-	-29.00
Worcester	0	7	-	-7.00	0	6	-	-6.00	1	3	33	-0.75

By race type

	Hurdles				**Chases**			
	W	R	%	£1 stake	W	R	%	£1 stake
Handicap	19	178	11	-82.34	26	203	13	-9.09
Novice	13	92	14	-43.40	6	44	14	-5.40
Maiden	5	49	10	-18.45	0	0	-	+0.00

By jockey

	Hurdles				**Chases**				**Bumpers**			
	W	R	%	£1 stake	W	R	%	£1 stake	W	R	%	£1 stake
Aidan Coleman	24	154	16	-61.89	16	103	16	+1.35	1	10	10	-8.50
Killian Moore	2	43	5	-26.00	4	29	14	+5.25	0	2	-	-2.00
Richie McLernon	3	64	5	-36.09	3	31	10	-2.00	0	0	-	+0.00
Jonjo O'Neill	4	30	13	-18.13	1	12	8	-3.00	0	0	-	+0.00
Richard Johnson	1	1	100	+2.50	1	2	50	+2.50	0	0	-	+0.00
Barry Geraghty	0	7	-	-7.00	2	8	25	+2.33	0	0	-	+0.00
Noel Fehily	0	1	-	-1.00	1	5	20	-3.09	0	0	-	+0.00
Jack Savage	0	0	-	+0.00	1	11	9	-3.50	0	0	-	+0.00
Alain Cawley	0	1	-	-1.00	0	0	-	+0.00	0	0	-	+0.00
Charlie Davies	0	0	-	+0.00	0	1	-	-1.00	0	0	-	+0.00

By month

	Hurdles				**Chases**				**Bumpers**			
	W	R	%	£1 stake	W	R	%	£1 stake	W	R	%	£1 stake
May 2017	5	28	18	-6.13	7	38	18	+4.91	0	1	-	-1.00
June	4	17	24	-6.23	3	21	14	-4.50	0	0	-	+0.00
July	4	20	20	-6.53	2	14	14	+1.00	0	0	-	+0.00
August	1	14	7	-12.09	1	10	10	-6.25	0	0	-	+0.00
September	2	16	13	+4.00	2	17	12	-1.90	0	0	-	+0.00
October	8	45	18	-6.57	4	28	14	-3.17	1	7	14	-5.50
November	2	48	4	-35.50	3	25	12	-9.25	0	2	-	-2.00
December	4	34	12	-13.50	4	20	20	+29.00	0	0	-	+0.00
January 2018	3	35	9	-23.63	0	12	-	-12.00	0	0	-	+0.00
February	1	14	7	-12.43	0	12	-	-12.00	0	2	-	-2.00
March	0	21	-	-21.00	1	7	14	-2.50	0	0	-	+0.00
April	0	19	-	-19.00	2	12	17	+1.50	0	1	-	-1.00

By horse

	Wins-Runs	%	£1 level stakes	Win prize	Total prize
Go Conquer	2-5	40	+8.00	£68,660.50	£71,340.50
Festive Affair	2-7	29	+10.00	£23,884.08	£30,352.08
I'dliketheoption	1-3	33	+1.00	£19,461.00	£19,811.00
Another Hero	1-1	100	+8.00	£15,640.00	£15,640.00
Mustmeetalady	1-5	20	+12.00	£15,640.00	£15,640.00
A Little Magic	1-2	50	+1.50	£14,521.64	£14,521.64
In The Rough	1-2	50	+4.00	£6,256.00	£14,281.00
Mad Jack Mytton	2-5	40	+1.60	£10,813.60	£13,823.60
Terry The Fish	3-7	43	+2.88	£9,617.04	£13,104.54
Mont Royale	1-10	10	+1.00	£7,507.20	£11,202.20
Spookydooky	1-4	25	+0.50	£9,846.00	£11,190.44
For Instance	2-3	67	+2.60	£10,341.96	£10,914.36
Timeforwest	1-7	14	-2.50	£9,615.00	£10,642.60

Jonjo O'Neill

All runners

	Wins-Runs	%	Win prize	Total prize	£1 level stakes
Hurdle	34-311	11	£135,734.06	£226,825.18	-158.60
Chase	29-216	13	£280,920.42	£378,637.03	-15.16
Bumper	1-13	8	£1,689.48	£3,139.56	-11.50
TOTAL	64-540	12	£418,343.96	£608,601.77	-185.26

By course - last four seasons

	\multicolumn{4}{c}{Hurdles}								
	W	R	%	£1 stake	W	R	%	£1 stake	W	R	%	£1 stake
Aintree	4	38	11	-21.90	2	31	6	-4.50	0	4	-	-4.00
Ascot	1	22	5	-1.00	2	29	7	-15.50	0	0	-	+0.00
Ayr	1	5	20	+1.50	0	5	-	-5.00	0	0	-	+0.00
Bangor-On-Dee	4	43	9	-24.63	5	40	13	-7.25	3	5	60	+12.75
Carlisle	3	11	27	-0.92	1	11	9	-8.00	1	3	33	+0.50
Cartmel	3	11	27	-5.20	3	8	38	+10.50	0	0	-	+0.00
Catterick	1	12	8	-7.00	1	9	11	-5.25	1	1	100	+5.00
Cheltenham	3	61	5	-30.25	8	82	10	-5.79	0	5	-	-5.00
Chepstow	8	55	15	-8.83	1	33	3	-24.00	2	6	33	+3.50
Doncaster	4	51	8	-31.00	7	30	23	+21.25	0	1	-	-1.00
Exeter	4	34	12	-19.21	2	28	7	-17.00	0	1	-	-1.00
Fakenham	1	4	25	-2.56	1	8	13	-4.75	0	0	-	+0.00
Ffos Las	6	41	15	-18.29	4	25	16	-8.50	1	3	33	+10.00
Fontwell	3	13	23	+2.75	5	18	28	+5.00	0	1	-	-1.00
Haydock	3	25	12	-3.00	2	22	9	-7.50	0	0	-	+0.00
Hereford	2	9	22	+22.50	0	3	-	-3.00	0	0	-	+0.00
Hexham	0	1	-	-1.00	0	0	-	+0.00	0	0	-	+0.00
Huntingdon	12	66	18	-14.38	8	30	27	+9.75	2	5	40	+6.25
Kelso	0	1	-	-1.00	1	2	50	-0.75	0	0	-	+0.00
Kempton	5	46	11	-26.49	3	32	9	-11.50	0	2	-	-2.00
Leicester	1	16	6	-13.25	3	17	18	-8.25	0	0	-	+0.00
Lingfield	1	6	17	-4.43	0	4	-	-4.00	0	0	-	+0.00
Lingfield (A.W)	0	0	-	+0.00	0	0	-	+0.00	1	2	50	+3.00
Ludlow	1	34	3	-31.38	6	46	13	-19.25	1	1	100	+8.00
Market Rasen	14	83	17	-6.35	13	76	17	-25.54	0	8	-	-8.00
Newbury	2	37	5	-27.10	3	29	10	-11.50	0	3	-	-3.00
Newcastle	0	1	-	-1.00	0	0	-	+0.00	0	0	-	+0.00
Newton Abbot	2	28	7	-19.25	0	24	-	-24.00	0	0	-	+0.00
Perth	0	0	-	+0.00	0	2	-	-2.00	0	0	-	+0.00
Plumpton	1	9	11	-6.25	0	0	-	+0.00	0	0	-	+0.00
Sandown	1	26	4	-22.00	1	14	7	-10.50	0	2	-	-2.00
Sedgefield	1	3	33	+3.50	0	2	-	-2.00	0	1	-	-1.00
Southwell	10	92	11	-50.76	11	41	27	+15.48	1	7	14	-3.25
Stratford	2	31	6	-22.90	2	33	6	-26.33	1	6	17	-0.50
Taunton	1	18	6	-16.17	1	12	8	+3.00	0	1	-	-1.00
Towcester	2	23	9	-11.00	2	7	29	-1.25	0	2	-	-2.00
Uttoxeter	16	113	14	-41.79	10	82	12	-24.65	2	9	22	-3.25
Warwick	12	75	16	+19.99	8	40	20	+14.41	1	10	10	-7.75
Wetherby	10	38	26	+1.95	3	21	14	-11.50	0	1	-	-1.00
Wincanton	0	10	-	-10.00	1	10	10	-2.00	0	0	-	+0.00
Worcester	19	121	16	-29.91	22	97	23	+3.52	2	10	20	-5.63

2018-19 RFO Jumps Racing Guide

By race type

	Hurdles				Chases			
	W	R	%	£1 stake	W	R	%	£1 stake
Handicap	14	138	10	-71.42	7	109	6	-77.03
Novice	17	84	20	+2.98	4	56	7	-42.63
Maiden	2	37	5	-32.43	0	0	-	+0.00

By jockey

	Hurdles				Chases				Bumpers			
	W	R	%	£1 stake	W	R	%	£1 stake	W	R	%	£1 stake
Richard Johnson	19	136	14	-86.09	7	79	9	-57.26	12	25	48	+53.20
Micheal Nolan	6	32	19	+39.95	2	15	13	-7.25	0	5	-	-5.00
Tom O'Brien	4	28	14	-13.50	2	26	8	-20.50	1	6	17	-2.75
Mr David Maxwell	0	3	-	-3.00	3	13	23	+4.50	0	0	-	+0.00
Ciaran Gethings	2	3	67	+6.50	0	0	-	+0.00	0	0	-	+0.00
Sean Houlihan	2	18	11	-12.50	0	3	-	-3.00	0	2	-	-2.00
Noel Fehily	1	1	100	+2.25	0	0	-	+0.00	0	0	-	+0.00
Barry Geraghty	1	4	25	-2.00	0	0	-	+0.00	0	0	-	+0.00
Liam Heard	1	13	8	-5.50	0	2	-	-2.00	0	0	-	+0.00
Miss N Parker	0	1	-	-1.00	0	0	-	+0.00	0	0	-	+0.00

By month

	Hurdles				Chases				Bumpers			
	W	R	%	£1 stake	W	R	%	£1 stake	W	R	%	£1 stake
May 2017	4	16	25	-4.37	1	9	11	-7.09	1	2	50	+0.00
June	0	7	-	-7.00	1	6	17	-3.90	1	3	33	+0.50
July	0	11	-	-11.00	0	1	-	-1.00	1	1	100	+0.36
August	2	6	33	+5.00	0	5	-	-5.00	0	0	-	+0.00
September	3	13	23	+4.33	1	4	25	-2.27	0	0	-	+0.00
October	6	38	16	-16.82	3	25	12	-11.88	1	2	50	+4.00
November	7	46	15	+21.75	3	30	10	-15.50	2	4	50	+10.00
December	1	20	5	-18.00	0	16	-	-16.00	0	5	-	-5.00
January 2018	4	17	24	-7.84	2	14	14	-3.13	1	2	50	+5.00
February	0	18	-	-18.00	1	12	8	-9.25	1	6	17	-4.17
March	3	30	10	-21.25	0	13	-	-13.00	2	8	25	+1.25
April	6	42	14	-26.69	2	13	15	-7.50	3	13	23	+23.50

By horse

	Wins-Runs	%	£1 level stakes	Win prize	Total prize
Rock The Kasbah	1-3	33	+0.00	£19,494.00	£51,294.00
Gumball	3-7	43	-2.49	£13,970.70	£46,122.81
Ozzie The Oscar	2-5	40	+3.00	£25,135.00	£31,893.90
Kayf Adventure	2-8	25	-2.50	£17,147.05	£28,956.73
Poppy Kay	2-6	33	+0.38	£19,027.00	£25,092.50
Show On The Road	2-8	25	-2.05	£17,544.60	£23,728.08
Rolling Dylan	2-7	29	+0.75	£15,388.95	£20,479.83
Springtown Lake	2-6	33	-3.35	£11,214.72	£20,300.72
War Sound	0-8	-	-8.00	£0.00	£19,918.54
Scoop The Pot	2-4	50	+2.00	£14,954.40	£16,957.80
Westend Story	2-4	50	+1.25	£12,216.24	£16,143.24
Wait For Me	1-6	17	-4.27	£5,064.00	£15,826.20
Crooks Peak	2-3	67	+8.00	£13,785.40	£13,785.40

2018-19 RFO Jumps Racing Guide

Philip Hobbs

All runners

	Wins-Runs	%	Win prize	Total prize	£1 level stakes
Hurdle	36-264	14	£203,547.96	£367,231.88	-99.89
Chase	14-148	9	£120,216.53	£295,446.41	-95.51
Bumper	13-46	28	£39,421.02	£46,912.96	+35.45
TOTAL	63-458	14	£363,185.51	£709,591.25	-159.95

By course - last four seasons

	Hurdles W	R	%	£1 stake	Chases W	R	%	£1 stake	Bumpers W	R	%	£1 stake
Aintree	4	35	11	-24.05	3	33	9	-7.50	0	6	-	-6.00
Ascot	4	31	13	-3.09	4	38	11	-8.50	2	4	50	+9.00
Ayr	1	7	14	+4.00	0	5	-	-5.00	0	0	-	+0.00
Bangor-On-Dee	2	11	18	-3.50	0	6	-	-6.00	0	3	-	-3.00
Carlisle	0	3	-	-3.00	1	2	50	-0.17	0	0	-	+0.00
Cartmel	0	2	-	-2.00	1	1	100	+2.50	0	0	-	+0.00
Catterick	1	2	50	-0.33	1	2	50	-0.75	0	1	-	-1.00
Cheltenham	8	77	10	-8.76	13	102	13	-27.75	3	13	23	-0.13
Chepstow	13	54	24	-8.65	11	52	21	-5.17	1	13	8	-9.75
Doncaster	2	13	15	-8.90	2	8	25	+0.75	0	0	-	+0.00
Exeter	23	94	24	-11.92	11	70	16	-17.34	3	12	25	-4.72
Fakenham	0	0	-	+0.00	1	2	50	-0.27	1	2	50	-0.17
Ffos Las	4	16	25	-7.92	2	8	25	+7.00	1	4	25	-1.50
Fontwell	7	35	20	-17.23	4	14	29	-2.43	0	4	-	-4.00
Haydock	3	26	12	-3.50	2	19	11	-9.50	0	4	-	-4.00
Hereford	3	14	21	-8.74	0	4	-	-4.00	1	2	50	+5.00
Hexham	2	2	100	+1.35	1	2	50	+0.00	1	1	100	+2.50
Huntingdon	4	28	14	-11.75	1	11	9	-3.50	2	7	29	-1.84
Kelso	1	2	50	-0.33	0	2	-	-2.00	0	0	-	+0.00
Kempton	6	45	13	-32.03	2	30	7	-21.50	0	9	-	-9.00
Leicester	3	8	38	+4.33	3	7	43	+1.25	0	0	-	+0.00
Lingfield	0	2	-	-2.00	0	3	-	-3.00	0	0	-	+0.00
Ludlow	13	52	25	-10.07	6	32	19	-7.46	1	9	11	-0.50
Market Rasen	5	17	29	+2.48	1	13	8	-10.25	2	6	33	-1.13
Musselburgh	0	1	-	-1.00	2	2	100	+2.53	0	0	-	+0.00
Newbury	10	49	20	+40.30	9	52	17	-7.67	1	6	17	+3.00
Newcastle	0	1	-	-1.00	0	2	-	-2.00	0	1	-	-1.00
Newton Abbot	17	71	24	+9.07	3	39	8	-26.08	5	9	56	+5.86
Perth	4	5	80	+7.13	2	6	33	-0.13	0	0	-	+0.00
Plumpton	4	14	29	-6.50	0	3	-	-3.00	0	0	-	+0.00
Sandown	6	28	21	+2.72	6	39	15	-7.00	0	4	-	-4.00
Sedgefield	2	5	40	-1.00	0	2	-	-2.00	0	0	-	+0.00
Southwell	3	11	27	-1.72	1	4	25	+1.50	1	7	14	-4.63
Stratford	3	18	17	+6.44	11	37	30	+22.33	0	2	-	-2.00
Taunton	7	75	9	-46.25	1	19	5	-13.00	3	10	30	+2.63
Towcester	1	7	14	-3.25	0	2	-	-2.00	0	2	-	-2.00
Uttoxeter	11	49	22	-1.97	3	35	9	-27.74	2	6	33	+7.38
Warwick	7	38	18	-9.44	6	27	22	-8.00	6	21	29	+0.65
Wetherby	5	13	38	-3.69	4	15	27	+7.08	0	0	-	+0.00
Wincanton	7	78	9	-46.00	6	43	14	-24.63	4	17	24	+23.25
Worcester	17	59	29	+32.50	10	41	24	+2.44	2	5	40	+4.50

By race type

		Hurdles				Chases		
	W	R	%	£1 stake	W	R	%	£1 stake
Handicap	13	92	14	-14.00	20	95	21	+29.98
Novice	9	71	13	-32.80	7	35	20	-9.87
Maiden	2	19	11	-5.60	0	0	-	+0.00

By jockey

		Hurdles				Chases				Bumpers		
	W	R	%	£1 stake	W	R	%	£1 stake	W	R	%	£1 stake
Paddy Brennan	18	105	17	-26.90	12	57	21	+4.89	5	33	15	-5.95
Barry Geraghty	1	1	100	+10.00	1	1	100	+8.00	2	3	67	+2.30
Alain Cawley	2	22	9	-6.00	1	9	11	+3.00	1	6	17	+1.00
Miss Lilly Pinchin	0	8	-	-8.00	3	10	30	+3.00	0	1	-	-1.00
Robert Dunne	0	0	-	+0.00	2	2	100	+9.83	0	0	-	+0.00
Miss B Hampson	1	4	25	+11.00	1	1	100	+1.75	0	0	-	+0.00
Richard Patrick	1	3	33	-0.38	0	1	-	-1.00	1	3	33	+0.50
LBdr Sally Randell	1	1	100	+4.50	0	0	-	+0.00	0	0	-	+0.00
Brian Hughes	0	0	-	+0.00	1	2	50	-0.09	0	0	-	+0.00
Mr Zac Baker	0	0	-	+0.00	1	3	33	-0.13	0	0	-	+0.00

By month

		Hurdles				Chases				Bumpers		
	W	R	%	£1 stake	W	R	%	£1 stake	W	R	%	£1 stake
May 2017	2	16	13	-3.50	3	6	50	+15.75	0	0	-	+0.00
June	1	11	9	-8.38	2	7	29	-1.77	0	0	-	+0.00
July	1	13	8	-11.27	2	10	20	-0.50	1	4	25	-0.75
August	2	7	29	+5.50	2	7	29	+0.67	0	1	-	-1.00
September	2	8	25	+11.00	1	6	17	-1.50	0	2	-	-2.00
October	6	23	26	-8.10	1	10	10	-5.00	2	7	29	+5.50
November	4	25	16	-2.00	4	8	50	+21.25	4	10	40	+11.80
December	3	23	13	-10.03	2	12	17	-5.20	1	8	13	-4.00
January 2018	1	11	9	-8.50	0	5	-	-5.00	0	5	-	-5.00
February	0	9	-	-9.00	6	11	55	+22.28	1	3	33	-1.70
March	2	16	13	+1.50	0	8	-	-8.00	0	6	-	-6.00
April	1	15	7	-4.00	2	17	12	-3.67	0	7	-	-7.00

By horse

	Wins-Runs	%	£1 level stakes	Win prize	Total prize
Master Dee	1-4	25	+5.00	£56,950.00	£78,539.37
Colin's Sister	1-5	20	+6.00	£22,887.20	£55,357.85
Cap Soleil	2-4	50	+0.10	£24,386.00	£49,184.00
Poetic Rhythm	2-5	40	+1.88	£42,819.70	£46,110.10
Chase The Spud	1-4	25	+3.00	£31,713.75	£31,713.75
Perfect Candidate	1-5	20	+3.00	£28,475.00	£31,155.00
Jennys Surprise	2-6	33	+14.00	£16,262.92	£29,319.89
Lovely Job	3-6	50	+1.42	£20,988.45	£26,722.65
Mighty Leader	3-7	43	+26.50	£25,277.07	£25,277.07
Tangolan	2-7	29	+2.50	£20,704.00	£21,631.60
Barney Dwan	2-5	40	-1.29	£13,453.08	£19,393.01
Ratify	4-5	80	+17.33	£18,074.70	£18,437.22
Socksy	1-5	20	+0.00	£5,848.20	£17,509.06

2018-19 RFO Jumps Racing Guide

Fergal O'Brien

All runners

	Wins-Runs	%	Win prize	Total prize	£1 level stakes
Hurdle	25-177	14	£185,497.03	£318,029.60	-46.77
Chase	25-107	23	£250,025.12	£349,177.33	+29.31
Bumper	9-53	17	£24,060.52	£41,573.15	-10.15
TOTAL	59-337	18	£459,582.67	£708,780.08	-27.61

By course - last four seasons

	Hurdles W	R	%	£1 stake	Chases W	R	%	£1 stake	Bumpers W	R	%	£1 stake
Aintree	0	8	-	-8.00	0	16	-	-16.00	0	7	-	-7.00
Ascot	0	4	-	-4.00	2	5	40	+5.00	0	5	-	-5.00
Ayr	3	3	100	+20.40	2	6	33	+1.38	0	1	-	-1.00
Bangor-On-Dee	2	8	25	-1.75	3	12	25	-5.02	0	4	-	-4.00
Carlisle	0	3	-	-3.00	0	7	-	-7.00	0	1	-	-1.00
Cartmel	0	5	-	-5.00	0	3	-	-3.00	0	0	-	+0.00
Catterick	1	1	100	+1.50	0	2	-	-2.00	0	0	-	+0.00
Cheltenham	2	40	5	-27.00	7	45	16	+23.75	3	22	14	-4.13
Chepstow	4	21	19	+28.00	0	12	-	-12.00	3	8	38	+8.50
Doncaster	0	5	-	-5.00	0	3	-	-3.00	0	1	-	-1.00
Exeter	2	18	11	-10.50	4	14	29	+32.00	2	3	67	+2.30
Fakenham	0	6	-	-6.00	0	1	-	-1.00	0	1	-	-1.00
Ffos Las	0	7	-	-7.00	2	6	33	+5.25	0	3	-	-3.00
Fontwell	1	3	33	+1.00	1	4	25	+0.50	1	4	25	+17.00
Haydock	2	7	29	-3.23	1	5	20	+2.00	0	1	-	-1.00
Hereford	1	8	13	-2.00	0	4	-	-4.00	0	0	-	+0.00
Hexham	1	4	25	-1.50	1	3	33	-1.33	1	1	100	+6.00
Huntingdon	2	22	9	-6.00	4	11	36	+7.46	1	5	20	+0.00
Kelso	0	1	-	-1.00	0	1	-	-1.00	0	0	-	+0.00
Kempton	0	8	-	-8.00	1	7	14	+2.00	0	3	-	-3.00
Leicester	1	10	10	-7.50	6	22	27	+34.63	0	0	-	+0.00
Lingfield	1	3	33	+3.00	0	5	-	-5.00	0	0	-	+0.00
Lingfield (A.W)	0	0	-	+0.00	0	0	-	+0.00	0	2	-	-2.00
Ludlow	4	22	18	+15.00	3	20	15	-3.13	0	6	-	-6.00
Market Rasen	9	39	23	+6.08	6	32	19	+10.30	2	7	29	+13.00
Musselburgh	0	1	-	-1.00	1	3	33	-1.09	0	0	-	+0.00
Newbury	2	14	14	-9.13	2	15	13	-1.00	1	6	17	-4.00
Newcastle	1	2	50	+2.00	0	3	-	-3.00	0	0	-	+0.00
Newton Abbot	1	18	6	-3.00	3	14	21	-0.25	0	3	-	-3.00
Perth	6	26	23	+7.75	10	31	32	+20.50	2	6	33	+0.25
Plumpton	1	11	9	-7.25	0	0	-	+0.00	0	1	-	-1.00
Sandown	4	9	44	+24.50	2	7	29	-1.88	2	5	40	+8.50
Sedgefield	1	8	13	-6.50	0	2	-	-2.00	0	1	-	-1.00
Southwell	2	28	7	-4.00	0	5	-	-5.00	2	11	18	-1.83
Stratford	3	30	10	-16.77	0	18	-	-18.00	1	7	14	+0.00
Taunton	0	13	-	-13.00	2	7	29	-1.75	0	1	-	-1.00
Towcester	9	23	39	+19.96	1	11	9	-7.00	0	6	-	-6.00
Uttoxeter	6	44	14	-20.97	7	25	28	+34.75	2	8	25	+12.50
Warwick	2	23	9	+5.63	0	16	-	-16.00	0	5	-	-5.00
Wetherby	3	7	43	+12.63	1	3	33	+2.50	2	8	25	+14.80
Wincanton	0	9	-	-9.00	1	7	14	-2.00	0	1	-	-1.00
Worcester	3	35	9	-18.60	1	19	5	-13.00	0	5	-	-5.00

By race type

	Hurdles W	R	%	£1 stake	Chases W	R	%	£1 stake
Handicap	25	211	12	-64.15	8	112	7	-75.75
Novice	12	109	11	-73.92	6	49	12	-23.87
Maiden	3	23	13	-18.03	0	0	-	+0.00

By jockey

	Hurdles W	R	%	£1 stake	Chases W	R	%	£1 stake	Bumpers W	R	%	£1 stake
Noel Fehily	21	137	15	-38.04	8	62	13	-23.15	3	18	17	-4.80
Tom Scudamore	6	60	10	-30.40	3	19	16	-6.20	1	3	33	+0.00
Philip Donovan	4	27	15	-4.00	0	0	-	+0.00	0	0	-	+0.00
Richard Johnson	2	6	33	+0.20	0	0	-	+0.00	0	1	-	-1.00
Robert Dunne	1	9	11	-2.00	1	9	11	-7.80	0	0	-	+0.00
James Best	1	13	8	-6.50	1	7	14	-1.00	0	1	-	-1.00
A P Heskin	0	0	-	+0.00	1	1	100	+0.33	0	0	-	+0.00
S Twiston-Davies	1	2	50	+6.00	0	0	-	+0.00	0	0	-	+0.00
Tom O'Brien	1	2	50	+1.50	0	0	-	+0.00	0	0	-	+0.00
Mr James King	0	19	-	-19.00	1	11	9	-8.00	0	4	-	-4.00

By month

	Hurdles W	R	%	£1 stake	Chases W	R	%	£1 stake	Bumpers W	R	%	£1 stake
May 2017	5	17	29	+13.91	1	4	25	-1.63	1	3	33	+0.00
June	3	23	13	-11.00	1	9	11	-1.00	0	3	-	-3.00
July	4	32	13	-15.26	0	9	-	-9.00	0	2	-	-2.00
August	5	23	22	-0.57	2	7	29	-0.13	0	0	-	+0.00
September	3	24	13	-4.76	0	9	-	-9.00	0	1	-	-1.00
October	2	29	7	-14.00	2	15	13	-8.70	0	3	-	-3.00
November	4	47	9	-34.06	3	22	14	-9.90	0	6	-	-6.00
December	1	30	3	-26.00	3	20	15	-4.67	0	2	-	-2.00
January 2018	4	28	14	-13.67	1	9	11	-2.50	0	1	-	-1.00
February	2	28	7	-21.43	1	10	10	-8.80	1	3	33	+6.00
March	1	24	4	-16.50	1	10	10	-5.50	1	2	50	-0.43
April	4	23	17	+0.00	0	9	-	-9.00	1	6	17	-3.38

By horse

	Wins-Runs	%	£1 level stakes	Win prize	Total prize
Kalondra	2-5	40	+7.80	£19,538.80	£37,440.70
Knight Of Noir	3-6	50	+10.00	£18,676.20	£21,619.62
Rossetti	2-6	33	+4.00	£19,508.10	£19,742.10
Doing Fine	0-4	-	-4.00	£0.00	£18,798.80
Tikkanbar	2-4	50	+1.83	£17,486.50	£17,915.30
Solighoster	2-6	33	+1.20	£15,882.00	£17,338.20
Solomn Grundy	1-7	14	+0.00	£8,057.52	£16,898.54
Pilgrims Bay	0-3	-	-3.00	£0.00	£14,896.00
Bishops Court	1-6	17	-3.00	£9,495.00	£13,601.99
Rainy Day Dylan	2-7	29	+2.00	£10,266.84	£12,284.55
Dalaman	3-4	75	+8.94	£10,071.90	£11,216.70
Vancouver	2-5	40	+7.50	£9,152.70	£10,798.35
Chirico Vallis	2-5	40	-2.57	£7,893.00	£10,487.88

Neil Mulholland

All runners

	Wins-Runs	%	Win prize	Total prize	£1 level stakes
Hurdle	38-328	12	£177,654.60	£288,232.94	-143.33
Chase	15-133	11	£89,002.66	£205,120.99	-69.82
Bumper	4-32	13	£8,772.30	£14,868.36	-15.80
TOTAL	57-493	12	£275,429.56	£508,222.29	-228.95

By course - last four seasons

	Hurdles W	R	%	£1 stake	Chases W	R	%	£1 stake	Bumpers W	R	%	£1 stake
Aintree	1	3	33	+4.00	1	12	8	+3.00	0	3	-	-3.00
Ascot	1	11	9	-3.00	2	8	25	-1.75	0	0	-	+0.00
Ayr	0	2	-	-2.00	0	3	-	-3.00	0	0	-	+0.00
Bangor-On-Dee	3	28	11	-17.10	1	7	14	-5.67	0	3	-	-3.00
Carlisle	1	4	25	-2.75	0	5	-	-5.00	0	3	-	-3.00
Cartmel	2	12	17	-7.18	1	6	17	-0.50	0	0	-	+0.00
Catterick	2	5	40	-1.67	0	5	-	-5.00	0	1	-	-1.00
Cheltenham	2	35	6	-25.50	8	38	21	+11.89	0	2	-	-2.00
Chepstow	6	43	14	-15.30	2	24	8	-10.50	0	3	-	-3.00
Doncaster	2	21	10	-12.25	1	9	11	-6.00	0	0	-	+0.00
Exeter	4	49	8	-33.75	2	11	18	-3.00	0	1	-	-1.00
Fakenham	12	30	40	+20.74	2	12	17	-8.23	0	0	-	+0.00
Ffos Las	4	33	12	-7.63	2	23	9	-4.00	2	6	33	+22.00
Fontwell	18	75	24	+19.69	12	44	27	+0.55	4	13	31	-5.28
Haydock	0	11	-	-11.00	0	4	-	-4.00	0	0	-	+0.00
Hereford	1	9	11	-7.67	0	4	-	-4.00	2	4	50	+5.83
Hexham	0	3	-	-3.00	0	0	-	+0.00	1	1	100	+2.00
Huntingdon	2	17	12	-6.89	4	16	25	-3.80	0	4	-	-4.00
Kelso	0	1	-	-1.00	0	1	-	-1.00	0	0	-	+0.00
Kempton	0	22	-	-22.00	2	15	13	+14.00	0	1	-	-1.00
Leicester	1	8	13	+5.00	0	6	-	-6.00	0	0	-	+0.00
Lingfield	2	17	12	+22.00	1	10	10	+0.00	0	0	-	+0.00
Lingfield (A.W)	0	0	-	+0.00	0	0	-	+0.00	1	3	33	+0.25
Ludlow	3	23	13	-12.63	1	10	10	-2.00	0	3	-	-3.00
Market Rasen	2	17	12	-11.25	4	20	20	-5.25	1	2	50	-0.09
Musselburgh	1	4	25	+0.00	0	1	-	-1.00	0	0	-	+0.00
Newbury	4	18	22	+6.13	0	19	-	-19.00	0	1	-	-1.00
Newcastle	0	2	-	-2.00	1	4	25	-1.25	1	1	100	+3.50
Newton Abbot	6	54	11	-22.18	3	26	12	-5.75	0	5	-	-5.00
Perth	1	3	33	-0.90	0	2	-	-2.00	0	0	-	+0.00
Plumpton	5	42	12	-29.76	5	20	25	+1.13	1	6	17	+3.00
Sandown	1	12	8	-10.00	4	18	22	+11.00	0	0	-	+0.00
Sedgefield	8	21	38	+11.84	6	10	60	+4.69	1	2	50	+1.00
Southwell	4	40	10	-23.36	4	22	18	-11.40	1	5	20	+36.00
Stratford	7	41	17	-12.38	2	15	13	-10.95	1	2	50	+13.00
Taunton	6	55	11	-19.50	1	11	9	-7.00	0	6	-	-6.00
Towcester	4	8	50	+8.35	2	7	29	-1.50	1	4	25	-1.13
Uttoxeter	11	65	17	-12.59	2	20	10	-4.00	0	2	-	-2.00
Warwick	3	21	14	-5.56	5	16	31	-0.97	1	2	50	+2.50
Wetherby	5	18	28	+3.83	4	9	44	+2.49	1	2	50	+0.00
Wincanton	7	80	9	-16.90	4	38	11	-22.50	1	9	11	-6.25
Worcester	16	84	19	-1.63	8	46	17	-2.47	0	8	-	-8.00

Top trainers by winners

Won	All runs Ran	%	Trainer	Won	First time out Ran	%	Won	Horses Ran	%
156	801	19	**Dan Skelton**	49	215	23	90	215	42
141	524	27	**Nicky Henderson**	46	154	30	85	154	55
127	576	22	**Paul Nicholls**	30	150	20	68	150	45
98	540	18	**Donald McCain**	16	113	14	58	113	51
80	527	15	**Nigel Twiston-Davies**	23	128	18	56	128	44
79	536	15	**Colin Tizzard**	16	111	14	50	111	45
64	553	12	**Jonjo O'Neill**	22	146	15	51	146	35
63	460	14	**Philip Hobbs**	22	143	15	46	143	32
60	338	18	**Fergal O'Brien**	27	106	25	43	106	41
59	502	12	**Neil Mulholland**	17	137	12	39	137	28
58	389	15	**Alan King**	18	125	14	36	125	29
53	245	22	**Harry Fry**	24	71	34	34	71	48
52	461	11	**Evan Williams**	17	103	17	37	103	36
52	405	13	**Gary Moore**	13	111	12	34	111	31
52	278	19	**Warren Greatrex**	15	75	20	38	75	51
52	293	18	**Peter Bowen**	6	59	10	30	59	51
47	356	13	**Tom George**	15	105	14	34	105	32
47	292	16	**Kim Bailey**	11	84	13	23	84	27
47	250	19	**Olly Murphy**	16	70	23	30	70	43
46	368	13	**Lucinda Russell**	10	92	11	31	92	34
46	349	13	**Micky Hammond**	7	85	8	31	85	36
44	389	11	**Charlie Longsdon**	6	95	6	29	95	31
43	188	23	**Dr Richard Newland**	5	42	12	22	42	52
40	298	13	**Sue Smith**	4	58	7	27	58	47
39	158	25	**Tom Lacey**	10	41	24	20	41	49
36	243	15	**Ben Pauling**	14	76	18	30	76	39
35	170	21	**Jamie Snowden**	8	48	17	21	48	44
34	305	11	**Venetia Williams**	11	87	13	29	87	33
34	162	21	**Anthony Honeyball**	11	45	24	24	45	53
34	249	14	**Brian Ellison**	10	65	15	23	65	35
33	361	9	**David Pipe**	9	93	10	27	93	29
33	162	20	**Henry Daly**	8	37	22	17	37	46
31	292	11	**Seamus Mullins**	7	70	10	19	70	27
29	150	19	**Nick Williams**	5	38	13	19	38	50
29	197	15	**Nicky Richards**	6	54	11	20	54	37
29	194	15	**Chris Gordon**	2	39	5	18	39	46
28	181	15	**Kerry Lee**	5	39	13	15	39	38
28	205	14	**Emma Lavelle**	10	62	16	21	62	34
27	135	20	**Harry Whittington**	10	43	23	12	43	28
27	344	8	**Tim Vaughan**	6	107	6	24	107	22
27	155	17	**Henry Oliver**	4	36	11	18	36	50
25	207	12	**David Dennis**	2	43	5	16	43	37
25	174	14	**Rose Dobbin**	4	39	10	15	39	38
24	202	12	**Ian Williams**	9	60	15	20	60	33
24	202	12	**Philip Kirby**	6	50	12	17	50	34
24	190	13	**Jeremy Scott**	3	46	7	15	46	33
24	85	28	**Keith Dalgleish**	11	27	41	14	27	52

Top trainers by prize-money

Total prize-money	Trainer	Win prize-money	Wins	Class 1-3 Won	Class 1-3 Ran	Class 1-3 %	Class 4-6 Won	Class 4-6 Ran	Class 4-6 %
£3,477,604	Nicky Henderson	£2,612,359	141	72	323	22	69	201	34
£2,513,233	Paul Nicholls	£1,612,108	127	69	391	18	58	185	31
£1,975,899	Colin Tizzard	£1,272,105	79	40	291	14	39	245	16
£1,896,193	Nigel Twiston-Davies	£1,201,080	80	47	291	16	33	236	14
£1,738,235	Dan Skelton	£1,065,532	156	47	324	15	109	477	23
£1,553,695	W P Mullins	£831,911	10	10	74	14	0	0	—
£1,338,270	Gordon Elliott	£1,054,952	21	12	64	19	9	42	21
£964,237	Tom George	£527,124	47	23	201	11	24	155	15
£923,496	Alan King	£553,491	58	27	197	14	31	192	16
£838,514	Donald McCain	£556,818	98	26	152	17	72	388	19
£787,617	Harry Fry	£502,550	53	30	165	18	23	80	29
£783,136	Evan Williams	£446,876	52	17	169	10	35	292	12
£711,945	Fergal O'Brien	£462,748	60	20	138	14	40	200	20
£709,992	Philip Hobbs	£363,186	63	25	230	11	38	230	17
£608,929	Jonjo O'Neill	£418,344	64	18	211	9	46	342	13
£608,624	Sue Smith	£366,302	40	16	118	14	24	180	13
£587,244	Gary Moore	£353,061	52	20	153	13	32	252	13
£546,799	Warren Greatrex	£365,201	52	18	113	16	34	165	21
£534,170	Henry De Bromhead	£323,363	3	3	35	9	0	0	—
£521,972	Charlie Longsdon	£317,715	44	10	150	7	34	239	14
£517,296	Neil Mulholland	£283,487	59	13	141	9	46	361	13
£517,224	Peter Bowen	£357,318	52	19	130	15	33	163	20
£497,554	David Pipe	£260,504	33	14	150	9	19	211	9
£479,405	Nick Williams	£287,898	29	10	85	12	19	65	29
£472,646	Kim Bailey	£265,591	47	14	102	14	33	190	17
£468,431	Venetia Williams	£302,226	34	16	138	12	18	167	11
£463,667	Dr Richard Newland	£301,953	43	16	97	16	27	91	30
£449,563	Kerry Lee	£227,450	28	18	104	17	10	77	13
£441,827	Nicky Richards	£296,127	29	12	87	14	17	110	15
£427,333	Anthony Honeyball	£263,466	34	15	65	23	19	97	20
£396,275	Ben Pauling	£287,044	36	14	103	14	22	140	16
£388,164	Ian Williams	£219,535	24	7	83	8	17	119	14
£388,123	Brian Ellison	£251,332	34	11	109	10	23	140	16
£382,935	Olly Murphy	£292,048	47	4	36	11	43	214	20
£371,695	Neil King	£186,304	19	6	69	9	13	114	11
£359,309	Tom Lacey	£284,089	39	9	40	23	30	118	25
£355,071	Lucinda Russell	£227,452	46	6	59	10	40	309	13
£323,017	Micky Hammond	£207,254	46	4	64	6	42	285	15
£321,754	Emma Lavelle	£214,620	28	14	96	15	14	109	13
£311,854	Jamie Snowden	£224,101	35	13	58	22	22	112	20
£306,736	Chris Gordon	£159,648	29	9	68	13	20	126	16
£268,299	Seamus Mullins	£150,578	31	8	63	13	23	229	10
£247,854	Stuart Edmunds	£164,410	23	8	37	22	15	84	18
£238,663	Harry Whittington	£184,037	27	7	29	24	20	106	19
£234,332	Rebecca Curtis	£182,194	9	6	47	13	3	42	7
£233,604	Henry Daly	£163,371	33	6	55	11	27	107	25
£232,327	David Dennis	£131,332	25	4	44	9	21	163	13

Top jockeys

Won	Ran	%	Jockey	Best Trainer	Won	Ran
176	901	20	Richard Johnson	Philip Hobbs	38	240
142	811	18	Brian Hughes	Donald McCain	24	93
131	612	21	Harry Skelton	Dan Skelton	128	551
110	532	21	Noel Fehily	Harry Fry	33	118
108	568	19	Sam Twiston-Davies	Paul Nicholls	47	215
104	669	16	Aidan Coleman	Jonjo O'Neill	41	267
82	482	17	Sean Bowen	Peter Bowen	35	187
77	367	21	Nico de Boinville	Nicky Henderson	60	217
76	440	17	Harry Cobden	Colin Tizzard	40	201
74	610	12	Tom Scudamore	David Pipe	24	221
70	441	16	Paddy Brennan	Fergal O'Brien	35	195
63	360	18	Daryl Jacob	Ben Pauling	19	121
58	348	17	James Bowen	Peter Bowen	16	90
53	445	12	Tom O'Brien	Ian Williams	17	106
53	424	13	Jamie Moore	Gary Moore	35	176
50	288	17	Gavin Sheehan	Jamie Snowden	23	93
49	313	16	Danny Cook	Sue Smith	30	176
48	351	14	Will Kennedy	Donald McCain	44	272
46	383	12	Nick Scholfield	Jeremy Scott	11	64
45	312	14	Wayne Hutchinson	Alan King	38	244
44	439	10	Henry Brooke	Martin Todhunter	8	42
43	231	19	Harry Bannister	Harry Whittington	18	97
40	368	11	Leighton Aspell	Oliver Sherwood	11	118
40	251	16	David Bass	Kim Bailey	29	182
38	204	19	Bryony Frost	Paul Nicholls	26	88
38	276	14	A P Heskin	Tom George	24	185
37	239	15	Ross Chapman	Iain Jardine	15	83
33	279	12	Ciaran Gethings	Stuart Edmunds	17	68
31	137	23	Barry Geraghty	Nicky Henderson	12	26
31	232	13	Craig Nichol	Rose Dobbin	11	89
30	253	12	Charlie Deutsch	Venetia Williams	21	150
29	308	9	Robert Dunne	Tom Lacey	9	36
28	346	8	Adam Wedge	Evan Williams	20	229
27	260	10	Derek Fox	Lucinda Russell	26	187
27	208	13	Andrew Tinkler	Henry Daly	10	65
26	316	8	Sean Quinlan	Jennie Candlish	14	154
25	170	15	Ryan Day	Nicky Richards	17	97
24	216	11	Mitchell Bastyan	Evan Williams	12	103
24	328	7	Richie McLernon	Alexandra Dunn	7	53
24	252	10	Tom Cannon	Chris Gordon	12	76
24	256	9	Jamie Hamilton	Malcolm Jefferson	5	28
23	224	10	Jack Quinlan	Amy Murphy	7	44
23	180	13	Jeremiah McGrath	Nicky Henderson	14	85
21	199	11	Kielan Woods	Graeme McPherson	12	95
20	227	9	Jamie Bargary	Nigel Twiston-Davies	16	148
20	205	10	Sean Houlihan	Bob Buckler	7	23
20	255	8	Callum Bewley	Keith Dalgleish	5	26
20	141	14	Richard Patrick	Kerry Lee	14	66

Big Race Dates, Fixtures and Track Facts

2018-19 *RFO Jumps Racing Guide*

Fixtures

Key - Flat, **Jumps**

October

1	Mon	Catterick, Bath, Kempton, **Newton Abbot**
2	Tue	Ayr, **Southwell**, Kempton, **Sedgefield**
3	Wed	Newcastle, **Bangor**, Salisbury, Nottingham
4	Thu	**Huntingdon**, Chelmsford City, **Warwick**, Lingfield
5	Fri	**Hexham**, Wolverhampton, Ascot, **Fontwell**
6	Sat	Redcar, Newmarket, Ascot, Wolverhampton, **Fontwell**
7	Sun	**Kelso**, **Uttoxeter**
8	Mon	Pontefract, **Stratford**, Kempton, Windsor
9	Tue	Catterick, Leicester, Brighton, Newcastle
10	Wed	**Ludlow**, Kempton, Nottingham, **Towcester**
11	Thu	Ayr, **Worcester**, Chelmsford City, **Exeter**
12	Fri	York, Newmarket, **Newton Abbot**, Wolverhampton
13	Sat	**Hexham**, Newmarket, Chelmsford City, York, **Chepstow**
14	Sun	**Chepstow**, Goodwood
15	Mon	Musselburgh, Yarmouth, Kempton, Windsor
16	Tue	**Hereford**, Kempton, **Huntingdon**, Leicester
17	Wed	Newcastle, Nottingham, Bath, **Wetherby**
18	Thu	**Carlisle**, **Uttoxeter**, Brighton, Chelmsford City
19	Fri	Haydock, **Fakenham**, **Wincanton**, Newcastle, Redcar
20	Sat	Catterick, **Market Rasen**, Ascot, **Stratford**, **Ffos Las**, Wolverhampton
21	Sun	**Sedgefield**, Kempton
22	Mon	Pontefract, Kempton, **Plumpton**, Windsor
23	Tue	Newcastle, Yarmouth, **Exeter**, Kempton
24	Wed	Newcastle, Newmarket, **Fontwell**, **Worcester**
25	Thu	**Carlisle**, **Ludlow**, Chelmsford City, **Southwell**
26	Fri	Doncaster, **Cheltenham**, Kempton, Newbury
27	Sat	Doncaster, **Cheltenham**, Kempton, **Kelso**, Newbury
28	Sun	**Aintree**, **Wincanton**
29	Mon	**Ayr**, Leicester, Chelmsford City, Redcar
30	Tue	Catterick, **Bangor**, **Chepstow**, Wolverhampton
31	Wed	**Fakenham**, Kempton, Nottingham, **Taunton**

November

1	Thu	**Sedgefield**, **Stratford**, Lingfield, Wolverhampton
2	Fri	**Wetherby**, Newmarket, Kempton, **Uttoxeter**
3	Sat	**Ayr**, Newmarket, **Ascot**, Newcastle, **Wetherby**
4	Sun	**Carlisle**, **Huntingdon**
5	Mon	**Hereford**, Kempton, **Plumpton**
6	Tue	Redcar, Wolverhampton, **Exeter**, Kempton
7	Wed	**Musselburgh**, Nottingham, **Chepstow**, Newcastle
8	Thu	**Sedgefield**, **Market Rasen**, Chelmsford City, **Newbury**
9	Fri	**Hexham**, **Warwick**, **Fontwell**, Newcastle

2018-19 RFO Jumps Racing Guide

10	Sat	**Aintree**, Chelmsford City, Doncaster, **Wincanton**, **Kelso**
11	Sun	**Ffos Las**, **Sandown**
12	Mon	**Carlisle**, Southwell, **Kempton**
13	Tue	**Hereford**, Chelmsford City, **Huntingdon**, **Lingfield**
14	Wed	**Ayr**, **Bangor**, **Exeter**, Kempton
15	Thu	**Ludlow**, Chelmsford City, Southwell, **Taunton**
16	Fri	**Newcastle**, **Cheltenham**, Lingfield, Wolverhampton
17	Sat	**Wetherby**, **Cheltenham**, Lingfield, **Uttoxeter**, Wolverhampton
18	Sun	**Cheltenham**, **Fontwell**
19	Mon	**Leicester**, Kempton, **Plumpton**
20	Tue	**Fakenham**, Lingfield, **Southwell**
21	Wed	**Hexham**, **Warwick**, **Chepstow**, Kempton
22	Thu	Newcastle, **Market Rasen**, **Wincanton**, Wolverhampton
23	Fri	**Catterick**, **Ascot**, **Ffos Las**, Kempton
24	Sat	**Haydock**, **Huntingdon**, **Ascot**, Wolverhampton, Lingfield
25	Sun	**Uttoxeter**, **Exeter**
26	Mon	**Musselburgh**, **Ludlow**, **Kempton**
27	Tue	**Sedgefield**, Southwell, **Lingfield**
28	Wed	Newcastle, **Hereford**, **Wetherby**, Wolverhampton
29	Thu	**Ayr**, **Towcester**, Chelmsford City, **Taunton**
30	Fri	**Doncaster**, Southwell, **Newbury**, Newcastle

December

1	Sat	**Doncaster**, **Bangor**, **Newbury**, **Newcastle**, Wolverhampton
2	Sun	**Carlisle**, **Leicester**
3	Mon	**Musselburgh**, Wolverhampton, **Plumpton**
4	Tue	**Fakenham**, Lingfield, **Southwell**
5	Wed	**Haydock**, **Ludlow**, Kempton, Lingfield
6	Thu	**Leicester**, Chelmsford City, **Market Rasen**, **Wincanton**
7	Fri	**Sedgefield**, **Exeter**, Kempton, **Sandown**
8	Sat	**Aintree**, Wolverhampton, **Chepstow**, **Wetherby**, **Sandown**
9	Sun	**Kelso**, **Huntingdon**
10	Mon	**Musselburgh**, Wolverhampton, **Lingfield**
11	Tue	Southwell, **Fontwell**, **Uttoxeter**
12	Wed	**Hexham**, **Leicester**, Kempton, Lingfield
13	Thu	**Newcastle**, **Warwick**, Chelmsford City, **Taunton**
14	Fri	**Doncaster**, **Bangor**, Kempton, **Cheltenham**
15	Sat	**Doncaster**, **Cheltenham**, Newcastle, **Hereford**, Wolverhampton
16	Sun	**Carlisle**, **Southwell**
17	Mon	Wolverhampton, **Ffos Las**, **Plumpton**
18	Tue	**Catterick**, **Fakenham**, Southwell
19	Wed	Newcastle, **Ludlow**, Lingfield, **Newbury**
20	Thu	Southwell, Chelmsford City, **Towcester**, **Exeter**
21	Fri	Southwell, **Ascot**, **Uttoxeter**, Wolverhampton
22	Sat	**Haydock**, **Ascot**, **Newcastle**, Lingfield
26	Wed	**Sedgefield**, **Huntingdon**, **Fontwell**, **Wetherby**, **Market Rasen**, **Kempton**, Wolverhampton, **Wincanton**
27	Thu	**Wetherby**, Wolverhampton, **Chepstow**, **Kempton**
28	Fri	**Catterick**, **Leicester**, Lingfield
29	Sat	**Doncaster**, Southwell, **Newbury**, **Kelso**

146

30 Sun...**Haydock**, Lingfield, **Taunton**
31 Mon...**Uttoxeter**, Lingfield, **Warwick**

January

1 Tue .... Southwell, **Catterick**, **Cheltenham**, Exeter, Fakenham, ...**Musselburgh**
2 Wed...**Ayr**, Wolverhampton, **Hereford**, **Newcastle**
3 Thu...................................**Ludlow**, **Towcester**, Southwell, Chelmsford
4 Fri.....................................**Lingfield**, **Wetherby**, Kempton, Wolverhampton
5 Sat........................Lingfield, Kempton, **Newcastle**, **Sandown**, **Wincanton**
6 Sun...Newcastle, **Plumpton**
7 Mon.....................................Wolverhampton, **Chepstow**, **Musselburgh**
8 Tue .... Newcastle, **Ayr**, **Bangor**
9 Wed.....................................Lingfield, Kempton, **Doncaster**, **Taunton**
10 Thu ....Southwell, Chelmsford, **Catterick**, **Leicester**
11 Fri .... Lingfield, Wolverhampton, **Huntingdon**, **Sedgefield**
12 Sat................ Lingfield, Newcastle, **Kempton**, **Warwick**, **Wetherby**
13 Sun..Southwell, **Kelso**
14 Mon.......................................Wolverhampton, **Ffos Las**, **Fontwell**
15 Tue ....Kempton, **Lingfield**, **Newcastle**
16 Wed............................... Lingfield, Kempton, **Newbury**, **Plumpton**
17 Thu ....Newcastle, **Ludlow**, **Market Rasen**, **Wincanton**
18 Fri ....Lingfield, Kempton, **Chepstow**, **Musselburgh**
19 Sat................... Lingfield, Wolverhampton, **Ascot**, **Haydock**, **Taunton**
20 Sun...**Ayr**, Exeter
21 Mon...Wolverhampton, **Sedgefield**, **Warwick**
22 Tue ....Newcastle, **Kelso**, **Leicester**
23 Wed................................ Lingfield, Kempton, **Catterick**, **Hereford**
24 Thu ....Southwell, Chelmsford, **Fakenham**, **Wetherby**
25 Fri ....Lingfield, Newcastle, **Doncaster**, **Huntingdon**
26 Sat................Lingfield, Chelmsford, **Cheltenham**, **Doncaster**, **Uttoxeter**
27 Sun...**Fontwell**, **Sedgefield**
28 Mon..Wolverhampton, **Kempton**, **Ludlow**
29 Tue ....Southwell, **Lingfield**, **Newcastle**
30 Wed................. Lingfield, Wolverhampton, **Leicester**, **Plumpton**
31 Thu ....Southwell, Newcastle, **Towcester**, **Wincanton**

February

1 Fri .... Lingfield, Newcastle, **Catterick**, **Chepstow**
2 Sat.................Lingfield, Kempton, **Musselburgh**, **Sandown**, **Wetherby**
3 Sun...Southwell, **Musselburgh**
4 Mon .... Wolverhampton, **Carlisle**, **Taunton**
5 Tue .... Southwell, **Market Rasen**, **Sedgefield**
6 Wed...Kempton, Wolverhampton, **Ayr**, **Ludlow**
7 Thu ....Chelmsford, **Doncaster**, **Ffos Las**, **Huntingdon**
8 Fri ....Southwell, Newcastle, **Bangor**, **Kempton**
9 Sat................. Lingfield, Wolverhampton, **Newbury**, **Uttoxeter**, **Warwick**
10 Sun...Southwell, **Exeter**
11 Mon..Wolverhampton, **Catterick**, **Hereford**
12 Tue ....Newcastle, **Ayr**, **Lingfield**
13 Wed.......................................Southwell, Kempton, **Plumpton**, **Towcester**

147

14	Thu	Chelmsford, **Fontwell**, **Kelso**, **Leicester**
15	Fri	Lingfield, Newcastle, **Fakenham**, **Sandown**
16	Sat	Lingfield, Kempton, **Ascot**, **Haydock**, **Wincanton**
17	Sun	**Huntingdon**, **Market Rasen**
18	Mon	Southwell, **Carlisle**, **Lingfield**
19	Tue	Wolverhampton, **Taunton**, **Wetherby**
20	Wed	Newcastle, Wolverhampton, **Doncaster**, **Ludlow**
21	Thu	Southwell, Chelmsford, **Huntingdon**, **Sedgefield**
22	Fri	Lingfield, Southwell, **Exeter**, **Warwick**
23	Sat	Lingfield, Wolverhampton, **Chepstow**, **Kempton**, **Newcastle**
24	Sun	**Carlisle**, **Fontwell**
25	Mon	Wolverhampton, **Ayr**, **Plumpton**
26	Tue	Wolverhampton, **Catterick**, **Leicester**
27	Wed	Southwell, Kempton, **Musselburgh**, **Wincanton**
28	Thu	Newcastle, Southwell, **Ludlow**, **Taunton**

March

1	Fri	Lingfield, Newcastle, **Doncaster**, **Newbury**
2	Sat	Lingfield, Chelmsford, **Doncaster**, **Kelso**, **Newbury**
3	Sun	**Huntingdon**, **Sedgefield**
4	Mon	Wolverhampton, **Fakenham**, **Southwell**
5	Tue	Southwell, **Exeter**, **Newcastle**
6	Wed	Lingfield, Kempton, **Catterick**, **Fontwell**
7	Thu	Southwell, Chelmsford, **Carlisle**, **Wincanton**
8	Fri	Lingfield, Newcastle, **Leicester**, **Sandown**
9	Sat	Wolverhampton, Kempton, **Ayr**, **Hereford**, **Sandown**
10	Sun	**Musselburgh**, **Warwick**
11	Mon	Kempton, **Plumpton**, **Stratford**, **Taunton**
12	Tue	**Cheltenham Festival**, Southwell, Wolverhampton, **Sedgefield**
13	Wed	**Cheltenham Festival**, Lingfield, Kempton, **Huntingdon**
14	Thu	**Cheltenham Festival**, Southwell, **Hexham**, **Towcester**
15	Fri	**Cheltenham Festival**, Lingfield, Chelmsford, **Fakenham**
16	Sat	Wolverhampton, **Fontwell**, **Kempton**, **Newcastle**, **Uttoxeter**
17	Sun	**Carlisle**, **Ffos Las**
18	Mon	**Exeter**, **Plumpton**, **Southwell**
19	Tue	**Huntingdon**, **Taunton**, **Wetherby**
20	Wed	**Chepstow**, **Haydock**, **Market Rasen**
21	Thu	**Chepstow**, **Ludlow**, **Sedgefield**
22	Fri	Lingfield, Newcastle, **Musselburgh**, **Newbury**
23	Sat	Lingfield, Kempton, **Bangor**, **Kelso**, **Newbury**
24	Sun	**Carlisle**, **Exeter**
25	Mon	Lingfield, Wolverhampton, **Wincanton**
26	Tue	Wolverhampton, **Hereford**, **Hexham**
27	Wed	Lingfield, Southwell, Kempton, **Market Rasen**
28	Thu	Wolverhampton, Chelmsford, **Newcastle**, **Warwick**
29	Fri	Lingfield, Newcastle, **Fontwell**, **Wetherby**
30	Sat	Kempton, Southwell, Doncaster, **Stratford**, **Uttoxeter**
31	Sun	Doncaster, **Ascot**

April

1	Mon	Newcastle, Ayr, **Ludlow**

2018-19 RFO Jumps Racing Guide

2	Tue	Lingfield, Wolverhampton, Musselburgh
3	Wed	Southwell, Kempton, **Market Rasen**, **Wincanton**
4	Thu	**Aintree**, Southwell, Chelmsford, **Taunton**
5	Fri	**Aintree**, Wolverhampton, Leicester, **Sedgefield**
6	Sat	**Aintree**, Lingfield, Wolverhampton, **Chepstow**, **Newcastle**
7	Sun	**Ffos Las**, **Plumpton**
8	Mon	Redcar, Windsor, **Kelso**
9	Tue	Pontefract, **Exeter**, **Southwell**
10	Wed	Lingfield, Kempton, Nottingham, **Warwick**
11	Thu	Chelmsford, Newcastle, **Towcester**, **Wetherby**
12	Fri	Kempton, Newbury, **Ayr**, **Fontwell**
13	Sat	Wolverhampton, Newbury, Thirsk, **Ayr**, **Bangor**
14	Sun	**Stratford**, **Wincanton**
15	Mon	Pontefract, Windsor, **Hexham**
16	Tue	Wolverhampton, Newmarket, **Exeter**
17	Wed	Southwell, Beverley, Newmarket, **Cheltenham**
18	Thu	Chelmsford, Newmarket, Ripon, **Cheltenham**
19	Fri	Lingfield, Newcastle, Bath
20	Sat	Kempton, Musselburgh, Brighton, Nottingham, **Carlisle**, **Haydock**, **Newton Abbot**
21	Sun	Southwell, **Ffos Las**, **Market Rasen**, **Plumpton**
22	Mon	Wolverhampton, Redcar, **Chepstow**, **Fakenham**, **Huntingdon**, **Plumpton**
23	Tue	Lingfield, Wolverhampton, Yarmouth, **Ludlow**, **Sedgefield**
24	Wed	Epsom, **Fontwell**, **Perth**, **Southwell**, **Taunton**
25	Thu	Chelmsford, Beverley, **Perth**, **Warwick**, **Kempton**
26	Fri	Doncaster, Sandown, **Perth**, **Chepstow**, **Towcester**
27	Sat	Wolverhampton, Haydock, Leicester, Ripon, Doncaster, **Sandown**
28	Sun	Salisbury, Wetherby
29	Mon	Southwell, Wolverhampton, Ayr, Thirsk, Windsor
30	Tue	Chelmsford, Brighton, Nottingham, Yarmouth, Ayr

May

1	Wed	Southwell, Ascot, Pontefract, Bath, Brighton
2	Thu	Southwell, Chelmsford, Musselburgh, Redcar, Salisbury
3	Fri	Newcastle, Chepstow, Lingfield, Musselburgh, **Cheltenham**
4	Sat	Goodwood, Newmarket, Thirsk, Doncaster, **Uttoxeter**, **Hexham**
5	Sun	Hamilton, Newmarket
6	Mon	Bath, Beverley, Windsor, **Kempton**, **Warwick**
7	Tue	Wolverhampton, Wetherby, **Ayr**, **Fakenham**, **Exeter**
8	Wed	Southwell, Chester, **Kelso**, **Newton Abbot**, **Fontwell**
9	Thu	Chelmsford, Chester, **Huntingdon**, **Worcester**, **Wincanton**
10	Fri	Wolverhampton, Ascot, Chester, Nottingham, Ripon, **Market Rasen**
11	Sat	Ascot, Lingfield, Nottingham, Thirsk, **Hexham**, **Warwick**, **Haydock**
12	Sun	**Ludlow**, **Plumpton**
13	Mon	Wolverhampton, Musselburgh, Windsor, **Kempton**, **Towcester**
14	Tue	Beverley, Chepstow, **Sedgefield**, **Southwell**, **Wincanton**
15	Wed	Yarmouth, York, Bath, **Newton Abbot**, **Perth**

149

2018-19 RFO Jumps Racing Guide

16	Thu	Salisbury, York, Newmarket, **Perth**, **Fontwell**
17	Fri	Newbury, Newmarket, York, Hamilton, **Aintree**
18	Sat	Newbury, Newmarket, Thirsk, Doncaster, **Bangor**, **Uttoxeter**
19	Sun	Ripon, **Market Rasen**, **Stratford**
20	Mon	Carlisle, Redcar, Leicester, Windsor, **Towcester**
21	Tue	Wolverhampton, Brighton, Nottingham, **Hexham**, **Huntingdon**
22	Wed	Kempton, Ayr, Yarmouth, **Warwick**, **Southwell**
23	Thu	Chelmsford, Chepstow, Goodwood, Lingfield, Sandown
24	Fri	Bath, Goodwood, Haydock, Pontefract, **Worcester**
25	Sat	Chester, Goodwood, Haydock, York, Salisbury, **Cartmel**, **Ffos Las**
26	Sun	**Fontwell**, **Kelso**, **Uttoxeter**
27	Mon	Chelmsford, Leicester, Redcar, Windsor, **Cartmel**, **Huntingdon**
28	Tue	Southwell, Brighton, Leicester, Redcar, Ayr
29	Wed	Beverley, Hamilton, **Newton Abbot**, **Cartmel**, **Warwick**
30	Thu	Lingfield, Wetherby, Yarmouth, Carlisle, Sandown
31	Fri	Wolverhampton, Chelmsford, Carlisle, Epsom, Doncaster, **Stratford**

June

1	Sat	Doncaster, Epsom, Musselburgh, Lingfield, **Hexham**, **Worcester**, **Stratford**
2	Sun	Nottingham, **Fakenham**
3	Mon	Wolverhampton, Brighton, Thirsk, Windsor, Lingfield, Newcastle, **Bangor**, **Southwell**
5	Wed	Kempton, Nottingham, Ripon, **Fontwell**, **Newton Abbot**
6	Thu	Chelmsford, Hamilton, Haydock, Ripon, **Ffos Las**
7	Fri	Brighton, Bath, Goodwood, Haydock, **Market Rasen**, **Uttoxeter**
8	Sat	Beverley, Chelmsford, Haydock, Newmarket, Chepstow, Lingfield
9	Sun	Goodwood, **Perth**
10	Mon	Leicester, Pontefract, Windsor, **Stratford**
11	Tue	Lingfield, Salisbury, Carlisle, Thirsk
12	Wed	Kempton, Haydock, Yarmouth, Hamilton, **Fontwell**
13	Thu	Newbury, Nottingham, Yarmouth, Haydock, **Uttoxeter**
14	Fri	Chepstow, Sandown, York, Goodwood, **Aintree**, **Newton Abbot**
15	Sat	Bath, Chester, Sandown, York, Leicester, **Hexham**, **Worcester**
16	Sun	Doncaster, Salisbury
17	Mon	Carlisle, Catterick, Nottingham, Windsor
18	Tue	Royal Ascot, Thirsk, Beverley, Brighton, **Stratford**
19	Wed	Royal Ascot, Chelmsford, Hamilton, Ripon, **Uttoxeter**
20	Thu	Royal Ascot, Chelmsford, Lingfield, Ripon, **Ffos Las**
21	Fri	Royal Ascot, Redcar, Ayr, Goodwood, Newmarket, **Market Rasen**
22	Sat	Royal Ascot, Ayr, Newmarket, Redcar, Haydock, Lingfield, **Perth**
23	Sun	Pontefract, **Hexham**, **Worcester**
24	Mon	Wolverhampton, Chepstow, Windsor, **Southwell**
25	Tue	Beverley, Brighton, Newbury, **Newton Abbot**
26	Wed	Kempton, Carlisle, Salisbury, Bath, **Worcester**
27	Thu	Newcastle, Newmarket, Nottingham, Hamilton, Leicester
28	Fri	Newcastle, Doncaster, Yarmouth, Chester, Newmarket, **Cartmel**
29	Sat	Chester, Newcastle, Newmarket, Windsor, York, Doncaster, Lingfield
30	Sun	Windsor, **Cartmel**, **Uttoxeter**

July

1	Mon	Wolverhampton, Pontefract, Catterick, Windsor
2	Tue	Brighton, Hamilton, Chepstow, **Stratford**
3	Wed	Kempton, Musselburgh, Thirsk, Bath, **Worcester**
4	Thu	Haydock, Yarmouth, Epsom, Newbury, **Perth**
5	Fri	Chelmsford, Doncaster, Sandown, Beverley, Haydock, **Newton Abbot**
6	Sat	Chelmsford, Beverley, Haydock, Leicester, Sandown, Carlisle, Nottingham
7	Sun	Ayr, **Market Rasen**
8	Mon	Ayr, Ripon, Windsor, **Worcester**
9	Tue	Wolverhampton, Pontefract, Brighton, **Uttoxeter**
10	Wed	Kempton, Catterick, Lingfield, Yarmouth, Bath
11	Thu	Carlisle, Doncaster, Newmarket, Epsom, Newbury
12	Fri	Ascot, Newmarket, York, Chepstow, Chester, **Ffos Las**
13	Sat	Ascot, Chester, Newmarket, York, Hamilton, Salisbury, **Newton Abbot**
14	Sun	**Perth, Stratford**
15	Mon	Wolverhampton, Ayr, Ripon, Windsor
16	Tue	Bath, Beverley, Nottingham, **Southwell**
17	Wed	Wolverhampton, Catterick, Lingfield, Yarmouth, **Uttoxeter**
18	Thu	Chepstow, Hamilton, Leicester, Epsom, **Worcester**
19	Fri	Haydock, Newbury, Nottingham, Hamilton, Newmarket, Pontefract
20	Sat	Newbury, Newmarket, Ripon, Doncaster, Haydock, **Cartmel**, **Market Rasen**
21	Sun	Redcar, **Newton Abbot, Stratford**
22	Mon	Ayr, Beverley, Windsor, **Cartmel**
23	Tue	Wolverhampton, Chelmsford, Musselburgh, **Southwell**
24	Wed	Bath, Catterick, Lingfield, Leicester, Sandown
25	Thu	Sandown, Yarmouth, Doncaster, Newbury, **Worcester**
26	Fri	Ascot, Thirsk, Chepstow, Newmarket, York, **Uttoxeter**
27	Sat	Newcastle, Ascot, Chester, Newmarket, York, Lingfield, Salisbury
28	Sun	Pontefract, **Uttoxeter**
29	Mon	Ayr, Ffos Las, Windsor, **Newton Abbot**
30	Tue	Beverley, Goodwood, Yarmouth, **Perth, Worcester**
31	Wed	Goodwood, Redcar, Leicester, Sandown, **Perth**

August

1	Thu	Goodwood, Nottingham, Epsom, Ffos Las, **Stratford**
2	Fri	Wolverhampton, Goodwood, Bath, Musselburgh, Newmarket, **Bangor**
3	Sat	Chelmsford, Doncaster, Goodwood, Newmarket, Thirsk, Hamilton, Lingfield
4	Sun	Chester, **Market Rasen**
5	Mon	Kempton, Ripon, Carlisle, Windsor
6	Tue	Catterick, Newbury, Nottingham, Ripon
7	Wed	Kempton, Bath, Brighton, Pontefract, Yarmouth
8	Thu	Newcastle, Brighton, Haydock, Yarmouth, Sandown
9	Fri	Chelmsford, Brighton, Musselburgh, Thirsk, Haydock, Newmarket
10	Sat	Chelmsford, Ascot, Haydock, Newmarket, Redcar, Ayr, Lingfield

2018-19 *RFO Jumps Racing Guide*

11	Sun	Leicester, Windsor
12	Mon	Wolverhampton, Ayr, Catterick, Windsor
13	Tue	Lingfield, Ffos Las, Nottingham, Carlisle
14	Wed	Kempton, Beverley, Salisbury, **Newton Abbot**, **Worcester**
15	Thu	Lingfield, Beverley, Salisbury, Chepstow, Yarmouth
16	Fri	Wolverhampton, Chelmsford, Newbury, Nottingham, Newmarket, Thirsk
17	Sat	Doncaster, Newbury, Newmarket, Ripon, Bath, **Perth**, **Market Rasen**
18	Sun	Pontefract, **Southwell**
19	Mon	Lingfield, Catterick, Windsor, **Bangor**
20	Tue	Kempton, Brighton, Hamilton, Yarmouth, **Newton Abbot**
21	Wed	Kempton, Bath, Carlisle, York, **Worcester**
22	Thu	Chepstow, York, Leicester, **Stratford**, **Fontwell**
23	Fri	Chelmsford, Ffos Las, Newmarket, York, Goodwood, Salisbury
24	Sat	Chelmsford, Goodwood, Newmarket, York, Redcar, Windsor, **Cartmel**
25	Sun	Beverley, Goodwood, Yarmouth
26	Mon	Southwell, Chepstow, Epsom, Ripon, **Cartmel**
27	Tue	Epsom, Ripon, Bath, Musselburgh
28	Wed	Kempton, Catterick, Lingfield, Musselburgh, **Worcester**
29	Thu	Chelmsford, Carlisle, Ffos Las, **Fontwell**, **Sedgefield**
30	Fri	Newcastle, Wolverhampton, Sandown, Thirsk, Hamilton, **Bangor**
31	Sat	Wolverhampton, Chelmsford, Lingfield, Beverley, Chester, Sandown, **Newton Abbot**

September

1	Sun	Brighton, **Worcester**
2	Mon	Brighton, Chepstow, Windsor, **Hexham**
3	Tue	Catterick, Goodwood, Kempton, Salisbury
4	Wed	Chelmsford, Bath, Hamilton, **Southwell**, **Uttoxeter**
5	Thu	Chelmsford, Haydock, Salisbury, Lingfield, **Sedgefield**
6	Fri	Newcastle, Kempton, Ascot, Haydock, Musselburgh
7	Sat	Kempton, Wolverhampton, Ascot, Haydock, Thirsk, **Stratford**
8	Sun	York, **Fontwell**
9	Mon	Wolverhampton, Brighton, **Newton Abbot**, **Perth**
10	Tue	Catterick, Leicester, **Worcester**, **Kelso**
11	Wed	Kempton, Carlisle, Doncaster, **Uttoxeter**
12	Thu	Chelmsford, Chepstow, Doncaster, Epsom
13	Fri	Chester, Doncaster, Sandown, Salisbury
14	Sat	Chelmsford, Bath, Chester, Doncaster, Lingfield, Musselburgh
15	Sun	Bath, Ffos Las
16	Mon	Kempton, Brighton, Thirsk, **Worcester**
17	Tue	Newcastle, Chepstow, Redcar, Yarmouth
18	Wed	Beverley, Sandown, Yarmouth, **Kelso**
19	Thu	Chelmsford, Southwell, Ayr, Pontefract, Yarmouth
20	Fri	Newcastle, Ayr, Newbury, **Newton Abbot**
21	Sat	Chelmsford, Wolverhampton, Ayr, Catterick, Newbury, Newmarket
22	Sun	Hamilton, **Plumpton**
23	Mon	Kempton, Hamilton, Leicester, **Warwick**
24	Tue	Lingfield, Chelmsford, Beverley, **Warwick**

25	Wed	Kempton, Newcastle, Goodwood, Redcar, **Perth**
26	Thu	Chelmsford, Southwell, Newmarket, Pontefract, **Perth**
27	Fri	Newcastle, Haydock, Newmarket, **Worcester**
28	Sat	Chelmsford, Chester, Haydock, Newmarket, Ripon, **Market Rasen**
29	Sun	Epsom, Musselburgh
30	Mon	Wolverhampton, Bath, Hamilton, **Newton Abbot**

October

1	Tue	Kempton, Ayr, **Sedgefield**, **Southwell**
2	Wed	Kempton, Newcastle, Nottingham, **Bangor**, **Huntingdon**
3	Thu	Lingfield, Chelmsford, Wolverhampton, Salisbury, **Warwick**
4	Fri	Southwell, Ascot, **Fontwell**, **Hexham**
5	Sat	Wolverhampton, Ascot, Newmarket, Redcar, **Fontwell**
6	Sun	**Kelso**, **Uttoxeter**
7	Mon	Newcastle, Pontefract, Windsor, **Stratford**
8	Tue	Chelmsford, Brighton, Catterick, Leicester
9	Wed	Kempton, Newcastle, Nottingham, **Ludlow**, **Towcester**
10	Thu	Kempton, Southwell, Ayr, **Exeter**, **Worcester**
11	Fri	Newcastle, Newmarket, York, **Chepstow**
12	Sat	Wolverhampton, Newmarket, York, **Chepstow**, **Hexham**
13	Sun	Goodwood, **Newton Abbot**
14	Mon	Wolverhampton, Musselburgh, Windsor, Yarmouth
15	Tue	Kempton, Leicester, **Hereford**, **Huntingdon**
16	Wed	Kempton, Southwell, Bath, Nottingham, **Wetherby**
17	Thu	Chelmsford, Wolverhampton, Brighton, **Carlisle**, **Wincanton**
18	Fri	Newcastle, Haydock, Redcar, **Fakenham**, **Uttoxeter**
19	Sat	Wolverhampton, Ascot, Catterick, **Ffos Las**, **Market Rasen**, **Stratford**
20	Sun	**Kempton**, Sedgefield
21	Mon	Southwell, Pontefract, Windsor, **Plumpton**
22	Tue	Newcastle, Kempton, Yarmouth, **Exeter**
23	Wed	Kempton, Wolverhampton, Newmarket, **Fontwell**, **Worcester**
24	Thu	Chelmsford, Wolverhampton, **Carlisle**, **Ludlow**, **Southwell**
25	Fri	Newcastle, Doncaster, Newbury, **Cheltenham**
26	Sat	Chelmsford, Doncaster, Newbury, **Cheltenham**, **Kelso**
27	Sun	**Aintree**, **Wincanton**
28	Mon	Kempton, Leicester, Redcar, **Ayr**
29	Tue	Southwell, Catterick, **Bangor**, **Chepstow**
30	Wed	Kempton, Wolverhampton, Nottingham, **Fakenham**, **Taunton**
31	Thu	Lingfield, Chelmsford, Kempton, **Newton Abbot**, **Stratford**

November

1	Fri	Newcastle, Newmarket, **Uttoxeter**, **Wetherby**
2	Sat	Chelmsford, Newmarket, **Ascot**, **Ayr**, **Wetherby**
3	Sun	**Carlisle**, **Huntingdon**
4	Mon	Kempton, Newcastle, **Hereford**, **Plumpton**
5	Tue	Southwell, Kempton, Redcar, **Exeter**
6	Wed	Kempton, Wolverhampton, Nottingham, **Chepstow**, **Musselburgh**
7	Thu	Chelmsford, Southwell, **Market Rasen**, **Newbury**, **Sedgefield**
8	Fri	Newcastle, **Fontwell**, **Hexham**, **Warwick**
9	Sat	Southwell, Doncaster, **Aintree**, **Kelso**, **Wincanton**

2018-19 *RFO Jumps Racing Guide*

10	Sun	**Ffos Las**, Sandown
11	Mon	**Carlisle**, Kempton, Stratford
12	Tue	**Hereford**, Huntingdon, Lingfield
13	Wed	Ayr, **Bangor**, Exeter
14	Thu	**Ludlow**, Sedgefield, Taunton
15	Fri	**Cheltenham**, Newcastle, Southwell
16	Sat	Lingfield, Wolverhampton, **Cheltenham**, Uttoxeter, Wetherby
17	Sun	**Cheltenham**, Fontwell
18	Mon	Wolverhampton, Southwell, **Leicester**, Plumpton
19	Tue	Kempton, Chelmsford, **Fakenham**, Lingfield
20	Wed	Kempton, **Chepstow**, Hexham, Warwick
21	Thu	Newcastle, Chelmsford, **Market Rasen**, Wincanton
22	Fri	Newcastle, **Ascot**, Catterick, Ffos Las
23	Sat	Lingfield, Wolverhampton, **Ascot**, Haydock, Huntingdon
24	Sun	**Exeter**, Uttoxeter
25	Mon	**Kempton**, Ludlow, Musselburgh
26	Tue	Wolverhampton, **Sedgefield**, Southwell
27	Wed	Southwell, Kempton, **Hereford**, Wetherby
28	Thu	Lingfield, Chelmsford, **Taunton**, Towcester
29	Fri	Southwell, Kempton, **Doncaster**, Newbury
30	Sat	Wolverhampton, **Bangor**, Doncaster, Newbury, Newcastle

December

1	Sun	**Carlisle**, Leicester
2	Mon	Wolverhampton, **Musselburgh**, Plumpton
3	Tue	Wolverhampton, **Lingfield**, Southwell
4	Wed	Lingfield, Kempton, **Haydock**, Ludlow
5	Thu	Southwell, **Leicester**, Market Rasen, Wincanton
6	Fri	Newcastle, **Exeter**, Sandown, Sedgefield
7	Sat	Wolverhampton, **Aintree**, Chepstow, Sandown, Wetherby
8	Sun	**Huntingdon**, Kelso
9	Mon	Lingfield, Newcastle, **Musselburgh**
10	Tue	Wolverhampton, **Fontwell**, Uttoxeter
11	Wed	Lingfield, Kempton, **Hexham**, Leicester
12	Thu	Chelmsford, **Newcastle**, Taunton, Warwick
13	Fri	Chelmsford, **Bangor**, Cheltenham, Doncaster
14	Sat	Newcastle, Wolverhampton, **Cheltenham**, Doncaster, Hereford
15	Sun	**Carlisle**, Southwell
16	Mon	Wolverhampton, **Ffos Las**, Plumpton
17	Tue	**Catterick**, Fakenham, Lingfield
18	Wed	Lingfield, Newcastle, **Ludlow**, Newbury
19	Thu	Southwell, Wolverhampton, **Exeter**, Towcester
20	Fri	Southwell, Wolverhampton, **Ascot**, Uttoxeter
21	Sat	Lingfield, **Ascot**, Haydock, Newcastle
26	Thu	Wolverhampton, **Fontwell**, Huntingdon, Kempton, **Market Rasen**, Sedgefield, Wetherby, Wincanton
27	Fri	Wolverhampton, **Chepstow**, Kempton, Wetherby
28	Sat	Lingfield, **Catterick**, Leicester, Newbury
29	Sun	Southwell, **Doncaster**, Kelso
30	Mon	Lingfield, **Haydock**, Taunton
31	Tue	Lingfield, **Uttoxeter**, Warwick

2018-19 RFO Jumps Racing Guide

Big-race dates

November
- 3 Wetherby .... Charlie Hall Chase
- 10 Wincanton .... Elite Hurdle
- 17 Cheltenham .... BetVictor Gold Cup
- 24 Haydock .... Betfair Chase
- 24 Haydock .... Ascot Hurdle

December
- 1 Newbury .... Ladbrokes Gold Cup
- 1 Newcastle .... Fighting Fifth Hurdle
- 8 Sandown .... Tingle Creek Trophy
- 8 Aintree .... Becher Chase
- 15 Cheltenham .... Caspian Caviar Gold Cup
- 22 Ascot .... Long Walk Hurdle
- 26 Kempton .... King George VI Chase
- 27 Chepstow .... Welsh Grand National
- 29 Newbury .... Challow Novices' Hurdle

January
- 5 Sandown .... Tolworth Hurdle
- 12 Warwick .... Classic Chase
- 19 Ascot .... Clarence House Chase
- 19 Haydock .... Peter Marsh Chase
- 26 Cheltenham .... Festival Trials Day

February
- 9 Newbury .... Betfair Hurdle
- 16 Ascot .... Ascot Chase
- 16 Haydock .... Grand National Trial
- 23 Kempton .... BetBright Chase

March
- 9 Sandown .... Imperial Cup
- 12 Cheltenham .... Champion Hurdle
- 13 Cheltenham .... Champion Chase
- 14 Cheltenham .... Stayers' Hurdle
- 15 Cheltenham .... Cheltenham Gold Cup

April
- 4 Aintree .... Betfred Bowl
- 5 Aintree .... Melling Chase
- 6 Aintree .... Crabbie's Grand National
- 13 Ayr .... Scottish Grand National
- 22 Fairyhouse .... Irish Grand National
- 27 Sandown .... bet365 Gold Cup

Big-race records

Year	Winner	Age-wgt	Trainer	Jockey	SP	Ran
\multicolumn{7}{c}{*BetVictor Gold Cup (2m4½f) Cheltenham*}

BetVictor Gold Cup (2m4½f) Cheltenham

Year	Winner	Age-wgt	Trainer	Jockey	SP	Ran
2008	Imperial Commander	7-10-7	N Twiston-Davies	P Brennan	13-2	19
2009	Tranquil Sea	7-10-13	E O'Grady	A McNamara	11-2f	16
2010	Little Josh	8-10-8	N Twiston-Davies	S Twiston-Davies (3)	20-1	18
2011	Great Endeavour	7-10-3	D Pipe	T Murphy	8-1	20
2012	Al Ferof	7-11-8	P Nicholls	R Walsh	8-1	18
2013	Johns Spirit	6-10-2	J O'Neill	R McLernon	7-1	20
2014	Caid Du Berlais	5-10-13	P Nicholls	S Twiston-Davies	10-1	18
2015	Annacotty	7-11-0	A King	I Popham	12-1	20
2016	Taquin Du Seuil	9-11-11	J O'Neill	A Coleman	8-1	17
2017	Splash Of Ginge	9-10-6	N Twiston-Davies	T Bellamy	25-1	17

COURSE form is the key factor as 21 of the last 26 winners had previously been successful at Cheltenham and two of the exceptions had been placed at the Cheltenham Festival. That's even more remarkable considering winners tend to be so inexperienced, with 11 of the last 15 being second-season chasers aged five to eight. Splash Of Ginge is the only winner to have had more than 15 chase runs since fellow nine-year-old The Outback Way in 1999 and the last older winner was Clear Cut in 1975. There have been several great weight-carrying performances down the years, most recently Taquin Du Seuil and Al Ferof, but they are the only winners since Exotic Dancer in 2006 to have carried more than 11st.

Betfair Chase (3m1½f) Haydock

Year	Winner	Age-wgt	Trainer	Jockey	SP	Ran
2008	Snoopy Loopy	10-11-7	P Bowen	S Durack	33-1	6
2009	Kauto Star	9-11-7	P Nicholls	R Walsh	4-6f	7
2010	Imperial Commander	9-11-7	N Twiston-Davies	P Brennan	10-11f	7
2011	Kauto Star	11-11-7	P Nicholls	R Walsh	6-1	6
2012	Silviniaco Conti	6-11-7	P Nicholls	R Walsh	7-4	5
2013	Cue Card	7-11-7	C Tizzard	J Tizzard	9-1	8
2014	Silviniaco Conti	8-11-7	P Nicholls	N Fehily	10-3	9
2015	Cue Card	9-11-7	C Tizzard	P Brennan	7-4	5
2016	Cue Card	10-11-7	C Tizzard	P Brennan	15-8f	6
2017	Bristol De Mai	6-11-7	N Twiston-Davies	D Jacob	11-10f	6

FIRST run in 2005, this race has quickly become the first port of call for proven top-class staying chasers. As such 12 of the 13 winners had already secured a top-two finish at Grade 1 level and the sole exception, Snoopy Loopy, is the only winner priced bigger

DENMAN: showed weight is no barrier to success when twice winning what was then the Hennessy Gold Cup and many others have followed suit

than 9-1. Tactical speed is vital at Haydock and form over shorter trips has been more telling than proven stamina – every winner since Kingscliff in the inaugural running had previously won over 2m or 2m1f whereas four hadn't even won over the big-race trip itself. The last six winners had all had a prep run, with the Charlie Hall the most popular port of call.

Ladbrokes Trophy (3m2f) Newbury

Year	Horse	Age-Wt	Trainer	Jockey	SP	Ran
2008	**Madison Du Berlais**	7-11-4	D Pipe	T Scudamore	25-1	15
2009	**Denman**	9-11-12	P Nicholls	R Walsh	11-4f	19
2010	**Diamond Harry**	7-10-0	N Williams	D Jacob	6-1	18
2011	**Carruthers**	8-10-4	M Bradstock	M Batchelor	10-1	18
2012	**Bobs Worth**	7-11-6	N Henderson	B Geraghty	4-1f	19
2013	**Triolo D'Alene**	6-11-1	N Henderson	B Geraghty	20-1	21
2014	**Many Clouds**	7-11-6	O Sherwood	L Aspell	8-1	19
2015	**Smad Place**	8-11-4	A King	W Hutchison	7-1	15
2016	**Native River**	6-11-1	C Tizzard	R Johnson	7-2f	19
2017	**Total Recall**	8-10-8	W Mullins	P Townend	9-2f	20

JUST about the most high-quality handicap of the season, won by some very special horses including twice by Denman as well as subsequent Gold Cup and Grand National winners since then. The increasing quality has seen 11 of the last 15 winners carry 11st or more to victory after 16 out of 18 prior to Strong Flow in 2003 had been below that benchmark. Twelve of the 19 winners since 1999 were second-season chasers (including three winners of the RSA Chase) and one of the exceptions, Strong Flow, was a novice, so lack of experience isn't a worry, especially as Be My Royal was also a winning novice in 2002 before being disqualified due to a banned substance. In contrast, no horse older than nine has won since Diamond Edge in 1981, with 85 beaten in the meantime. The Badger Ales Trophy is best of the traditional trials, although six of the last 12 winners were making their seasonal debuts.

Tingle Creek Trophy (2m) Sandown

2008	Master Minded	5-11-7	P Nicholls	A McCoy	4-7f	7
2009	Twist Magic	7-11-7	P Nicholls	R Walsh	9-4	5
2010*	Master Minded	7-11-7	P Nicholls	N Fehily	10-11f	9
2011	Sizing Europe	9-11-7	H de Bromhead	A Lynch	11-8f	7
2012	Sprinter Sacre	6-11-7	N Henderson	B Geraghty	4-11f	7
2013	Sire De Grugy	7-11-7	G Moore	J Moore	7-4jf	9
2014	Dodging Bullets	6-11-7	P Nicholls	S Twiston-Davies	9-1	10
2015	Sire De Grugy	9-11-7	G Moore	J Moore	10-3	7
2016	Un De Sceaux	8-11-7	W Mullins	R Walsh	5-4f	6
2017	Politologue	6-11-7	P Nicholls	H Cobden	7-2	6

*run at Cheltenham

THIS changed from a handicap to a Grade 1 conditions event prior to the 1994 renewal and has grown to rank alongside the Champion Chase in terms of quality. Moscow Flyer's epic 2004 win over Well Chief and Azertyuiop was the most memorable running and since then the Irish legend has been matched by Master Minded, Sprinter Sacre, Sire De Grugy and Dodging Bullets in doubling up at Cheltenham, while Un De Sceaux went on to win the Ryanair. As well as going on to big things, winners also tend to have proved themselves already at the highest level as 15 of the last 19 winners had already landed a Grade 1 chase. As a result no winner has returned bigger than 9-1 since the race gained top-flight status.

Caspian Caviar Gold Cup (2m5f) Cheltenham

2008	Abandoned					
2009	Poquelin	6-11-8	P Nicholls	R Walsh	7-2f	17
2010	Poquelin	7-11-12	P Nicholls	I Popham (5)	16-1	16
2011	Quantitativeeasing	6-10-7	N Henderson	B Geraghty	6-1	16
2012	Unioniste	4-10-0	P Nicholls	H Derham (5)	15-2	14
2013	Double Ross	8-10-8	N Twiston-Davies	S Twiston-Davies	14-1	13
2014	Niceonefrankie	8-11-5	V Williams	A Coleman	16-1	12
2015	Village Vic	8-10-0	P Hobbs	R Johnson	8-1	14
2016	Frodon	4-10-10	P Nicholls	S Twiston-Davies	14-1	16
2017	Guitar Pete	7-10-5	N Richards	R Day (3)	9-1	10

NOT surprisingly, the BetVictor Gold Cup, held at the same venue four weeks earlier, is the most useful guide to this event as seven of the last 13 winners ran in that race, with Exotic Dancer doing the double (to emulate Pegwell Bay and Senor El Betrutti in the previous 20 years) and Quantitativeeasing, Poquelin (for his 2009 victory) and Monkerhostin improving on their second-placed efforts. Even compared to the BetVictor, it's a great race for young horses. Four-year-olds Frodon and Unioniste are the best example and three winners since 2006 were only six, while Double Ross was another successful novice in 2013, whereas Fragrant Dawn was the last winner older than eight in 1993. The race has featured some notable weight-carrying performances and five of the last 11 winners carried 11st 4lb or more.

Long Walk Hurdle (3m½f) Ascot

2008	Punchestowns	5-11-7	N Henderson	B Geraghty	3-1f	11
2009*	Big Buck's	6-11-7	P Nicholls	R Walsh	1-2f	8
2010*	Big Buck's	7-11-7	P Nicholls	A McCoy	2-13f	6
2011	Big Buck's	8-11-7	P Nicholls	R Walsh	3-10f	7

2018-19 RFO Jumps Racing Guide

2012	Reve De Sivola	7-11-7	N Williams	R Johnson	9-2	7
2013	Reve De Sivola	8-11-7	N Williams	R Johnson	9-4	5
2014	Reve De Sivola	9-11-7	N Williams	D Jacob	13-2	5
2015	Thistlecrack	7-11-7	C Tizzard	T Scudamore	2-1f	8
2016	Unowhatimeanharry	8-11-7	H Fry	B Geraghty	6-5f	11
2017	Sam Spinner	6-11-7	J O'Keeffe	J Colliver	9-2	8

*run at Newbury

DEFENDING champions deserve the utmost respect because ten of the 18 runnings since 2000 have been won by just three horses – Baracouda leads the way with four victories from 2000 to 2004 (he was also second at 4-11 to Deano's Beeno in between), Big Buck's reeled off a hat-trick from 2009 to 2011 and Reve De Sivola did likewise from 2012 to 2014 before finishing second the following year. Four-year-olds fare better than they do at Cheltenham aged five – Silver Wedge and Ocean Hawk were successful in the 1990s – but generally you want an older horse with seven of the last eight winners aged at least seven. Thirteen of the last 25 winners came via the Long Distance Hurdle at Newbury, with nine doing the double.

King George VI Chase (3m) Kempton

2008	Kauto Star	8-11-10	P Nicholls	R Walsh	10-11f	10
2009	Kauto Star	9-11-10	P Nicholls	R Walsh	8-13f	13
2010*	Long Run	6-11-10	N Henderson	Mr S W-Cohen	9-2	9
2011	Kauto Star	11-11-10	P Nicholls	R Walsh	3-1	7
2012	Long Run	7-11-10	N Henderson	Mr S W-Cohen	15-8f	9
2013	Silviniaco Conti	7-11-10	P Nicholls	N Fehily	7-2	9
2014	Silviniaco Conti	8-11-10	P Nicholls	N Fehily	15-8f	10
2015	Cue Card	9-11-10	C Tizzard	P Brennan	9-2	9
2016	Thistlecrack	8-11-10	C Tizzard	T Scudamore	11-10f	5
2017	Might Bite	9-11-10	N Henderson	N de Boinville	6-4f	8

*run in January 2011

A RACE the best horses often manage to win several times. It's not just the amazing Kauto Star, who landed a fifth win in 2011, as Silviniaco Conti, Long Run, Kicking King, See More Business and One Man are also multiple winners since the days of the legendary Desert Orchid. That also emphasises the importance of experience as 15 of the last 19 winners were in at least their third season of chasing – although, staggeringly, Thistlecrack somehow managed to prevail as a novice in 2016 before Might Bite proved good enough to defy several trends last year. Thistlecrack is also the only winner not to have previously landed a Grade 1 chase since Teeton Mill in 1998. Kempton's relatively sharp three miles provides slightly less of a stamina test than other major tracks, particularly Cheltenham, and the importance of tactical speed is shown by the fact that the 13 winners prior to Thistlecrack and Might Bite had all landed a Graded chase from 2m4f to 2m6f. That means those who have just failed to see out the Gold Cup trip often make amends here, such as One Man and Florida Pearl, while Kauto Star was also more vulnerable in March, there were stamina doubts about Kicking King prior to his first win and Edredon Bleu was a 2m performer stepping into the unknown.

Christmas Hurdle (2m) Kempton

2008	Harchibald	9-11-7	N Meade	P Carberry	7-1	7
2009	Go Native	6-11-7	N Meade	D Condon	5-2	7
2010*	Binocular	7-11-7	N Henderson	A McCoy	13-8f	6

KALASHNIKOV: yet another novice to win the Betfair Hurdle on handicap debut

2011	**Binocular**	7-11-7	N Henderson	A McCoy	5-4f	5
2012	**Darlan**	5-11-7	N Henderson	A McCoy	3-1	7
2013	**My Tent Or Yours**	6-11-7	N Henderson	A McCoy	11-8	6
2014	**Faugheen**	6-11-7	W Mullins	R Walsh	4-11f	6
2015	**Faugheen**	7-11-7	W Mullins	R Walsh	1-4f	5
2016	**Yanworth**	6-11-7	A King	B Geraghty	5-4f	5
2017	**Buveur D'Air**	6-11-7	N Henderson	B Geraghty	2-11f	4

*run in January 2011

FORGET Harchibald's trend-busting win in 2008 as this sharp two miles is ideal for young, improving types. Apart from Harchibald and 1-4 certainty Faugheen in 2015, every winner since 2000 would have been aged five or six had Binocular not had his first win forced over into 2011 by bad weather and then pipped Rock On Ruby by a nose at the end of that year. Six of the last 11 winners were getting off the mark for the season and three of the five exceptions had won the Fighting Fifth.

Welsh Grand National (3m5f) Chepstow

2008	**Notre Pere**	7-11-0	T Dreaper	A Lynch	16-1	20
2009	**Dream Alliance**	8-10-8	P Hobbs	T O'Brien	20-1	18
2010*	**Synchronised**	8-11-6	J O'Neill	A McCoy	5-1	18
2011	**Le Beau Bai**	8-10-1	R Lee	C Poste	10-1	20
2012	**Monbeg Dude**	8-10-1	M Scudamore	P Carberry	10-1	17
2013	**Mountainous**	8-10-0	R Lee	P Moloney	20-1	20
2014	**Emperor's Choice**	7-10-8	V Williams	A Coleman	9-1	19
2015**	**Mountainous**	11-10-6	K Lee	J Moore	9-1	20

| 2016 | Native River | 6-11-12 | C Tizzard | R Johnson | 11-4f | 20 |
| 2017*** | Raz De Maree | 13-11-1 | G Cromwell | J Bowen (5) | 16-1 | 20 |

*run in January 2011   **run in January 2016   ***run in January 2018

CHEPSTOW lost a key trial for this race with the Rehearsal Chase moving to Newcastle, but it has basically been replaced by another handicap in early December – aptly named the Welsh Grand National Trial – and course form remains pivotal. Six of the last 11 winners had previously triumphed at the track, making 13 of the last 20 in all, and last year's winner Raz De Maree had finished second in the race 12 months earlier. As with most staying handicap chases run in the mud, horses at the foot of the weights are massively favoured. Only nine winners since 1976 carried more than 11st, with James Bowen's claim taking Raz De Maree below the threshold last year, and the last three show the quality needed as Synchronised and Native River went on to win the Gold Cup and Halcon Genelardais was fourth in that race. Generally punters should not even rule out any horse from out of the handicap, with Mountainous the latest to defy extra weight in 2013, and Kendal Cavalier was as much as 13lb wrong in 1997. Native River is the only winning favourite since 2004 and the only horse to come via what was the Hennessy since 1987.

Betfair Hurdle (2m½f) Newbury

2009	Abandoned					
2010	Get Me Out Of Here	6-10-6	J O'Neill	A McCoy	6-1	23
2011	Recession Proof	5-10-8	J Quinn	D Costello	12-1	15
2012	Zarkandar	5-11-1	P Nicholls	R Walsh	11-4f	20
2013	My Tent Or Yours	6-11-2	N Henderson	A McCoy	5-1f	19
2014	Splash Of Ginge	6-10-10	N Twiston-Davies	R Hatch (7)	33-1	20
2015	Violet Dancer	5-10-9	G Moore	Joshua Moore	20-1	23
2016	Agrapart	5-10-10	N Williams	L Kelly (5)	16-1	22
2017	Ballyandy	6-11-1	N Twiston-Davies	S Twiston-Davies	3-1f	16
2018	Kalashnikov	5-11-5	A Murphy	J Quinlan	8-1cf	20

A TOP-CLASS handicap hurdle which has been rewarded for a big increase in prize-money in recent times. Young improvers with Grade 1 potential are preferred to experienced handicappers – the last 11 winners were five or six, seven of the last nine were novices and the same number were making their handicap debuts. Ten of the last 20 winners carried more than 11st, yet no horse has defied a burden in excess of 11st 7lb since Persian War in 1968. Eight of the last 25 winners were officially ahead of the handicapper having had their mark raised since the publication of the weights.

Grand National Trial (3m4½f) Haydock

2009	Rambling Minster	11-11-0	K Reveley	J Reveley (3)	18-1	16
2010	Silver By Nature	8-10-11	L Russell	P Buchanan	7-1	14
2011	Silver By Nature	9-11-12	L Russell	P Buchanan	10-1	14
2012	Giles Cross	10-10-5	V Dartnall	D O'Regan	4-1f	14
2013	Well Refreshed	9-10-0	G Moore	J Moore (3)	9-2f	14
2014	Rigadin De Beauchene	9-10-8	V Williams	R Dunne (3)	16-1	14
2015	Lie Forrit	11-11-6	L Russell	P Buchanan	8-1	12
2016	Bishops Road	8-11-7	K Lee	R Johnson	13-2	8
2017	Vieux Lion Rouge	8-11-6	D Pipe	T Scudamore	8-1	13
2018	Yala Enki	8-10-11	V Williams	C Deutsch	8-1	8

THIS race is usually run on soft ground and can be a real test of stamina, so it's extremely rare for winners not to have already triumphed over at least 3m1f despite most being surprisingly short of experience. None of the last 15 winners had run more than 14 times over fences in Britain or Ireland even though four were aged in double figures during that time and none younger than eight. This was a graveyard for favourites, with none successful from Frantic Tan in 2001 to Giles Cross in 2012, but six of the last seven winners were priced in single figures. Neptune Collonges followed up his 2012 second by winning at Aintree, but the race has been overrated as a National trial with the winner no better than fifth since 2000 and several running poorly when well fancied.

Betdaq Chase (3m) Kempton

Year	Horse	Age-Wt	Trainer	Jockey	SP	Ran
2009	Nacarat	8-10-13	T George	A McCoy	10-1	20
2010	Razor Royale	8-10-5	N Twiston-Davies	P Brennan	11-1	13
2011	Quinz	7-11-0	P Hobbs	R Johnson	8-1	16
2012	Nacarat	11-11-8	T George	P Brennan	9-2	10
2013	Opening Batsman	7-10-5	H Fry	N Fehily	12-1	13
2014	Bally Legend	9-10-12	C Keevil	I Popham	28-1	13
2015	Rocky Creek	9-11-11	P Nicholls	S Twiston-Davies	8-1	14
2016	Theatre Guide	9-10-6	C Tizzard	P Brennan	6-1	15
2017	Pilgrims Bay	7-10-2	N Mulholland	J Best	25-1	13
2018	Master Dee	9-11-5	F O'Brien	B Geraghty	8-1	15

IT'S remarkable how many horses manage to defy big weights to win this top prize as 12 of the last 19 winners carried more than 11st including Gungadu, Farmer Jack, Marlborough and Gloria Victis from the top of the handicap. Course form is a handy asset with 11 of the last 19 winners having previously been successful at Kempton, while Pilgrims Bay and Bally Legend are the only winners priced bigger than 12-1 since 1997. This is the first major handicap chase of the year in which novices have been a big factor, including three of the last eight winners in Pilgrims Bay, Opening Batsman and Quinz.

LABAIK: provided a shock all round when winning the Supreme in 2017 – not least for trends followers as horses who started on the Flat are best avoided

Imperial Cup (2m) Sandown

2009	Dave's Dream	6-10-13	N Henderson	B Geraghty	12-1	19
2010	Qaspal	6-10-3	P Hobbs	A McCoy	11-4f	23
2011	Alarazi	7-10-3	L Wadham	D Elsworth	10-1	24
2012	Paintball	5-10-7	C Longsdon	N Fehily	20-1	24
2013	First Avenue	8-11-1	L Mongan	N Baker (10)	20-1	19
2014	Baltimore Rock	5-10-12	D Pipe	T Scudamore	7-1	14
2015	Ebony Express	6-11-7	Dr R Newland	W Kennedy	33-1	23
2016	Flying Angel	5-10-10	N Twiston-Davies	R Hatch (3)	9-1	14
2017	London Prize	6-11-2	I Williams	T O'Brien	10	13
2018	Mr Antolini	8-10-1	N Twiston-Davies	J Bargary (3)	20-1	17

THIS falls on the eve of the Cheltenham Festival and, with the sponsors putting up a bonus for horses doubling up, a strong and competitive field is always assured. Unexposed youngsters hold the key as 12 of the last 16 winners were novices – seven having raced no more than four times over hurdles – and nine of the last 21 were five-year-olds, with two of the exceptions aged just four. David Pipe has won three of the last 12 runnings to maintain a strong family tradition as his father Martin also won three of the last five in which he had runners. No winner has carried more than 11st 2lb since 2003.

Supreme Novices' Hurdle (2m½f) Cheltenham

2009	Go Native	6-11-7	N Meade	P Carberry	12-1	20
2010	Menorah	5-11-7	P Hobbs	R Johnson	12-1	18
2011	Al Ferof	6-11-7	P Nicholls	R Walsh	10-1	15
2012	Cinders And Ashes	5-11-7	D McCain	J Maguire	10-1	19
2013	Champagne Fever	6-11-7	W Mullins	R Walsh	5-1	12
2014	Vautour	5-11-7	W Mullins	R Walsh	7-2jf	18
2015	Douvan	5-11-7	W Mullins	R Walsh	2-1f	12
2016	Altior	6-11-7	N Henderson	N de Boinville	4-1	14
2017	Labaik	6-11-7	G Elliott	J Kennedy	25-1	14
2018	Summerville Boy	6-11-7	T George	N Fehily	9-1	19

THIS traditionally gets Ireland off to a flying start at the Cheltenham Festival as the raiders have taken 12 of the last 20 runnings, including three in a row for Willie Mullins from 2013 to 2015. That run reversed the dreadful record of favourites, though Douvan is still the only successful outright market leader since Brave Inca in 2004 and just three of the last 13 horses sent off at 2-1 or shorter came out on top. Among the ten short-priced horses beaten, Cue Card, Dunguib and Cousin Vinny had won the previous year's Champion Bumper so don't be sucked in by winners of that race, with Champagne Fever the only one to follow up since Montelado in 1992. That said, a background in bumpers is much preferred as just three top-four finishers in the last decade had started on the Flat, with Labaik the only winner. Nineteen of the last 22 winners had won last time out and 17 had run within the previous 45 days, showing the benefit of recent match practice.

Racing Post Arkle Chase (2m) Cheltenham

2009	Forpadydeplasterer	7-11-7	T Cooper	B Geraghty	8-1	17
2010	Sizing Europe	8-11-7	H de Bromhead	A Lynch	6-1	12
2011	Captain Chris	7-11-7	P Hobbs	R Johnson	6-1	10
2012	Sprinter Sacre	6-11-7	N Henderson	B Geraghty	8-11f	6
2013	Simonsig	7-11-7	N Henderson	B Geraghty	8-15f	7
2014	Western Warhorse	6-11-4	D Pipe	T Scudamore	33-1	9

2015	Un De Sceaux	7-11-4	W Mullins	R Walsh	4-6f	11
2016	Douvan	6-11-4	W Mullins	R Walsh	1-4f	7
2017	Altior	7-11-4	N Henderson	N de Boinville	1-4f	9
2018	Footpad	6-11-4	W Mullins	R Walsh	5-6f	5

A TYPICAL Arkle winner tends to be well fancied with proven class over hurdles and plenty of chasing experience. Nine of the last 12 winners had won a Graded race over hurdles (seven at Grade 1 level) and all but one of the exceptions had been placed, while only Western Warhorse and Simonsig hadn't run at least three times over fences since Well Chief in 2004. Western Warhorse is also the only winner priced bigger than 11-1 since 1989 in the middle of a run of six wins in seven years for odds-on shots, all trained by Nicky Henderson or Willie Mullins. The abolition of an overly generous weight-for-age allowance in 2008 has ended the dominance of French-bred five-year-olds, with seven of the last 12 winners aged seven or eight, although that's as old as you want to go. No horse older than eight has won since Danish Flight in 1989 and since 2000 alone that includes several fancied horses such as Ned Kelly, Adamant Approach, Barton, Captain Cee Bee, Overturn, Rock On Ruby and Royal Caviar.

Ultima H'cap Chase (3m1f) Cheltenham

2009	Wichita Lineman	8-10-9	J O'Neill	A McCoy	5-1f	21
2010	Chief Dan George	10-10-10	J Moffatt	P Aspell	33-1	24
2011	Bensalem	8-11-2	A King	R Thornton	5-1	19
2012	Alfie Sherrin	9-10-0	J O'Neill	R McLernon	14-1	19
2013	Golden Chieftain	8-10-5	C Tizzard	B Powell (5)	28-1	24
2014	Holywell	7-11-6	J O'Neill	R McLernon	10-1	23
2015	The Druids Nephew	8-11-3	N Mulholland	B Geraghty	8-1	24
2016	Un Temps Pour Tout	7-11-7	D Pipe	T Scudamore	11-1	23
2017	Un Temps Pour Tout	8-11-12	D Pipe	T Scudamore	9-1	23
2018	Coo Star Sivola	6-10-13	N Williams	L Kelly (3)	5-1f	18

YOUTH has taken over this contest. Fifteen of the last 17 winners were novices (six) or second-season chasers (nine) and The Druids Nephew is the only one to have raced more than 11 times over fences since 2007 hero Joes Edge, whereas just two horses older than ten have even made the frame since 1997. A strong stayer is essential as only three of the last 22 winners lacked previous winning form at 3m or further and all three had been placed over that trip on soft ground. Long-standing trends in favour of those near the bottom of the weights have been turned around in recent years by four of the last five winners carrying more than 11st to victory, although Un Temps Pour Tout is the only horse to defy a mark of more than 150 since 1983 when landing his second victory in 2017. That has also helped those near the front of the market, with the last five winners no bigger than 11-1 after three of the previous seven had been 28-1 or bigger.

Unibet Champion Hurdle (2m½f) Cheltenham

2009	Punjabi	6-11-10	N Henderson	B Geraghty	22-1	23
2010	Binocular	6-11-10	N Henderson	A McCoy	9-1	12
2011	Hurricane Fly	7-11-10	W Mullins	R Walsh	11-4f	11
2012	Rock On Ruby	7-11-10	P Nicholls	N Fehily	11-1	10
2013	Hurricane Fly	9-11-10	W Mullins	R Walsh	13-8f	9
2014	Jezki	6-11-10	J Harrington	B Geraghty	9-1	9
2015	Faugheen	7-11-10	W Mullins	R Walsh	4-5f	8
2016	Annie Power	8-11-3	W Mullins	R Walsh	5-2f	12

| 2017 | **Buveur D'Air** | 6-11-10 | N Henderson | N Fehily | 5-1 | 11 |
| 2018 | **Buveur D'Air** | 7-11-10 | N Henderson | B Geraghty | 4-6f | 11 |

BUVEUR D'AIR is the fourth multiple winner of this race in the last 20 years, emulating Istabraq, Hardy Eustace and Hurricane Fly, with the last-named perhaps the most notable as he became the first horse to regain the crown since Comedy Of Errors in 1975. He was also unusual as a nine-year-old winner because younger horses have been faring much better in recent times. Katchit defied the biggest trend of all as a winning five-year-old in 2008 and six others have been placed in the last ten years, with seven of the nine subsequent winners aged six or seven. Previous festival form is the key and, as well as the former champions, plenty of horses step up having been placed the previous year, with wins for Hurricane Fly, Binocular, Punjabi and Brave Inca since 2006 after they were third 12 months earlier. Of the other winners in that time, Buveur D'Air, Jezki and Sublimity had top-four finishes in the Supreme, Faugheen and Rock On Ruby were first and second in the Neptune, Katchit won the Triumph and Annie Power would have won the Mares' Hurdle but for falling at the last.

Ballymore Novices' Hurdle (2m5f) Cheltenham

2009	**Mikael D'Haguenet**	5-11-7	W Mullins	R Walsh	5-2f	14
2010	**Peddlers Cross**	5-11-7	D McCain	J Maguire	7-1	17
2011	**First Lieutenant**	6-11-7	M Morris	D Russell	7-1	12
2012	**Simonsig**	6-11-7	N Henderson	B Geraghty	2-1f	17
2013	**The New One**	5-11-7	N Twiston-Davies	S Twiston-Davies	5-1	8
2014	**Faugheen**	6-11-7	W Mullins	R Walsh	6-4f	15
2015	**Windsor Park**	6-11-7	D Weld	D Russell	9-2	10
2016	**Yorkhill**	6-11-7	W Mullins	R Walsh	3-1	11
2017	**Willoughby Court**	6-11-7	B Pauling	D Bass	14-1	15
2018	**Samcro**	6-11-7	G Elliott	J Kennedy	8-11f	14

MUCH like the Supreme, this has traditionally been a race in which to oppose the short-priced favourite but has seen the picture change in recent years with the success of Ireland, whose horses account for seven of the last 11 winners including favourites Samcro, Faugheen and Mikael D'Haguenet. You have to go back to 2005 for the last winner to have started on the Flat, yet speed is often vital in a race that has proved a fair Champion Hurdle trial and the best horses from around this trip earlier in the season often lack enough toe on quicker ground, with all 16 Challow Hurdle winners to run getting beaten. In contrast, seven winners since 1998 had won a Grade 1 from 2m-2m2f from just 21 runners. French Holly was the first of those and he is also the only winner older than six since 1974, with 54 beaten subsequently. Seven of the last 19 winners had recorded a top-six finish in one of the big bumpers at Cheltenham, Aintree and Punchestown the previous spring.

RSA Chase (3m½f) Cheltenham

2009	**Cooldine**	7-11-4	W Mullins	R Walsh	9-4f	15
2010	**Weapon's Amnesty**	7-11-4	C Byrnes	D Russell	10-1	9
2011	**Bostons Angel**	7-11-4	Mrs J Harrington	R Power	16-1	12
2012	**Bobs Worth**	7-11-4	N Henderson	B Geraghty	9-2	9
2013	**Lord Windermere**	7-11-4	J Culloty	D Russell	8-1	11
2014	**O'Faolains Boy**	7-11-4	R Curtis	B Geraghty	12-1	15
2015	**Don Poli**	6-11-4	W Mullins	B Cooper	13-8f	8
2016	**Blaklion**	7-11-4	N Twiston-Davies	R Hatch	8-1	8

PRESENTING PERCY: the sixth winning favourite in 12 years in the RSA Chase

| 2017 | **Might Bite** | 8-11-4 | N Henderson | N de Boinville | 7-2f | 12 |
| 2018 | **Presenting Percy** | 7-11-4 | P Kelly | D Russell | 5-2f | 10 |

SIX winning favourites in 12 years have redressed the balance somewhat, but this still justifies its reputation as a race for upsets with plenty of bubbles getting burst. Eight beaten favourites this century had come into the race unbeaten over fences, with only Denman and Don Poli surviving with their records intact. It's worth bearing in mind that many horses in the field will be getting better and better with experience having wasted little time over hurdles as 15 of the last 17 winners had raced no more than once in that sphere outside their novice campaign. It's therefore vital to have had enough runs over fences, with Don Poli the only winner since Florida Pearl in 1998 not to have run in at least three chases and the only one in more than 50 years not to have run since the turn of the year. Seven-year-olds have a remarkable record with nine of the last 11 winners, while four of the last seven winners ran in the previous season's Albert Bartlett. There have been six Irish-trained winners in the last decade and four had run big races in the Flogas Novice Chase at Leopardstown.

Coral Cup (2m5f) Cheltenham

2009	**Ninetieth Minute**	6-10-3	T Taaffe	P W Flood	14-1	27
2010	**Spirit River**	5-11-2	N Henderson	B Geraghty	14-1	28
2011	**Carlito Brigante**	5-11-0	G Elliott	D Russell	16-1	22
2012	**Son Of Flicka**	8-10-6	D McCain	J Maguire	16-1	28
2013	**Medinas**	6-11-10	A King	W Hutchinson	33-1	28
2014	**Whisper**	6-11-11	N Henderson	N de Boinville (5)	14-1	28
2015	**Aux Ptits Soins**	5-10-7	P Nicholls	S Twiston-Davies	9-1	25
2016	**Diamond King**	8-11-3	G Elliott	D Russell	12-1	26
2017	**Supasundae**	7-11-4	J Harrington	R Power	16-1	25
2018	**Bleu Berry**	7-11-2	W Mullins	M Walsh	20-1	26

2018-19 RFO Jumps Racing Guide

THIS race has brought pain for punters, with just one winning outright favourite since its outright inception in 1993 and one winner priced in single figures since 2008. Siding with younger, progressive horses should be a good start as ten of the last 13 winners were second-season hurdlers. A light but successful campaign is also key as the last 11 winners had run no more than four times earlier in the season, though not necessarily with an eye on a plot. After all, 14 of the last 16 had managed a victory, nine of them last time out, and this is such a quality race these days that connections being too clever with the handicapper risk not getting a run at all. That has also given those near the top of the handicap a chance, shown by the fact that seven of the last nine winners carried 11st or more including Medinas and Whisper under big weights.

Queen Mother Champion Chase (2m) Cheltenham

Year	Horse	Weight	Trainer	Jockey	SP	Ran
2009	Master Minded	6-11-10	P Nicholls	R Walsh	4-11f	12
2010	Big Zeb	9-11-10	C Murphy	B Geraghty	10-1	9
2011	Sizing Europe	9-11-10	H de Bromhead	A Lynch	10-1	11
2012	Finian's Rainbow	9-11-10	N Henderson	B Geraghty	4-1	8
2013	Sprinter Sacre	7-11-10	N Henderson	B Geraghty	1-4f	7
2014	Sire De Grugy	8-11-10	G Moore	J Moore	11-4f	11
2015	Dodging Bullets	7-11-10	P Nicholls	S Twiston-Davies	9-2	9
2016	Sprinter Sacre	10-11-10	N Henderson	N de Boinville	5-1	10
2017	Special Tiara	10-11-10	H de Bromhead	N Fehily	11-1	10
2018	Altior	8-11-10	N Henderson	N de Boinville	Evsf	9

THE 2006 hero Newmill is the only winner in more than 25 years sent off bigger than 11-1 and, while it would be wrong to say that was easy to predict, it was nonetheless forecast in the pages of the RFO – Nick Watts tipped Newmill ante-post at 100-1! Newmill is also one of only three winners out of the last 19 to return bigger than 5-1 in a race that generally proves the most predictable of Cheltenham's championship races. The previous year's Arkle is the best pointer as Altior, Sprinter Sacre (for his first win), Sizing Europe, Voy Por Ustedes, Azertyuiop and Moscow Flyer have all followed up since 2003 and Douvan (injured when a 2-9 shot in 2017) is the only winner among the last 15 to run the following year not to be at least placed, while Dodging Bullets and Finian's Rainbow were also the highest-placed representatives from the Arkle when victorious. Also look at the Tingle Creek as five of the last 14 winners had won the Sandown Grade 1 earlier in the season, including three in a row from 2013 to 2015. However, defending champions have a poor record with just one of the last 15 to take part hanging on to their crown.

Weatherbys Champion Bumper (2m½f) Cheltenham

Year	Horse	Weight	Trainer	Jockey	SP	Ran
2009	Dunguib	6-11-5	P Fenton	Mr B O'Connell	9-2	24
2010	Cue Card	4-10-12	C Tizzard	J Tizzard	40-1	24
2011	Cheltenian	5-11-5	P Hobbs	R Johnson	14-1	24
2012	Champagne Fever	5-11-5	W Mullins	Mr P Mullins	16-1	20
2013	Briar Hill	5-11-5	W Mullins	R Walsh	25-1	23
2014	Silver Concorde	6-11-5	D Weld	Mr R McNamara	16-1	22
2015	Moon Racer	6-11-5	D Pipe	T Scudamore	9-2f	23
2016	Ballyandy	5-11-5	N Twiston-Davies	S Twiston-Davies	5-1	23
2017	Fayonagh	6-10-12	G Elliott	Mr J Codd	7-1	22
2018	Relegate	5-10-12	W Mullins	Ms K Walsh	25-1	23

BONANZA time for Ireland, winners of 19 of the 26 runnings with nine-time winner Willie Mullins leading the way in style. British trainers have cottoned on to the strength of

Irish bumper form and also now try to buy the best Irish prospects, so in total 16 of the 18 winners this century made their debut in Ireland, with Ballyandy and Cue Card the exceptions. Cue Card is also the only successful four-year-old since Dato Star in 1995 as older horses tend to prove too strong, with the early dominance of five-year-olds now challenged by more and more top-class six-year-olds being held back for the race. Favourites have a poor record with just three winners, while horses who have been off the track since the turn of the year have accounted for seven of the last 17 winners from very few runners.

Pertemps Final (3m) Cheltenham

2009	Kayf Aramis	7-10-5	V Williams	A Coleman	16-1	22
2010	Buena Vista	9-10-4	D Pipe	H Frost (3)	16-1	24
2011	Buena Vista	10-10-8	D Pipe	C O'Farrell (5)	20-1	23
2012	Cape Tribulation	8-10-11	M Jefferson	D O'Regan	14-1	24
2013	Holywell	6-11-4	J O'Neill	R McLernon	25-1	24
2014	Fingal Bay	8-11-12	P Hobbs	R Johnson	9-2f	23
2015	Call The Cops	6-10-12	N Henderson	A Tinkler	9-1	23
2016	Mall Dini	6-10-11	P Kelly	D Russell	14-1	24
2017	Presenting Percy	6-11-11	P Kelly	D Russell	11-1	24
2018	Delta Work	5-10-10	G Elliott	D Russell	6-1	23

THERE'S greater competition to merely get a run in all Cheltenham handicaps these days and that seems to have had a particularly profound effect on this race, giving younger horses much more of a chance against older, battle-hardened performers whose connections have perhaps had more of an opportunity to try to work their way down to a good mark without risking their spot. That certainly seems borne out by a run of four six-year-old winners in five years from 2013 to 2017 – the last winner of that age had been in 2005 – followed by the first winning five-year-old since 1988 when Delta Work triumphed last year. The change has certainly been good news for punters because three of the last five winners were sent off in single figures after ten in a row had been bigger, including two at 50-1. It's still best to stick to lower weights, though, as eight of the last 11 winners carried no more than 10st 12lb and the bottom weight carried just 11st 2lb when one of the exceptions, Presenting Percy, won in 2017.

Ryanair Chase (2m5f) Cheltenham

2009	Imperial Commander	8-11-10	N Twiston-Davies	P Brennan	6-1	10
2010	Albertas Run	9-11-10	J O'Neill	A McCoy	14-1	13
2011	Albertas Run	10-11-10	J O'Neill	A McCoy	6-1	11
2012	Riverside Theatre	8-11-10	N Henderson	B Geraghty	7-2f	12
2013	Cue Card	7-11-10	C Tizzard	J Tizzard	7-2	8
2014	Dynaste	8-11-10	D Pipe	T Scudamore	3-1f	11
2015	Uxizandre	7-11-10	A King	T McCoy	16-1	14
2016	Vautour	7-11-10	W Mullins	R Walsh	Evsf	15
2017	Un De Sceaux	9-11-10	W Mullins	R Walsh	7-4f	8
2018	Balko Des Flos	7-11-10	H de Bromhead	D Russell	8-1	6

UPGRADED to Grade 1 status in 2008, this race has got stronger and stronger since its inception just three years earlier. The noticeable pattern over time has been that younger horses have taken over from their older rivals, with second-season chasers winning in five of the last six years and Un De Sceaux the only winning nine-year-old since 2011 after five of the first seven winners had been at least old, including three ten-year-olds.

Un De Sceaux and Cue Card were notable older failures last year, clearing the way for Balko Des Flos, who became only the second winner not to have already been successful at Cheltenham. In the early days of the race that made the BetVictor Gold Cup and the Caspian Caviar Gold Cup the key guides, but as the race has got classier it's Grade 1 form that is needed and five of the last nine winners were previous Cheltenham Festival heroes, with Uxizandre also beaten less than a length. Stamina is a more important asset than speed as seven of the last 11 winners had posted their best Racing Post Rating at 3m or beyond (two at intermediate trips and two at around 2m), while six of those 11 were also beaten in that season's King George.

Stayers' Hurdle (3m) Cheltenham

Year	Horse	Age-Wt	Trainer	Jockey	SP	Ran
2009	Big Buck's	6-11-10	P Nicholls	R Walsh	6-1	14
2010	Big Buck's	7-11-10	P Nicholls	R Walsh	5-6f	14
2011	Big Buck's	8-11-10	P Nicholls	R Walsh	10-11f	13
2012	Big Buck's	9-11-10	P Nicholls	R Walsh	5-6f	11
2013	Solwhit	9-11-10	C Byrnes	P Carberry	17-2	13
2014	More Of That	6-11-10	J O'Neill	B Geraghty	15-2	10
2015	Cole Harden	6-11-10	W Greatrex	G Sheehan	14-1	16
2016	Thistlecrack	8-11-10	C Tizzard	T Scudamore	Evsf	12
2017	Nichols Canyon	7-11-10	W Mullins	R Walsh	10-1	12
2018	Penhill	7-11-10	W Mullins	P Townend	12-1	15

THREE horses – Big Buck's, Inglis Drever and Baracouda – shared nine of the last 11 runnings from 2002 to 2012 between them and this would be an even more amazing race for former champions if all but one subsequent winner hadn't been prevented from returning 12 months on. That's largely because 3m form is rarely turned around – horses beaten in the race previously rarely step up, with Derring Rose in 1981 the last to win having finished out of the first two 12 months earlier, and only three winners this century had been beaten in a 3m Graded hurdle earlier in the season. For that reason the market has been a strong guide in this time – 16 of the last 18 winners came from the first four in the betting – with the danger to the defending champion or established form horse coming from those stepping up in trip. In fact a lack of proven stamina shouldn't be considered a negative at all as seven of the last 13 first-time winners were triumphing over 3m for the first time and class is more important as Cole Harden and Thistlecrack are the only winners since Princeful in 1998 not to have won a Graded race shorter than 2m5f.

Triumph Hurdle (2m1f) Cheltenham

Year	Horse	Age-Wt	Trainer	Jockey	SP	Ran
2009	Zaynar	4-11-0	N Henderson	B Geraghty	11-2	18
2010	Soldatino	4-11-0	N Henderson	B Geraghty	6-1	17
2011	Zarkandar	4-11-0	P Nicholls	D Jacob	13-2	23
2012	Countrywide Flame	4-11-0	J Quinn	D Costello	33-1	20
2013	Our Conor	4-11-0	D Hughes	B Cooper	4-1	17
2014	Tiger Roll	4-11-0	G Elliott	D Russell	10-1	15
2015	Peace And Co	4-11-0	N Henderson	B Geraghty	2-1f	16
2016	Ivanovich Gorbatov	4-11-0	A O'Brien	B Geraghty	9-2f	15
2017	Defi Du Seuil	4-11-0	P Hobbs	R Johnson	5-2f	15
2018	Farclas	4-11-0	G Elliott	J Kennedy	9-1	9

THE juvenile championship has benefited greatly from the advent of the Fred Winter in 2005, with the loss of many of the also-rans helping the cream to rise to the top. Of the 14 subsequent winners, only the subsequent Champion Hurdle third Countrywide Flame was sent off bigger than 10-1. At the same time experience has become less of a factor, with Zarkandar even winning after just one outing over hurdles and three of the last five winners never having run on the Flat, which used to be almost guaranteed with 12 of the previous 13 having done so. If still considering one coming via the Flat, bear in mind that Our Conor is the only winner in recent times who ran on the Flat but wasn't tried over at least 1m4f. The last six Irish-trained winners had run in the Grade 1 Spring Hurdle at Leopardstown on their previous start, while six of the last ten British-trained winners had landed the Finesse Hurdle at Cheltenham or the Adonis Hurdle at Kempton. Nineteen of the last 25 winners passed the post first on their previous run (Scolardy had been disqualified before winning in 2002).

County Hurdle (2m1f) Cheltenham

2009	American Trilogy	5-11-0	P Nicholls	R Walsh	20-1	27
2010	Thousand Stars	6-10-5	W Mullins	Ms K Walsh	20-1	28
2011	Final Approach	5-10-12	W Mullins	R Walsh	10-1	26
2012	Alderwood	8-11-1	T Mullins	A McCoy	20-1	26
2013	Ted Veale	6-10-6	T Martin	B Cooper	10-1	28
2014	Lac Fontana	5-10-11	P Nicholls	D Jacob	11-1	28
2015	Wicklow Brave	6-11-4	W Mullins	P Townend	25-1	24
2016	Superb Story	5-10-12	D Skelton	H Skelton	8-1	26
2017	Arctic Fire	8-11-12	W Mullins	P Townend	20-1	25
2018	Mohaayed	6-10-11	D Skelton	B Andrews (3)	33-1	24

MUCH like in the Imperial Cup, another fiercely competitive 2m handicap hurdle, young horses have a big edge. Ten five-year-olds have won in the last 17 years and the 15 winners prior to Arctic Fire in 2017 were all novices (six) or had been novices the previous season (nine), although the last winner without handicap experience was Thumbs Up in 1993 with more than 60 having failed since. Ireland have won eight of the last 12 runnings, which is remarkable given that Pedrobob was only the second in 25 years when he won in 2007, and five of the last nine Irish winners were at least placed in the Coral Hurdle at Leopardstown or the Betfair Hurdle at Newbury. The last two exceptions, Arctic Fire and Wicklow Brave, were both trained by Willie Mullins and are also the only winners to carry more than 11st 1lb since Spirit Leader in 2003.

Albert Bartlett Novices' Hurdle (3m) Cheltenham

2009	Weapon's Amnesty	6-11-7	C Byrnes	D Russell	8-1	17
2010	Berties Dream	7-11-7	P J Gilligan	A Lynch	33-1	19
2011	Bobs Worth	6-11-7	N Henderson	B Geraghty	15-8f	18
2012	Brindisi Breeze	6-11-7	L Russell	C Gillies	7-1	20
2013	At Fishers Cross	6-11-7	R Curtis	A McCoy	11-8f	13
2014	Very Wood	5-11-7	N Meade	P Carberry	33-1	18
2015	Martello Tower	7-11-4	M Mullins	A Heskin	14-1	19
2016	Unowhatimeanharry	8-11-5	H Fry	N Fehily	11-1	19
2017	Penhill	6-11-5	W Mullins	P Townend	16-1	15
2018	Kilbricken Storm	7-11-5	C Tizzard	H Cobden	33-1	20

THOUGH not run as a Grade 1 until 2008, this has always been a level-weights affair since its inception three years earlier. Unowhatimeanharry won as an eight-year-old in 2016 and there have been five winning seven-year-olds, including 33-1 shot Kilbricken Storm last year, which is very unusual for a top novice hurdle. The importance of stamina and experience is also shown by the fact that all 14 winners had run at least three times

LORD WINDERMERE (left): the most baffling Gold Cup winner of recent times, but he was a solid trends pick as a second-season chaser and RSA winner

over hurdles (six of them at least six times) and 11 had also been tried over at least 3m. Seven of the nine non-Irish winners (French-trained Moulin Riche won the inaugural running) had run at least twice at Cheltenham and finished first or second, five of them winning, while Kilbricken Storm had also won his only start at the track.

Cheltenham Gold Cup (3m2½f) Cheltenham

2009	**Kauto Star**	9-11-10	P Nicholls	R Walsh	7-4f	16
2010	**Imperial Commander**	9-11-10	N Twiston-Davies	P Brennan	7-1	11
2011	**Long Run**	6-11-10	N Henderson	Mr S W-Cohen	7-2f	13
2012	**Synchronised**	9-11-10	J O'Neill	A McCoy	8-1	14
2013	**Bobs Worth**	8-11-10	N Henderson	B Geraghty	11-4f	9
2014	**Lord Windermere**	8-11-10	J Culloty	D Russell	20-1	13
2015	**Coneygree**	8-11-10	M Bradstock	N de Boinville	7-1	16
2016	**Don Cossack**	9-11-10	G Elliott	B Cooper	9-4f	9
2017	**Sizing John**	7-11-10	J Harrington	R Power	7-1	13
2018	**Native River**	8-11-10	C Tizzard	R Johnson	5-1	15

AS the Gold Cup has increasingly become the be-all and end-all for top staying chasers, winners tend to be proven top-class performers who have been wrapped in cotton wool during the season. Don Cossack is the only winner since Kauto Star in 2007 to have run more than three times earlier in the campaign and even he had been off since early January, while the last 19 winners had already struck at the top level. That's certainly made the race more predictable as eight of the last 16 favourites have won, with just one winner since 1999 priced bigger than 8-1. Lord Windermere was the exception, but even he was a solid trends pick having won the previous year's RSA Chase, which has provided four of the last 11 winners with Lord Windermere, Bobs Worth and Denman doing the double. That trio are among a raft of winners for inexperienced horses, with eight of the last 14 in their first or second season over fences, headed of course by the remarkable Coneygree, who was the first winning novice since Captain Christy in 1974. The key races during the season are the King George and the Lexus Chase as 15 of the last 19 winners ran in one of those contests. Horses older than nine struggle, with Cool Dawn the last to win in 1998 – there have since been 15 sent off at 8-1 or shorter including four favourites – while Native River was the first horse to make the necessary improvement after being beaten in their first attempt at the race since See More Business in 1999, with 66 beaten in the interim.

Christie's Foxhunter Chase (3m2½f) Cheltenham

Year	Horse	Age-Wt	Trainer	Jockey	SP	Ran
2009	Cappa Bleu	7-12-0	Mrs E Crow	Mr R Burton	11-2	24
2010	Baby Run	10-12-0	N Twiston-Davies	Mr S Twiston-Davies	9-2jf	24
2011	Zemsky	8-12-0	I Ferguson	Mr D O'Connor	33-1	24
2012	Salsify	7-12-0	R Sweeney	Mr C Sweeney	7-1	22
2013	Salsify	8-12-0	R Sweeney	Mr C Sweeney	2-1f	23
2014	Tammys Hill	9-12-0	L Lennon	Mr J Smyth	15-2	24
2015	On The Fringe	10-12-0	E Bolger	Ms N Carberry	6-1	24
2016	On The Fringe	11-12-0	E Bolger	Ms N Carberry	13-8f	24
2017	Pacha Du Polder	10-12-0	P Nicholls	Miss B Frost	16-1	23
2018	Pacha Du Polder	11-12-0	P Nicholls	Miss H Tucker	25-1	24

THIS is regarded as a lottery by many punters and six of the last 13 winners were at least 16-1, but with the other seven no bigger than 15-2 it's clearly been kind to some. Pacha Du Polder last year became the third winner since 2013 to successfully defend their crown, but the key is to rule out any horse older than ten barring these former champions, with the 2000 winner Cavalero the only first-time winner aged 11 or older since 1989. It's also vital to side with in-form horses rather than formerly classy horses on the downgrade as 24 of the last 32 winners had been successful last time out. Cappa Bleu was very unusual in winning on his debut under rules in 2009, while six of the subsequent nine runnings have gone to Ireland.

Grand Annual H'cap Chase (2m½f) Cheltenham

Year	Horse	Age-Wt	Trainer	Jockey	SP	Ran
2009	Oh Crick	6-10-0	A King	W Hutchinson	7-1	18
2010	Pigeon Island	7-10-1	N Twiston-Davies	P Brennan	16-1	19
2011	Oiseau De Nuit	9-11-6	C Tizzard	S Clements (7)	40-1	23
2012	Bellvano	8-10-2	N Henderson	P Carberry	20-1	21
2013	Alderwood	9-10-11	T Mullins	A McCoy	3-1f	23
2014	Savello	8-11-5	T Martin	D Russell	16-1	23
2015	Next Sensation	8-11-2	M Scudamore	T Scudamore	16-1	20
2016	Solar Impulse	6-11-0	P Nicholls	S Twiston-Davies	28-1	24
2017	Rock The World	9-11-5	J Harrington	R Power	10-1	24
2018	Le Prezien	7-11-8	P Nicholls	B Geraghty	15-2	22

CHELTENHAM is one of the few places where you see 2m handicaps run at such a fast and furious pace and those who have excelled at the course before, especially in this race, tend to go well. Eight of the last 11 British-trained winners had previously been successful at Cheltenham, with one of the exceptions, Next Sensation, placed in this race, and while Irish horses are an increasing factor with seven winners in the last 19 runnings even then Rock The World and Tiger Cry had been placed in a previous running and Alderwood had won a County Hurdle. It takes a strong, mature horse to cope with the demands of the Grand Annual yet you also want one unexposed enough to still be ahead of the handicapper. Ten of the last 15 winners were eight or older even though most of those at head of the market are younger, including ten favourites in that time, but even so just one of the last 17 winners had run more than 12 times over fences.

Betway Bowl (3m1f) Aintree

2009	Madison Du Berlais	8-11-10	D Pipe	T Scudamore	12-1	10
2010	What A Friend	7-11-7	P Nicholls	R Walsh	5-2	5
2011	Nacarat	10-11-7	T George	P Brennan	7-2	6
2012	Follow The Plan	9-11-7	O McKiernan	T Doyle	50-1	11
2013	First Lieutenant	8-11-7	M Morris	T Cooper	7-2	8
2014	Siliviniaco Conti	8-11-7	P Nicholls	N Fehily	9-4	6
2015	Siliviniaco Conti	9-11-7	P Nicholls	N Fehily	7-4f	7
2016	Cue Card	10-11-7	C Tizzard	P Brennan	6-5f	9
2017	Tea For Two	8-11-7	N Williams	L Kelly	10-1	7
2018	Might Bite	9-11-7	N Henderson	N de Boinville	4-5f	7

THIS race is Aintree's version of the Gold Cup, but it rarely attracts the winner of the big one and the record of the three who have tried to do the double – Imperial Commander, Desert Orchid and Dawn Run – won't tempt many more to try it as all of them failed to complete. That's part of a wider trend because, of the 22 winners to have come via the Gold Cup, 14 of them finished outside the top four at Cheltenham. Not only were they likely to have avoided a harder race, but Prestbury Park form can always be turned around at this sharp, flat course that, despite being left-handed, has more in common with Kempton. Indeed, form at the Sunbury track seems to be key as 11 of the last 19 winners had been first or second in a King George, with Silviniaco Conti winning both races twice while Might Bite and Cue Card also did the double. Of the exceptions, Tea For Two and Madison Du Berlais had produced their best runs at Kempton and Nacarat had twice won the Racing Post Chase.

Randox Health Grand National (4m2½f) Aintree

2009	Mon Mome	9-11-0	V Williams	L Treadwell	100-1	40
2010	Don't Push It	10-11-5	J O'Neill	A McCoy	10-1jf	40
2011	Ballabriggs	10-11-0	D McCain	J Maguire	14-1	40
2012	Neptune Collonges	11-11-6	P Nicholls	D Jacob	33-1	40
2013	Auroras Encore	11-10-3	S Smith	R Mania	66-1	40
2014	Pineau De Re	11-10-6	Dr R Newland	L Aspell	25-1	40
2015	Many Clouds	8-11-9	O Sherwood	L Aspell	25-1	39
2016	Rule The World	9-10-7	M Morris	D Mullins	33-1	39
2017	One For Arthur	8-10-11	L Russell	D Fox	14-1	40
2018	Tiger Roll	8-10-13	G Elliott	D Russell	10-1	38

FOR such a unique challenge, it's remarkable that previous Grand Nationals are such a poor guide to this race – 21 of the last 26 winners had never run in it before and four of the five exceptions failed to complete, with no horse winning it more than once since Red Rum and Amberleigh House the only winner in this period to have placed previously as others get weighted out of contention. The Becher and the Topham over the same fences have thrown up a fair number of winners, but the best guides are other major staying handicaps like the Ladbrokes Trophy, the Welsh National and the Irish National. A light weight used to be the key trend and remains a big help – 59 of the 66 top-11 finishers in the last six years were below 11st – but the condensing of the handicap in recent years has given class horses more of a chance, with Many Clouds, Neptune Collonges, Ballabriggs, Don't Push It and Mon Mome all defying 11st or more in the last eight years after Hedgehunter in 2005 had been the first since Corbiere 22 years earlier. Winners still tend to have hidden their ability from the handicapper that season as ten of the last 19 winners hadn't won at all over fences and 16 of them no more than once. Don't back at

OUR DUKE: very much the exception to the rule in the Irish National

starting price but take the best available odds non-runner no-bet in the days before the race as prices tend to shorten dramatically close to start time.

Scottish Grand National (4m) Ayr

2009	**Hello Bud**	11-10-9	N Twiston-Davies	P Brennan	12-1	17
2010	**Merigo**	9-10-0	A Parker	T Murphy	18-1	30
2011	**Beshabar**	9-10-4	T Vaughan	R Johnson	15-2	28
2012	**Merigo**	11-10-2	A Parker	T Murphy	15-2	24
2013	**Godsmejudge**	7-11-3	A King	W Hutchinson	12-1	24
2014	**Al Co**	9-10-0	P Bowen	J Moore	40-1	29
2015	**Wayward Prince**	11-10-1	H Parrott	R Dunne	25-1	29
2016	**Vicente**	7-11-3	P Nicholls	S Twiston-Davies	14-1	28
2017	**Vicente**	8-11-10	P Nicholls	S Twiston-Davies	9-1jf	30
2018	**Joe Farrell**	9-10-6	R Curtis	A Wedge	33-1	29

THIS has been a lean race for punters, with 9-1 shot Vicente the only winning favourite since Paris Pike in 2000 and some real skinners in that time, topped by 66-1 shot Iris De Balme romping to victory in 2008. Vicente had fallen at the first in the Grand National, but in general running at Aintree is a big negative as he is the only winner to come via the National since Little Polveir in 1987. Similarly, ignore Cheltenham Festival winners as none have followed up in more than 30 years, though the ground tends to be fast which can also render soft-ground winter form redundant. Instead it's best to look back at previous Scottish Nationals, with Vicente and Merigo winning four of the last nine renewals between them and Godsmejudge also finishing second 12 months after his 2013 victory. There are no conclusive trends with regard to weight – 12 of the last 29 winners carried the minimum of 10st, ranging up to 26lb out of the handicap, but seven of the last 20 carried more than 11st and Vicente, Grey Abbey and Young Kenny defied welter burdens. The best bet is to side with a novice, with ten winners in 25 years from small representation.

Irish Grand National (3m5f) Fairyhouse

2009	Niche Market	8-10-5	R Buckler	H Skelton (5)	33-1	28
2010	Bluesea Cracker	8-10-4	J Motherway	A J McNamara	25-1	26
2011	Organisedconfusion	6-9-13	A Moore	Miss N Carberry	12-1	25
2012	Lion Na Bearnai	10-10-5	T Gibney	A Thornton	33-1	29
2013	Liberty Counsel	10-9-10	D Love	B Dalton (5)	50-1	28
2014	Shutthefrontdoor	7-10-13	J O'Neill	B Geraghty	8-1f	26
2015	Thunder And Roses	7-10-6	S Hughes	K Walsh	20-1	28
2016	Rogue Angel	8-10-9	M Morris	G Fox (3)	16-1	27
2017	Our Duke	7-11-4	J Harrington	R Power	9-2f	28
2018	General Principle	9-10-0	G Elliott	JJ Slevin	20-1	30

OUR DUKE was a stunning winner of this race in 2017, but that was all the more remarkable because light weights are generally so strongly favoured – 17 of the last 18 winners carried less than 11st. The main reason is that this tends to be a race for young horses just starting to realise their potential as they step up in trip, with Rogue Angel the only winner since Mudahim in 1998 to have run more than 13 times over fences and Our Duke the ninth in that time carrying novice status. That can also make it a hard race to call, with ten of the last 13 winners sent off 20-1 or bigger. British raiders have traditionally had an awful record, but that's changed in recent times with Shutthefrontdoor the fourth successful raider in 11 years when he won in 2014.

bet365 Gold Cup (3m5f) Sandown

2009	Hennessy	8-10-7	C Llewellyn	A McCoy	13-2	14
2010	Church Island	11-10-5	M Hourigan	A Heskin (7)	20-1	19
2011	Poker De Sivola	8-10-12	F Murphy	T Murphy	11-1	18
2012	Tidal Bay	11-11-12	P Nicholls	D Jacob	9-1	19
2013	Quentin Collonges	9-10-12	H Daly	A Tinkler	14-1	19
2014	Hadrian's Approach	7-11-0	N Henderson	B Geraghty	10-1	19
2015	Just A Par	8-10-3	P Nicholls	S Bowen (3)	14-1	20
2016	The Young Master	7-11-1	N Mulholland	Mr S Waley-Cohen (3)	8-1	20
2017	Henllan Harri	9-10-0	P Bowen	S Bowen	40-1	13
2018	Step Back	8-10-0	M Bradstock	J Moore	7-1	20

AS in so many staying chases, light weights are favoured – 25 of the last 30 winners carried less than 11st (including The Young Master with Sam Waley-Cohen's 3lb claim) and the best winner of recent times, Tidal Bay, was a rare beast indeed when defying 11st 12lb. However, that still hasn't helped punters as the race is a graveyard for favourites, with Mr Frisk the last outright market leader to prevail when becoming the only horse to follow up a Grand National victory in 1990. He's one of ten winners to have come via Aintree since 1973 and seven of them had failed to get beyond Becher's on the second circuit. Most winners had run at the Cheltenham Festival – 27 of the last 44 in all – but none of them had won there.

2018-19 RFO Jumps Racing Guide

Track Facts

WANT course statistics? Look no further – this section contains all the numbers you'll need for every jumps track in Britain.

Course by course, we've set out four-year trainer and jockey statistics, favourites' records, winning pointers and three-dimensional racecourse maps, plus details of how to get there and fixtures for the new season.

Following this, from page 220, we've got details of course records and standard times for each track. Note that we have been unable to produce standard times in a few cases as there have not been enough recent races over the trip at the track in question.

See also our statistical assessment of last season's records from Britain's top ten trainers (page 119).

AINTREE	177-178
ASCOT	179
AYR	180
BANGOR	181
CARLISLE	182
CARTMEL	183
CATTERICK	184
CHELTENHAM	185-186
CHEPSTOW	187
DONCASTER	188
EXETER	189
FAKENHAM	190
FFOS LAS	191
FONTWELL	192
HAYDOCK	193
HEREFORD	194
HEXHAM	195
HUNTINGDON	196
KELSO	197
KEMPTON	198
LEICESTER	199
LINGFIELD	200
LUDLOW	201
MARKET RASEN	202
MUSSELBURGH	203
NEWBURY	204
NEWCASTLE	205
NEWTON ABBOT	206
PERTH	207
PLUMPTON	208
SANDOWN	209
SEDGEFIELD	210
SOUTHWELL	211
STRATFORD	212
TAUNTON	213
TOWCESTER	214
UTTOXETER	215
WARWICK	216
WETHERBY	217
WINCANTON	218
WORCESTER	219

2018-19 RFO Jumps Racing Guide

AINTREE

Ormskirk Rd, Liverpool,
L9 5AS. Tel: 0151 523 2600

How to get there Road: M6, M62, M57, M58. Rail: Liverpool Lime Street and taxi.

Features The left-handed 2m2f giant triangular Grand National course is perfectly flat. Inside it, the sharp left-handed Mildmay course is 1m4f in circumference.

2018-19 Fixtures
October 28, November 10, December 8, April 4-6

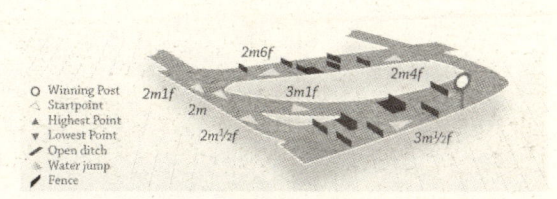

Trainers	Wins-Runs	%	Hurdles	Chases	£1 level stks
Nicky Henderson	25-116	22	16-69	7-36	+22.61
Paul Nicholls	14-127	11	4-42	9-77	-45.63
Colin Tizzard	12-47	26	4-16	8-31	+101.49
Tom George	10-64	16	2-14	6-45	+17.33
Nigel Twiston-Davies	8-84	10	3-34	5-46	-36.25
Dan Skelton	8-73	11	6-45	2-24	-47.83
W P Mullins	8-52	15	5-24	2-23	-12.40
Philip Hobbs	7-74	9	4-35	3-33	-37.05
Jonjo O'Neill	6-73	8	4-38	2-31	-29.90
Peter Bowen	5-59	8	2-31	2-23	-29.25
Rebecca Curtis	5-46	11	3-17	1-26	-27.14
David Pipe	4-58	7	2-23	2-35	-12.38
Alan King	4-54	7	3-30	1-14	-30.38

Jockeys	Wins-Rides	%	£1 level stks	Best Trainer	W-R
Richard Johnson	12-91	13	+8.64	Philip Hobbs	4-43
Nico de Boinville	11-49	22	+13.42	Nicky Henderson	10-35
Noel Fehily	8-55	15	-14.50	Harry Fry	2-15
Barry Geraghty	8-52	15	-4.22	Rebecca Curtis	2-7
Brian Hughes	7-93	8	-10.04	Malcolm Jefferson	3-16
Aidan Coleman	7-76	9	-43.83	Jonjo O'Neill	3-20
Sean Bowen	7-64	11	-30.25	Peter Bowen	4-39
Tom Scudamore	6-65	9	+7.91	David Pipe	4-40
Harry Skelton	6-61	10	-41.13	Dan Skelton	6-56
Daryl Jacob	6-55	11	-26.00	Nicky Henderson	4-16
Sam Twiston-Davies	5-67	7	-27.38	Paul Nicholls	5-43
Paddy Brennan	5-47	11	-17.97	Tom George	3-22
A P Heskin	5-30	17	+19.50	Tom George	5-26

Favourites
Hurdle 36.1% +4.02   Chase 29.5% -2.32   TOTAL 32.4% -4.43

2018-19 *RFO Jumps Racing Guide*

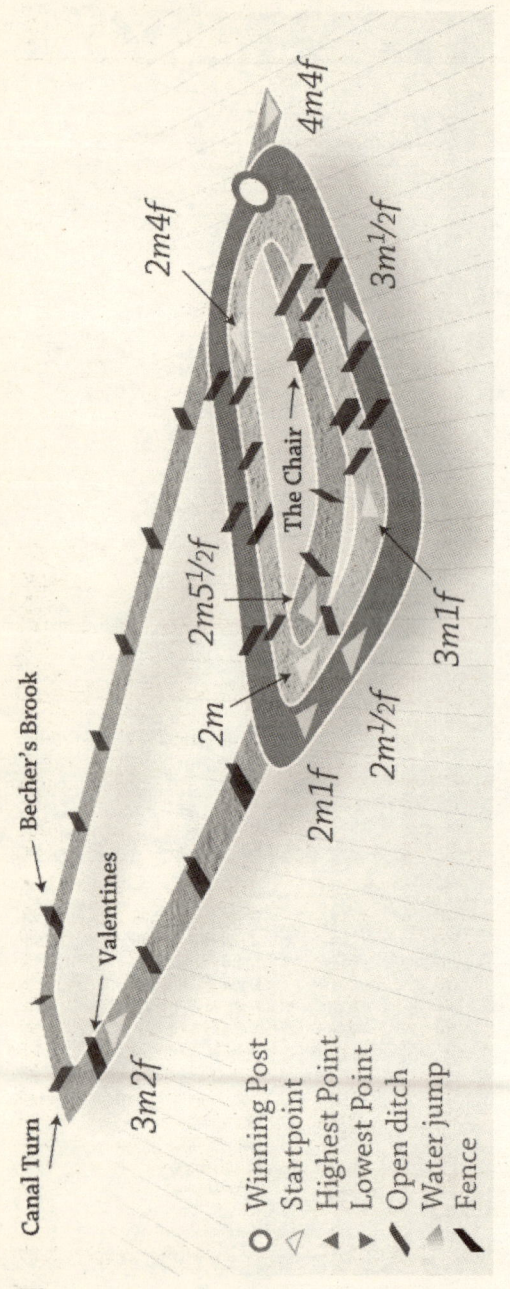

Aintree's Grand National course – used in the Becher Chase, the Grand Sefton Chase, the Topham Chase, the Foxhunters' Chase and the Grand National

2018-19 *RFO Jumps Racing Guide*

ASCOT

Ascot, Berkshire SL5 7JX
0870 7227 227

How to get there Road: M4 junction 6 or M3 junction 3 on to A332. Rail: Frequent service from Reading or Waterloo

Features Right-handed

2018-19 Fixtures
November 3, 23-24, December 21-22, January 19, February 16, March 31

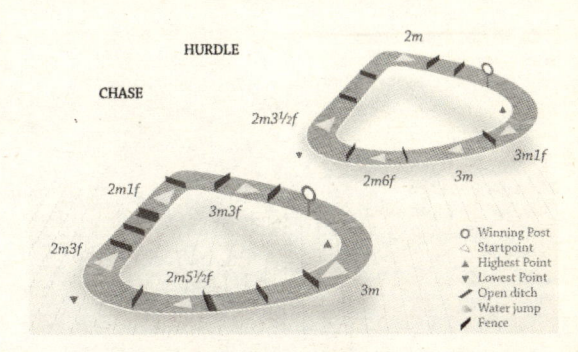

Trainers	Wins-Runs	%	Hurdles	Chases	£1 level stks
Nicky Henderson	26-133	20	16-85	8-35	-30.45
Paul Nicholls	25-129	19	8-53	16-70	-15.23
Harry Fry	14-53	26	11-30	3-18	+1.04
Philip Hobbs	10-73	14	4-31	4-38	-2.09
Alan King	9-67	13	7-52	1-9	-32.47
Venetia Williams	9-63	14	3-13	6-48	+17.25
Gary Moore	7-71	10	2-29	5-33	-17.50
Colin Tizzard	6-58	10	3-18	3-35	-27.72
Charlie Longsdon	6-48	13	2-20	3-21	+24.00
David Pipe	6-38	16	4-24	2-14	-0.25
W P Mullins	5-13	38	2-7	3-5	-5.74
Oliver Sherwood	4-25	16	0-14	3-9	-3.38
Jonjo O'Neill	3-51	6	1-22	2-29	-16.50

Jockeys	Wins-Rides	%	£1 level stks	Best Trainer	W-R
Barry Geraghty	21-74	28	+29.41	Nicky Henderson	6-27
Nico de Boinville	14-53	26	+10.18	Nicky Henderson	13-36
Aidan Coleman	13-86	15	+28.75	Venetia Williams	7-29
Sam Twiston-Davies	12-66	18	-15.14	Paul Nicholls	11-48
Noel Fehily	10-60	17	-6.41	Harry Fry	5-32
Jamie Moore	8-50	16	+13.50	Gary Moore	7-32
R Walsh	7-13	54	+2.75	W P Mullins	4-8
Richard Johnson	6-60	10	-21.15	Philip Hobbs	4-33
Leighton Aspell	6-44	14	+7.63	Oliver Sherwood	4-18
Daryl Jacob	6-42	14	-15.62	Nicky Henderson	2-10
Wayne Hutchinson	6-41	15	-16.60	Alan King	6-37
Tom O'Brien	5-50	10	-7.50	Philip Hobbs	4-21
Tom Scudamore	5-48	10	-20.75	David Pipe	3-22

Favourites
Hurdle 38.5% -0.77   Chase 31.2% -17.03   TOTAL 33.7% -26.26

AYR

2018-19 RFO Jumps Racing Guide

Whitletts Road, Ayr, KA8 0JE
Tel: 01292 264 179

How to get there Road: south from Glasgow on A77 or A75, A70, A76. Rail: Ayr

Features Left-handed 1m4f oval, easy turns, slight uphill finish

2018-19 Fixtures
October 29, November 3, 14, 29, January 2, 8, 20, February 6, 12, 25, March 9, April 12-13

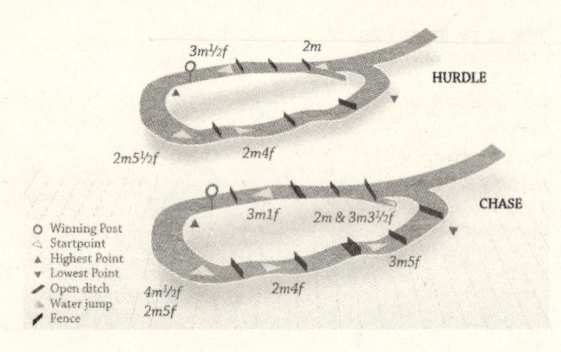

Trainers	Wins-Runs	%	Hurdles	Chases	£1 level stks
Nicky Richards	34-143	24	19-88	7-37	-13.58
Lucinda Russell	29-237	12	13-125	13-86	-94.12
N W Alexander	21-191	11	10-111	10-64	-68.72
Donald McCain	14-71	20	7-33	6-30	-19.74
S R B Crawford	13-107	12	9-67	2-22	-50.98
James Ewart	11-89	12	6-44	2-20	-18.20
Iain Jardine	10-51	20	7-35	1-8	+4.23
Martin Todhunter	10-50	20	4-22	6-27	+18.23
Dan Skelton	10-44	23	6-26	3-16	-4.01
Stuart Coltherd	9-50	18	6-28	3-21	+20.00
Ian Duncan	8-71	11	5-41	3-22	+8.75
Sandy Thomson	8-47	17	4-22	2-16	-15.03
Malcolm Jefferson	8-41	20	4-15	3-18	+0.30

Jockeys	Wins-Rides	%	£1 level stks	Best Trainer	W-R
Brian Hughes	45-210	21	+3.62	Donald McCain	7-13
Brian Harding	20-113	18	-1.57	Nicky Richards	12-51
Craig Nichol	15-128	12	-16.08	Nicky Richards	8-34
Derek Fox	13-128	10	-18.83	Lucinda Russell	9-80
Henry Brooke	11-103	11	-21.63	Martin Todhunter	3-24
Peter Buchanan	10-56	18	+7.13	Lucinda Russell	8-43
Ryan Day	10-48	21	-11.42	Nicky Richards	7-30
Ross Chapman	9-41	22	+11.73	Iain Jardine	5-17
Harry Skelton	9-38	24	-2.01	Dan Skelton	9-34
Stephen Mulqueen	8-77	10	-53.11	Nicky Richards	3-6
Lucy Alexander	7-90	8	-30.50	N W Alexander	6-61
Dale Irving	7-49	14	-1.25	James Ewart	5-20
Jamie Hamilton	7-48	15	-0.87	Alison Hamilton	3-18

Favourites
Hurdle 38.5% -11.73   Chase 38% +11.22   TOTAL 39% -2.88

BANGOR

Bangor-on-Dee, nr Wrexham
Clwyd. Tel: 01948 860 438

How to get there Road: A525. Rail: Wrexham

Features Left-handed, 1m4f round, quite sharp, final fence gets plenty of fallers

2018-19 Fixtures
October 3, 30, November 14, December 1, 14, January 8, February 8, March 23, April 13

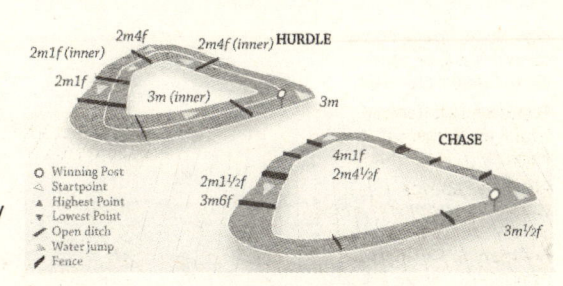

Trainers	Wins-Runs	%	Hurdles	Chases	£1 level stks
Donald McCain	50-248	20	36-158	12-65	+29.43
Dan Skelton	21-71	30	12-45	8-19	+6.87
Alan King	16-50	32	10-26	3-12	+3.19
Jonjo O'Neill	12-88	14	4-43	5-40	-19.13
Warren Greatrex	11-37	30	6-22	2-7	-1.86
Rebecca Curtis	10-52	19	5-22	4-19	-5.67
Nigel Twiston-Davies	10-52	19	3-21	5-21	-18.36
Charlie Longsdon	9-54	17	6-33	3-17	-19.03
Henry Daly	9-40	23	6-21	1-11	+36.75
Venetia Williams	8-72	11	1-29	7-40	-28.34
Peter Bowen	8-45	18	5-19	2-20	+2.58
Jennie Candlish	7-54	13	4-34	3-14	-26.90
Kim Bailey	6-42	14	3-22	2-16	-24.07

Jockeys	Wins-Rides	%	£1 level stks	Best Trainer	W-R
Will Kennedy	22-119	18	+29.92	Donald McCain	20-81
Harry Skelton	17-56	30	+11.78	Dan Skelton	17-51
Richard Johnson	14-70	20	-2.02	Charlie Longsdon	4-6
Wayne Hutchinson	12-61	20	-23.31	Alan King	11-31
Noel Fehily	12-59	20	-13.95	Harry Fry	5-15
Brian Hughes	11-53	21	+20.38	Donald McCain	4-6
Gavin Sheehan	11-42	26	+13.95	Warren Greatrex	7-21
Tom Scudamore	10-44	23	-6.13	David Pipe	6-17
Sean Bowen	8-45	18	+7.00	Peter Bowen	6-27
Sean Quinlan	8-40	20	+1.50	Jennie Candlish	5-31
Richie McLernon	7-43	16	+15.00	George Moore	2-2
Paddy Brennan	7-31	23	-2.30	Fergal O'Brien	3-10
James Cowley	7-28	25	+0.13	Donald McCain	7-27

Favourites
Hurdle 34.3% -40.20   Chase 42.3% +14.04   TOTAL 37.6% -29.45

2018-19 RFO Jumps Racing Guide

CARLISLE

Blackwell, Carlisle, CA2 4TS
Tel: 01228 522 973

How to get there Road: M6 Jctn 42. Rail: 2m from Citadel Station, Carlisle

Features Pear-shaped, 1m5f circuit, right-handed, undulating, uphill home straight

2018-19 Fixtures
October 18, 25, November 4, 12, December 2, 16, February 4, 18, 24, March 7, 17, 24, April 20

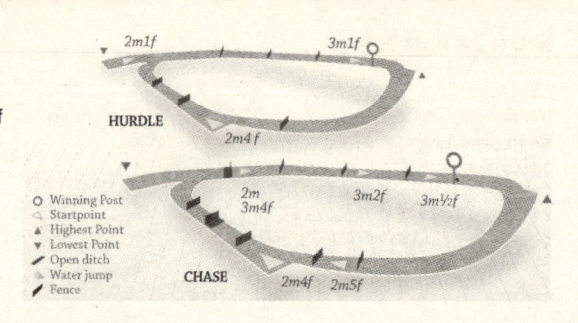

Trainers	Wins-Runs	%	Hurdles	Chases	£1 level stks
Donald McCain	26-165	16	16-106	8-48	-17.14
Sue Smith	16-99	16	2-29	13-62	-19.09
Nicky Richards	15-71	21	9-36	2-29	+11.94
S R B Crawford	12-29	41	5-11	0-7	+11.01
Brian Ellison	10-52	19	5-28	4-18	-20.79
Malcolm Jefferson	10-41	24	1-4	7-28	-2.67
Micky Hammond	9-101	9	6-52	3-42	-50.35
Jennie Candlish	9-61	15	1-31	8-25	-18.13
Alan Swinbank	9-29	31	6-19	2-5	+11.28
Rose Dobbin	8-62	13	2-28	6-27	-18.75
Venetia Williams	8-31	26	2-10	5-18	+8.91
Nigel Hawke	8-24	33	5-15	1-5	+5.13
Lucinda Russell	6-125	5	2-59	4-58	-85.25

Jockeys	Wins-Rides	%	£1 level stks	Best Trainer	W-R
Brian Hughes	38-197	19	-49.09	Malcolm Jefferson	10-40
Will Kennedy	17-77	22	+25.57	Donald McCain	14-63
Danny Cook	14-73	19	-10.13	Sue Smith	10-46
Brian Harding	12-94	13	-27.96	Nicky Richards	10-32
Craig Nichol	11-79	14	-21.75	Rose Dobbin	5-33
Richard Johnson	10-39	26	-3.89	S R B Crawford	2-3
Paul Moloney	8-28	29	+8.79	Alan Swinbank	7-23
Sean Quinlan	7-68	10	-38.42	Jennie Candlish	4-29
James Reveley	7-40	18	+13.08	Philip Kirby	2-4
Daragh Bourke	7-28	25	+31.25	Maurice Barnes	5-20
Sam Twiston-Davies	7-20	35	+1.73	Paul Nicholls	4-6
Aidan Coleman	6-29	21	-12.34	Venetia Williams	2-12
Henry Brooke	5-104	5	-76.47	Jennie Candlish	2-11

Favourites
Hurdle 39.4% -15.80   Chase 37% -14.43   TOTAL 38.8% -31.39

CARTMEL

Grange-over-Sands, Penrith
CA10 2HG. Tel: 01593 536 340

How to get there Road: M6 Jctn 36, A591. Rail: Cark-in-Cartmel or Grange-over-Sands

Features Tight, left-handed 1m circuit, undulating, half-mile run-in from last (longest in Britain)

2018-19 Fixtures
Summer jumping only

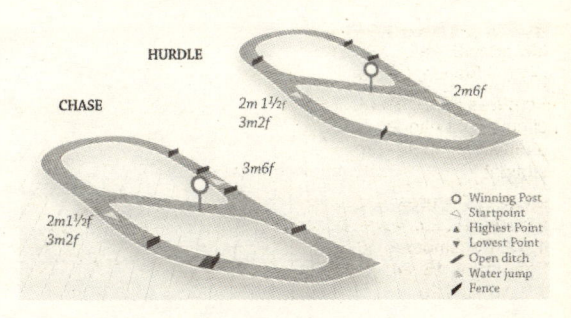

HURDLE 2m 1½f / 3m2f / 2m6f
CHASE 2m1½f / 3m2f / 3m6f

○ Winning Post
◁ Startpoint
▲ Highest Point
▼ Lowest Point
/ Open ditch
≈ Water jump
/ Fence

Trainers	Wins-Runs	%	Hurdles	Chases	£1 level stks
James Moffatt	21-153	14	14-107	7-46	+8.13
Donald McCain	19-97	20	16-61	3-36	-10.52
Peter Bowen	11-37	30	6-19	5-18	+13.13
Gordon Elliott	10-38	26	8-25	2-13	-4.55
Martin Todhunter	8-46	17	4-25	4-21	-6.63
Kenneth Slack	8-23	35	8-21	0-2	+51.00
Dianne Sayer	7-92	8	2-57	5-35	-50.17
Micky Hammond	6-51	12	1-26	5-25	-9.25
Jonjo O'Neill	6-19	32	3-11	3-8	+5.30
Richard Ford	5-20	25	1-8	4-12	+5.87
Maurice Barnes	4-27	15	0-13	4-14	+5.00
S R B Crawford	4-23	17	1-13	3-10	-7.60
Julia Brooke	4-20	20	4-15	0-5	+2.33

Jockeys	Wins-Rides	%	£1 level stks	Best Trainer	W-R
Brian Hughes	25-158	16	-23.99	James Moffatt	8-57
Henry Brooke	25-121	21	+52.74	Martin Todhunter	5-20
Richard Johnson	17-84	20	-20.85	Gordon Elliott	6-30
Sean Bowen	9-28	32	+8.13	Peter Bowen	8-25
Brian Harding	6-34	18	+42.23	Pauline Robson	2-4
Tom Scudamore	5-25	20	+2.38	David Pipe	2-6
Jonathan England	5-22	23	+28.50	Maurice Barnes	2-6
A P McCoy	5-15	33	-3.34	Donald McCain	4-9
Sean Quinlan	4-44	9	-24.75	Sue Smith	2-8
Will Kennedy	4-36	11	-19.38	Donald McCain	4-29
Paul Moloney	4-30	13	-2.00	Evan Williams	2-7
Wilson Renwick	4-19	21	+0.50	Brian Ellison	1-1
Sam Twiston-Davies	4-18	22	-2.61	Dr Richard Newland	2-5

Favourites
Hurdle 32.5% -15.24   Chase 31.4% -10.57   TOTAL 32% -25.82

2018-19 RFO Jumps Racing Guide

CATTERICK

Catterick Bridge, Richmond, N Yorks
DL10 7PE. Tel: 01748 811 478

How to get there Road: A1.
Rail: Darlington

Features Left-handed, 1m2f oval, undulating, sharp turns, favours small, handy horses

2018-19 Fixtures
November 23, December 18, 28, January 1, 10, 23, February 1, 11, 26, March 6

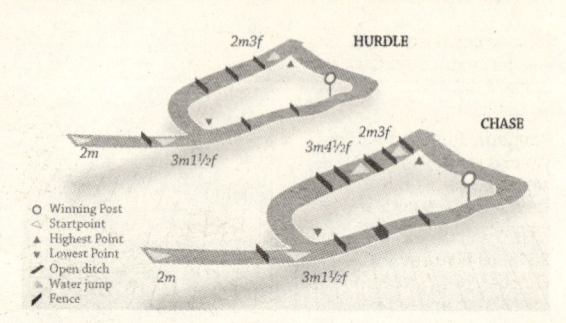

Trainers	Wins-Runs	%	Hurdles	Chases	£1 level stks
Sue Smith	25-78	32	6-36	19-36	+62.08
Donald McCain	24-135	18	17-90	6-36	-17.52
Brian Ellison	15-54	28	9-32	4-17	-12.95
Micky Hammond	10-141	7	5-87	5-46	-51.50
Kenneth Slack	8-33	24	5-21	3-12	+7.25
Dan Skelton	8-28	29	5-17	2-10	-6.61
John Ferguson	7-9	78	5-6	0-1	+11.74
Michael Easterby	4-24	17	2-12	2-11	-5.88
John Quinn	4-21	19	4-17	0-2	-9.97
Sam England	4-14	29	1-4	3-10	+7.00
Pam Sly	4-9	44	3-7	1-2	+10.56
Alan King	4-6	67	3-5	1-1	+1.74
Philip Kirby	3-42	7	3-35	0-1	-25.50

Jockeys	Wins-Rides	%	£1 level stks	Best Trainer	W-R
Brian Hughes	24-132	18	-21.65	Peter Niven	2-5
Danny Cook	24-82	29	+15.49	Sue Smith	16-43
Will Kennedy	11-51	22	-5.47	Donald McCain	7-33
Aidan Coleman	8-25	32	+2.11	John Ferguson	4-5
Henry Brooke	7-103	7	-54.13	Kenneth Slack	3-13
Joe Colliver	7-59	12	+0.90	Micky Hammond	4-43
Sean Quinlan	6-45	13	-10.75	Sue Smith	3-10
Jonathan England	6-35	17	+3.00	Sam England	3-13
Ross Chapman	6-18	33	+3.50	Kenneth Slack	2-4
A P McCoy	6-11	55	+6.28	Benjamin Arthey	1-1
Harry Skelton	5-25	20	-9.76	Dan Skelton	5-23
Richard Johnson	5-12	42	+10.92	Donald McCain	1-1
Finian O'Toole	4-48	8	-28.00	Micky Hammond	3-36

Favourites
Hurdle 44.8% -1.88   Chase 46.2% +18.39   TOTAL 46.1% +20.06

2018-19 RFO Jumps Racing Guide

CHELTENHAM

Prestbury Park, Cheltenham, GL50 4SH. Tel: 01242 513 014

How to get there Road: A435, five miles north of M5 Jctns 9, 10, 11

Features There are two left-handed courses - the Old Course is 1m4f around, the New Course slightly longer. Both are undulating and end with a testing uphill finish

2018-19 Fixtures
October 26-27, November 16-18, December 14-15, January 1, 26, March 12-15, April 17-18

BLOW BY BLOW: an incredible eighth winner at the 2018 Cheltenham Festival for Gordon Elliott, who has the best strike-rate at the track among the top trainers

New Course

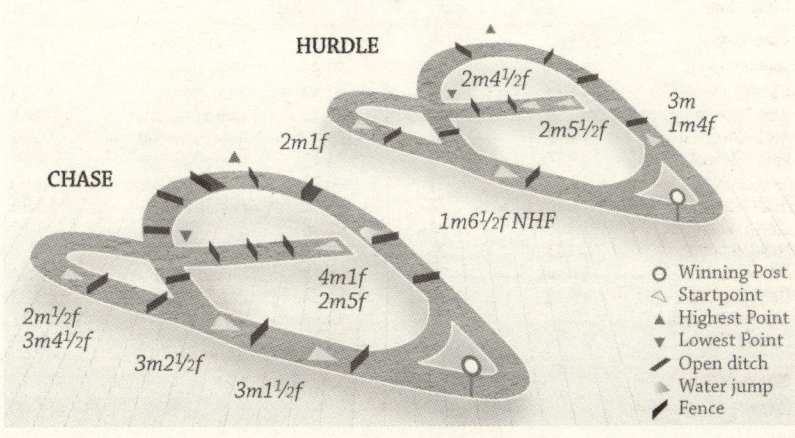

HURDLE
2m4½f
2m1f
2m5½f
3m
1m4f
1m6½f NHF

CHASE
2m½f
3m4½f
3m2½f
3m1½f
4m1f
2m5f

○ Winning Post
◁ Startpoint
▲ Highest Point
▼ Lowest Point
Open ditch
Water jump
Fence

185

2018-19 RFO Jumps Racing Guide

Old Course

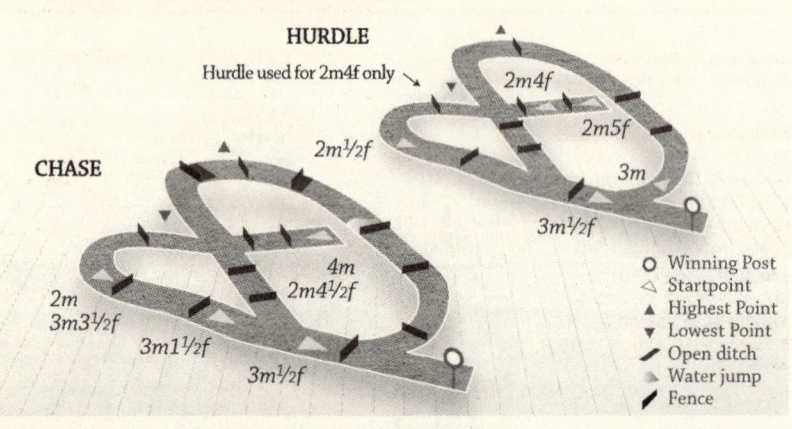

HURDLE

Hurdle used for 2m4f only

2m4f
2m5f
3m
3m½f
2m½f

CHASE

4m
2m4½f
2m
3m3½f
3m1½f
3m½f

○ Winning Post
◁ Startpoint
▲ Highest Point
▼ Lowest Point
◢ Open ditch
≋ Water jump
▮ Fence

Trainers	Wins-Runs	%	Hurdles	Chases	£1 level stks
Nicky Henderson	36-302	12	26-198	9-92	-126.73
Paul Nicholls	33-296	11	13-129	17-162	+29.26
W P Mullins	29-239	12	17-146	11-70	-34.74
Nigel Twiston-Davies	24-212	11	11-84	11-118	-57.40
Philip Hobbs	24-192	13	8-77	13-102	-36.63
Gordon Elliott	20-128	16	10-68	9-55	+75.85
Colin Tizzard	19-181	10	7-58	12-117	-45.72
Alan King	17-141	12	10-91	6-38	-18.92
Dan Skelton	14-140	10	11-98	3-37	-37.79
David Pipe	13-161	8	4-75	7-80	-76.63
Fergal O'Brien	12-107	11	2-40	7-45	-7.38
Harry Fry	12-80	15	9-48	2-25	-19.99
Jonjo O'Neill	11-148	7	3-61	8-82	-41.04

Jockeys	Wins-Rides	%	£1 level stks	Best Trainer	W-R
Barry Geraghty	31-185	17	-39.87	Nicky Henderson	9-59
Richard Johnson	26-221	12	-53.89	Philip Hobbs	16-123
Sam Twiston-Davies	22-219	10	-30.43	Paul Nicholls	15-141
Noel Fehily	21-179	12	-26.48	Neil Mulholland	7-25
Aidan Coleman	19-187	10	-24.42	Martin Keighley	4-15
Nico de Boinville	19-92	21	+7.28	Nicky Henderson	13-69
R Walsh	18-70	26	-14.43	W P Mullins	18-64
Tom Scudamore	15-166	9	-67.18	David Pipe	9-98
Paddy Brennan	15-132	11	-15.13	Fergal O'Brien	8-53
Davy Russell	14-79	18	+35.53	Gordon Elliott	4-19
Harry Skelton	13-111	12	-44.29	Dan Skelton	12-105
Harry Cobden	10-60	17	+40.71	Colin Tizzard	5-23
Daryl Jacob	9-111	8	-78.05	Nigel Twiston-Davies	5-17

Favourites

Hurdle 30.9% -35.57   Chase 30.3% -33.40   TOTAL 30.4% -71.45

2018-19 RFO Jumps Racing Guide

Chepstow, Gwent, NP6 5YH
Tel: 01291 622 260

CHEPSTOW

How to get there Road: three miles west of Severn Bridge (M4). Rail: Chepstow

Features Left-handed, undulating oval, nearly 2m round, suits long-striding front-runners

2018-19 Fixtures
October 13-14, 30, November 7, 21, December 8, 27, January 7, 18, February 1, 23, March 20-21, April 6, 22, 26

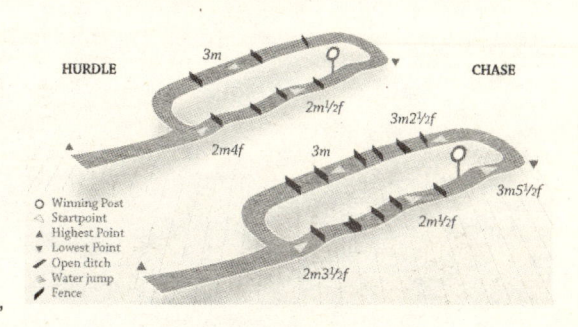

HURDLE — 3m, 2m½f, 2m4f
CHASE — 3m2½f, 3m, 3m5½f, 2m½f, 2m3½f

○ Winning Post
◁ Startpoint
▲ Highest Point
▼ Lowest Point
╱ Open ditch
≋ Water jump
╱ Fence

Trainers	Wins-Runs	%	Hurdles	Chases	£1 level stks
Evan Williams	28-159	18	18-93	9-59	+34.49
Philip Hobbs	25-119	21	13-54	11-52	-23.57
Paul Nicholls	24-114	21	14-60	7-44	-24.10
Peter Bowen	19-104	18	7-55	9-37	+7.53
Nigel Twiston-Davies	16-83	19	7-34	6-37	+13.39
Venetia Williams	15-99	15	2-42	12-51	-16.23
Colin Tizzard	14-146	10	6-60	8-67	-68.00
David Pipe	14-91	15	6-54	5-28	-17.05
Tom George	14-58	24	6-28	3-22	-3.69
Jonjo O'Neill	11-94	12	8-55	1-33	-29.33
Matt Sheppard	11-65	17	6-37	5-27	+24.88
Rebecca Curtis	10-101	10	6-33	4-50	-31.00
Warren Greatrex	9-47	19	9-37	0-4	-1.04

Jockeys	Wins-Rides	%	£1 level stks	Best Trainer	W-R
Richard Johnson	33-137	24	+12.38	Philip Hobbs	14-59
Sean Bowen	25-100	25	+71.98	Peter Bowen	15-57
Tom Scudamore	22-119	18	-4.01	David Pipe	10-49
Sam Twiston-Davies	21-109	19	-37.38	Paul Nicholls	12-57
Adam Wedge	12-87	14	-23.59	Evan Williams	11-60
Tom O'Brien	11-77	14	-13.36	Philip Hobbs	3-23
Paul Moloney	11-69	16	+23.85	Evan Williams	8-35
Stan Sheppard	11-48	23	+28.88	Matt Sheppard	8-38
Nick Scholfield	10-71	14	-24.97	Paul Nicholls	4-14
Paddy Brennan	10-63	16	-17.42	Tom George	5-17
Aidan Coleman	9-88	10	-28.43	Venetia Williams	3-17
Gavin Sheehan	8-59	14	-21.20	Warren Greatrex	3-20
Daryl Jacob	8-53	15	-18.78	Nicky Henderson	2-2

Favourites
Hurdle 37.2% -16.38   Chase 34% -6.02   TOTAL 35.2% -35.27

2018-19 RFO Jumps Racing Guide

DONCASTER

Grand Street, Leger Way, Doncaster
DN2 6BB. Tel: 01302 320 666/7

How to get there Road: M18 Jctn 3, A638, A18 towards Hull. Rail: Doncaster Central

Features Left-handed, flat, 2m round, run-in of just over a furlong, rarely heavy, favours speed horses

2018-19 Fixtures
November 30, December 1, 14-15, 29, January 9, 25-26, February 7, 20, March 1-2

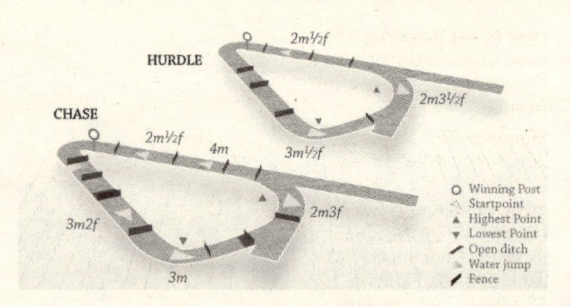

○ Winning Post
⊸ Startpoint
▲ Highest Point
▼ Lowest Point
◠ Open ditch
≋ Water jump
／ Fence

Trainers	Wins-Runs	%	Hurdles	Chases	£1 level stks
Nicky Henderson	25-72	35	17-44	8-21	+2.17
Alan King	21-89	24	13-54	7-27	+13.10
Paul Nicholls	14-56	25	6-24	7-31	-7.71
Jonjo O'Neill	11-82	13	4-51	7-30	-10.75
Emma Lavelle	11-37	30	7-16	1-12	+15.58
Ben Pauling	10-41	24	6-25	4-12	+8.15
Ian Williams	9-60	15	5-40	3-19	+7.13
Charlie Longsdon	8-79	10	3-37	4-36	-27.03
Kim Bailey	8-50	16	5-32	2-14	-22.90
Keith Reveley	7-63	11	3-35	4-23	-25.50
Nicky Richards	7-39	18	4-25	2-10	+8.25
Warren Greatrex	7-38	18	2-21	4-12	-22.47
Brian Ellison	7-33	21	2-17	3-13	-7.34

Jockeys	Wins-Rides	%	£1 level stks	Best Trainer	W-R
Nico de Boinville	13-49	27	-2.21	Nicky Henderson	8-27
David Bass	11-45	24	-4.33	Kim Bailey	6-29
James Reveley	10-67	15	+49.83	Keith Reveley	6-49
Nick Scholfield	10-33	30	+26.42	Paul Nicholls	5-13
Leighton Aspell	9-43	21	-1.43	Emma Lavelle	4-10
Wayne Hutchinson	9-37	24	-4.77	Alan King	7-25
A P McCoy	9-26	35	+1.44	John Ferguson	2-6
Brian Hughes	8-115	7	-86.26	Malcolm Jefferson	3-18
Aidan Coleman	8-57	14	-17.92	Emma Lavelle	2-5
Richard Johnson	8-56	14	-24.21	Philip Hobbs	3-16
Noel Fehily	8-36	22	-6.17	Neil Mulholland	2-9
Henry Brooke	7-54	13	-7.75	Peter Atkinson	2-3
Kielan Woods	7-52	13	+1.00	Graeme McPherson	4-26

Favourites
Hurdle 43.4% +5.12   Chase 37.8% -3.45   TOTAL 40.5% -3.59

EXETER

Kennford, nr Exeter, Devon
EX6 7XS. Tel: 01392 832 599

How to get there Road: five miles south of M5, A38. Rail: Exeter Central or Exeter St Davids

Features Right-handed, 2m, hilly, stiff half-mile home straight with 300-yard run-in

2018-19 Fixtures
October 11, 23, November 6, 14, 25, December 7, 20, January 1, 20, February 10, 22, March 5, 18, 24, April 9, 16

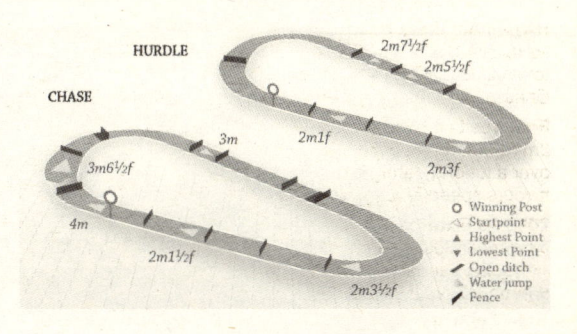

Trainers	Wins-Runs	%	Hurdles	Chases	£1 level stks
Philip Hobbs	37-176	21	23-94	11-70	-33.97
Paul Nicholls	36-115	31	23-68	12-41	-14.62
Harry Fry	24-61	39	16-40	6-15	+42.78
Colin Tizzard	23-139	17	11-70	12-61	-46.86
David Pipe	17-158	11	13-110	3-35	-47.47
Alan King	14-73	19	7-44	6-22	-13.18
Evan Williams	14-54	26	10-33	4-19	+27.38
Victor Dartnall	10-77	13	7-51	3-22	-34.88
Venetia Williams	10-67	15	3-26	7-39	+0.13
Sue Gardner	9-97	9	7-72	2-16	-43.88
Chris Down	8-73	11	5-58	3-9	-7.75
Anthony Honeyball	8-48	17	5-29	2-15	+15.08
Fergal O'Brien	8-35	23	2-18	4-14	+23.80

Jockeys	Wins-Rides	%	£1 level stks	Best Trainer	W-R
Richard Johnson	35-158	22	-37.02	Philip Hobbs	23-98
Noel Fehily	25-102	25	+23.07	Harry Fry	18-41
Sam Twiston-Davies	23-109	21	-37.96	Paul Nicholls	19-61
Nick Scholfield	20-148	14	-45.21	Paul Nicholls	8-20
Tom Scudamore	18-124	15	-46.59	David Pipe	8-71
Aidan Coleman	15-95	16	-17.25	Venetia Williams	4-26
Tom O'Brien	13-102	13	-37.99	Philip Hobbs	6-31
James Best	12-140	9	-53.75	Robert Walford	4-20
Paddy Brennan	10-44	23	+50.75	Fergal O'Brien	4-12
Lucy Gardner	8-80	10	-33.88	Sue Gardner	8-80
Harry Cobden	8-55	15	-37.61	Paul Nicholls	4-12
Brendan Powell	8-55	15	-1.63	Colin Tizzard	5-27
Gavin Sheehan	8-44	18	-10.44	Warren Greatrex	4-17

Favourites
Hurdle 43.3% +3.61   Chase 33.8% -33.85   TOTAL 38.5% -44.52

2018-19 RFO Jumps Racing Guide

FAKENHAM

Fakenham, Norfolk, NR21 7NY
Tel: 01328 862 388

How to get there Road: A1065 from Swaffham, A148 King's Lynn, A1067 from Norwich. Rail: Kings Lynn, Norwich

Features Left-handed, 1m circuit, undulating, unsuitable for long-striding horses

2018-19 Fixtures October 19, 31, November 20, December 4, 18, January 1, 24, February 15, March 4, 15, April 22

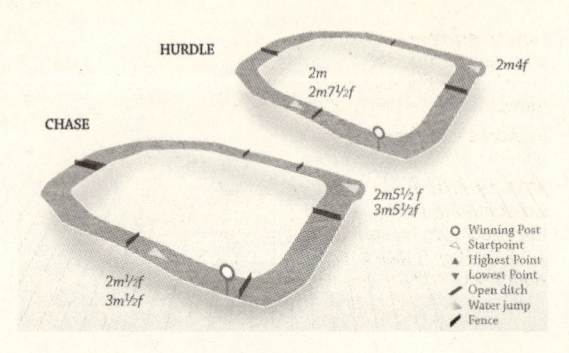

HURDLE
2m
2m7½f
2m4f

CHASE
2m5½f
3m5½f
2m½f
3m½f

○ Winning Post
◁ Startpoint
▲ Highest Point
▼ Lowest Point
╱ Open ditch
⌇ Water jump
╱ Fence

Trainers	Wins-Runs	%	Hurdles	Chases	£1 level stks
Dan Skelton	16-61	26	9-38	6-21	-6.42
Lucy Wadham	16-58	28	8-35	5-16	+16.10
Olly Murphy	14-46	30	12-36	2-7	+13.94
Neil Mulholland	14-42	33	12-30	2-12	+12.51
Nicky Henderson	12-31	39	6-20	2-6	-6.96
Neil King	9-64	14	4-35	4-27	+24.48
Alex Hales	6-38	16	3-27	3-11	-2.27
Pam Sly	6-26	23	2-15	4-8	+12.55
Charlie Mann	6-23	26	2-8	4-15	+13.00
David Pipe	6-14	43	4-9	2-5	-0.69
Henry Daly	6-11	55	2-2	4-8	+7.38
Tim Vaughan	5-46	11	4-32	1-13	-30.15
Paul Henderson	5-26	19	2-8	3-18	+5.00

Jockeys	Wins-Rides	%	£1 level stks	Best Trainer	W-R
Harry Skelton	16-48	33	+10.88	Dan Skelton	12-39
Richard Johnson	15-53	28	-5.13	Olly Murphy	6-13
Tom Scudamore	10-31	32	+1.76	David Pipe	5-11
Leighton Aspell	9-41	22	-2.25	Lucy Wadham	6-24
Noel Fehily	9-25	36	+4.85	Neil Mulholland	8-16
James Banks	8-43	19	-0.50	Emma-Jane Bishop	3-10
Jack Quinlan	7-80	9	-44.88	Michael Wigham	2-12
Brian Hughes	7-21	33	+52.38	David Thompson	3-3
Trevor Whelan	6-60	10	+14.13	Neil King	6-41
Sam Twiston-Davies	6-19	32	+11.13	J R Jenkins	1-1
Harry Bannister	6-17	35	+10.38	Charlie Mann	4-10
Nico de Boinville	6-15	40	-3.80	Nicky Henderson	4-9
Kielan Woods	5-48	10	-22.47	Alex Hales	3-16

Favourites
Hurdle 38.7% -14.68 Chase 40.3% -14.31 TOTAL 39.7% -30.01

2018-19 RFO Jumps Racing Guide

FFOS LAS

Trimsaran, Carmarthenshire
SA17 4DE. Tel: 01554 811 092

How to get there Road: M4 Jctn 48, follow A4138 to Llanelli. Rail: Llanelli, Kidwelly, Carmarthen

Features Left-handed, flat, galloping

2018-19 Fixtures
October 20, November 11, 23, December 17, January 14, February 7, March 17, April 7, 21

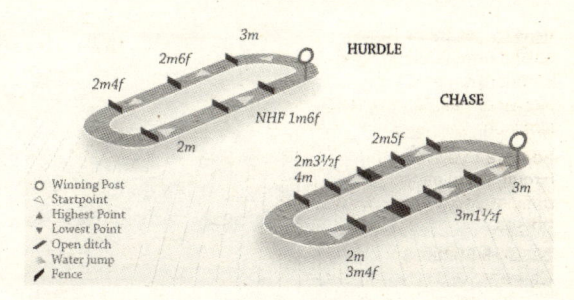

○ Winning Post
◁ Startpoint
▲ Highest Point
▼ Lowest Point
╱ Open ditch
≋ Water jump
╱ Fence

HURDLE: 3m, 2m6f, 2m4f, NHF 1m6f, 2m

CHASE: 2m5f, 2m3½f, 4m, 3m, 3m1½f, 2m, 3m4f

Trainers	Wins-Runs	%	Hurdles	Chases	£1 level stks
Evan Williams	38-255	15	26-144	7-91	-32.09
Peter Bowen	31-203	15	15-111	15-67	-64.30
Nigel Twiston-Davies	30-133	23	18-77	9-41	+6.84
Rebecca Curtis	28-112	25	11-62	13-34	+19.09
Debra Hamer	12-70	17	4-35	8-32	+8.38
Bernard Llewellyn	11-74	15	10-65	1-7	+1.02
Jonjo O'Neill	11-69	16	6-41	4-25	-16.79
Warren Greatrex	10-42	24	6-26	1-8	-9.84
Nicky Henderson	10-27	37	8-18	0-4	-6.89
David Pipe	9-65	14	5-43	1-11	-23.16
Tim Vaughan	8-113	7	3-67	5-40	-67.00
David Rees	8-80	10	3-44	5-35	+11.50
Neil Mulholland	8-62	13	4-33	2-23	+10.38

Jockeys	Wins-Rides	%	£1 level stks	Best Trainer	W-R
Sean Bowen	28-138	20	-11.02	Peter Bowen	21-104
Adam Wedge	20-129	16	-19.86	Evan Williams	20-109
Sam Twiston-Davies	20-97	21	+2.36	Nigel Twiston-Davies	16-76
Tom Scudamore	19-96	20	-5.00	David Pipe	8-37
Richard Johnson	17-96	18	-25.92	Tim Vaughan	6-43
Paul Moloney	15-109	14	+2.14	Evan Williams	10-60
David Bass	13-36	36	+45.28	Kim Bailey	7-18
Gavin Sheehan	10-51	20	-8.12	Warren Greatrex	7-27
Trevor Whelan	9-63	14	+54.17	Debra Hamer	5-33
Jamie Moore	8-60	13	-20.00	Peter Bowen	5-36
Jonathan Moore	8-40	20	-9.19	Rebecca Curtis	8-39
Noel Fehily	7-43	16	-0.13	Jonjo O'Neill	2-5
Tom O'Brien	6-64	9	-35.25	Ian Williams	1-2

Favourites
Hurdle 41.3% -5.51   Chase 34.6% -12.00   TOTAL 38.4% -26.52

2018-19 RFO Jumps Racing Guide

FONTWELL

Fontwell Park, nr Arundel, W Sussex
BN18 0SX. Tel: 01243 543 335

How to get there Road: A29 to Bognor Regis. Rail: Barnham

Features Left-handed, 1m4f circuit, quite sharp

2018-19 Fixtures
October 5-6, 24, November 9, 18, December 11, 26, January 14, 27, February 14, 24, March 6, 16, 29, April 12, 24

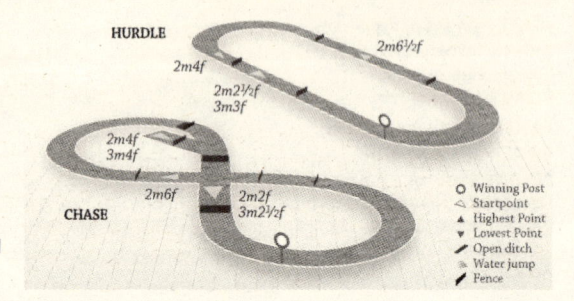

HURDLE
2m4f
2m6½f
2m2½f
3m3f
2m4f
3m4f
2m6f
2m2f
3m2½f
CHASE

○ Winning Post
◁ Startpoint
▲ Highest Point
▼ Lowest Point
/ Open ditch
~ Water jump
/ Fence

Trainers	Wins-Runs	%	Hurdles	Chases	£1 level stks
Gary Moore	40-277	14	24-177	10-76	-48.02
Neil Mulholland	34-132	26	18-75	12-44	+14.96
Chris Gordon	31-213	15	20-137	10-61	-32.69
Paul Nicholls	29-70	41	8-30	21-38	+10.15
Anthony Honeyball	23-68	34	10-35	9-24	+33.92
Colin Tizzard	20-96	21	9-46	10-40	-16.43
Dan Skelton	16-71	23	6-39	9-21	-12.53
Alan King	14-52	27	11-35	1-9	-9.78
Charlie Longsdon	13-65	20	6-31	5-26	-14.67
Seamus Mullins	12-122	10	4-63	7-51	-6.17
Dr Richard Newland	12-32	38	7-23	5-9	+8.87
Jeremy Scott	11-57	19	4-30	7-25	-10.43
Philip Hobbs	11-53	21	7-35	4-14	-23.66

Jockeys	Wins-Rides	%	£1 level stks	Best Trainer	W-R
Tom Cannon	35-250	14	-52.31	Chris Gordon	21-133
Jamie Moore	31-192	16	-53.82	Gary Moore	26-130
Noel Fehily	27-103	26	-12.64	Neil Mulholland	17-54
Richard Johnson	22-106	21	-5.89	Philip Hobbs	7-27
Aidan Coleman	22-86	26	+22.37	Lawney Hill	5-13
Sam Twiston-Davies	19-68	28	-11.77	Paul Nicholls	11-30
Leighton Aspell	18-158	11	-48.11	Oliver Sherwood	5-50
Nick Scholfield	16-90	18	+18.17	Jeremy Scott	6-21
Harry Cobden	15-49	31	+3.03	Colin Tizzard	7-22
Tom O'Brien	14-103	14	-31.21	Suzy Smith	3-15
David Noonan	14-63	22	-3.41	Anthony Honeyball	9-21
Tom Scudamore	14-62	23	-7.42	David Pipe	5-22
Gavin Sheehan	14-60	23	+9.85	Warren Greatrex	8-20

Favourites

Hurdle 37% -31.61   Chase 39.8% -17.13   TOTAL 37.7% -67.29

2018-19 RFO Jumps Racing Guide

HAYDOCK

Newton-Le-Willows, Lancashire
WA12 0HQ. Tel: 01942 725 963

How to get there Road: M6 Jctn 23 on A49 to Wigan. Rail: Wigan or Warrington Bank Quay (main line)

Features Flat, left-handed, 1m5f circuit, quarter-mile run-in, chase track much sharper (like hurdles track) since introduction of portable fences

2018-19 Fixtures
November 24, December 5, 22, 30, January 19, February 16, March 20, April 20

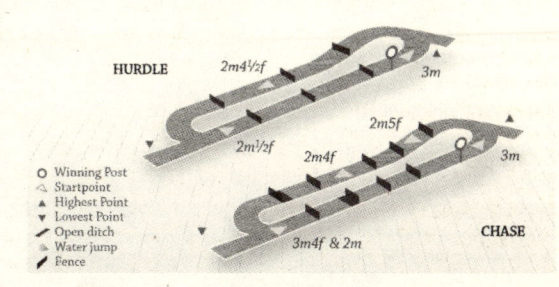

Trainers	Wins-Runs	%	Hurdles	Chases	£1 level stks
Nigel Twiston-Davies	17-85	20	10-37	7-46	-5.58
Donald McCain	14-70	20	6-45	8-22	-4.97
Paul Nicholls	13-57	23	4-34	9-21	-12.24
Venetia Williams	11-59	19	3-18	7-40	+57.88
David Pipe	11-54	20	5-29	6-25	+48.00
Sue Smith	10-97	10	5-38	5-57	-4.47
Nicky Henderson	8-35	23	5-26	2-7	-8.31
Dan Skelton	7-66	11	6-50	1-16	-29.13
Lucinda Russell	7-56	13	5-27	2-28	+23.33
Evan Williams	6-56	11	6-29	0-26	-1.00
Tom George	6-35	17	4-13	1-19	-6.00
Philip Hobbs	5-49	10	3-26	2-19	-17.00
Jonjo O'Neill	5-47	11	3-25	2-22	-10.50

Jockeys	Wins-Rides	%	£1 level stks	Best Trainer	W-R
Daryl Jacob	14-38	37	+35.71	Nigel Twiston-Davies	6-8
Will Kennedy	12-46	26	+3.38	Donald McCain	11-35
Sam Twiston-Davies	9-52	17	-27.20	Nigel Twiston-Davies	7-22
Richard Johnson	9-51	18	+2.75	Philip Hobbs	3-25
Paddy Brennan	9-36	25	-1.86	Fergal O'Brien	3-10
Brian Hughes	7-82	9	-55.72	Malcolm Jefferson	4-23
Danny Cook	7-63	11	+5.83	Sue Smith	6-52
Aidan Coleman	7-50	14	+62.41	Venetia Williams	2-13
Sean Bowen	7-22	32	+11.53	Peter Bowen	4-9
Harry Skelton	6-52	12	-19.13	Dan Skelton	5-45
Tom Scudamore	6-47	13	+5.50	David Pipe	6-24
Harry Cobden	5-25	20	+11.25	Paul Nicholls	3-14
Charlie Deutsch	5-14	36	+12.00	Venetia Williams	3-12

Favourites
Hurdle 35.9% +2.08   Chase 28.7% -19.92   TOTAL 33.5% -17.02

2018-19 RFO Jumps Racing Guide

HEREFORD

Roman Road, Holmer, Hereford
HR 4 9QU. Tel 01981 250 436

How to get there Road: A49 1m north of Hereford.
Rail: Hereford

Features Right-handed, predominately galloping track with stiffer fences than at many minor courses

2018-19 Fixtures
October 16, November 5, 13, 28, December 15, January 2, 23, February 11, March 9, 26

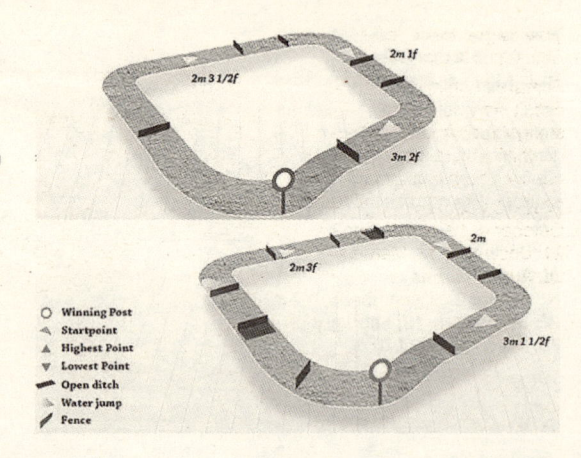

- ○ Winning Post
- ◁ Startpoint
- ▲ Highest Point
- ▽ Lowest Point
- ▬ Open ditch
- ╱ Water jump
- ╱ Fence

Trainers	Wins-Runs	%	Hurdles	Chases	£1 level stks
Venetia Williams	8-40	20	4-25	3-14	+8.23
Henry Oliver	5-18	28	2-9	3-7	+25.50
Warren Greatrex	5-17	29	3-9	1-4	-1.17
Nigel Twiston-Davies	4-24	17	1-9	3-9	-8.75
Philip Hobbs	4-20	20	3-14	0-4	-7.74
Dan Skelton	4-20	20	2-12	2-7	-4.22
Kerry Lee	3-32	9	1-9	2-22	-16.25
Neil Mulholland	3-17	18	1-9	0-4	-5.83
Tom George	3-16	19	2-11	1-4	-3.00
Rebecca Curtis	3-14	21	0-6	2-5	-5.63
Tom Symonds	3-12	25	3-7	0-2	+20.33
Nikki Evans	3-10	30	3-9	0-1	+6.75
David Rees	3-9	33	0-1	3-6	+9.88

Jockeys	Wins-Rides	%	£1 level stks	Best Trainer	W-R
Richard Johnson	6-47	13	-29.22	Philip Hobbs	3-13
Charlie Deutsch	6-28	21	+15.25	Venetia Williams	6-23
Noel Fehily	6-16	38	+1.40	Harry Fry	3-4
Aidan Coleman	5-22	23	+6.63	Tom Symonds	1-1
Sean Bowen	5-19	26	+7.00	David Rees	1-1
Andrew Tinkler	5-15	33	+5.73	Alastair Ralph	1-1
Sam Twiston-Davies	4-17	24	-4.58	Nigel Twiston-Davies	2-6
Ben Poste	3-26	12	+1.33	Tom Symonds	2-7
Tom O'Brien	3-22	14	-5.68	Henry Oliver	1-1
Tom Scudamore	3-18	17	+0.33	Neil Mulholland	2-2
Gavin Sheehan	3-12	25	-2.13	David Dennis	1-1
Jake Greenall	3-7	43	+18.00	Oliver Greenall	2-4
Jamie Moore	2-17	12	-6.25	Kerry Lee	2-14

Favourites
Hurdle 29.2% -22.25   Chase 37.2% +3.19   TOTAL 33.6% -18.44

194

2018-19 RFO Jumps Racing Guide

HEXHAM

High Yarridge, Hexham, Northumberland
NE46 2JP. Tel: 01434 606 881

How to get there Road: A69. Rail: Hexham

Features Left-handed, 1m4f circuit, very stiff, back straight runs nearly all downhill before steep uphill run from home turn

2018-19 Fixtures
October 4, 13, November 9, 21, December 12, March 14, 26, April 15

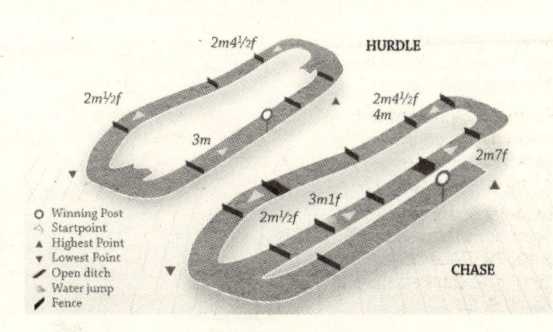

Course diagram key:
- ○ Winning Post
- Startpoint
- ▲ Highest Point
- ▼ Lowest Point
- ✱ Open ditch
- Water jump
- Fence

HURDLE: 2m4½f, 2m½f, 3m, 2m4½f/4m, 2m7f

CHASE: 3m1f, 2m½f

Trainers	Wins-Runs	%	Hurdles	Chases	£1 level stks
Lucinda Russell	26-177	15	9-93	16-78	+19.22
Maurice Barnes	17-102	17	7-47	10-51	-0.88
Micky Hammond	15-115	13	10-56	5-51	-44.68
Malcolm Jefferson	11-55	20	5-32	1-9	-25.00
Brian Ellison	11-52	21	8-39	2-11	+5.54
Donald McCain	10-83	12	10-64	0-12	-54.96
Jonathan Haynes	10-72	14	9-54	1-13	+9.28
Stuart Coltherd	10-63	16	3-31	7-32	+17.25
Mark Walford	10-55	18	5-31	5-22	+6.13
Nicky Richards	10-35	29	6-22	4-12	+8.43
Martin Todhunter	9-71	13	6-41	3-29	-15.88
George Bewley	9-57	16	3-34	6-20	+16.25
James Ewart	9-50	18	4-22	5-23	+0.25

Jockeys	Wins-Rides	%	£1 level stks	Best Trainer	W-R
Brian Hughes	29-181	16	-72.54	Malcolm Jefferson	11-46
Thomas Dowson	16-109	15	+38.00	Jonathan Haynes	6-32
Henry Brooke	15-139	11	-29.20	Micky Hammond	3-16
Jamie Hamilton	12-86	14	-17.67	Henry Hogarth	5-13
Dale Irving	11-58	19	+7.38	James Ewart	5-17
Derek Fox	10-100	10	-43.42	Lucinda Russell	6-51
Craig Nichol	10-96	10	-44.78	Keith Dalgleish	2-7
Danny Cook	10-52	19	-1.10	Brian Ellison	4-14
James Reveley	10-44	23	+11.37	Stuart Coltherd	2-5
Wilson Renwick	10-41	24	-1.81	Donald McCain	4-13
Richard Johnson	10-21	48	+9.93	John C McConnell	2-2
Brian Harding	9-82	11	-40.83	Nicky Richards	7-16
Jonathon Bewley	9-51	18	+53.75	George Bewley	8-50

Favourites
Hurdle 36.2% -45.95 Chase 35.9% -6.99 TOTAL 37.7% -45.70

2018-19 RFO Jumps Racing Guide

HUNTINGDON

Brampton, Huntingdon, Cambs
PE18 8NN. Tel: 01480 453 373

How to get there Road: Follow signs off A14. Rail: Huntingdon

Features Right-handed, flat track, short run-in of around 200 yards

2018-19 Fixtures
October 4, 16, November 4, 13, 24, December 9, 26, January 11, 25, February 7, 17, 21, March 3, 13, 19, April 22

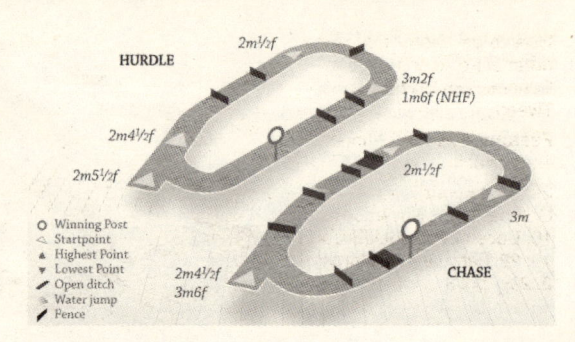

Trainers	Wins-Runs	%	Hurdles	Chases	£1 level stks
Nicky Henderson	26-82	32	16-49	8-15	-13.00
Jonjo O'Neill	22-101	22	12-66	8-30	+1.63
Alan King	20-91	22	12-56	5-19	-21.69
Dan Skelton	18-114	16	10-68	6-29	-36.00
Kim Bailey	18-84	21	11-43	5-28	+31.98
John Ferguson	15-29	52	10-21	1-3	+12.10
Gary Moore	13-85	15	9-57	4-24	+24.96
Ben Pauling	11-52	21	6-32	3-14	+88.42
David Dennis	11-38	29	6-25	5-12	+34.46
Charlie Longsdon	9-69	13	4-43	5-20	-24.52
Ian Williams	9-59	15	4-41	5-15	-13.50
Tim Vaughan	7-52	13	4-36	2-12	-17.33
Philip Hobbs	7-46	15	4-28	1-11	-17.09

Jockeys	Wins-Rides	%	£1 level stks	Best Trainer	W-R
Richard Johnson	24-105	23	+4.33	Philip Hobbs	5-22
Noel Fehily	20-76	26	-0.64	Nicky Henderson	5-8
Aidan Coleman	17-86	20	+2.92	John Ferguson	4-13
Wayne Hutchinson	15-73	21	-17.61	Alan King	13-60
Harry Skelton	14-103	14	-39.00	Dan Skelton	13-77
A P McCoy	14-29	48	+6.51	John Ferguson	4-5
Leighton Aspell	13-106	12	-40.99	Lucy Wadham	4-23
Sam Twiston-Davies	13-65	20	+10.75	Paul Nicholls	3-12
David Bass	13-65	20	+56.49	Kim Bailey	9-43
Trevor Whelan	10-90	11	-12.13	Neil King	4-43
Jamie Moore	10-72	14	+39.25	Gary Moore	5-37
Tom O'Brien	9-69	13	-28.84	Dr Richard Newland	1-1
Gavin Sheehan	9-51	18	-5.05	Warren Greatrex	4-16

Favourites
Hurdle 36.5% -31.20   Chase 34.4% -21.97   TOTAL 35.8% -63.55

2018-19 RFO Jumps Racing Guide
KELSO

Kelso, Roxburghshire.
Tel: 01668 281 611

How to get there Road: 1m north of Kelso on B6461 to Ednam. Rail: Berwick-on-Tweed

Features Tight, left-handed, 1m3f circuit

2018-19 Fixtures
October 7, 27, November 10, December 9, 29, January 13, 22, February 14, March 2, 23, April 8

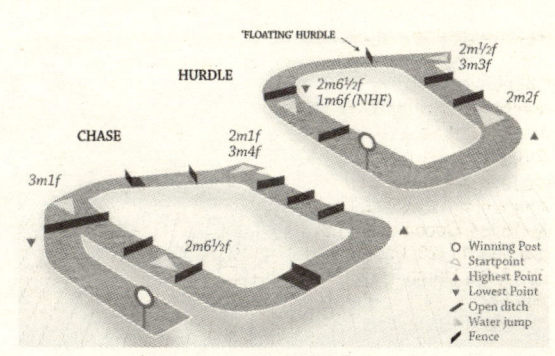

Trainers	Wins-Runs	%	Hurdles	Chases	£1 level stks
Lucinda Russell	29-207	14	12-115	15-82	-39.22
Nicky Richards	24-112	21	16-60	7-42	-10.81
Donald McCain	21-119	18	11-76	9-38	-25.34
N W Alexander	19-153	12	15-90	4-51	+3.08
James Ewart	14-71	20	8-39	5-23	+36.63
Rose Dobbin	12-110	11	6-74	5-29	-47.81
Malcolm Jefferson	12-55	22	7-24	3-21	-10.09
Sandy Thomson	11-86	13	5-45	6-40	+41.58
Chris Grant	9-60	15	3-33	5-20	+14.60
Iain Jardine	8-45	18	2-27	3-11	-7.95
Micky Hammond	7-58	12	3-27	3-28	-23.25
Keith Dalgleish	7-18	39	6-13	0-1	+39.73
Paul Nicholls	7-18	39	2-4	5-14	-1.54

Jockeys	Wins-Rides	%	£1 level stks	Best Trainer	W-R
Brian Hughes	38-203	19	-22.82	Malcolm Jefferson	9-45
Brian Harding	26-130	20	-17.21	Nicky Richards	15-50
Craig Nichol	15-141	11	-68.26	Rose Dobbin	7-53
Derek Fox	13-113	12	-36.63	Lucinda Russell	9-73
Lucy Alexander	12-97	12	+10.13	N W Alexander	9-71
Callum Bewley	10-74	14	+44.00	Keith Dalgleish	3-5
Peter Buchanan	10-67	15	-14.25	Lucinda Russell	8-45
Danny Cook	8-55	15	-1.80	Brian Ellison	2-8
Blair Campbell	8-26	31	+37.04	Lucinda Russell	6-18
Henry Brooke	7-84	8	-52.63	Kenneth Slack	3-5
Jamie Hamilton	7-66	11	-29.54	Malcolm Jefferson	3-9
Mr T Hamilton	7-34	21	+27.58	Mrs Wendy Hamilton	3-5
Ross Chapman	7-32	22	+8.50	Iain Jardine	5-13

Favourites
Hurdle 36.1% -28.44   Chase 37.4% +7.13   TOTAL 35.5% -36.27

2018-19 RFO Jumps Racing Guide

KEMPTON

Staines Rd East, Sunbury-on-Thames
TW16 5AQ. Tel: 01932 782 292

How to get there Road: M3 Jctn 1, A308 towards Kingston-on-Thames. Rail: Kempton Park from Waterloo

Features A sharp right-handed track with the emphasis very much on speed

2018-19 Fixtures October 21, November 12, 26, December 26-27, January 12, 28, February 8, 23, March 16, April 25

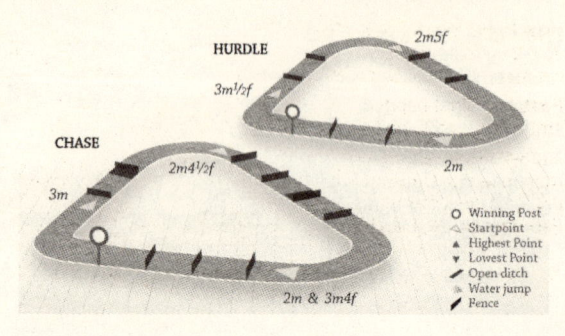

Trainers	Wins-Runs	%	Hurdles	Chases	£1 level stks
Nicky Henderson	50-196	26	28-117	16-55	-27.12
Paul Nicholls	32-150	21	12-68	19-75	-20.34
Alan King	21-148	14	17-96	3-37	-69.43
Colin Tizzard	11-67	16	5-27	6-36	+28.60
Harry Fry	11-61	18	10-37	1-17	-24.13
Nigel Twiston-Davies	11-59	19	4-23	7-32	-14.89
Chris Gordon	11-56	20	4-27	6-27	+29.43
Dan Skelton	9-112	8	7-75	2-28	-80.46
Tom George	9-57	16	0-7	9-48	-1.75
Philip Hobbs	8-84	10	6-45	2-30	-62.53
Jonjo O'Neill	8-80	10	5-46	3-32	-39.99
Charlie Longsdon	8-55	15	2-28	6-26	-1.05
David Pipe	7-42	17	6-26	1-16	+2.13

Jockeys	Wins-Rides	%	£1 level stks	Best Trainer	W-R
Sam Twiston-Davies	24-122	20	-30.41	Paul Nicholls	12-84
Barry Geraghty	23-85	27	+6.17	Nicky Henderson	12-40
Nico de Boinville	23-84	27	-2.08	Nicky Henderson	17-57
Noel Fehily	20-126	16	-58.53	Harry Fry	5-34
Aidan Coleman	17-115	15	-42.44	Venetia Williams	3-20
Tom Cannon	16-78	21	+71.35	Chris Gordon	7-27
Richard Johnson	15-102	15	-50.03	Philip Hobbs	7-41
Wayne Hutchinson	14-92	15	-29.60	Alan King	13-81
Daryl Jacob	10-79	13	-18.85	Ben Pauling	3-10
Paddy Brennan	9-70	13	+19.75	Tom George	5-27
Harry Skelton	8-82	10	-33.96	Dan Skelton	6-75
Nick Scholfield	8-62	13	+2.85	Paul Nicholls	6-19
David Bass	8-45	18	+9.50	Kim Bailey	5-24

Favourites
Hurdle 44% -0.30   Chase 44.3% +3.55   TOTAL 43.5% -2.09

2018-19 RFO Jumps Racing Guide

LEICESTER

Leicester, LE2 4AL
Tel: 0116 271 6515

How to get there Road: M1 Jctn 21, 2m south of city centre on A6. Rail: Leicester

Features Right-handed, 1m6f circuit, stiff uphill run-in

2018-19 Fixtures
November 19, December 2, 6, 12, 28, January 10, 22, 30, February 14, 26, March 8

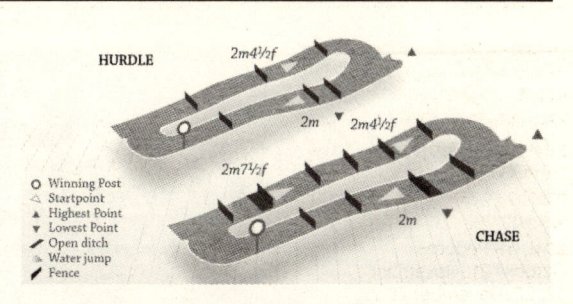

HURDLE 2m4½f 2m 2m4½f 2m7½f 2m CHASE

○ Winning Post
△ Startpoint
▲ Highest Point
▼ Lowest Point
/ Open ditch
≈ Water jump
/ Fence

Trainers	Wins-Runs	%	Hurdles	Chases	£1 level stks
Nigel Twiston-Davies	14-54	26	5-22	9-32	+28.46
Tom George	13-39	33	2-8	11-31	+12.63
Caroline Bailey	9-33	27	4-11	5-22	+2.49
David Pipe	9-25	36	5-14	4-11	+8.90
Fergal O'Brien	7-32	22	1-10	6-22	+27.13
Robin Dickin	7-25	28	1-5	6-20	+14.63
Philip Hobbs	6-15	40	3-8	3-7	+5.58
Venetia Williams	5-30	17	2-14	3-16	-17.38
Dan Skelton	5-26	19	2-12	3-14	-1.15
Jonjo O'Neill	4-33	12	1-16	3-17	-21.50
Matt Sheppard	4-22	18	1-8	3-14	-0.75
Zoe Davison	4-20	20	1-7	3-13	+15.00
Ian Williams	4-18	22	2-10	2-8	-8.18

Jockeys	Wins-Rides	%	£1 level stks	Best Trainer	W-R
Sam Twiston-Davies	14-44	32	+15.88	Nigel Twiston-Davies	9-30
Richard Johnson	11-45	24	-9.37	Philip Hobbs	5-12
Paddy Brennan	9-48	19	+11.75	Fergal O'Brien	5-17
Aidan Coleman	9-44	20	-14.60	Jonjo O'Neill	3-10
Tom Scudamore	7-36	19	-4.60	David Pipe	6-19
A P Heskin	7-22	32	+2.54	Tom George	6-18
Charlie Poste	5-27	19	+6.50	Robin Dickin	3-13
Harry Skelton	5-26	19	+2.13	Dan Skelton	4-20
Jack Quinlan	5-25	20	+1.38	Robin Dickin	3-9
Liam Treadwell	5-24	21	+14.13	Venetia Williams	3-7
Will Kennedy	5-19	26	-4.31	Ian Williams	3-5
Jamie Bargary	5-17	29	+12.38	Nigel Twiston-Davies	3-7
David Bass	4-23	17	-0.25	Kim Bailey	3-17

Favourites
Hurdle 44.7% +9.04   Chase 39.6% -8.63   TOTAL 41.7% +0.41

LINGFIELD

Lingfield, Surrey, RH7 6PQ
Tel: 01342 834 800

How to get there Road: M25 Jctn 6, south on A22. Rail: Lingfield from London Bridge and Victoria

Features Left-handed, 1m4f circuit, hilly

2018-19 Fixtures November 13, 27, December 10, January 4, 15, 29, February 12, 18

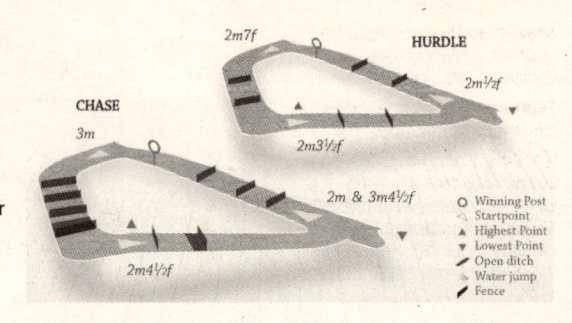

Course diagram:
- CHASE: 3m, 2m4½f, 2m & 3m4½f
- HURDLE: 2m7f, 2m½f, 2m3½f
- Legend: Winning Post, Startpoint, Highest Point, Lowest Point, Open ditch, Water jump, Fence

Trainers	Wins-Runs	%	Hurdles	Chases	£1 level stks
Gary Moore	8-78	10	4-45	4-33	-24.75
Chris Gordon	8-38	21	4-22	4-16	-8.15
Nigel Twiston-Davies	8-26	31	5-15	3-11	+25.58
Seamus Mullins	7-40	18	3-22	4-18	+12.25
Warren Greatrex	7-18	39	5-13	2-5	-0.78
Dan Skelton	5-14	36	3-11	2-3	+12.00
Zoe Davison	4-25	16	3-16	1-9	-8.50
Tim Vaughan	4-24	17	1-11	3-13	-11.40
Martin Keighley	4-14	29	3-10	1-4	+9.17
Nicky Henderson	4-6	67	3-5	1-1	-0.25
Neil Mulholland	3-27	11	2-17	1-10	+22.00
Venetia Williams	3-22	14	1-7	2-15	-9.00
Anna Newton-Smith	3-18	17	2-9	1-9	+0.00

Jockeys	Wins-Rides	%	£1 level stks	Best Trainer	W-R
Leighton Aspell	9-42	21	+6.74	Oliver Sherwood	2-7
Tom Cannon	8-51	16	-14.15	Chris Gordon	7-23
Tom Scudamore	8-38	21	-4.51	Anabel K Murphy	2-2
Gavin Sheehan	7-21	33	+4.78	Warren Greatrex	5-13
Jeremiah McGrath	6-16	38	+1.93	Nicky Henderson	3-4
Jamie Moore	5-41	12	-5.25	Gary Moore	5-30
Andrew Thornton	4-24	17	+14.50	Seamus Mullins	4-13
Noel Fehily	4-19	21	+4.92	Harry Fry	2-2
Paddy Brennan	4-19	21	-1.25	Colin Tizzard	1-1
Alan Johns	4-18	22	-8.78	Tim Vaughan	3-17
Aidan Coleman	4-18	22	+0.57	Venetia Williams	2-6
Sam Twiston-Davies	4-12	33	+7.58	Nigel Twiston-Davies	4-9
Daryl Jacob	4-12	33	+2.10	Dr Richard Newland	2-2

Favourites
Hurdle 42.5% -1.61   Chase 37.7% -0.64   TOTAL 40.3% -2.24

LUDLOW

2018-19 RFO Jumps Racing Guide

Bromfield, Ludlow, Shrewsbury, Shropshire. Tel: 01981 250 052

How to get there Road: 2m north of Ludlow on A49. Rail: Ludlow

Features Flat, right-handed, has sharp turns and a testing run-in of 450 yards

2018-19 Fixtures
October 10, 25, November 15, 26, December 5, 19, January 3, 17, 28, February 6, 20, 28, March 21, April 1, 23

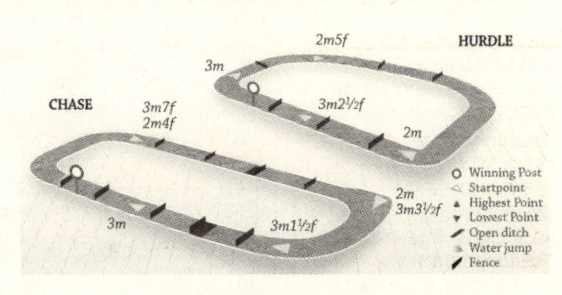

Course diagram labels: CHASE 3m7f, 2m4f, 3m, 3m1½f, 3m, 2m5f, 3m2½f, 2m, 2m, 3m3½f, HURDLE

Key: Winning Post, Startpoint, Highest Point, Lowest Point, Open ditch, Water jump, Fence

Trainers	Wins-Runs	%	Hurdles	Chases	£1 level stks
Nicky Henderson	24-80	30	15-48	2-13	-6.90
Evan Williams	23-166	14	9-73	11-81	-48.32
Dan Skelton	21-99	21	18-70	2-16	-13.89
Philip Hobbs	20-93	22	13-52	6-32	-18.03
Kim Bailey	16-93	17	9-56	1-25	-25.36
Tom George	16-83	19	2-29	14-50	-13.00
Henry Daly	15-88	17	8-41	6-33	-27.93
Nigel Twiston-Davies	11-109	10	6-60	5-44	-74.46
Venetia Williams	11-98	11	3-47	8-49	-45.03
Matt Sheppard	9-56	16	3-27	6-27	+6.00
Alan King	9-48	19	6-37	2-9	-11.13
Jonjo O'Neill	8-81	10	1-34	6-46	-42.63
David Pipe	8-52	15	4-32	3-19	+18.86

Jockeys	Wins-Rides	%	£1 level stks	Best Trainer	W-R
Richard Johnson	30-140	21	-38.12	Philip Hobbs	11-56
Paddy Brennan	22-81	27	+27.75	Tom George	12-37
Harry Skelton	20-77	26	+2.12	Dan Skelton	20-73
David Bass	18-63	29	+98.25	Kim Bailey	14-50
Paul Moloney	10-76	13	-36.18	Evan Williams	8-57
Adam Wedge	9-86	10	-28.76	Evan Williams	9-64
Andrew Tinkler	9-50	18	+16.38	Alastair Ralph	3-6
Aidan Coleman	8-89	9	-50.29	Venetia Williams	4-24
Tom O'Brien	8-56	14	-8.35	Ian Williams	4-13
Wayne Hutchinson	8-43	19	-21.63	Alan King	7-33
Kielan Woods	8-36	22	+33.00	Graeme McPherson	4-11
Jeremiah McGrath	8-19	42	+23.66	Nicky Henderson	7-13
Tom Scudamore	7-49	14	+4.37	David Pipe	5-22

Favourites
Hurdle 43% -5.36   Chase 40.1% +25.35   TOTAL 41.2% +12.97

MARKET RASEN

Legsby Road, LN8 3EA
Tel: 01673 843 434

2018-19 RFO Jumps Racing Guide

How to get there Road: A46 to Market Rasen, course on A631. Rail: Market Rasen (1m walk)

Features Right-handed, easy fences, run-in of 250 yards

2018-19 Fixtures
October 20, November 8, 22, December 6, 26, January 17, February 5, 17, March 20, 27, April 3, 21

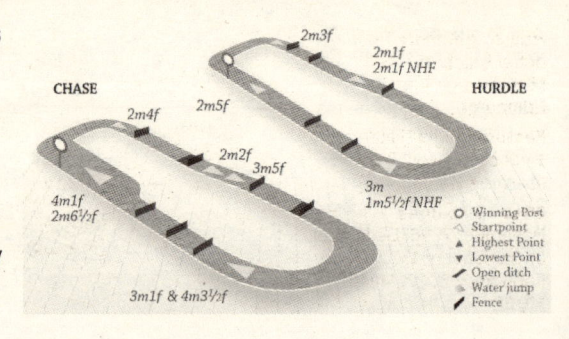

Course diagram labels: CHASE, HURDLE, 2m3f, 2m1f, 2m1f NHF, 2m4f, 2m5f, 2m2f, 2m5f, 3m, 1m5½f NHF, 4m1f, 2m6½f, 3m1f & 4m3½f

Legend: Winning Post, Startpoint, Highest Point, Lowest Point, Open ditch, Water jump, Fence

Trainers	Wins-Runs	%	Hurdles	Chases	£1 level stks
Dan Skelton	40-140	29	28-89	11-40	+19.23
Jonjo O'Neill	27-167	16	14-83	13-76	-39.89
Nicky Henderson	20-55	36	12-34	3-10	+9.82
Brian Ellison	19-126	15	13-82	3-36	-41.13
Fergal O'Brien	17-78	22	9-39	6-32	+29.38
Charlie Longsdon	14-101	14	8-51	6-37	-47.09
Dr Richard Newland	14-57	25	10-40	4-17	+12.52
Peter Bowen	13-69	19	6-32	5-29	-20.08
Malcolm Jefferson	11-60	18	7-32	2-10	-3.38
David Dennis	10-50	20	6-29	3-17	-2.71
David Pipe	10-47	21	4-24	6-20	-13.10
Sue Smith	9-75	12	4-36	5-37	-40.63
Micky Hammond	9-63	14	8-40	1-20	+10.80

Jockeys	Wins-Rides	%	£1 level stks	Best Trainer	W-R
Harry Skelton	32-120	27	-3.57	Dan Skelton	32-105
Aidan Coleman	29-156	19	-20.20	Jonjo O'Neill	11-55
Richard Johnson	28-154	18	-62.79	Philip Hobbs	7-23
Paddy Brennan	21-91	23	+42.95	Fergal O'Brien	12-46
Brian Hughes	19-154	12	-63.70	Malcolm Jefferson	7-41
Tom Scudamore	18-100	18	-17.51	David Pipe	9-35
A P McCoy	16-58	28	-17.34	Jonjo O'Neill	6-26
Gavin Sheehan	15-78	19	-11.07	Warren Greatrex	7-28
Danny Cook	14-85	16	-27.96	Sue Smith	8-34
Sam Twiston-Davies	14-74	19	-20.02	Dr Richard Newland	8-33
Noel Fehily	14-74	19	-34.87	Harry Fry	4-15
Sean Bowen	13-63	21	-6.54	Peter Bowen	9-38
Daryl Jacob	12-40	30	+30.44	Emma Lavelle	3-7

Favourites
Hurdle 39% -26.14   Chase 38.3% -9.68   TOTAL 39.5% -29.63

2018-19 RFO Jumps Racing Guide

MUSSELBURGH

East Lothian
Tel: 01316 652 859

How to get there Road: A1 out of Edinburgh. Rail: Musselburgh from Edinburgh

Features Right-handed, 1m2f circuit, very flat with sharp turns

2018-19 Fixtures
November 7, 26, December 3, 10, January 1, 7, 18, February 2-3, 27, March 10, 22

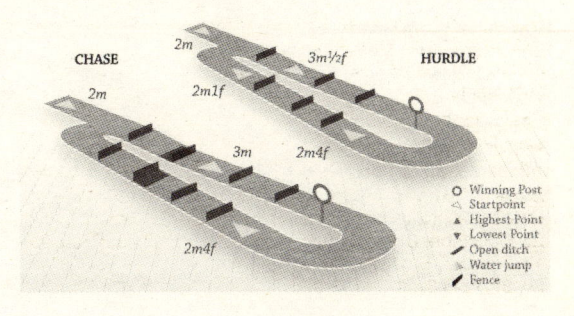

Trainers	Wins-Runs	%	Hurdles	Chases	£1 level stks
Lucinda Russell	29-211	14	17-122	11-74	-4.45
Donald McCain	20-107	19	12-68	6-35	+1.55
Sandy Thomson	14-64	22	8-37	6-25	+33.30
Keith Dalgleish	13-42	31	7-29	4-6	+1.09
Paul Nicholls	10-26	38	4-16	6-10	+6.72
James Ewart	9-68	13	8-48	0-10	-0.95
Rose Dobbin	8-66	12	1-32	6-31	-18.75
Nicky Henderson	7-21	33	7-18	0-2	-5.96
Jim Goldie	6-73	8	6-69	0-1	-33.59
Tim Vaughan	6-35	17	3-20	3-14	-0.25
John Quinn	6-16	38	6-15	0-1	+11.05
Brian Ellison	5-90	6	3-64	1-16	-60.09
Chris Grant	5-54	9	2-21	2-22	-29.00

Jockeys	Wins-Rides	%	£1 level stks	Best Trainer	W-R
Brian Hughes	39-164	24	-4.74	Keith Dalgleish	7-11
Derek Fox	14-91	15	-6.63	Lucinda Russell	13-72
Danny Cook	9-71	13	-3.54	Sandy Thomson	3-9
James Reveley	9-46	20	+2.49	Pauline Robson	2-6
Will Kennedy	9-45	20	+11.75	Donald McCain	7-28
Craig Nichol	8-90	9	-52.67	Lucinda Russell	3-18
Richard Johnson	7-29	24	-13.15	Gordon Elliott	3-6
Henry Brooke	6-77	8	-23.42	David Thompson	2-2
Peter Buchanan	6-39	15	+26.38	Lucinda Russell	6-34
Brian Harding	5-68	7	-44.25	Jim Goldie	2-6
Ryan Day	5-29	17	-4.38	Keith Dalgleish	1-2
Jason Maguire	5-28	18	-13.70	Donald McCain	5-27
Rachael McDonald	5-24	21	+10.25	Sandy Thomson	5-19

Favourites
Hurdle 39.7% -8.97   Chase 40.6% +9.50   TOTAL 40.7% +4.24

NEWBURY

Newbury, Berkshire, RG14 7NZ
Tel: 01635 400 15 or 414 85

How to get there Road: Follow signs from M4 or A34. Rail: Newbury Racecourse

Features Flat, left-handed, 1m6f circuit, suits galloping sorts with stamina, tough fences

2018-19 Fixtures
November 8, 30, December 1, 19, 29, January 16, February 9, March 1-2, 22-23

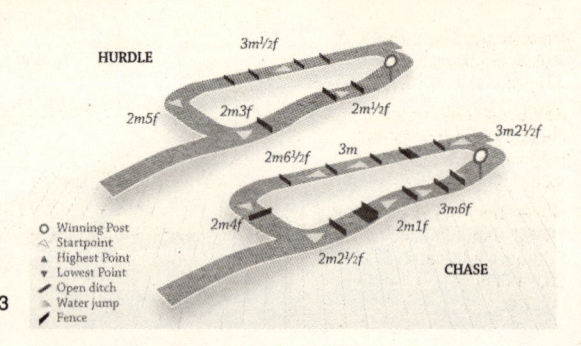

Trainers	Wins-Runs	%	Hurdles	Chases	£1 level stks
Nicky Henderson	34-158	22	26-96	4-39	-37.20
Philip Hobbs	20-107	19	10-49	9-52	+35.63
Paul Nicholls	18-131	14	6-54	12-74	-26.25
Alan King	17-126	13	8-75	4-29	-43.47
David Pipe	16-81	20	9-49	7-29	+19.03
Colin Tizzard	14-67	21	3-24	10-36	+1.95
Harry Fry	10-56	18	6-32	2-15	-9.88
Ben Pauling	9-45	20	5-31	3-9	-10.14
Warren Greatrex	8-60	13	5-39	2-12	-16.38
Dan Skelton	8-57	14	5-44	3-12	-9.63
Nigel Twiston-Davies	7-75	9	5-27	1-38	-28.59
Rebecca Curtis	7-54	13	1-22	6-27	-2.67
Gary Moore	6-75	8	4-50	2-19	-6.63

Jockeys	Wins-Rides	%	£1 level stks	Best Trainer	W-R
Richard Johnson	28-137	20	+81.58	Philip Hobbs	17-78
Nico de Boinville	21-74	28	+12.05	Nicky Henderson	16-50
Noel Fehily	17-105	16	-5.79	Harry Fry	6-37
Tom Scudamore	16-95	17	+12.15	David Pipe	11-51
Barry Geraghty	15-83	18	-12.35	Nicky Henderson	8-33
Wayne Hutchinson	12-95	13	-27.41	Alan King	11-80
Sam Twiston-Davies	11-118	9	-53.88	Paul Nicholls	7-73
Gavin Sheehan	11-78	14	-6.38	Warren Greatrex	7-36
Aidan Coleman	8-114	7	-83.78	Harry Whittington	2-4
Paddy Brennan	8-74	11	-36.13	Fergal O'Brien	5-25
Tom O'Brien	7-66	11	-11.00	Hughie Morrison	2-7
Harry Skelton	7-45	16	-6.63	Dan Skelton	7-37
A P McCoy	7-35	20	-12.50	Jonjo O'Neill	2-16

Favourites
Hurdle 38% -12.70   Chase 25.6% -31.77   TOTAL 31.9% -51.11

2018-19 RFO Jumps Racing Guide

High Gosforth Park, Newcastle
NE3 5HP. Tel: 01912 362 020

NEWCASTLE

How to get there Road: Follow signs from A1. Rail: 4m from Newcastle Central

Features Left-handed, 1m6f circuit, tough fences, half-mile straight is all uphill

2018-19 Fixtures
November 16, December 1, 13, 22, January 2, 5, 15, 29, February 23, March 5, 16, 28, April 6

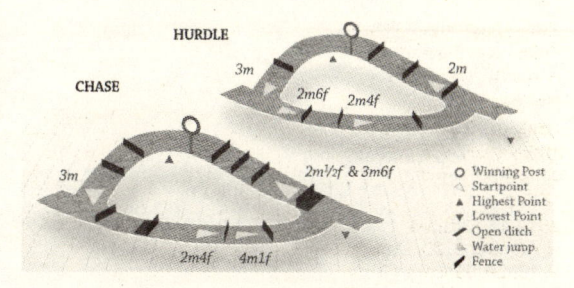

Trainers	Wins-Runs	%	Hurdles	Chases	£1 level stks
Sue Smith	17-96	18	4-34	12-55	-16.85
N W Alexander	14-92	15	7-42	7-43	-10.80
Lucinda Russell	12-101	12	6-49	6-46	-48.97
Nicky Richards	11-49	22	4-20	3-21	-8.24
Malcolm Jefferson	8-26	31	3-6	3-13	-0.52
Keith Dalgleish	8-20	40	2-12	4-6	+21.00
Keith Reveley	7-43	16	4-28	2-9	-14.38
Brian Ellison	7-41	17	3-18	4-20	-13.99
Sandy Thomson	7-34	21	3-17	3-15	-13.47
Philip Kirby	7-29	24	5-21	2-4	-2.33
Micky Hammond	6-65	9	4-28	2-30	-28.13
Donald McCain	6-59	10	4-35	2-17	-27.70
Rose Dobbin	5-51	10	3-32	2-16	-29.06

Jockeys	Wins-Rides	%	£1 level stks	Best Trainer	W-R
Brian Hughes	29-133	22	-25.87	Malcolm Jefferson	8-22
Danny Cook	14-64	22	-10.45	Sue Smith	13-47
Brian Harding	12-66	18	-13.86	Nicky Richards	7-23
James Reveley	9-55	16	-0.22	Keith Reveley	4-28
Craig Nichol	8-82	10	-47.61	Keith Dalgleish	2-5
Lucy Alexander	8-53	15	+2.50	N W Alexander	7-40
Joe Colliver	7-37	19	+6.88	Micky Hammond	6-25
Stephen Mulqueen	6-38	16	-14.30	N W Alexander	4-23
Wilson Renwick	6-30	20	-5.38	Keith Dalgleish	2-5
Steven Fox	6-24	25	+20.00	Sandy Thomson	2-8
Tony Kelly	5-53	9	-18.50	Rebecca Menzies	2-13
Thomas Dowson	5-45	11	-2.75	Philip Kirby	2-6
Adam Nicol	5-42	12	-23.33	Philip Kirby	4-17

Favourites
Hurdle 35.2% -22.32   Chase 38.7% -5.57   TOTAL 37.4% -25.48

205

2018-19 RFO Jumps Racing Guide

NEWTON ABBOT

Devon, TQ12 3AF
Tel: 01626 532 35

How to get there Road: On A380 from Newton Abbot to Torquay. Rail: Newton Abbot

Features Tight, left-handed, 1m1f circuit

2018-19 Fixtures
October 1, 12, April 20

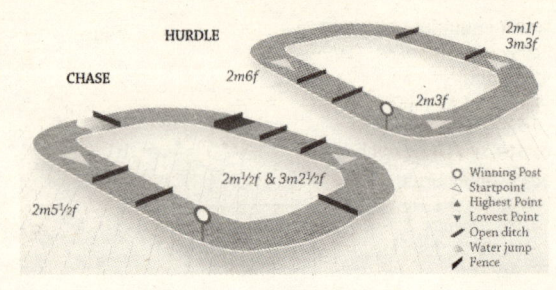

HURDLE — 2m1f, 3m3f, 2m6f, 2m3f
CHASE — 2m5½f, 2m½f & 3m2½f

○ Winning Post
△ Startpoint
▲ Highest Point
▼ Lowest Point
◇ Open ditch
≈ Water jump
∕ Fence

Trainers	Wins-Runs	%	Hurdles	Chases	£1 level stks
Paul Nicholls	42-125	34	18-55	23-66	-26.85
Philip Hobbs	25-119	21	17-71	3-39	-11.14
Martin Hill	13-102	13	9-77	3-21	-12.28
Evan Williams	13-93	14	7-49	6-42	-36.86
David Bridgwater	12-41	29	4-16	8-23	+5.66
John Ferguson	12-29	41	8-24	2-3	+10.50
Jimmy Frost	11-142	8	8-103	3-39	-68.88
Tim Vaughan	11-72	15	10-52	0-13	-12.71
Jeremy Scott	11-67	16	3-42	8-25	-1.00
David Pipe	10-109	9	6-77	4-24	-63.02
Colin Tizzard	10-83	12	5-44	4-35	-26.75
Harry Fry	10-38	26	6-28	2-5	-1.50
Chris Down	9-87	10	8-74	1-10	-33.90

Jockeys	Wins-Rides	%	£1 level stks	Best Trainer	W-R
Sam Twiston-Davies	40-149	27	-48.04	Paul Nicholls	30-84
Richard Johnson	36-163	22	-32.64	Philip Hobbs	13-55
Tom Scudamore	26-152	17	-19.07	David Bridgwater	9-21
Aidan Coleman	19-73	26	+32.58	John Ferguson	8-13
Nick Scholfield	17-114	15	-17.33	Jeremy Scott	7-28
Tom O'Brien	15-105	14	-35.64	Philip Hobbs	6-20
Noel Fehily	15-79	19	-7.77	Harry Fry	6-20
Bryony Frost	11-83	13	-39.32	Paul Nicholls	7-12
Paul Moloney	11-66	17	-12.30	Evan Williams	7-29
A P McCoy	11-42	26	-13.99	John Ferguson	3-8
Harry Cobden	10-67	15	-5.79	Michael Blake	4-10
James Best	9-115	8	-29.75	Linda Blackford	2-5
Daryl Jacob	8-48	17	+21.75	Emma Lavelle	3-7

Favourites
Hurdle 35.4% -20.91   Chase 38.6% -18.30   TOTAL 37.1% -40.02

2018-19 RFO Jumps Racing Guide

PERTH

Scone Palace Park, Perth
PH2 6BB. Tel: 01683 220 131

How to get there Road: A93. Rail: Free bus service from Perth

Features Flat, right-handed, 1m2f circuit

2018-19 Fixtures
April 24-26

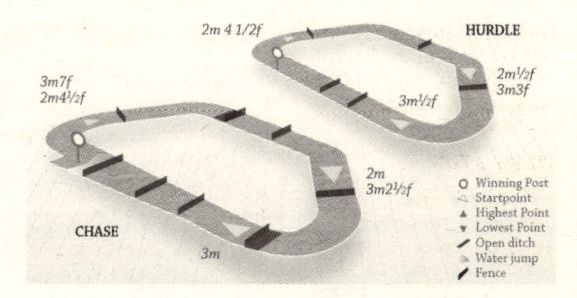

HURDLE
2m½f
3m3f
2m4½f
3m½f
3m7f
2m4½f
2m
3m2½f
CHASE
3m

○ Winning Post
△ Startpoint
▲ Highest Point
▼ Lowest Point
／ Open ditch
≋ Water jump
／ Fence

Trainers	Wins-Runs	%	Hurdles	Chases	£1 level stks
Gordon Elliott	55-218	25	36-128	15-70	-28.23
Lucinda Russell	22-283	8	16-191	5-77	-110.09
Lisa Harrison	22-149	15	13-90	9-43	-1.08
Donald McCain	19-83	23	10-51	7-26	+9.30
Nicky Richards	18-105	17	11-69	6-29	+5.46
Fergal O'Brien	18-63	29	6-26	10-31	+28.50
Nigel Twiston-Davies	16-75	21	8-41	6-28	-10.33
S R B Crawford	15-123	12	7-76	4-28	-46.19
David Pipe	12-20	60	6-12	6-8	+18.61
Tom George	11-52	21	3-15	8-35	-12.80
Dianne Sayer	10-85	12	9-64	1-21	-22.00
Jackie Stephen	9-63	14	4-37	5-21	-2.50
Alistair Whillans	7-70	10	5-45	2-22	-18.25

Jockeys	Wins-Rides	%	£1 level stks	Best Trainer	W-R
Richard Johnson	53-201	26	-35.18	Gordon Elliott	35-142
Brian Hughes	28-211	13	-63.67	Malcolm Jefferson	4-22
Craig Nichol	19-151	13	-50.73	Nicky Richards	7-30
Paddy Brennan	18-87	21	-5.50	Fergal O'Brien	11-41
Tom Scudamore	17-42	40	+13.77	David Pipe	11-18
Sam Twiston-Davies	16-70	23	-6.46	Nigel Twiston-Davies	7-45
Henry Brooke	11-128	9	-48.50	Donald McCain	2-8
Ryan Day	10-68	15	-10.67	Lisa Harrison	8-31
Callum Bewley	9-96	9	-15.63	Lisa Harrison	6-55
Brian Harding	9-87	10	-37.36	Nicky Richards	5-31
Tony Kelly	9-56	16	+16.25	Jackie Stephen	6-35
Will Kennedy	9-24	38	+31.10	Donald McCain	8-17
Derek Fox	8-106	8	-63.14	Lucinda Russell	7-85

Favourites
Hurdle 37.8% -28.11   Chase 29.8% -45.86   TOTAL 35.2% -75.58

207

2018-19 RFO Jumps Racing Guide

PLUMPTON

Plumpton, Sussex
Tel: 01273 890 383

How to get there Road: A274 or A275 to B2116. Rail: Plumpton

Features Quirky, undulating, left-handed 1m1f circuit, uphill straight, has several course specialists

2018-19 Fixtures
October 22, November 5, 19, December 3, 17, January 6, 16, 30, February 13, 25, March 11, 18, April 7, 21-22

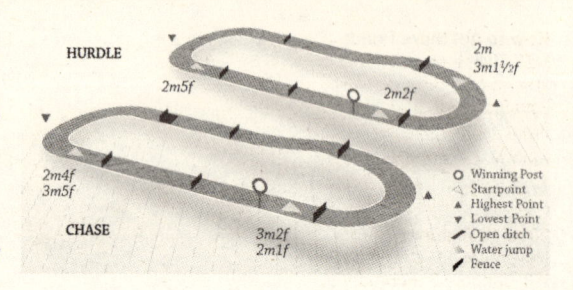

HURDLE
2m5f
2m
3m1½f
2m2f
2m4f
3m5f
CHASE
3m2f
2m1f

○ Winning Post
◁ Startpoint
▲ Highest Point
▼ Lowest Point
✎ Open ditch
≈ Water jump
✎ Fence

Trainers	Wins-Runs	%	Hurdles	Chases	£1 level stks
Gary Moore	47-242	19	28-152	19-81	-42.14
Chris Gordon	25-133	19	16-94	8-30	+49.03
Anthony Honeyball	14-48	29	6-25	5-16	-7.63
Sheena West	12-72	17	7-56	5-15	+16.33
Neil Mulholland	11-68	16	5-42	5-20	-25.63
Colin Tizzard	11-61	18	6-36	5-22	-19.92
Paul Henderson	11-59	19	4-27	7-32	-9.37
Alan King	11-37	30	9-28	2-7	-9.51
David Pipe	10-43	23	6-25	3-11	+13.76
Charlie Mann	10-27	37	4-15	6-12	+31.52
Seamus Mullins	9-97	9	6-51	3-42	-52.17
Neil King	9-57	16	3-33	6-23	-15.92
David Bridgwater	9-57	16	1-26	7-29	-29.47

Jockeys	Wins-Rides	%	£1 level stks	Best Trainer	W-R
Tom Cannon	25-178	14	+3.54	Chris Gordon	16-76
Joshua Moore	24-128	19	-34.28	Gary Moore	23-103
Jamie Moore	22-144	15	-41.67	Gary Moore	17-95
Marc Goldstein	21-155	14	+42.33	Sheena West	11-61
Tom Scudamore	18-77	23	+8.56	David Pipe	7-27
Noel Fehily	17-59	29	-4.42	Neil Mulholland	5-30
Gavin Sheehan	14-59	24	+15.91	Warren Greatrex	7-23
Leighton Aspell	12-98	12	-46.37	Oliver Sherwood	6-25
Aidan Coleman	11-60	18	-20.48	Anthony Honeyball	5-16
Tom O'Brien	10-65	15	-16.33	Paul Henderson	5-17
Paddy Brennan	10-44	23	+7.70	Colin Tizzard	3-7
Wayne Hutchinson	10-38	26	-15.60	Alan King	9-27
Harry Cobden	9-34	26	+3.00	Colin Tizzard	3-11

Favourites
Hurdle 40.3% -5.11   Chase 42.2% +4.90   TOTAL 39.9% -11.72

2018-19 RFO Jumps Racing Guide

SANDOWN

Esher, Surrey, KT10 9AJ
Tel: 01372 463 072 or 464 348

How to get there Road: M25 anti-clockwise Jctn 10 and A3, M25 clockwise Jctn 9 and A224. Rail: Esher (from Waterloo)

Features Right-handed, 1m5f circuit, tough fences and stiff uphill finish

2018-19 Fixtures November 11, December 7-8, January 5, February 2, 15, March 8-9, April 27

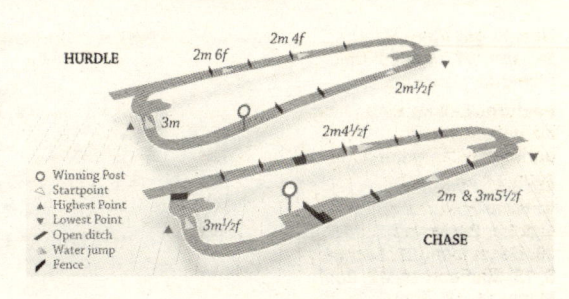

Trainers	Wins-Runs	%	Hurdles	Chases	£1 level stks
Nicky Henderson	38-128	30	27-88	10-37	+14.97
Paul Nicholls	20-160	13	7-60	13-97	-40.42
Gary Moore	18-104	17	8-61	9-42	+23.03
Philip Hobbs	12-71	17	6-28	6-39	-8.28
Nigel Twiston-Davies	10-55	18	6-26	4-29	+48.66
Alan King	10-48	21	8-35	2-10	+0.71
Fergal O'Brien	8-21	38	4-9	2-7	+31.13
Charlie Longsdon	6-53	11	0-15	6-37	+18.25
David Pipe	6-48	13	2-36	4-11	-26.54
Lucy Wadham	6-34	18	2-16	4-17	+3.83
W P Mullins	6-17	35	3-8	2-7	+19.19
Oliver Sherwood	5-35	14	2-19	3-15	+2.25
Neil Mulholland	5-30	17	1-12	4-18	+1.00

Jockeys	Wins-Rides	%	£1 level stks	Best Trainer	W-R
Jamie Moore	19-79	24	+26.94	Gary Moore	11-49
Daryl Jacob	18-58	31	+39.12	Nicky Henderson	7-13
Richard Johnson	15-86	17	-10.19	Philip Hobbs	10-42
Noel Fehily	14-74	19	+1.07	Neil Mulholland	4-12
Sam Twiston-Davies	13-100	13	+2.58	Paul Nicholls	9-68
Nico de Boinville	11-54	20	-20.02	Nicky Henderson	10-39
Leighton Aspell	9-65	14	-13.25	Lucy Wadham	3-20
Barry Geraghty	9-41	22	-0.91	Nicky Henderson	8-24
Joshua Moore	8-47	17	+27.88	Gary Moore	6-34
Aidan Coleman	6-97	6	-48.50	Venetia Williams	2-38
Wayne Hutchinson	6-38	16	-14.29	Alan King	6-30
Paddy Brennan	5-40	13	-3.50	Fergal O'Brien	4-8
Sean Bowen	5-24	21	+44.91	Charlie Longsdon	1-1

Favourites
Hurdle 35.2% -1.24   Chase 39.8% +11.71   TOTAL 36.5% +5.35

209

SEDGEFIELD

Sedgefield, Cleveland, TS21 2HW
Tel: 01740 621 925

How to get there Road: 2m from A1 on A689. Rail: Stockton, Darlington

Features Left-handed, 1m2f circuit, sharp and undulating, no water jump

2018-19 Fixtures
October 2, 21, November 1, 8, 27, December 7, 26, January 11, 21, 27, February 5, 21, March 3, 12, 21, April 5, 23

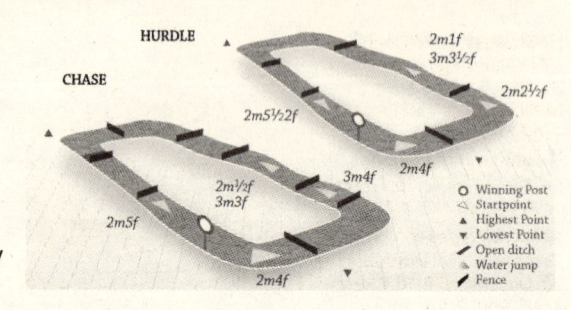

Trainers	Wins-Runs	%	Hurdles	Chases	£1 level stks
Donald McCain	44-235	19	32-163	10-58	-21.96
Micky Hammond	31-222	14	16-130	13-80	-56.74
Brian Ellison	29-131	22	19-85	6-32	-29.95
Malcolm Jefferson	21-85	25	7-43	9-22	-2.50
Kenneth Slack	20-71	28	12-52	8-18	+30.58
Sue Smith	17-149	11	11-75	6-67	-60.52
Dan Skelton	16-54	30	12-36	4-14	-3.61
Neil Mulholland	15-33	45	8-21	6-10	+17.52
Chris Grant	13-124	10	5-72	4-29	-12.53
Dianne Sayer	13-69	19	11-54	2-14	+29.75
Joanne Foster	9-70	13	1-27	8-43	-0.90
Sam England	9-47	19	4-23	5-24	+5.90
Ben Haslam	9-46	20	5-28	4-18	+13.50

Jockeys	Wins-Rides	%	£1 level stks	Best Trainer	W-R
Brian Hughes	62-291	21	+47.30	Malcolm Jefferson	19-67
Henry Brooke	30-181	17	-22.25	Kenneth Slack	12-31
Danny Cook	17-102	17	-28.35	Brian Ellison	8-32
Wilson Renwick	15-66	23	+8.69	Donald McCain	9-28
James Reveley	13-46	28	-2.72	Keith Reveley	5-10
Will Kennedy	12-103	12	-29.75	Donald McCain	9-71
Brian Harding	12-78	15	+10.03	Keith Dalgleish	3-7
Joe Colliver	12-67	18	-15.38	Micky Hammond	10-48
Sean Quinlan	11-100	11	-44.75	Sue Smith	6-39
Harry Skelton	11-35	31	+2.86	Dan Skelton	11-28
Finian O'Toole	10-105	10	-34.79	Micky Hammond	9-84
Jonathan England	10-71	14	-9.10	Sam England	8-38
Adam Nicol	8-92	9	-42.25	Philip Kirby	3-34

Favourites
Hurdle 41.8% -11.56   Chase 36.1% -19.01   TOTAL 39.2% -41.21

2018-19 RFO Jumps Racing Guide

SOUTHWELL

Rolleston, nr Newark, Notts
NG25 0TS. Tel: 01636 814 481

How to get there Road: A1 to Newark and A617 to Southwell or A52 to Nottingham (off M1) and A612 to Southwell. Rail: Rolleston

Features Flat, left-handed, 1m2f circuit

2018-19 Fixtures
October 2, 25, November 20, December 4, 16, March 4, 18, April 9, 24

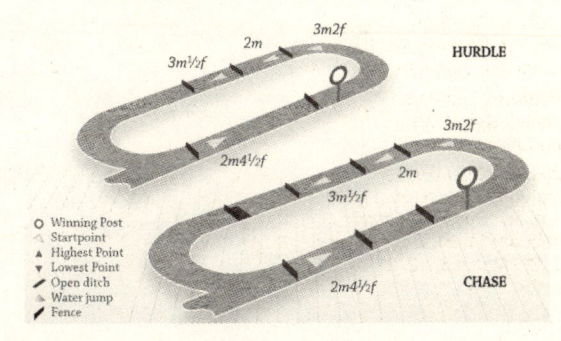

Trainers	Wins-Runs	%	Hurdles	Chases	£1 level stks
Jonjo O'Neill	22-140	16	10-92	11-41	-38.54
Dan Skelton	20-116	17	14-75	6-25	-49.28
Tom George	19-57	33	14-33	4-13	+10.53
Caroline Bailey	16-84	19	10-50	6-33	+20.25
Nicky Henderson	13-43	30	5-24	0-5	-7.01
Ben Pauling	12-40	30	8-26	1-5	-3.65
Tim Vaughan	10-73	14	6-44	4-20	+7.25
Charlie Longsdon	10-69	14	7-42	2-16	-7.21
Neil Mulholland	9-67	13	4-40	4-22	+1.24
Kim Bailey	9-51	18	6-33	2-11	-3.78
Peter Bowen	9-46	20	4-23	5-13	+5.56
Seamus Mullins	8-49	16	2-26	3-17	+18.13
Caroline Fryer	8-34	24	5-22	3-12	+22.78

Jockeys	Wins-Rides	%	£1 level stks	Best Trainer	W-R
Richard Johnson	28-130	22	-13.33	Charlie Longsdon	3-9
Harry Skelton	27-120	23	+4.09	Dan Skelton	18-82
Paddy Brennan	23-87	26	+30.11	Tom George	11-28
Aidan Coleman	17-127	13	-56.50	Jonjo O'Neill	6-41
Sean Bowen	17-70	24	+38.56	Peter Bowen	8-37
Nico de Boinville	16-60	27	-3.43	Ben Pauling	6-19
A P McCoy	15-43	35	+0.38	Jonjo O'Neill	5-21
Tom Scudamore	12-70	17	-18.52	Michael Scudamore	3-11
Sam Twiston-Davies	12-59	20	+1.76	Nigel Twiston-Davies	5-21
Noel Fehily	12-57	21	-5.10	Neil Mulholland	3-22
Gavin Sheehan	12-54	22	+80.60	Jamie Snowden	3-5
Brian Hughes	11-92	12	-34.02	Mike Sowersby	3-16
Richie McLernon	11-61	18	-7.58	Jonjo O'Neill	6-20

Favourites
Hurdle 44.1% +36.27   Chase 33.7% -30.88   TOTAL 39.3% -4.85

2018-19 RFO Jumps Racing Guide

STRATFORD

Luddington Road, Stratford
CV37 9SE. Tel: 01789 267 949

How to get there Road: M40 Jctn 15, A3400, B439, A46. Rail: Stratford-Upon-Avon

Features Sharp, left-handed, 1m2f circuit

2018-19 Fixtures October 8, 20, November 1, March 11, 30, April 14

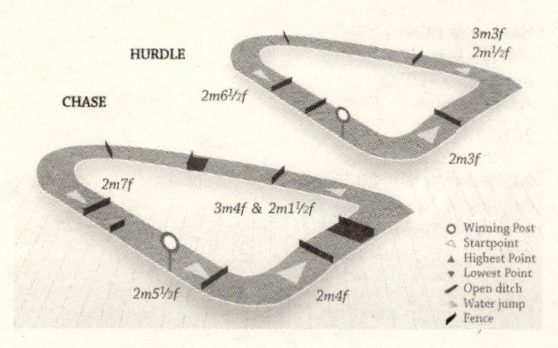

HURDLE 3m3f 2m½f
CHASE 2m6½f
2m3f
2m7f
3m4f & 2m1½f
2m5½f 2m4f

○ Winning Post
◁ Startpoint
▲ Highest Point
▼ Lowest Point
／ Open ditch
≈ Water jump
▬ Fence

Trainers	Wins-Runs	%	Hurdles	Chases	£1 level stks
Dan Skelton	19-109	17	12-71	5-31	-30.74
Warren Greatrex	17-55	31	9-35	3-11	+17.99
John Ferguson	16-30	53	13-25	1-1	+8.01
Philip Hobbs	14-57	25	3-18	11-37	+26.78
Tom George	13-51	25	5-18	7-30	+34.59
Nigel Twiston-Davies	10-67	15	8-37	2-26	-19.38
Neil Mulholland	10-58	17	7-41	2-15	-10.33
Alan King	10-40	25	8-30	1-5	-4.15
David Dennis	9-59	15	7-40	2-19	+26.50
Peter Bowen	9-38	24	1-14	7-15	+13.67
Tim Vaughan	8-86	9	4-59	3-21	-39.21
Paul Nicholls	8-28	29	5-13	2-14	-7.88
David Bridgwater	7-74	9	4-42	3-29	-19.00

Jockeys	Wins-Rides	%	£1 level stks	Best Trainer	W-R
Richard Johnson	36-153	24	+11.67	Philip Hobbs	8-30
Aidan Coleman	22-97	23	+7.60	John Ferguson	9-14
Sam Twiston-Davies	16-92	17	-23.55	Paul Nicholls	6-17
Harry Skelton	16-78	21	-15.12	Dan Skelton	15-72
Tom Scudamore	13-99	13	-21.90	David Pipe	6-32
Tom O'Brien	13-75	17	+14.33	Ian Williams	4-12
Noel Fehily	12-68	18	-15.56	Neil Mulholland	4-17
Daryl Jacob	12-47	26	+9.58	Emma Lavelle	4-11
Gavin Sheehan	10-61	16	-12.90	Warren Greatrex	6-27
Sean Bowen	10-46	22	-0.98	Peter Bowen	5-23
Paddy Brennan	9-65	14	+6.17	Tom George	4-23
Andrew Tinkler	9-45	20	+16.00	Martin Keighley	5-26
Harry Bannister	9-30	30	+23.20	Charlie Mann	4-5

Favourites
Hurdle 38.1% -8.80   Chase 31.5% -27.46   TOTAL 35.1% -45.85

2018-19 RFO Jumps Racing Guide

TAUNTON

Orchard Portman, Taunton, Somerset
TA3 7BL. Tel: 01823 337 172

How to get there Road: M5 Jctn 25. Rail: Taunton

Features Right-handed, 1m2f circuit

2018-19 Fixtures
October 31, November 15, 29, December 13, 30, January 9, 19, February 4, 19, 28, March 11, 19, April 4, 24

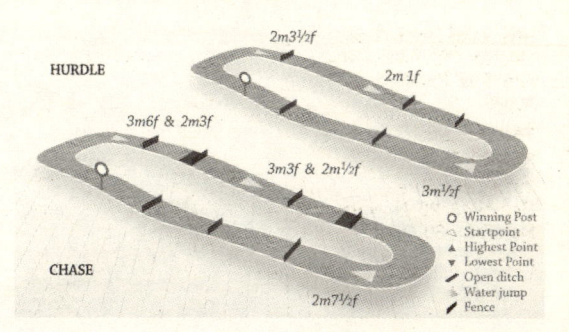

HURDLE — 2m3½f, 2m 1f
CHASE — 3m6f & 2m3f, 3m3f & 2m½f, 3m½f, 2m7½f

○ Winning Post
◁ Startpoint
▲ Highest Point
▼ Lowest Point
↗ Open ditch
≈ Water jump
/ Fence

Trainers	Wins-Runs	%	Hurdles	Chases	£1 level stks
Paul Nicholls	46-156	29	33-104	10-40	-14.01
Harry Fry	18-76	24	14-60	1-5	-21.07
Colin Tizzard	16-103	16	11-61	5-37	-6.85
David Pipe	15-145	10	10-118	5-23	-66.38
Philip Hobbs	11-104	11	7-75	1-19	-56.63
Nicky Henderson	11-32	34	9-26	1-3	+3.68
Dan Skelton	10-56	18	8-48	0-4	-25.15
Evan Williams	9-86	10	7-60	2-22	-29.83
Anthony Honeyball	9-48	19	7-35	1-9	-4.92
Jeremy Scott	9-48	19	5-30	4-13	+8.63
Johnny Farrelly	8-67	12	8-57	0-9	-10.63
Venetia Williams	8-39	21	5-19	3-20	+7.20
Alexandra Dunn	7-73	10	4-57	2-14	-12.25

Jockeys	Wins-Rides	%	£1 level stks	Best Trainer	W-R
Sam Twiston-Davies	26-102	25	-24.70	Paul Nicholls	23-73
Noel Fehily	16-70	23	-21.54	Harry Fry	9-28
Tom Scudamore	14-113	12	-48.58	David Pipe	7-65
Nick Scholfield	13-91	14	-36.55	Paul Nicholls	6-23
Harry Cobden	12-57	21	-15.00	Paul Nicholls	5-23
David Noonan	10-78	13	-27.92	Anthony Honeyball	4-17
James Best	9-111	8	-64.63	Jackie Du Plessis	3-19
Brendan Powell	9-62	15	-4.75	Johnny Farrelly	5-24
Micheal Nolan	9-50	18	+112.57	Jamie Snowden	3-7
Richard Johnson	8-85	9	-50.70	Philip Hobbs	5-47
Aidan Coleman	8-62	13	-30.43	Anthony Honeyball	3-9
Daryl Jacob	8-38	21	-3.06	Nicky Henderson	2-2
James Davies	7-51	14	+38.75	Chris Down	4-20

Favourites
Hurdle 40.4% -1.15   Chase 33.6% -12.27   TOTAL 38.2% -13.01

TOWCESTER

Easton Newston, Towcester
NN12 7HS. Tel: 01327 353 414

How to get there Road: M1 Jctn 15a, A43 West. Rail: Northampton (8m) and bus service

Features Right-handed, 1m6f circuit, uphill from back straight

2018-19 Fixtures January 3, 31, February 13, March 14, April 11, 26 (track unable to fulfil 2018 fixtures due to administration – remaining fixtures above to be confirmed)

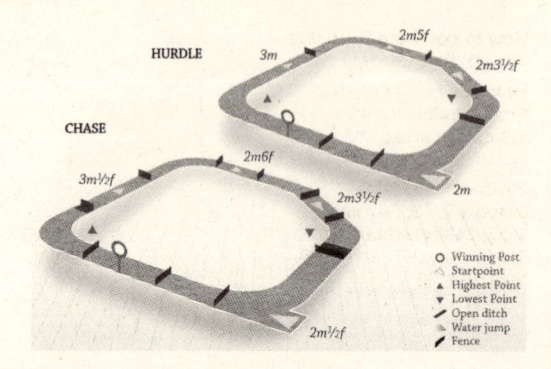

Trainers	Wins-Runs	%	Hurdles	Chases	£1 level stks
Kim Bailey	13-53	25	7-29	4-15	-0.41
Ben Pauling	11-46	24	5-32	6-13	+29.75
Nicky Henderson	11-30	37	8-16	1-4	-0.58
Fergal O'Brien	10-40	25	9-23	1-11	+6.96
Henry Oliver	10-33	30	5-21	5-10	+29.12
Henry Daly	9-32	28	3-18	5-10	+25.60
Charlie Longsdon	8-44	18	2-24	6-17	-14.05
Dan Skelton	8-33	24	5-21	2-7	-13.14
Alan King	8-32	25	5-21	0-2	-1.80
Martin Keighley	7-47	15	3-28	3-16	-13.75
Neil Mulholland	7-19	37	4-8	2-7	+5.73
Venetia Williams	6-40	15	1-20	4-19	-10.80
David Pipe	6-34	18	1-21	2-5	-11.03

Jockeys	Wins-Rides	%	£1 level stks	Best Trainer	W-R
David Bass	10-49	20	-4.32	Ben Pauling	4-14
Paddy Brennan	10-43	23	+9.88	Fergal O'Brien	8-20
Nico de Boinville	8-37	22	-11.36	Nicky Henderson	4-9
Jeremiah McGrath	8-25	32	+7.93	Nicky Henderson	4-7
Daryl Jacob	7-41	17	-0.66	Ben Pauling	2-5
Liam Treadwell	6-43	14	-10.60	Venetia Williams	3-16
Richard Johnson	6-36	17	-1.25	Henry Daly	2-3
Brendan Powell	5-44	11	-3.50	Brendan Powell	3-12
Richie McLernon	5-39	13	+59.00	Ben Haslam	1-2
Tom Scudamore	5-34	15	-22.53	David Pipe	4-17
Sam Twiston-Davies	5-28	18	+28.00	Nigel Twiston-Davies	3-13
Noel Fehily	5-27	19	-9.00	Neil Mulholland	2-7
Joshua Moore	5-26	19	+7.75	Gary Moore	3-10

Favourites
Hurdle 36.9% -20.54   Chase 37.1% -8.29   TOTAL 36.6% -36.86

2018-19 RFO Jumps Racing Guide

UTTOXETER

Wood Lane, Uttoxeter, Staffs
ST14 8BD. Tel: 01889 562 561

How to get there Road: M6 Jctn 14. Rail: Uttoxeter

Features Left-handed, 1m2f circuit, undulating with sweeping curves, suits galloping types

2018-19 Fixtures
October 7, 18, November 2, 17, 25, December 11, 21, 31, January 26, February 9, March 16, 30

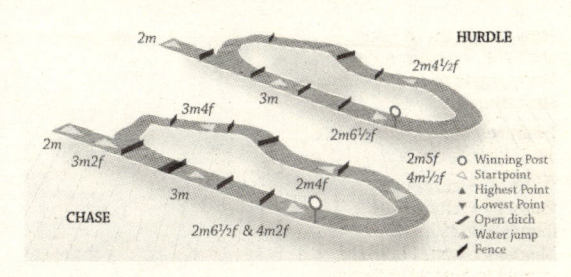

Trainers	Wins-Runs	%	Hurdles	Chases	£1 level stks
Jonjo O'Neill	28-204	14	16-113	10-82	-69.69
Dan Skelton	24-105	23	15-62	8-33	-13.52
Nigel Twiston-Davies	23-136	17	11-68	11-55	-26.76
Charlie Longsdon	23-105	22	12-57	11-42	+6.23
Warren Greatrex	21-59	36	8-34	3-9	+21.84
Nicky Henderson	19-62	31	13-37	4-18	-13.85
Philip Hobbs	16-90	18	11-49	3-35	-22.33
Dr Richard Newland	16-57	28	14-42	2-15	-11.44
Tim Vaughan	15-123	12	12-97	2-21	-38.47
David Pipe	15-108	14	4-59	8-37	-37.68
Fergal O'Brien	15-77	19	6-44	7-25	+26.28
Neil King	15-77	19	12-55	1-15	-14.46
Evan Williams	14-89	16	8-52	5-31	+33.35

Jockeys	Wins-Rides	%	£1 level stks	Best Trainer	W-R
Richard Johnson	40-216	19	-40.78	Philip Hobbs	9-43
Aidan Coleman	34-169	20	+2.71	Jonjo O'Neill	15-56
Harry Skelton	26-82	32	+33.53	Dan Skelton	23-69
Noel Fehily	24-96	25	-7.17	Harry Fry	6-11
Gavin Sheehan	23-86	27	+31.64	Warren Greatrex	13-32
Tom Scudamore	22-143	15	-53.20	David Pipe	12-67
Sam Twiston-Davies	21-117	18	-28.23	Dr Richard Newland	10-28
Sean Bowen	18-106	17	-23.72	Peter Bowen	9-46
Trevor Whelan	16-104	15	-20.29	Neil King	13-59
Paddy Brennan	15-87	17	+28.66	Fergal O'Brien	9-39
Tom O'Brien	13-115	11	-43.38	Ian Williams	3-20
Andrew Tinkler	13-86	15	-15.89	Martin Keighley	6-36
A P McCoy	13-54	24	-17.41	Jonjo O'Neill	3-26

Favourites
Hurdle 42.6% +27.48   Chase 36.4% -3.31   TOTAL 40.7% +26.21

2018-19 RFO Jumps Racing Guide

WARWICK

Hampton Street, Warwick
CV34 6HN. Tel: 01926 491 553

How to get there Road: M40 Jctn 15 on to A429 and follow signs to town centre. Rail: Warwick

Features Left-handed, 1m6f circuit, undulating

2018-19 Fixtures
October 4, November 9, 21, December 13, 31, January 12, 21, February 9, 22, March 10, 28, April 10, 25

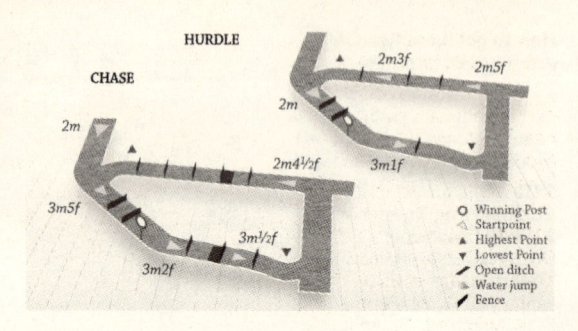

Trainers	Wins-Runs	%	Hurdles	Chases	£1 level stks
Dan Skelton	29-140	21	14-87	10-34	-33.67
Alan King	25-113	22	17-74	5-18	-42.34
Jonjo O'Neill	21-125	17	12-75	8-40	+26.65
Philip Hobbs	19-86	22	7-38	6-27	-16.79
Nigel Twiston-Davies	15-130	12	3-56	10-52	-60.04
Nicky Henderson	13-50	26	8-27	3-6	-10.46
Paul Nicholls	12-44	27	3-18	8-22	-7.79
Charlie Longsdon	11-90	12	6-52	5-28	-34.51
Venetia Williams	11-76	14	5-28	5-43	-27.57
Henry Daly	9-52	17	6-25	2-19	-10.88
Ben Pauling	9-43	21	2-22	0-6	+7.75
Neil Mulholland	9-39	23	3-21	5-16	-4.02
Warren Greatrex	8-44	18	2-27	1-4	+9.33

Jockeys	Wins-Rides	%	£1 level stks	Best Trainer	W-R
Richard Johnson	31-152	20	-34.92	Philip Hobbs	15-55
Harry Skelton	28-119	24	-16.18	Dan Skelton	27-110
Noel Fehily	25-94	27	+26.64	Neil Mulholland	7-24
Aidan Coleman	20-115	17	-27.94	Venetia Williams	5-20
Sam Twiston-Davies	18-97	19	-26.34	Paul Nicholls	10-26
Daryl Jacob	13-65	20	-17.97	Nicky Henderson	4-5
Wayne Hutchinson	11-78	14	-35.75	Alan King	8-60
Gavin Sheehan	11-64	17	+0.21	Warren Greatrex	4-23
Nico de Boinville	11-49	22	-1.41	Nicky Henderson	6-19
David Bass	10-60	17	-10.00	Ben Pauling	5-12
Jamie Moore	10-58	17	+109.75	Richard Lee	3-3
Tom O'Brien	9-66	14	-23.38	Stuart Edmunds	2-2
Sean Bowen	9-64	14	-30.68	Peter Bowen	3-34

Favourites
Hurdle 37.5% -37.73   Chase 40.1% -0.94   TOTAL 38.4% -38.79

2018-19 RFO Jumps Racing Guide

WETHERBY

York Road, Wetherby, West Yorks
L22 5EJ. Tel: 01937 582 035

How to get there Road: A1, A58 from Leeds, B1224 from York. Rail: Leeds, Harrogate, York

Features Long, left-handed circuit (1m4f chases, 1m2f hurdles), suits galloping types

2018-19 Fixtures
October 17, November 2-3, 17, 28, December 8, 26-27, January 4, 12, 24, February 2, 19, March 19, 29, April 11

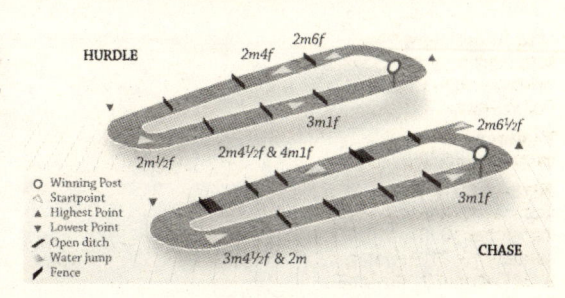

Trainers	Wins-Runs	%	Hurdles	Chases	£1 level stks
Dan Skelton	28-80	35	15-46	10-26	+11.40
Micky Hammond	24-232	10	15-149	6-70	+14.83
Sue Smith	20-162	12	6-75	13-81	-76.81
Warren Greatrex	17-60	28	13-41	3-10	+6.52
Philip Kirby	15-121	12	13-104	2-4	-21.82
Jonjo O'Neill	13-60	22	10-38	3-21	-10.55
Brian Ellison	11-79	14	6-46	3-24	-31.04
Neil Mulholland	10-29	34	5-18	4-9	+6.32
Rose Dobbin	9-55	16	6-32	2-20	+2.71
Michael Easterby	9-41	22	6-22	3-12	+28.33
Nigel Twiston-Davies	9-40	23	4-20	4-19	-8.05
Nicky Richards	9-31	29	5-14	3-12	+59.25
Philip Hobbs	9-28	32	5-13	4-15	+3.39

Jockeys	Wins-Rides	%	£1 level stks	Best Trainer	W-R
Brian Hughes	27-201	13	-47.78	Malcolm Jefferson	7-49
Harry Skelton	25-71	35	+3.98	Dan Skelton	23-62
Danny Cook	21-137	15	-52.60	Sue Smith	14-80
Richard Johnson	19-70	27	+12.90	Philip Hobbs	6-16
Adam Nicol	16-89	18	+31.93	Philip Kirby	8-49
Joe Colliver	14-100	14	+37.58	Micky Hammond	13-79
Paddy Brennan	11-25	44	+49.90	Fergal O'Brien	6-8
Craig Nichol	10-59	17	-0.13	Lucinda Russell	3-7
Gavin Sheehan	10-57	18	-28.46	Warren Greatrex	8-27
Noel Fehily	9-37	24	-6.68	Neil Mulholland	3-11
Tom Scudamore	9-35	26	-10.89	David Pipe	4-14
A P McCoy	9-24	38	+7.33	Jonjo O'Neill	4-9
Dougie Costello	8-60	13	+5.00	Warren Greatrex	3-10

Favourites
Hurdle 39.7% -22.66   Chase 38.2% -20.18   TOTAL 38.6% -51.40

217

2018-19 RFO Jumps Racing Guide

WINCANTON

Wincanton, Somerset
BA9 8BJ. Tel: 01963 323 44

How to get there Road: A303 to Wincanton, course on B3081, 1m from town centre. Rail: Gillingham

Features Right-handed, 1m4f circuit, dries fast

2018-19 Fixtures October 19, 29, November 10, 22, December 6, 26, January 5, 17, 31, February 16, 27, March 7, 25, April 3, 14

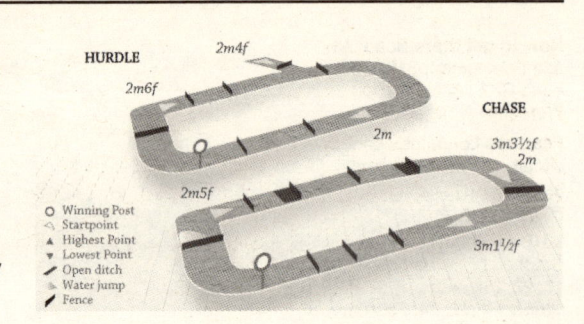

HURDLE — 2m4f, 2m6f, 2m, 2m5f
CHASE — 3m3½f, 2m, 3m1½f

○ Winning Post
⊲ Startpoint
▲ Highest Point
▼ Lowest Point
✓ Open ditch
≈ Water jump
✓ Fence

Trainers	Wins-Runs	%	Hurdles	Chases	£1 level stks
Paul Nicholls	76-221	34	49-126	21-71	-1.36
Colin Tizzard	30-207	14	13-102	17-76	-52.26
Philip Hobbs	17-138	12	7-78	6-43	-47.38
Harry Fry	16-79	20	9-55	3-12	-12.13
Neil Mulholland	12-127	9	7-80	4-38	-45.65
Emma Lavelle	12-56	21	6-25	3-22	+28.38
Alan King	12-54	22	7-40	3-9	+3.89
Jeremy Scott	9-84	11	4-48	4-25	-18.88
Anthony Honeyball	9-61	15	4-36	2-15	-20.68
Tom George	9-47	19	1-9	8-34	-9.79
Seamus Mullins	8-83	10	3-49	5-26	-20.20
Venetia Williams	8-68	12	4-24	4-44	-30.52
Warren Greatrex	8-38	21	6-30	1-4	+1.13

Jockeys	Wins-Rides	%	£1 level stks	Best Trainer	W-R
Sam Twiston-Davies	36-146	25	-36.57	Paul Nicholls	33-110
Harry Cobden	34-112	30	+0.21	Paul Nicholls	21-47
Nick Scholfield	18-118	15	-4.03	Paul Nicholls	4-21
Richard Johnson	17-111	15	-21.25	Philip Hobbs	9-59
Daryl Jacob	16-72	22	+11.42	Emma Lavelle	6-16
Tom O'Brien	13-100	13	-38.33	Philip Hobbs	5-29
Noel Fehily	12-85	14	-46.08	Harry Fry	6-37
Aidan Coleman	12-69	17	+3.80	Anthony Honeyball	4-11
Tom Scudamore	10-77	13	-25.04	David Pipe	4-26
Tom Bellamy	9-35	26	+18.38	Alan King	4-9
Gavin Sheehan	8-43	19	+3.25	Warren Greatrex	6-21
David Bass	8-31	26	+4.88	Kim Bailey	5-16
Wayne Hutchinson	7-45	16	-10.00	Alan King	3-27

Favourites
Hurdle 42.3% -11.71   Chase 37.5% -19.61   TOTAL 40% -35.62

2018-19 RFO Jumps Racing Guide

WORCESTER

Pitchcroft, Worcester
WR1 3EJ. Tel: 01905 253 64

How to get there Road: M5 Jctn 6 from north, M5 Jctn 7 or A38 from south. Rail: Worcester (Forgate Street)

Features Left-handed, 1m5f circuit, prone to flooding

2018-19 Fixtures
October 11, 24

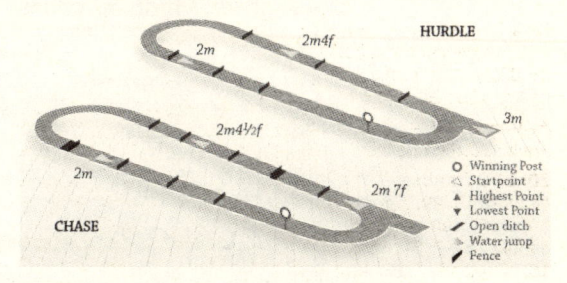

HURDLE — 2m, 2m4f, 3m
CHASE — 2m, 2m4½f, 2m7f

○ Winning Post
◁ Startpoint
▲ Highest Point
▼ Lowest Point
╱ Open ditch
⌇ Water jump
╱ Fence

Trainers	Wins-Runs	%	Hurdles	Chases	£1 level stks
Jonjo O'Neill	43-228	19	19-121	22-97	-32.01
Philip Hobbs	29-105	28	17-59	10-41	+39.44
Neil Mulholland	24-138	17	16-84	8-46	-12.09
Dan Skelton	23-122	19	12-71	9-39	-28.22
Nicky Henderson	22-68	32	14-39	3-11	+7.40
David Pipe	20-130	15	13-82	3-31	-43.89
Dr Richard Newland	17-61	28	15-46	2-15	-11.62
Nigel Twiston-Davies	15-83	18	7-50	5-23	-2.97
Charlie Longsdon	13-75	17	6-39	4-26	-0.71
Peter Bowen	13-74	18	5-30	6-33	-14.37
Kim Bailey	13-48	27	6-27	7-19	+6.29
John Ferguson	13-35	37	8-25	1-5	-7.07
Tim Vaughan	12-90	13	5-50	7-33	-21.80

Jockeys	Wins-Rides	%	£1 level stks	Best Trainer	W-R
Richard Johnson	49-244	20	-43.81	Philip Hobbs	21-65
A P McCoy	35-102	34	+18.51	Jonjo O'Neill	12-46
Sam Twiston-Davies	34-170	20	-30.22	Dr Richard Newland	9-36
Aidan Coleman	31-186	17	-58.01	Jonjo O'Neill	14-64
Noel Fehily	25-134	19	-20.98	Neil Mulholland	11-55
Tom Scudamore	22-187	12	-63.03	David Pipe	14-84
Harry Skelton	21-114	18	-5.85	Dan Skelton	18-100
Sean Bowen	16-98	16	-17.62	Peter Bowen	10-49
Tom O'Brien	15-112	13	-25.13	Robert Stephens	6-23
Nico de Boinville	15-98	15	-33.95	Nicky Henderson	7-32
Brendan Powell	13-109	12	+68.46	Brendan Powell	6-32
Paul Moloney	12-104	12	-37.18	Evan Williams	7-38
Daryl Jacob	11-70	16	+4.85	Emma Lavelle	3-10

Favourites
Hurdle 41.3% -4.78   Chase 37% -3.75   TOTAL 40.2% -11.30

Record and standard times

Aintree, Mildmay course

2m Ch	Nohalmdun (7 Apr 1990)	3m45.30s	3m49s
2m4f Ch	Wind Force (2 Apr 1993)	4m46.60s	4m48s
3m1f Ch	Cab On Target (2 Apr 1993)	6m03.40s	6m07s
2m1½f Hdl	Spinning (3 Apr 1993)	3m44.80s	3m53s
2m1f Hdl	Gabrial The Great (16 May 2014)	4m04.30s	4m00s
	Hawk High (25 Oct 2014)		
2m4f Hdl	Gallateen (2 Apr 1993)	4m37.10s	4m43s
3m½f Hdl	Andrew's First (1 Apr 1993)	5m50.70s	5m54s

Aintree, Grand National course

2m5f Ch	Always Waining (8 Apr 2011)	5m19.30s	5m21s
3m2f Ch	Eurotrek (19 Nov 2006)	6m46.60s	6m38s
4m2½f Ch	One For Arthur (8 Apr 2017)	9m03.50s	9m04s

Ascot

2m1f Ch	Quite By Chance (29 Oct 2016)	3m55.90s	4m04s
2m3f Ch	Master Dee (29 Oct 2016)	4m29.50s	4m34s
2m5f Ch	Kew Jumper (11 Apr 2008)	5m12.60s	5m08s
3m Ch	Exmoor Ranger (29 Oct 2011)	5m49.60s	5m43s
1m7½f Hdl	Brampour (29 Oct 2011)	3m33.30s	3m41s
2m3½f Hdl	Overturn (19 Nov 2011)	4m30.80s	4m28s
2m5½f Hdl	Emmaslegend (19 Nov 2011)	5m10.90s	5m00s
2m7½f Hdl	Heronry (30 Mar 2014)	5m34.10s	5m29s
3m½f Hdl	Unowhatimeanharry (17 Dec 2016)	5m54.30s	5m46s

Ayr

1m7½f Ch	Clay County (12 Oct 1991)	3m38.60s	3m40s
2m4½f Ch	Cloudy Dream (22 Apr 2017)	5m02.00s	4m58s
2m5½f Ch	Star To The North (9 May 2001)	5m10.20s	5m10s
3m½f Ch	Top 'N' Tale (12 May 1982)	5m57.70s	5m54s
3m3f Ch	Joaaci (15 Apr 2005)	6m50.20s	6m35s
4m Ch	Hot Weld (21 Apr 2007)	7m55.10s	8m02s
2m Hdl	Midnight Shadow (21 Apr 2018)	3m41.50s	3m40s
2m5½f Hdl	Cucumber Run (21 Apr 2012)	5m04.70s	5m02s
3m½f Hdl	Nautical Lad (6 Apr 1964)	5m42.00s	5m43s

Bangor

2m1½f Ch	Daulys Anthem (4 Aug 2017)	4m01.80s	4m05s
2m4½f Ch	The Disengager (24 Jul 2012)	4m49.70s	4m49s
3m Ch	He's The Gaffer (16 Aug 2008)	5m50.60s	5m45s
3m5½f Ch	Kaki Crazy (23 May 2001)	7m34.10s	7m10s
2m1½f Hdl	Andy Rew (24 Apr 1982)	3m44.50s	3m48s
2m3½f Hdl	Captain Peacock (3 Apr 2018)	4m30.80s	4m24s
2m7f Hdl	Silk Run (20 Aug 2018)	5m33.00s	5m20s

Carlisle

2m Ch	Germany Calling (15 Oct 2015)	3m53.70s	3m57s
2m4f Ch	New Alco (12 Nov 2007)	5m00.40s	4m57s
2m5f Ch	Amilliontimes (13 Oct 2016)	5m20.90s	5m13s
3m½f Ch	Ripalong Lad (9 Oct 2009)	6m00.70s	6m03s

3m2f Ch	Basford Ben (5 May 2016)	6m38.10s	6m27s
2m1f Hdl (Inner)	Idder (11 May 2017)	4m06.00s	4m02s
2m1f Hdl (Outer)	Supertop (25 Oct 1997)	4m02.60s	4m04s
2m3½f Hdl (Inner)	Officer Hoolihan (5 May 2016)	4m39.50s	4m39s
2m4f Hdl (Outer)	Gods Law (29 Sep 1990)	4m50.60s	4m45s
3m½f Hdl (Outer)	Maggie Blue (15 Oct 2015)	6m02.30s	5m48s
3m1f Hdl (Inner)	Takingrisks (26 Mar 2016)	6m17.90s	5m50s

Cartmel

2m1½f Ch	Altruism (28 May 2016)	4m05.80s	4m12s
2m5f Ch	Princeton Royale (24 Jun 2016)	5m04.40s	5m12s
3m1½f Ch	Better Times Ahead (28 Aug 1999)	6m13.40s	6m20s
3m5½f Ch	Chabrimal Minster (26 May 2007)	7m12.00s	7m20s
2m1f Hdl	Lisbon (25 May 2013)	3m56.20s	4m02s
2m6f Hdl	Shantou Tiger (19 Jul 2014)	5m10.40s	5m11s
3m1½f Hdl	Portonia (30 May 1994)	5m58.00s	6m03s

Catterick

1m7½f Ch	Preston Deal (18 Dec 1971)	3m44.60s	3m48s
2m3f Ch	Laissez Dire (30 Nov 2016)	4m47.70s	4m45s
3m1½f Ch	Clever General (7 Nov 1981)	6m14.00s	6m18s
3m6f Ch	Straidnahanna (12 Jan 2017)	7m46.00s	7m25s
1m7½f Hdl	Lunar Wind (22 Apr 1982)	3m36.50s	3m40s
2m3f Hdl	Smadynium (4 Dec 2013)	4m31.50s	4m32s
3m1½f Hdl	Seamus O'Flynn (8 Nov 1986)	6m03.80s	6m08s

Cheltenham, New Course

2m½f Ch	Samakaan (16 Mar 2000)	3m52.40s	3m56s
2m4f Ch	Black Hercules (17 Mar 2016)	4m55.20s	4m51s

ONE FOR ARTHUR: won the fastest National since the track was remeasured

2m5f Ch	Vautour (17 Mar 2016)	5m05.50s	5m03s
3m2f Ch	Theatre Guide (9 Dec 2016)	6m40.80s	6m26s
3m2½f Ch	Long Run (18 Mar 2011)	6m29.70s	6m37s
3m4f Ch	Gentle Ranger (16 Apr 2010)	7m14.50s	7m08s
4m½f Ch	Hot Weld (16 Mar 2006)	8m33.20s	8m22s
2m1f Hdl	Detroit City (17 Mar 2006)	3m51.20s	3m54s
2m4½f Hdl	William Henry (19 Apr 2017)	4m48.80s	4m47s
3m Hdl	Bacchanal (16 Mar 2000)	5m36.60s	5m41s

Cheltenham, Old Course

2m Ch	Edredon Bleu (15 Mar 2000)	3m44.70s	3m52s
2m4f Ch	Shantou Village (22 Oct 2016)	4m53.30s	4m45s
2m4½f Ch	Dark Stranger (15 Mar 2000)	4m49.60s	4m58s
3m½f Ch	Marlborough (14 Mar 2000)	5m59.70s	5m57s
3m1f Ch	Un Temps Pour Tout (15 Mar 2016)	6m17.80s	6m05s
3m3½f Ch	Shardam (15 Nov 2003)	7m01.00s	6m50s
4m Ch	Relaxation (15 Mar 2000)	8m00.60s	7m59s
2m½f Hdl	Annie Power (15 Mar 2016)	3m45.10s	3m51s
2m4f Hdl	Vroum Vroum Mag (15 Mar 2016)	4m45.00s	4m37s

VAUTOUR: the triple festival hero wins the 2017 Ryanair in a record time

2m5f Hdl	Monsignor (15 Mar 2000)	4m52.00s	4m54s
3m Hdl	Trackmate (18 Oct 2013)	5m46.96s	5m40s
3m1½f Hdl	Rubhahunish (14 Mar 2000)	6m03.40s	6m05s

Cheltenham, Cross-Country Course

3m6f Ch	Balthazar King (13 Mar 2012)	7m51.70s	8m04s

Chepstow

2m Ch	Valseur Du Grenval (2 Nov 2016)	3m53.70s	3m58s
2m3½f Ch	Balder Succes (12 Oct 2013)	4m42.50s	4m45s
2m7½f Ch	Broadheath (4 Oct 1986)	5m47.90s	5m45s
3m2f Ch	Jaunty Jane (26 May 1975)	6m39.40s	6m34s
2m Hdl	Tingle Bell (4 Oct 1986)	3m43.20s	3m47s
2m3½f Hdl	Ballyoptic (8 Oct 2016)	4m37.20s	4m34s
2m7½f Hdl	Chucklestone (11 May 1993)	5m33.60s	5m36s

Doncaster

2m½f Ch	Clic Work (29 Dec 2016)	3m57.00s	3m57s
2m3f Ch	Gold Present (26 Nov 2016)	4m40.70s	4m36s
2m4½f Ch	Kalane (29 Dec 2016)	5m01.70s	4m54s
3m Ch	Killala Quay (22 Feb 2017)	5m55.80s	5m54s
3m2f Ch	Dancing Shadow (9 Dec 2016)	6m35.80s	6m24s
2m½f Hdl	All Set To Go (10 Dec 2016)	3m53.50s	3m50s
2m3½f Hdl	Just Milly (29 Dec 2016)	4m32.30s	4m33s
3m1½f Hdl	Parish Business (29 Dec 2016)	5m47.50s	5m45s

Exeter

2m1½f Ch	Sir Valentino (1 Nov 2016)	3m57.50s	4m03s
2m3f Ch	West With The Wind (7 May 2013)	4m27.90s	4m30s
3m Ch	Dennis The Legend (13 May 2009)	5m42.80s	5m46s
3m6½f Ch	Thomas Wild (14 Apr 2015)	7m14.70s	7m24s
2m1f Hdl	Remind Me Later (21 Apr 2015)	3m49.20s	3m54s
2m2½f Hdl	Mr Brother Sylvest (18 Oct 2011)	4m14.70s	4m17s
2m5½f Hdl	I'm In Charge (6 Oct 2016)	5m05.20s	5m05s
2m7f Hdl	Very Cool (4 May 2010)	5m26.20s	5m29s

Fakenham

2m½f Ch	Cheekio Ora (23 Apr 1984)	3m44.90s	3m55s
2m5f Ch	Skipping Tim (25 May 1992)	5m10.30s	5m10s
3m Ch	Specialize (16 May 1999)	5m56.90s	5m52s
3m5f Ch	Rebeccas Choice (3 May 2016)	7m24.90s	7m10s
2m Hdl	Cobbet (9 May 2001)	3m45.70s	3m54s
2m4f Hdl	Ayem (16 May 1999)	4m41.20s	4m47s
2m7½f Hdl	Phare Isle (17 Apr 2017)	5m49.10s	5m40s

Ffos Las

2m Ch	Get Rhythm (22 Jun 2017)	3m57.60s	3m48s
2m3½f Ch	Cold Harbour (31 May 2011)	4m37.34s	4m40s
2m5f Ch	Putney Bridge (17 Jun 2010)	5m09.70s	5m05s
3m Ch	Sea Wall (18 Jun 2009)	5m49.60s	5m50s
3m1½f Ch	Backstage (28 Aug 2009)	6m07.10s	6m10s
3m4f Ch	The Bay Oak (16 Apr 2017)	7m28.10s	6m49s
2m Hdl	Comanche Chieftain (9 May 2017)	3m37.00s	3m36s
2m4f Hdl	Positively Dylan (9 May 2017)	4m40.80s	4m32s

THISTLECRACK: could have gone even quicker when strolling home in the 2016 King George but hasn't managed to win a single race since then

2m6f Hdl	Koultas King (22 Aug 2013)	5m15.40s	5m00s
3m Hdl	Chill Factor (21 Aug 2014)	5m39.00s	5m30s

Fontwell

2m1½f Ch	A Thousand Dreams (3 Jun 2002)	4m14.50s	4m20s
2m3f Ch	Chalcedony (3 Jun 2002)	4m38.10s	4m42s
2m5f Ch	Contes (3 Jun 2002)	5m13.90s	5m17s
3m1½f Ch	Il Capitano (6 May 2002)	6m24.30s	6m25s
3m3f Ch	Strolling Vagabond (18 Mar 2007)	7m11.10s	6m58s
2m1½f Hdl	Hyperion Du Moulin (3 Jun 2002)	4m06.80s	4m12s
2m3f Hdl	Hillswick (27 Aug 1999)	4m30.50s	4m33s
2m5½f Hdl	Mister Pickwick (3 Jun 2002)	5m06.70s	5m12s
3m1½f Hdl	Sir Mangan (2 Oct 2015)	6m14.00s	6m18s

Haydock

1m7½f Ch	Witness In Court (19 Apr 2014)	3m52.30s	4m00s
2m3f Ch	Purple 'N Gold (7 May 2016)	4m45.70s	4m50s
2m4½f Ch	Beggar's Wishes (12 May 2018)	5m21.50s	5m11s
2m5½f Ch	Javert (7 May 2016)	5m20.20s	5m23s

2m7f Ch	No Planning (19 Apr 2014)	5m41.50s	5m51s
3m3½f Ch	Blenheim Brook (19 Apr 2014)	7m07.70s	6m55s
1m7½f Hdl	She's Our Mare (1 May 1999)	3m32.30s	3m40s
2m3f Hdl	Carlton Jack (19 Apr 2014)	4m33.00s	4m27s
2m3f F Brush Hdl	Horizontal Speed (19 Apr 2014)	4m32.10s	4m34s
2m7f Hdl	Whataknight (7 May 2016)	5m28.90s	5m22s
2m7f F Brush Hdl	Dynaste (19 Nov 2011)	5m37.60s	5m28s

Haydock, Lancashire course

2m½f Ch	Cloudy Dream (18 Nov 2016)	4m19.80s	4m05s
2m4f Ch	Ballybolley (15 Apr 2017)	5m02.40s	5m02s
2m5½f Ch	Politologue (18 Nov 2016)	5m50.40s	5m20s
2m6f Ch	Magic Money (15 Apr 2017)	5m47.50s	5m25s
3m Ch	Willoughby Hedge (15 Apr 2017)	6m13.40s	6m05s
3m4½f Ch	Vieux Lion Rouge (18 Feb 2017)	7m25.10s	7m20s

Hexham

1m7½f Ch	Imjoeking (22 Jun 2014)	3m52.80s	3m56s
2m4f Ch	Mr Laggan (14 Sep 2003)	4m55.40s	5m03s
3m Ch	Silent Snipe (1 Jun 2002)	6m07.60s	6m10s
4m Ch	Simply Smashing (18 Mar 2010)	8m34.00s	8m15s
2m Hdl	Francies Fancy (19 June 2005)	3m57.80s	3m55s
2m4f Hdl	Pappa Charlie (27 May 1997)	4m31.50s	4m52s
2m7½f Hdl	Fingers Crossed (29 Apr 1991)	5m45.50s	5m45s

Huntingdon

2m½f Ch	No Greater Love (23 May 2007)	3m53.30s	3m56s
2m4f Ch	Peccadillo (26 Dec 2004)	4m46.40s	4m48s
2m7½f Ch	Ozzie Jones (18 Sep 1998)	5m44.40s	5m45s
3m7f Ch	Kinnahalla (24 Nov 2001)	8m02.70s	7m40s
1m7½f Hdl	Weather Front (31 Aug 2009)	3m32.70s	3m38s
2m3½f Hdl	Sabre Hongrois (4 Oct 2009)	4m30.20s	4m36s
2m4½f Hdl	Sound Of Laughter (14 Apr 1984)	4m45.80s	4m48s
3m1f Hdl	Orchard King (31 Aug 2009)	5m50.20s	5m56s

Kelso

2m1f Ch	Simply Ned (4 Oct 2015)	3m57.80s	4m02s
2m5½f Ch	Romany Ryme (16 Sep 2015)	5m19.80s	5m01s
2m7½f Ch	Leanna Ban (24 May 2015)	5m40.30s	5m38s
3m2f Ch	Looking Well (29 May 2016)	6m33.20s	6m16s
4m1½f Ch	Seven Towers (17 Jan 1997)	8m07.50s	7m56s
2m Hdl	Life And Soul (26 May 2013)	3m38.90s	3m43s
2m2f Hdl	Croco Bay (26 May 2013)	4m08.70s	4m13s
2m5f Hdl	Waterclock (16 Sept 2015)	4m49.50s	4m50s
2m6½f Hdl	Hit The Canvas (30 Sep 1995)	5m12.20s	5m18s
3m2f Hdl	Dook's Delight (19 May 1995)	6m10.10s	6m12s

Kempton

2m Ch	Special Tiara (27 Dec 2016)	3m46.25s	3m50s
2m2f Ch	Imperial Presence (7 May 2018)	4m19.37s	4m19s
2m4½f Ch	Max Ward (18 Mar 2017)	4m58.90s	4m58s
3m Ch	Thistlecrack (26 Dec 2016)	5m53.50s	5m54s
2m Hdl	Yanworth (26 Dec 2016)	3m45.20s	3m42s
2m5f Hdl	Work In Progress (28 Oct 2015)	4m57.80s	4m50s
3m½f Hdl	Secret Investor (7 May 2018)	5m59.35s	5m45s

Leicester

2m Ch	Thankyou Very Much (1 Dec 2016)	3m45.30s	3m51s
2m4f Ch	Oliver's Hill (28 Dec 2016)	4m54.20s	5m01s
2m6½f Ch	Forgotten Gold (27 Nov 2016)	5m37.40s	5m40s
1m7½f Hdl	Amantius (1 Dec 2016)	3m43.10s	3m35s
2m4½f Hdl	Ten Sixty (7 Dec 2016)	4m58.60s	4m45s

Lingfield

2m Ch	Authorized Too (8 Nov 2016)	3m57.80s	3m59s
2m4f Ch	Mr Medic (8 Nov 2016)	4m55.80s	4m59s
2m7½f Ch	Onderun (10 Dec 2016)	6m07.60s	5m48s
2m Hdl	Bobble Emerald (8 Nov 2016)	3m46.20s	3m50s
2m3½f Hdl	Phobiaphiliac (8 Nov 2016)	4m36.80s	4m40s

Ludlow

2m Ch	Pearl King (5 Apr 2007)	3m47.30s	3m53s
	Bullet Street (10 May 2015)	3m47.30s	
2m4f Ch	Handy Money (5 Apr 2007)	4m47.30s	4m54s
3m Ch	Braqueur D'Or (11 Oct 2017)	5m54.70s	5m44s
3m1½f Ch	Moving Earth (12 May 2005)	6m17.30s	6m12s
2m Hdl	Leoncavallo (13 May 2018)	3m32.80s	3m38s
2m5f Hdl	Templehills (5 Oct 2016)	4m55.80s	4m56s
3m Hdl	Dark Spirit (9 Oct 2013)	5m33.30s	5m38s

Market Rasen

2m1f Ch	Mister Wiseman (7 Jul 2013)	4m13.60s	4m14s
2m3f Ch	Bocciani (10 May 2013)	4m41.40s	4m45s
2m5½f Ch	Vintage Vinnie (24 Sep 2016)	5m17.40s	5m16s
3m Ch	Allerlea (1 May 1985)	6m01.00s	5m46s
3m3½f Ch	Carli King (26 Dec 2014)	7m26.10s	6m46s
2m½f Hdl	L'Inganno Felice (21 Jul 2018)	3m55.60s	3m55s
2m2½f Hdl	Attaglance (19 Feb 2012)	4m26.10s	4m25s
2m4½f Hdl	Fiulin (19 Feb 2012)	5m03.70s	4m47s
2m7f Hdl	Trustful (21 May 1977)	5m38.80s	5m39s

Musselburgh

2m1f Ch	Celtic Flames (16 Mar 2018)	4m13.10s	4m00s
2m4f Ch	Bohemian Spirit (18 Dec 2005)	4m44.50s	4m41s
3m Ch	Snowy (18 Dec 2005)	5m47.70s	5m40s
3m2½f Ch	Present Flight (6 Nov 2015)	6m47.10s	6m20s
4m1f Ch	Dancing Shadow (4 Feb 2017)	8m28.60s	7m50s
1m7½f Hdl	Superb Story (1 Jan 2017)	3m35.00s	3m35s
2m3½f Hdl	Strongpoint (9 Dec 2013)	4m34.70s	4m30s
2m6f Hdl	Mondlicht (24 Nov 2016)	5m27.60s	5m05s
3m Hdl	Monbeg Charmer (5 Feb 2017)	5m47.80s	5m32s
3m2f Hdl	El Bandit (5 Feb 2017)	6m26.90s	6m05s

Newbury

2m½f Ch	Valdez (30 Nov 2013)	3m57.34s	4m02s
2m2½f Ch	Highway Code (29 Nov 2013)	4m31.87s	4m22s
2m4f Ch	Espy (25 Oct 1991)	4m47.90s	4m49s
2m6½f Ch	Pepite Rose (24 Mar 2012)	5m28.93s	5m25s
2m7½f Ch	Long Run (17 Feb 2012)	5m42.53s	5m40s
3m2f Ch	Ikorodu Road (24 Mar 2012)	6m22.86s	6m31s

MR MEDIC (right): a Lingfield record-breaker and favourite of our man Birchy

2m½f Hdl	Dhofar (25 Oct 1985)	3m45.20s	3m48s
2m3f Hdl	Songsmith (24 Mar 2012)	4m26.70s	4m26s
2m4½f Hdl	Argento Luna (21 Mar 2009)	4m48.63s	4m49s
3m Hdl	Lansdowne (25 Oct 1996)	5m45.40s	5m45s

Newcastle

2m½f Ch	Greenheart (7 May 1990)	3m56.70s	3m59s
2m4f Ch	Snow Blessed (19 May 1984)	4m46.70s	4m53s
2m7½f Ch	Even Swell (30 Oct 1975)	5m48.10s	5m44s
4m½f Ch	Domaine Du Pron (21 Feb 1998)	8m30.40s	8m21s
2m½f Hdl	Padre Mio (25 Nov 1995)	3m40.70s	3m41s
2m4½f Hdl	Mils Mij (13 May 1989)	4m42.00s	4m44s
2m6f Hdl	Bygones Of Brid (28 Nov 2009)	5m24.90s	5m13s
3m Hdl	Withy Bank (29 Nov 1986)	5m40.10s	5m37s

Newton Abbot

2m½f Ch	Shantou Rock (13 Oct 2017)	3m49.70s	3m57s
2m5f Ch	The Unit (6 Aug 2018)	5m01.00s	5m08s
3m2f Ch	No Loose Change (8 Jul 2013)	6m09.50s	6m24s
2m1f Hdl	Windbound Lass (1 Aug 1988)	3m45.00s	3m50s
2m2½f Hdl	Rum And Butter (22 Aug 2013)	4m15.20s	4m17s
2m5½f Hdl	Virbian (30 Jun 1983)	4m55.40s	5m00s
3m2½f Hdl	Veneaux Du Cochet (1 Jul 2016)	6m09.90s	6m20s

Perth

| 2m Ch | Go West Young Man (15 Jul 2018) | 3m41.70s | 3m51s |
| 2m4f Ch | Strobe (14 Jul 2013) | 4m48.20s | 4m52s |

3m Ch	Problema Tic (9 Jun 2013)	5m46.20s	5m42s
3m6½f Ch	Laertes (24 Apr 2009)	7m43.70s	7m30s
2m Hdl	Court Minstrel (22 Aug 2015)	3m40.20s	3m42s
2m4f Hdl	Valiant Dash (19 May 1994)	4m41.20s	4m44s
3m Hdl	Imtihan (2 Jul 2009)	5m41.60s	5m35s
3m2½f Hdl	Noir Et Vert (28 Apr 2006)	6m37.20s	6m11s

Plumpton

2m1f Ch	Pearls Legend (17 Apr 2017)	4m04.40s	4m08s
2m3½f Ch	Dead Or Alive (10 May 2009)	4m42.80s	4m44s
3m1½f Ch	Sunday Habits (19 Apr 2003)	6m23.50s	6m15s
3m4½f Ch	Ecuyer Du Roi (15 Apr 2002)	7m19.80s	7m06s
2m Hdl	Royal Derbi (19 Sep 1988)	3m31.00s	3m38s
2m1½f Hdl	Arthington (24 Sep 2017)	4m08.50s	4m05s
2m4½f Hdl	Urban Warrior (21 Sep 2008)	4m46.80s	4m48s
3m1f Hdl	Listen And Learn (18 Sep 2016)	5m49.80s	5m57s

Sandown

1m7½f Ch	Dempsey (28 Apr 2007)	3m43.40s	3m46s
2m4f Ch	Coulton (29 Apr 1995)	4m57.10s	4m57s
2m6½f Ch	Menorah (29 Apr 2017)	5m41.40s	5m26s
3m Ch	Arkle (6 Nov 1965)	5m59.00s	5m58s
3m5f Ch	Cache Fleur (29 Apr 1995)	7m09.10s	7m15s
2m Hdl	Olympian (13 Mar 1993)	3m42.00s	3m45s

MENORAH: went out on a real high at Sandown in April 2017

2m4f Hdl	Oslot (28 Apr 2007)	4m35.70s	4m37s
2m5½f Hdl	L'Ami Serge (29 Apr 2017)	5m20.50s	5m00s
2m7½f Hdl	Rostropovich (26 Apr 2003)	5m39.10s	5m35s

Sedgefield

2m½f Ch	Mixboy (27 Sep 2016)	3m49.90s	3m50s
2m3½f Ch	The Backup Plan (27 Aug 2015)	4m38.80s	4m32s
2m5f Ch	Degooch (1 Sep 2016)	5m10.50s	4m58s
3m2½f Ch	Running In Heels (30 Aug 2018)	6m29.00s	6m30s
3m5f Ch	Buachaill Alainn (27 Oct 2016)	7m20.40s	7m14s
2m1f Hdl	Country Orchid (5 Sep 1997)	3m45.70s	3m50s
2m4f Hdl	Grams And Ounces (27 Aug 2015)	4m32.80s	4m32s
2m5f Hdl	Palm House (4 Sep 1992)	4m46.30s	4m52s
3m3f Hdl	Pikestaff (25 Jul 2005)	6m19.70s	6m20s

Southwell

1m7½f Ch	Unify (27 Sep 2016)	3m53.70s	3m58s
2m4½f Ch	Gentleman Anshan (17 May 2011)	5m06.60s	5m04s
3m Ch	Best Boy Barney (22 Jul 2014)	6m10.10s	6m04s
3m1½f Ch	Silent Man (17 Dec 2017)	7m08.50s	6m26s
1m7½f Hdl	Dealing River (22 Jul 2014)	3m44.30s	3m42s
2m4f Hdl	Red Not Blue (17 May 2011)	4m57.30s	4m57s
3m Hdl	Jawaab (22 Jul 2014)	5m55.40s	5m50s

Stratford

2m1f Ch	One For Billy (15 Jul 2018)	3m54.00s	4m02s
2m3½f Ch	Comanche Chieftain (2 Aug 2018)	4m31.70s	4m40s
2m5f Ch	Spare Change (16 Sep 2007)	4m56.60s	5m01s
2m6½f Ch	Danandy (19 Jul 2015)	5m24.90s	5m25s
3m3½f Ch	Mossey Joe (7 Jun 2013)	6m38.30s	6m40s
2m½f Hdl	Chusan (7 May 1956)	3m40.40s	3m46s
2m2½f Hdl	Lostock Hall (24 Aug 2016)	4m17.30s	4m21s
2m6f Hdl	Broken Wing (31 May 1986)	5m06.80s	5m10s
3m2½f Hdl	Burren Moonshine (11 Jun 2006)	6m13.10s	6m17s

Taunton

2m Ch	I Have Him (28 Apr 1995)	3m49.50s	4m00s
2m2f Ch	Wait No More (28 Mar 2012)	4m24.90s	4m35s
2m5½f Ch	Howlongisafoot (12 Nov 2015)	5m31.80s	5m21s
2m7f Ch	Glacial Delight (24 Apr 2006)	5m39.80s	5m45s
3m2½f Ch	Copperfacejack (1 Nov 2017)	6m51.00s	6m30s
3m4½f Ch	No Buts (27 Apr 2017)	7m21.70s	7m09s
2m½f Hdl	Indian Jockey (3 Oct 1996)	3m39.40s	3m50s
2m3f Hdl	Prairie Spirit (2 Apr 2009)	4m19.70s	4m27s
3m Hdl	On My Toes (15 Oct 1998)	5m30.20s	5m33s

Towcester

2m Ch	Pinkie Brown (5 Oct 2016)	3m51.90s	3m52s
2m4f Ch	Rakaia Rosa (4 May 2017)	4m53.40s	4m49s
2m5½f Ch	Midnight Shot (4 May 2017)	5m14.30s	5m16s
3m½f Ch	Lucky Luk (29 May 2009)	5m52.60s	5m53s
1m7½f Hdl	Moonday Sun (5 Oct 2016)	3m42.60s	3m43s
2m3f Hdl	Ballygrooby Bertie (19 May 2014)	4m31.50s	4m36s
2m5f Hdl	Plantagenet (11 Oct 2017)	4m58.60s	4m55s
3m Hdl	Dropshot (25 May 1984)	5m44.00s	5m40s

Uttoxeter

2m Ch	Festive Affair (2 Jul 2017)	3m45.70s	3m48s
2m4f Ch	Midnight Shot (24 Sep 2017)	4m54.70s	4m49s
2m6½f Ch	Brassick (26 Jul 2013)	5m35.60s	5m30s
3m Ch	Big Sound (9 Jun 2016)	6m00.10s	5m54s
3m2f Ch	Drop Out Joe (26 Jun 2016)	6m23.10s	6m25s
4m1½f Ch	Goulanes (15 Mar 2014)	8m41.30s	8m30s
2m Hdl	Mountainside (26 Jun 2016)	3m42.20s	3m39s
2m4f Hdl	Chicago's Best (11 Jun 1995)	4m39.10s	4m42s
2m5½f Hdl	Fealing Real (27 Jun 2010)	5m06.80s	5m05s
2m7½f Hdl	Princeton Royale (4 Oct 2015)	5m36.60s	5m32s

Warwick

2m Ch	Wells De Lune (20 Sep 2016)	3m51.00s	3m51s
2m4f Ch	Gone Too Far (22 Sep 2015)	4m55.60s	4m49s
3m Ch	Urcalin (1 Oct 2015)	5m52.60s	5m48s
3m1½f Ch	Belmount (26 Sep 2017)	6m20.20s	6m09s
3m5f Ch	Big Casino (24 Apr 2017)	7m37.10s	7m04s
2m Hdl (Outer)	High Knowl (17 Sep 1988)	3m30.80s	3m33s
2m Hdl (Inner)	Satanic Beat (1 Oct 2015)	3m38.60s	3m38s
2m3f Hdl (Outer)	Blairs Cove (13 May 2017)	4m32.50s	4m26s
2m3f Hdl (Inner)	Rebel Yeats (26 Sep 2017)	4m25.60s	4m21s
2m5f Hdl (Outer)	Bendomingo (13 May 2017)	4m57.10s	4m50s
2m5f Hdl (Inner)	Atlantic Gold (1 Oct 2015)	4m54.10s	4m50s
3m1f Hdl (Inner)	The Tourard Man (24 Apr 2017)	5m56.40s	5m45s
3m2f Hdl (Outer)	Braventara (4 Nov 2016)	6m18.50s	6m03s
3m2f Hdl (Inner)	Mr Shantu (22 Sep 2015)	6m08.60s	5m57s

Wetherby

1m7f Ch	Oliver's Gold (14 Oct 2015)	3m41.60s	3m43s
2m3½f Ch	Village Vic (14 Oct 2015)	4m44.80s	4m45s
2m5½f Ch	Rosquero (4 May 2016)	5m17.60s	5m14s
3m Ch	Irish Cavalier (29 Oct 2016)	5m59.70s	5m57s
2m Hdl	Lightening Rod (31 Oct 2014)	3m43.20s	3m45s
2m3½f Hdl	Mustmeetalady (14 Oct 2015)	4m40.90s	4m34s
2m5½f Hdl	Kaysersberg (15 Oct 2014)	5m02.10s	4m56s
3m Hdl	Lilly's Legend (21 May 2015)	5m46.30s	5m48s
	Minella Hero (21 May 2015)	5m46.30s	

Wincanton

1m7½f Ch	Kie (13 Apr 2014)	3m37.90s	3m50s
2m4f Ch	Meldrum Lad (23 Apr 2017)	4m54.20s	4m56s
3m1f Ch	Swansea Bay (8 Nov 2003)	6m09.70s	6m15s
3m2½f Ch	Gullible Gordon (24 Oct 2010)	6m37.20s	6m40s
1m7½f Hdl	Cliffs Of Dover (14 Oct 2016)	3m22.60s	3m31s
2m4f Hdl	Deserter (14 Oct 2016)	4m28.30s	4m31s
2m5½f Hdl	San Satiro (23 Apr 2017)	4m53.10s	4m52s

Worcester

2m½f Ch	Mercian King (12 Oct 2017)	3m51.60s	3m52s
2m4f Ch	Rene's Girl (12 Oct 2017)	4m39.90s	4m48s
2m7f Ch	Pawn Star (30 Aug 2016)	5m31.10s	5m35s
2m Hdl	Moonday Sun (30 Aug 2016)	3m37.30s	3m40s
2m4f Hdl	Mont Choisy (14 Oct 2015)	4m38.50s	4m44s
2m7f Hdl	Net Work Rouge (14 Oct 2015)	5m28.10s	5m22s

BELMOUNT: one of two record-breakers on Warwick's September 2017 card

2018-19 *RFO Jumps Racing Guide*

Win – free form!

THIS YEAR'S QUIZ could hardly be more simple and the prize should prove invaluable to our lucky winner. We're offering a free subscription to The Jumps Form Book 2018-19, the BHA's official form book – every week up to April 2019, you could be getting the previous week's results in full, together with notebook comments highlighting future winners, adjusted Official Ratings and Racing Post ratings.

All you have to do is this: identify the three horses pictured on the following pages. And here's a clue – they were the three highest-rated chasers of last season according to Racing Post Ratings, two of them for winning at the Cheltenham Festival and the other for galloping through the mud at Haydock.

Send your answers along with your details on the entry form below to:

2018-19 Jumps Annual Competition, Racing & Football Outlook, Floor 7, Vivo Building, South Bank Central, 30 Stamford Street, London, SE1 9LS.

Entries must reach us no later than first post on December 5. The winner's name and the right answers will be printed in the RFO's December 11 edition.

Six runners-up will each receive a copy of last year's form book.

Name

Address

Town

Postcode

In the event of more than one correct entry, the winner will be drawn at random from the correct entries. The Editor's decision is final and no correspondence will be entered into.

2018-19 *RFO Jumps Racing Guide*

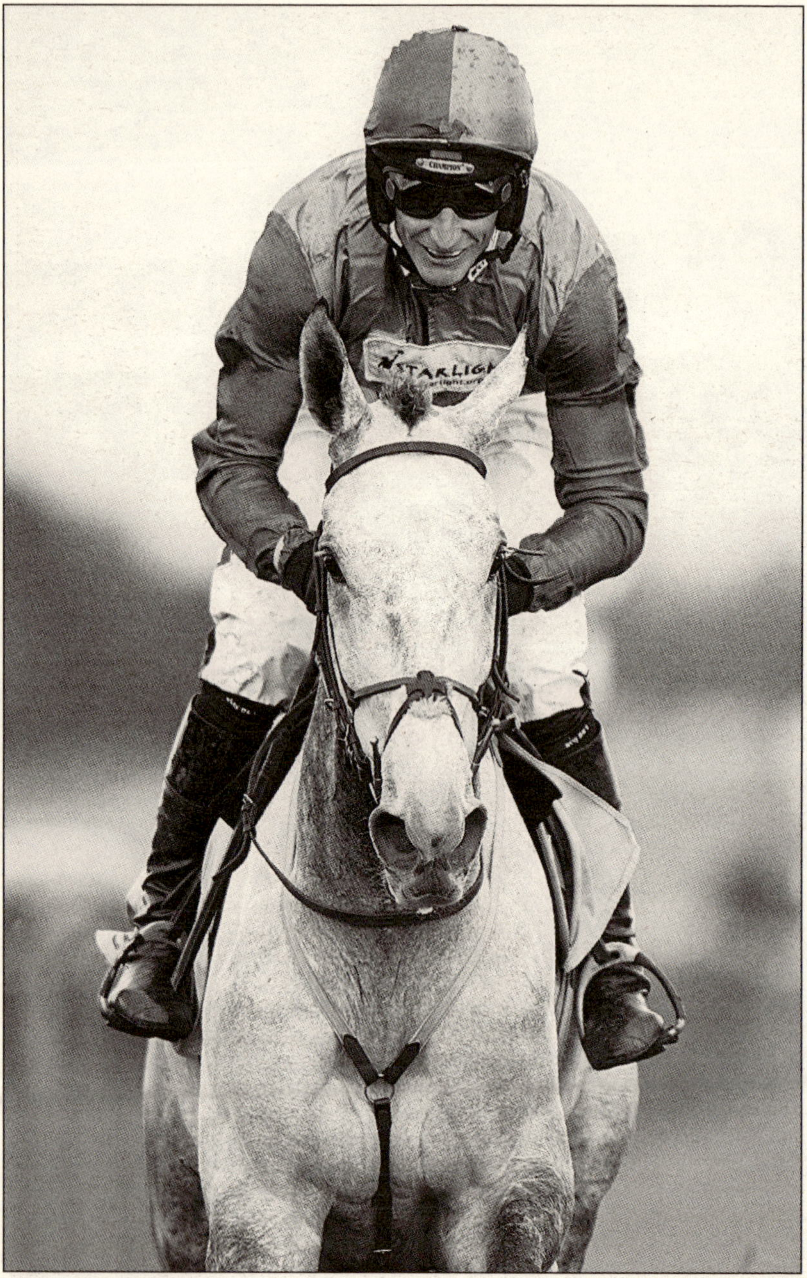

2018-19 RFO Jumps Racing Guide

BETTING CHART

ON	ODDS	AGAINST
50	Evens	50
52.4	11-10	47.6
54.5	6-5	45.5
55.6	5-4	44.4
58	11-8	42
60	6-4	40
62	13-8	38
63.6	7-4	36.4
65.3	15-8	34.7
66.7	2-1	33.3
68	85-40	32
69.2	9-4	30.8
71.4	5-2	28.6
73.4	11-4	26.6
75	3-1	25
76.9	100-30	23.1
77.8	7-2	22.2
80	4-1	20
82	9-2	18
83.3	5-1	16.7
84.6	11-2	15.4
85.7	6-1	14.3
86.7	13-2	13.3
87.5	7-1	12.5
88.2	15-2	11.8
89	8-1	11
89.35	100-12	10.65
89.4	17-2	10.6
90	9-1	10
91	10-1	9
91.8	11-1	8.2
92.6	12-1	7.4
93.5	14-1	6.5
94.4	16-1	5.6
94.7	18-1	5.3
95.2	20-1	4.8
95.7	22-1	4.3
96.2	25-1	3.8
97.2	33-1	2.8
97.6	40-1	2.4
98.1	50-1	1.9
98.5	66-1	1.3
99.0	100-1	0.99

The table above (often known as the 'Field Money Table') shows both bookmakers' margins and how much a backer needs to invest to win £100. To calculate a bookmaker's margin, simply add up the percentages of all the odds on offer. The sum by which the total exceeds 100% gives the 'over-round' on the book. To determine what stake is required to win £100 (includes returned stake) at a particular price, just look at the relevant row, either odds-against or odds-on.

RULE 4 DEDUCTIONS

When a horse is withdrawn before coming under starter's orders, but after a market has been formed, bookmakers are entitled to make the following deductions from win and place returns (excluding stakes) in accordance with Tattersalls' Rule 4(c).

	Odds of withdrawn horse	Deduction from winnings
(1)	3-10 or shorter	75p in the £
(2)	2-5 to 1-3	70p in the £
(3)	8-15 to 4-9	65p in the £
(4)	8-13 to 4-7	60p in the £
(5)	4-5 to 4-6	55p in the £
(6)	20-21 to 5-6	50p in the £
(7)	Evens to 6-5	45p in the £
(8)	5-4 to 6-4	40p in the £
(9)	13-8 to 7-4	35p in the £
(10)	15-8 to 9-4	30p in the £
(11)	5-2 to 3-1	25p in the £
(12)	100-30 to 4-1	20p in the £
(13)	9-2 to 11-2	15p in the £
(14)	6-1 to 9-1	10p in the £
(15)	10-1 to 14-1	5p in the £
(16)	longer than 14-1	no deductions

(17) When more than one horse is withdrawn without coming under starter's orders, total deductions shall not exceed 75p in the £.

Starting-price bets are affected only when there was insufficient time to form a new market.

Feedback!

If you have any comments or criticism about this book, or suggestions for future editions, please tell us.

Write
Nick Watts/Dylan Hill
2018-19 Jumps Annual
Racing & Football Outlook
Floor 7, Vivo Building, South Bank Central
30 Stamford Street
London SE1 9LS

email rfo@rfoutlook.co.uk

Horse index

All horses discussed, with page numbers, except for references in the big-race form and novice sections (pages 83-120), which have their own indexes

Acey Milan	20
Activial	8
Air Navigator	8
Al Boum Photo	71
Alberto's Dream	15
Alighted	44
Alnadam	58
Alrightjack	49
Altior	28, 33, 46, 77
Anemoi	49
Anibale Fly	39
Another Stowaway	20
Apple's Jade	36, 44
Bacardys	35
Baddesley Knight	63
Balko Des Flos	29, 45, 76
Ballyoptic	41
Banjo Girl	65
Baywing	55, 73
Bedrock	57
Begbie	47
Bellshill	20, 29, 37, 41, 43
Benatar	62
Benie Des Dieux	43
Big River	57
Bigmartre	49
Billingsley	61
Birchdale	47
Black Op	8
Blaklion	41
Boomerang	64
Boyhood	8
Brain Power	47
Brave Eagle	47
Breakfast	56
Brewin'Upastorm	58
Bristol De Mai	30
Broken Quest	73
Bullionaire	53
Burning Ambition	69
Buster Thomas	64
Buveur D'Air	31, 46, 77
Calipso Collonges	59
Call Me Lord	47
Canyon City	49
Capone	49
Captain Peacock	48
Carntop	48
Casa Tall	9
Casse Tete	62
Champagne Classic	44
Chapel Stile	55
Charlemar	49
Chef Des Obeaux	47
Claimantakinforgan	47
Clan Des Obeaux	21
Clondaw Castle	9
Closest Friend	67
Cloudy Dream	56
Commanche Red	63
Commander Of Fleet	21
Coneygree	49
Coningsby	15
Coole Hall	56
Court Liability	49
Cracking Smart	44
Cubswin	49
Daario Naharis	61
Danny Kirwan	21, 51
Dans Le Vent	48
Daphne Du Clos	21
De Rasher Counter	64
Dear Sire	56
Debacle	66
Debece	22
Defi Du Seuil	53
Definitly Red	55
Dentley De Mee	73
Diakali	62
Didtheyleaveuoutto	22, 64
Diego Du Charmil	34
Disko	29, 45
Dissavril	64
Don Poli	44
Dorking Boy	15
Dorking Cock	15
Dortmund Park	44
Dostal Phil	71
Double Shuffle	9
Double Treasure	48
Douvan	29, 33, 43
Downtown Getaway	47

Name	Page
Duel At Dawn	61
Duke Of Navan	55
Editeur Du Gite	62
Edwulf	44
Emerging Force	49
Emitom	47
Enniscoffey Oscar	63
Episode	62
Equus Amadeus	16
Eragon De Chanay	62
Espoir De Teillee	10
Euxton Lane	47
Fagan	60, 68
Fanfan Du Seuil	10
Farclas	44
Farne	49
Faugheen	35, 43, 78
Fin And Game	56
Flashing Glance	16
Flemcara	64
Fleminport	71
Florrie Knox	61
Footpad	22, 28, 33, 39, 43, 77
For Pleasure	61
Forest Bihan	55
Forest Des Aigles	57
Full Irish	64
Garrettstown	59
Gas Line Boy	59
General Principle	41, 44
Genius	49
Getabird	43
Gilgamboa	22, 69
Giving Glances	47
Glen Rocco	64
Glittering Love	73
God's Own	10
Gold Present	47
Got Away	48
Grand Morning	57
Great Field	23, 33
Guitar Pete	55
Gunfleet	64
Hainan	56
Hawthorn Cottage	66
Highway One O One	63
Hitherjacques Lady	48
Hogan's Height	48
Hunters Call	59
Huntsman Son	60
I Just Know	55
Identity Thief	35, 45
If The Cap Fits	32
I'm To Blame	57
It's Only Money	63
Ivilnoble	49
Jaisalmer	49
Jester Jet	16
Jonniesofa	57
Junction Fourteen	64
Jurby	48
Kalahari Queen	48
Kalashnikov	23, 66
Kateson	17
Keeper Hill	47
Kilbricken Storm	23, 51
Kiltealy Briggs	48
Kimberlite Candy	17
King Of Realms	60
King's Odyssey	23
King's Socks	24, 52
La Bague Au Roi	47
Lastbutnotleast	56
Laurina	32, 43
Le Reve	66
Leith Hill Legasi	74
Like The Sound	49
Lil Rockefeller	49
Lough Derg Spirit	47
Lovenormoney	47
Lust For Glory	72
Macksville	67
Manning Estate	48
Master Blueyes	47
Master Tommytucker	52
Meep Meep	17, 24, 72
Melon	32, 43, 78
Mengli Khan	24, 32
Mercers Court	49
Mercian Prince	66
Mia's Story	47
Michael's Mount	60
Mick Jazz	32, 44
Midnight Shadow	56
Might Bite	29, 38, 46, 76
Milansbar	49
Min	33
Missed Approach	24, 47
Mister Fisher	47
Monalee	29, 44
Monbeg Theatre	48
Mount Mews	56
Movewiththetimes	52
Mr Whipped	47
Naranja	48
Native River	29, 38, 50, 76
Natter Jack Croak	74
Nearly Perfect	49

Next Destination	35, 43	Sizing John	30, 45
On A Promise	55, 75	Smooth Stepper	60
On The Blind Side	25, 47	Southern Sam	48
On Tour	25	Step Back	41, 49
One For Arthur	41, 57	Summerville Boy	12, 32, 77
Ormesher	56	Supasundae	35, 45, 78
Pacha Du Polder	68	Sussex Ranger	62
Pallasator	36	Talkischeap	47
Papagana	48	Tazka	62
Penhill	25, 35, 43, 78	Terrefort	47
Petit Mouchoir	34	Testify	26, 56
Pickamix	49	Theatre Territory	47
Pleasant Company	41	Thebannerkingrebel	48
Point Of Principle	25	The Big Bite	12, 26
Politologue	30, 51, 77	The Boss's Dream	49
Polydora	17	The Dubai Way	49
Potters Legend	65	The Lincoln Lawyer	49
Presenting Percy	29, 38, 45, 76	The New One	77
Queens Cave	53	The Organist	48
Rathvinden	41	The Worlds End	12
Redemption Song	61	Thistlecrack	30
Redicean	47	Thomas Darby	59
Road To Respect	29, 45	Thomas Patrick	18
Robin Roe	59	Three Ways	48
Rocklander	11	Tiger Roll	40, 44
Roksana	58	Time To Move On	27
Rouge Vif	49	Total Recall	43, 76
Royal Sunday	61	Tower Bridge	44
Saint Calvados	49	Traffic Fluide	62
Samcro	32, 43, 78	Trevelyn's Corn	51
Sam Spinner	35, 54	Triopas	19
San Benedeto	34	Triplicate	44
Sangha River	59	Twenty Twenty	63
Santini	26, 47	Un De Sceaux	43, 76
Sceau Royal	34, 47	Uncle Alastair	55
Scorpion Sid	48	Uppertown Prince	56
Sebastopol	18	Vado Forte	19
Secret Legacy	60	Vinnie Lewis	49
Seddon	11, 72	Vintage Clouds	55
See The City	67	Virginia Chick	75
Seeyouatmidnight	57	Waiting Patiently	30, 55
Sevarano	48	Wakanda	56
Seven De Baune	60	We Have A Dream	27, 31, 47
Shanroe Santos	66	Western Ryder	47
Shantung	65	Whisper	76
Shattered Love	44	White Moon	51
Shaughnessy	48	Wicklow Brave	78
Silent Steps	49	William Of Orange	56
Silsol	68	Yalltari	75
Simply Ned	55	Yanmare	75
Simply The Betts	49	Yanworth	27
Singlefarmpayment	11	Zen Master	49
Sir Egbert	18		
Sir Jack Yeats	66		